LAW, VIRTUE AND JUSTICE

This book explores the relevance of virtue theory to law from a variety of perspectives. The concept of virtue is central in both contemporary ethics and epistemology. In contrast, in law, there has not been a comparable trend toward explaining normativity on the model of virtue theory. In the last few years, however, there has been an increasing interest in virtue theory among legal scholars. 'Virtue jurisprudence' has emerged as a serious candidate for a theory of law and adjudication. Advocates of virtue jurisprudence put primary emphasis on aretaic concepts rather than on duties or consequences. Aretaic concepts are, on this view, crucial for explaining law and adjudication. This book is a collection of essays examining the role of virtue in general jurisprudence as well as in specific areas of the law. Part I puts together a number of papers discussing various philosophical aspects of an approach to law and adjudication based on the virtues. Part II discusses the relationship between law, virtue and character development. Critically, the essays selected analyse this relationship by combining both eastern perspectives on virtue and character with western approaches. Parts III and IV examine problems of substantive areas of law, more specifically, criminal law and evidence law, from within a virtue-based framework. Last, Part V discusses the relevance of empathy to our understanding of justice and legal morality.

Volume 5 in the series Law and Practical Reason

Law and Practical Reason

The intention of this series is that it should encompass monographs and collections of essays that address the fundamental issues in legal philosophy. The foci are conceptual and normative in character, not empirical. Studies addressing the idea of law as a species of practical reason are especially welcome. Recognising that there is no occasion sharply to distinguish analytic and systematic work in the field from historico-critical research, the editors also welcome studies in the history of legal philosophy. Contributions to the series, inevitably crossing disciplinary lines, will be of interest to students and professionals in moral, political, and legal philosophy.

Volume 1: The Normative Claim of Law
Stefano Bertea

Volume 2: Community and Collective Rights: A Theoretical Framework for Rights held by Groups
Dwight Newman

Volume 3: New Essays on the Normativity of Law
Edited by Stefano Bertea and George Pavlakos

Volume 4: Hannah Arendt and the Law
Edited by Marco Goldoni and Christopher McCorkindale

Law, Virtue and Justice

Edited by

Amalia Amaya

and

Ho Hock Lai

·HART·
PUBLISHING

OXFORD AND PORTLAND, OREGON

2013

Published in the United Kingdom by Hart Publishing Ltd
16C Worcester Place, Oxford, OX1 2JW
Telephone: +44 (0)1865 517530
Fax: +44 (0)1865 510710
E-mail: mail@hartpub.co.uk
Website: http://www.hartpub.co.uk

Published in North America (US and Canada) by
Hart Publishing
c/o International Specialized Book Services
920 NE 58th Avenue, Suite 300
Portland, OR 97213-3786
USA
Tel: +1 503 287 3093 or toll-free: (1) 800 944 6190
Fax: +1 503 280 8832
E-mail: orders@isbs.com
Website: http://www.isbs.com

British Library Cataloguing in Publication Data
Data Available

ISBN: 978-1-84946-175-7

Typeset by Hope Services Abingdon Ltd
Printed and bound in Great Britain by
Lightning Source UK Ltd

Contents

IV. Legal Fact-Finding: Aretaic Perspectives

V. Law, Empathy and Justice

List of Contributors

Amalia Amaya, Researcher, Institute for Philosophical Research, National Autonomous University of Mexico.

Sandrine Berges, Assistant Professor of Philosophy, Bilkent University.

Susan J Brison, Associate Professor of Philosophy, Dartmouth College.

Sherman J Clark, Professor of Law, University of Michigan Law School.

John Deigh, Professor of Law and Philosophy, University of Texas.

Antony Duff, Professor of Philosophy, University of Stirling and Professor of Law, University of Minnesota Law School.

Kyron Huigens, Professor of Law, Benjamin N Cardozo School of Law, Yeshiva University.

Hendrik Kaptein, Senior University Lecturer, Leiden University.

Ho Hock Lai, Professor, Faculty of Law, National University of Singapore.

Claudio Michelon, Senior Lecturer, Edinburgh Law School.

Frederick Schauer, David and Mary Harrison Distinguished Professor of Law, University of Virginia.

Michael A Slote, UST Professor of Ethics, University of Miami.

Lawrence B Solum, Professor of Law, Georgetown University.

Mateusz Stępień, Assistant Professor, Department of Sociology of Law, Faculty of Law and Administration, Jagiellonian University in Cracow.

Linghao Wang, Assistant Professor, Xiamen University Law School, China.

Ekow N Yankah, Associate Professor of Law, Benjamin N Cardozo School of Law, Yeshiva University.

1

Of Law, Virtue and Justice – An Introduction

AMALIA AMAYA AND HO HOCK LAI

I. THE REVIVAL OF VIRTUE

IN THE LAST decades, there has been a blossoming of virtue-based approaches to a number of philosophical problems. Virtue theory has a prominent place in both contemporary ethics and epistemology.

A. Virtue Ethics

Virtue ethics has its origins in Classical Greece and it was the dominant approach in western moral philosophy until the Enlightenment. During the nineteenth century and the first half of the twentieth century, virtue theory faded from the landscape of moral philosophy, and the discussion on ethics centered around two traditions, namely, deontology and utilitarianism. Virtue ethics re-emerged in the late 1950s, with Elizabeth Anscombe's important article 'Modern Moral Philosophy', and has established itself as a major approach in normative ethics.[1] The revival of virtue ethics was motivated by an increasing dissatisfaction with deontology and utilitarianism. Proponents of virtue theories objected that these theories sidestepped or ignored a number of topics that any adequate moral philosophy should address, such as motives, moral character, moral education, the moral significance of friendship, family relations, and community bonds, questions about what sort of person one should be, the role of emotions in our moral life, and a concern with happiness and flourishing.[2] There is a wide variety of views that fall under the heading of virtue ethics, as critics have objected to different aspects of modern ethical theory and have developed a virtue-based approach

[1] Anscombe (1958), reprinted in Crisp and Slote (1997). For an introduction to virtue ethics, see Trianosky (1990); Pence (1993); and Annas (2005). Some of the most important monographs in virtue ethics include: Foot (1978) and (2001); MacIntyre (1984); Slote (1995) and (2001); McDowell (1998); Hursthouse (1999); Driver (2001); Arpaly (2003); Hurka (2003); Swanton (2003); Brewer (2009); Annas (2011). For some anthologies of virtue ethics, see French, Uehling and Wettstein (1988); Crisp (1996); Crisp and Slote (1997); Statman (1997); Darwall (2002); Gardiner (2005); and Chappell (2006).

[2] Hursthouse (1999: 2–3); Nussbaum (1999: 170–79); and Baron (2011: 11–12).

to ethics in different directions.[3] Despite differences, all varieties of virtue ethics take the notion of virtue as basic within ethical theory, and this sets them apart from deontology, which emphasises duties or rules, and utilitarianism, which focuses on the consequences of actions.

B. Virtue Epistemology

Virtue epistemology is one of the most important developments in contemporary epistemology.[4] The virtue turn in epistemology began with the publication of a paper by Ernest Sosa, 'The Raft and the Pyramid', where he argued that virtue theory could provide a solution to the impasse between foundationalism and coherentism.[5] The central commitment of virtue epistemology is that intellectual agents and communities, instead of beliefs, are the primary focus of epistemic evaluation. This commitment entails a distinctive direction of analysis: virtue epistemology explains the normative properties of beliefs in terms of the epistemic virtues of agents, rather than the other way around, and this differentiates it from non-virtue approaches to knowledge and justification. Two main kinds of virtue epistemology may be distinguished: virtue responsibilism and virtue reliabilism.[6] According to virtue reliabilism, intellectual virtues are reliable cognitive faculties, such as perception, intuition and memory.[7] According to virtue responsibilism, intellectual virtues are personality traits or qualities of character, such as open-mindedness, perseverance and intellectual autonomy, which are analogous to the moral virtues.[8] While virtue reliabilism is a descendant of early externalist epistemologies, responsibilism is aligned with internalist theories of knowledge and justification.[9] Mixed approaches, that aim at combining reliabilist with responsibilist components, have also been articulated and defended in the literature.[10]

[3] For some proposals as to how the domain of virtue ethics may be mapped out, see Oakley (1996) and Nussbaum (1999).

[4] For an introduction to virtue epistemology, see Greco (2002); Battaly (2008); Kvanvig (2010); and Greco and Turri (2011). Collections of articles in virtue epistemology may be found in Axtell (2000); Fairweather and Zagzebski (2001); Steup (2001); Brady and Pritchard (2003); and DePaul and Zagzebski (2003).

[5] Sosa (1980), reprinted in Sosa (1991).

[6] For this distinction, see Axtell (1997) and Battaly (2008).

[7] Sosa (1991) and (2007).

[8] See Code (1987) and Montmarquet (1993). Zagzebski (1996) is the most detailed and systematic articulation of a theory of knowledge and epistemic justification grounded in a moral model of intellectual virtues.

[9] See Axtell (1997: 2–3).

[10] See Greco (2000) and (2010), for a version of virtue reliabilism that makes, nonetheless, internal conditions for epistemic value crucial. Zagzbeski (1996), unlike other forms of virtue responsibilism, incorporates reliability as a component of virtue.

C. Virtue Theory: Conventional and Alternative

In both ethics and epistemology, virtue theory not only has provided new answers to traditional questions, but it has also led to an expansion of these fields of inquiry by drawing attention to new questions. Some moral philosophers have used virtue ethics to inquire into the nature, source, and content of moral reasons and have provided accounts of right action in which virtue plays a primary explanatory role.[11] Others, however, portray virtue ethics as a form of theorising that questions the conventional understanding of moral philosophy as a theory of right action and stress the need for moral philosophy to be also concerned with issues such as the overall course of an agent's life, the character of the inner moral life, and the nature of an agent's emotions, motivations and desires.[12] Likewise, in epistemology, while some philosophers have used the resources of virtue theory to address traditional epistemological problems, such as the analysis of knowledge and justification, others have deployed virtue theory to pursue a different set of problems, for example, issues about deliberation, the role of agency in inquiry, wisdom and understanding, and the social and political dimensions of knowledge.[13] In addition, the virtue turn has also led to an expansion of the methods and sources used in philosophical inquiry. Some philosophers working in the field of virtue ethics and virtue epistemology have relied heavily on literature and the arts to argue for their claims and have used methods other than the kind of conceptual analysis that is the landmark of analytic philosophy.[14] Thus, alongside 'conventional' or 'moderate' virtue approaches to ethics and epistemology,

[11] Hursthouse (1999) is a prominent example of the use of the resources of virtue ethics to address traditional problems in moral philosophy. Some virtue approaches to traditional problems in moral epistemology contend that all judgements of rights are reducible to judgements of character, but that we can and should use deontic concepts, provided we remember that these are derivative from virtue concepts. As opposed to reductionist versions of virtue ethics, replacement views contend that we should get rid of the deontic notions altogether. For this distinction, see Watson (1997). Louden (1984) has argued against the thesis of explanatory primacy that underscores both reductionist and eliminativist versions of virtue ethics, ie, the claim that right conduct should be explained exclusively in terms of virtue, and has argued for a view of morality that coordinates irreducible notions of virtue alongside irreducible notions of duty.

[12] Some contributions to the virtue ethical critique of modern moral philosophy, initiated by Anscombe (1958) and MacIntyre (1980), include Nussbaum (1990) and Brewer (2009).

[13] For attempts to employ virtue notions in the service of traditional epistemology, see Sosa (1991) and (2007); Zagzebski (1996); Greco (2000) and (2010). Whereas some virtue epistemologists adopt a strong stance and define both knowledge and justification in terms of virtue, others endorse a weaker version of virtue epistemology, according to which the notion of virtue only plays a secondary or peripheral role within traditional epistemology. On the distinction between different versions of conventional virtue epistemology, see Baehr (2008) and (2011). For virtue approaches to epistemology that focus on issues different from those that are central to traditional epistemology, see Code (1987); Kvanvig (1992) and (2003); Montmarquet (1993); Hookway (1994) and (2003); and Roberts and Wood (2007). Within these approaches, strong and weak varieties may also be distinguished, depending on whether virtue approaches are viewed as complementing or replacing traditional epistemological concerns (see Baehr (2008) and (2011) and Greco (2011)).

[14] See eg Nussbaum (1990); Arpaly (2003); and Fricker (2007).

there are some 'alternative' or 'radical' approaches that counsel a departure from traditional questions, sources and methods.[15]

D. New Directions and Intersections

Virtue theory is currently a very active area of research. In ethics, new ways of developing virtue-based approaches to morality and of understanding virtue have been recently proposed.[16] The emergence of virtue ethics has had an invigorating effect on both deontology and utilitarianism, for it has stimulated work on virtue within the terms of these theories and prompted a revision of the way in which these traditions, particularly the Kantian tradition, should be understood.[17] There is also a growing literature that aims at exploring the relationship between Kantian Ethics and Aristotelian Ethics.[18] Current research on the moral significance of virtue has also generated an interesting dialogue between contemporary ethics and the Ancient Greek tradition as well as an increasing interest in Ancient Chinese Ethics.[19] Finally, recent years have seen increasing attention being paid to the role of virtues in applied ethics, educational theory, and moral and social psychology, and these seem to be areas of moral inquiry that may be expected to grow in the future.[20]

Virtue epistemology has also significantly changed the landscape of contemporary epistemology, enriching current debates on the value of knowledge and epistemic luck, and inspiring work on topics such as understanding, wisdom and the epistemology of emotions.[21] Another growth area in virtue epistemology is the investigation of individual intellectual virtues and their corresponding vices.[22] An important consequence of the revival of virtue approaches to normativity has been the cross-fertilisation between ethics and epistemology as well as the production of interesting work at the intersection of these fields.[23] The political implications of a

[15] For the distinction between conventional and radical approaches to virtue ethics, see Solomon (2003). For an analogous distinction in the field of epistemology, see Baehr (2008); Battaly (2008: 640); Kvanvig (2010: 199); and Greco (2011).

[16] For references, see n 1 above.

[17] See O'Neill (1989) and Herman (1993). For consequentialist approaches to virtue, see Driver (2001) and Hurka (2003).

[18] See Engstrom and Whiting (1996); Sherman (1997); and Jost and Wuerth (2011).

[19] On the debate about the relationship between Greco-Roman and contemporary approaches to virtue, see Gill (2005). On Ancient Chinese Ethics and its relation to western virtue ethics, see Hutton (2002); Tan (2005); Van Norden (2007); Yu (2007) and (2010); Sim (2007) and (2011); and Tiwald (2010).

[20] On virtues and educational theory, see Carr and Steutel (1999). On virtue approaches to applied ethics, see Walker and Ivanhoe (2007) and Oakley and Cocking (2007). On the moral and social psychology of virtue, see Doris (2002); Miller (2009); and Sreenivasan (forthcoming).

[21] See, eg, Zagzebski (2001); Riggs (2006); Brun, Doğuoğlu and Kuenzle (2008); Haddock, Millar and Pritchard (2009) and (2010); and Brady (2010).

[22] See Fricker (2007); Roberts and Wood (2007); Baehr (2010) and (2011); Battaly (2010a); and Riggs (2010). Work on collective virtues nicely intersects with the emerging field of social epistemology. See Lahroodi (2007) and Fricker (2010).

[23] Some collections of essays bring together contributions to both virtue epistemology and virtue ethics. See eg DePaul and Zagzebski (2003); Brady and Pritchard (2003); and Battaly (2010b).

virtue approach to moral and epistemic issues have only begun to be explored, but the last few years have witnessed increasing interest in the subject.[24] In law, virtue theory has not had an impact comparable to the influence it has had in philosophical inquiry. Nonetheless, the concept of virtue is becoming increasingly important in various areas of legal study. It is to virtue theoretic approaches to law we now turn.

II. VIRTUE AND THE LAW

The amount of legal writing that examines virtue or that uses virtue as a framework is small compared to the amount of similar work in consequentialist and deontological legal theory. But virtue-centred scholarship in law has been growing in recent years.[25] This book is a contribution to the emerging field of 'virtue jurisprudence'. All but two of the chapters in this collection were written specially for a workshop on 'Virtues in Law' at the Twenty-Fourth World Congress on Philosophy of Law and Social Philosophy held in Beijing in September 2009. The two exceptions are the commentaries by Antony Duff and Frederick Schauer which were specially commissioned after the workshop.

Legal scholarship on virtue can pursue different aims and take a variety of forms and approaches. It need not adopt a (strictly) virtue-ethical approach to law. Just as it is possible for a philosopher to give an account of virtue without being a virtue ethicist,[26] it is possible for a lawyer to offer a study of virtue in the legal context without rooting it in virtue ethics.[27] A number of chapters in this volume fall into this category. For example, as Michelon makes clear, the focus of his essay is not on the relationship between virtue ethics and law as such but on the relationship of certain character traits, especially the virtue of practical wisdom, and the process of legal decision-making. Similarly, Clark's project, of which his contribution here forms part, does not involve the application of virtue ethics as a tool within law; instead, the aim is to establish connections between law, community character and human thriving.

[24] See Tessman (2005); Nussbaum (2006); Slote (2010); and Gaskarth (forthcoming). For some pioneering discussion, see Nussbaum (1990); Macedo (1990); Hursthouse (1990–91) and (1993); Galston (1991); Chapman and Galston (1992); and Dagger (1997). Part V of this book may also be regarded as a contribution to the emerging field of 'virtue politics'.

[25] Farrelly and Solum (2008). For an earlier collection that deals mainly with political theory but has contributions on law and by lawyers, see Chapman and Galston (1992).

[26] On the scope and even need for an account of virtue *within* consequentialism and deontology, see Crisp (1996: 5–8); Hursthouse (1999: 3) and (2010) (distinguishing between 'virtue theory' and 'virtue ethics'); n 17 above and accompanying text.

[27] eg contrast Kronman (1993) (articulating the virtues of the professional ideal of the lawyer-statesman) with Hursthouse (2008) (taking an explicitly virtue-ethical approach to dealing with problematic issues of client confidentiality).

A. Reliance on Different Versions of Virtue Ethics

When lawyers rely on virtue ethics, they commonly draw on Aristotelian or neo-Aristotelian versions.[28] Other important sources or traditions of virtue ethics have not received equal attention. Various chapters in this collection seek to broaden our field of vision: Berges looks to Plato;[29] Wang and Solum (writing jointly) and Stępień turn to Confucianism; and Slote offers a sentimentalist version of virtue ethics based on empathy that was inspired by a variety of sources, including Hume.

B. Primacy of Virtue

What distinguishes virtue ethics from the other major ethical approaches is the *primacy* given to virtue.[30] Virtue may play only an auxiliary role in legal theory. To illustrate, a normative theory of judging[31] or legal ethics[32] that is not virtue-ethical will very likely require or presuppose certain character traits. These traits serve an instrumental role; the judge or lawyer has to be a certain kind of person to be able to comply effectively with the prescriptions of the theory in question, whatever they may be. Examples of a strong virtue-ethical approach to law can be found in Solum's pioneering work on virtue-centred theory of judging[33] and in Amaya's chapter in this volume on legal justification. Amaya contends that a legal decision is justified if and only if it is a decision that a virtuous legal decision-maker would have taken in like circumstances. On this theory, virtue is not merely an epistemic device or an aid to rule-application where the justification for the decision lies in some logically prior notion of a right decision. Instead, virtue (in the counterfactual sense) constitutes the justification for the decision.

C. Attention to Particulars

Virtue ethics rejects the possibility of what deontology and consequentialism offer, namely, a form of decision-procedure for ethics. Familiar examples of such a procedure include Kant's categorical imperative and the maximisation of utility or

[28] On the relevance and impact of Aristotle's philosophy on law and legal theory, see Brooks and Murphy (2003) as well as the Proceedings of 'Aristotle and the Philosophy of Law' IVR Special Workshop (2007).

[29] See also Berges (2009).

[30] Farrelly and Solum (2008: 2–3) advocate the same approach to law, stating that '[t]he fundamental concepts of legal philosophy should not be welfare, efficiency, autonomy or equality; the fundamental notions of legal theory should be virtue and excellence . . . [J]urisprudence should turn from an emphasis on ideology, rights and utility to a focus on virtue'.

[31] Solum (2003: 167–69) and Duff (2003).

[32] Woolley and Wendel (2010). See also Dare (2009: 122).

[33] eg Solum (2003) and (2005a: 500–02). *cf* Duff (2003).

preference satisfaction. In contrast, virtue ethics insists on the need to attend to the relevant circumstances of individual cases. One must possess virtue to be able to perceive well the relevant circumstances and respond well to them. Moral decision-making cannot be controlled (completely) by general rules and abstract principles. The importance of attending to the particular circumstances of a given situation figures in a number of chapters in this volume.[34] Huigens argues that the assessment of criminal fault involves a particularistic assessment of the quality of the defendant's practical reasoning. The particularistic nature of legal fact-finding is highlighted by Ho and challenged by Schauer.[35]

D. Human Flourishing as the End

A third characteristic of virtue ethics is the conception of human flourishing (*eudaimonia*) as the end. In the legal context, this translates into the belief that the proper aim of law is to promote virtue and to prevent vice. This is, of course, putting it crudely. As Clark tells us, there are many ways in which law and politics 'intentionally or inadvertently' (can) shape our character. In the case of criminal law, no one can reasonably suggest that we should, even if we can, criminalise every vice or compel citizens to behave virtuously in every respect.[36] Thus, Yankah argues that, even if prostitution retards virtue in those who are involved in the trade, it does not necessarily follow that it should be criminalised; we also need to consider whether such criminalisation contributes as a whole to the flourishing of society and there are reasons to think that it does not.[37]

E. Other Relations Between Law and Virtue/Vice

Virtue is not limited in its role as the possible end or justification of law. There are many other possible connections between law and virtue, and between law and vice. The roles of virtue in legal reasoning – reasoning by judges and by fact-finders[38] – have already been noted. Additionally, it has been argued that virtue provides the content of the legal standards or norms in particular areas of law (such as negligence);[39] that 'justice' is a natural virtue and the conception of justice as lawfulness illuminates the natural law thesis on the essential connection between

[34] For discussion on particularised judgement and the Aristotelian virtue of equity in the context of law, see Shiner (1994); Solum (1994); and Zahnd (1996).

[35] See Bowers (2010) (particularism in the exercise of the discretion to prosecute).

[36] On the extent to which the law may be used to promote virtue, see generally Koller (2007) and George (2008).

[37] Yankah (2011) takes a similar line of argument to the prohibition on the smoking of marijuana.

[38] On the role of virtue in legal fact-finding, see also Amaya (2008) and Ho (2008).

[39] eg according to Feldman (2000), the negligence standard embodies the virtues of prudence and benevolence.

law and justice;[40] that our relation to the law may be accounted for in virtue-theoretic terms, specifically by the claim that law-abidance is a virtue;[41] that citizens[42] and officials must possess the appropriate virtues for a legal system to function well (the virtues of the lawyer are considered by Kaptein[43] and those of the judge are examined by Michelon and Stępień in this collection, and also by Solum[44] and many others[45] elsewhere); that legal practices such as judicial review[46] and the appointment and election of judges[47] should be shaped by considerations of virtue; and that legal rules, processes and institutions both influence and manifest community character, and should be evaluated in terms of their tendency to promote civic virtue or vice (this is a thesis that Clark has pursued over the years).[48] Whether vice is the proper object of criminal liability is the topic of an exchange in this volume. Huigens, who is a leading proponent of a virtue-centred approach to criminal law, locates criminal fault in objectionable practical reasoning.[49] Duff, disagreeing with him, would go only so far as to allow that some excusatory defences, such as duress, may be interpreted and rationalised partly in virtue-theoretical terms.[50]

F. Fields of Virtue Theorising in Law

The transformative potential of virtue theory in law is indicated by the great diversity of substantive legal fields that have been critically re-examined through the lens of virtue. In 2005, Solum observed that there was a growing number of exceptions to the 'hegemony of deontological and utilitarian theories . . . among legal theorists', including 'work on antitrust law, bioethics, civil rights law, corporate law, criminal law, employment law, environment law, terrorism law and policy, torts, legal ethics, military justice, pedagogy and public interest law.'[51]

40 Solum (2006).

41 Edmundson (2006).

42 Koller (2007).

43 See also Kronman (1993) (virtues of the ideal lawyer-statesman) and Cassidy (2006) (character of the virtuous prosecutor).

44 eg Solum (2003) and (2006).

45 Blasi (1988); Luban (1992); Shklar (1992); Scharffs (1998); Modak-Truran (2000); Sherry (2003); Siegel (2008); Horwitz (2009); Soeharno (2009); and Lund (2012).

46 Farrelly (2008) offers a dialogical model of judicial review as a prescription of the relation between the legislature and the judiciary in a virtuous polity. See also Sherry (2003) and Gaebler (2011) (providing a neo-Aristotelian critique of judicial review).

47 Solum (1988), (2005b) and (2005c) and Failinger (2004) and (2005).

48 See his essay in this book and also Clark (1999), (2004), (2005) and (2006).

49 For a selection of his other writings on virtue and criminal law, see Huigens (1995), (1998), (2002), (2003) and (2009). On virtue ethics and criminal punishment, see also Gelfand (2004) and Schaeffer (2010). For a survey of character-based theories of punishment and an argument against such theories, see Yankah (2004). On the influence of moral character on blame judgements, see Nadler (2012).

50 See also Duff (2006). For an earlier exchange between the two writers, see Duff (2008) and Huigens (2008).

51 Solum (2005a: 494–95); see footnotes, ibid, for citations of the relevant literature.

Since then, new writing has appeared[52] and virtue scholarship in law has become even more wide-ranging. The approach has been applied to other subjects, notably, contract law,[53] property law,[54] intellectual property law,[55] constitutional law,[56] corporate governance,[57] medical law,[58] theory of adjudication[59] and international criminal justice.[60]

G. Objections to Virtue Legal Theories

This 'aretaic turn' – the adoption of virtue, in lieu of consequences and moral rules, as the primary basis of normativity – can yield, and has yielded, important new insights. But it also faces many criticisms. For example, it is sometimes said of this approach generally or of a particular theory taking this approach that it cannot give adequate action-guidance;[61] that it is paternalistic (an objection addressed by Berges in her chapter); that it intrudes excessively into the 'private' realm and is illiberal (a charge made by Duff in this volume and elsewhere);[62] that it undermines the 'rule of law';[63] and that it is at odds with our interest in having reasons given for judicial decisions to the extent that it allows judges to cite their own virtue as justification for their decisions.[64] Advocates of virtue legal theory have responded to these criticisms either by way of denying the charges or by pointing to aspects of their theories which, they claim, refute these criticisms. That there is still much left in the debate on these issues, and much else on which to debate, are indications of the richness of the field. It is our hope that this book will excite thoughts on both the potential and limitations of virtue-centered legal scholarship.

[52] eg in legal ethics see Graham (1995–96); Milde (2002); Saguil (2006); Cassidy (2006); Oakley and Cocking (2007); Hursthouse (2008); Markovits (2008); Dare (2009); and Cordell (2011); in criminal law, see Schaeffer (2010); and in environmental law, see Anon (2010).

[53] Cimino (2009); Katz (forthcoming).

[54] Lametti (2003) and (2010b); Alexander (2009); Peñalver (2009) Alexander and Peñalver (2012), ch 5. cf Claeys (2009) and Wyman (2009).

[55] Lametti (2010a), (2010b), and (forthcoming), Opderbeck (2007). For a philosophical perspective, see Benkler and Nissenbaum (2006).

[56] Solum (2005a) and Strang (2012).

[57] Mescher and Howieson (2005); McConvill (2005); and Colombo (2012).

[58] Discussion of virtue ethics has found its way into textbooks and monographs on medical law: eg, Maclean (2008) and Pattinson (2011).

[59] Barzun (2010: 1167–71) (interpreting Jerome Frank's account of adjudication as a virtue theory of adjudication).

[60] Gaskarth (forthcoming).

[61] Contesting this in the context of tort law: Feldman (2000: 1449–1500).

[62] eg Duff (2003). See also Yankah (2009).

[63] This criticism has been directed at virtue theories that (on the critic's reading) (i) supposedly allow judges to decide cases according to their own lights (for responses to this, see section IV(b) of the chapter by Amaya and section III of the chapter by Stępień in this volume) and (ii) urge lawyers to be guided by their personal moral convictions in the discharge of their professional duties (Dare (2009)).

[64] Duff (2003: 207). *cf* Amaya's chapter in this volume.

III. AN OVERVIEW OF THIS BOOK

This book is divided into five parts. Part I ('Law, Virtue and Legal Reasoning') examines some issues concerning the role of virtue in law-making and law-application. It begins with a chapter by Claudio Michelon, the aim of which is to contribute to the plausibility of the thesis that legal decision-making by public officials can only be carried out properly if those officials possess certain virtues. In Michelon's view, the greatest obstacle to assigning virtues a major role in legal decision-making is the fear of subjectivity in decisions taken by public officials. However, argues Michelon, once we replace an oversimplified, 'topological' view of subjectivity by a more complex, 'relational' conception, we may come to see that this fear is misplaced and, thus, that subjectivity may plausibly play a prominent role in legal decision-making. With a view to advancing an acceptable account of how the decision-maker's subjectivity could come into play in legal decision-making, Michelon provides an analysis of practical wisdom, particularly, of its perceptive aspects. Next, he argues that an appropriate use of the kind of perception that is constitutive of practical wisdom requires the possession of certain moral virtues. Consequently, in Michelon's view, the possession of certain moral virtues is necessary for practical wisdom and, thus, for proper legal decision-making. This chapter concludes by contrasting this picture of legal decision-making with some methodological-deontological approaches to practical wisdom and to the role it plays in legal contexts.[65]

The next chapter, by Amalia Amaya, explores the possibility of developing a virtue theory of legal justification. After distinguishing different ways in which one might give virtue a role in a theory of legal justification, Amaya argues for a strong aretaic approach to legal justification according to which a legal decision is justified if and only if it is a decision that a virtuous legal decision-maker would have taken in like circumstances. This counterfactual analysis of legal justification in terms of virtue, claims Amaya, avoids some of the problems affecting causal approaches to legal justification, which make justification depend on the virtue of the causal process that actually lead to the legal decision. The proposed account of justification, she argues, also has the resources to meet a number of potential objections that may be addressed against virtue approaches to legal justification. The chapter concludes by examining some implications of a virtue theory of legal justification or discussions about the nature and scope of reason in law.[66]

In the last essay of this Part, Sandrine Berges examines the prospects of developing a virtue-based theory of the ends of law according to which laws should promote and protect virtue that does not fall prey to the objection from paternalism. Plato, argues Berges, might be claimed to provide an answer to the problem of paternalism in virtue jurisprudence. If virtue ethicists can limit their claim to

[65] See also Michelon (2006).
[66] Elaborated in Amaya (2011).

the idea that laws should promote wisdom, as Plato seems to do, then the threat of paternalism disappears, for wisdom may be promoted without endangering autonomy. However, despite appearances to the contrary, a Platonic Virtue Jurisprudence, claims Berges, fails to avoid the pitfalls of paternalism. First, although Plato seems to believe that laws concerning education should aim at helping citizens to develop wisdom, on his proposal only a small proportion of the population should receive the necessary education. Secondly, the education Plato proposes is not merely wisdom promoting but is also concerned with promoting temperance and courage. Nonetheless, she concludes, the teaching of temperance and courage alongside wisdom is not as objectionable as the teaching of these virtues without wisdom, for it could be argued that courage and wisdom are part of what it takes to be autonomous. Thus, at the end of the day, the teaching of courage and wisdom may be at the service of a virtue jurisprudence that is paternalistic only in the minimal sense of being wisdom promoting.[67]

Part II explores the relationships between 'Law, Virtue and Character', bringing together western and eastern perspectives on this subject. Sherman Clark's chapter explores the connections between law, character, and human thriving.[68] More specifically, he addresses two main questions: first, how does the law impact on or influence the kind of people we become; and second, what sort of people should we try to become if we hope to thrive, that is, to live a full and satisfying human life. With a view to answering the former question, Clark discusses six ways in which law and politics have an influence on people's character, namely, by requiring or forbidding conduct which is thought to display traits of character; by requiring or prohibiting conduct that might engender such traits; by facilitating or hindering institutions that promote the construction of traits of character; by providing or precluding opportunities for exemplars to flourish; by providing contexts for argument about what sort of people we are or would like to be; and by facilitating or obstructing public discussion about character and thriving. In response to the latter question, Clark identifies four traits of character as crucial to human thriving in a modern democratic society: courage, temperance, wisdom, and, most critically, a trait of character that corresponds to the classical term of 'piety', but for which Clark uses the term 'aspiration', that is, the willingness and ability to strive for higher, better, things than we can precisely define. Aspiration, argues Clark, is an essential vehicle for human thriving, and as lawyers and academics we may help to develop this fundamental capacity through our public policy advocacy, scholarship and teaching.

Wang Linghao and Lawrence Solum's essay offers a sketch of Confucian virtue jurisprudence, an aretaic theory of law that is rooted in the tradition of Confucian thought.[69] The chapter is divided into two parts. The first part provides an overview of Confucian social and ethical thought and describes in detail the following

[67] On paternalism and a virtue-based approach to the function of laws modelled on Plato's virtue theory, see further Berges (2007) and (2009).

[68] See also references in n 48 above.

[69] See also Greer and Lim (1998).

four concepts: *Li*, that is, rules of conduct; *Ren*, the cardinal virtue that unifies the particular moral excellences and, in a narrower sense, the virtue of benevolence; *Yi*, that is, a character trait related to the motivational attitude to abide by *Li*; and the concept of *name* and the associated practice of correcting names. These concepts are the building blocks of the Confucian virtue jurisprudence that the authors develop in the second part of the chapter. From a Confucian perspective, the fundamental question of legal theory is the aim of law. Law's proper function, argue the authors, is the creation of a social order on the basis of coordinative harmony and autonomous harmony. The former kind of harmony is related to the social coordinative function of *Li*: everyone has a proper position in the community regulated by *Li*. The latter kind of harmony is related to the expressive function of *Li*: individuals can express their emotions or exercise their virtues with the help of *Li* and follow their desires without creating a breach of *Li*. Thus, the end of law is to create harmony in both the society and the individual by establishing a social order that rests on norms that can be internalised by autonomous agents who possess certain virtues.

Last, Mateusz Stępień's chapter provides an analysis of judges' professional self-development. Three different models of judicial decision-making are distinguished: the formal positivist model, in which decision-making is mostly a matter of rule-application; the responsive model, which gives a prominent role to consequentialist reasoning; and the aretaic model, in which decisions are grounded on the judicial virtues. Judges' professional self-development may be understood, argues Stępień, as a transition that goes from the formal positivist model, though the responsive model, to the aretaic model of judicial decision-making. Confucian virtue theory, claims Stępień, provides valuable guidance as to how judges may pursue the path of professional self-development and, ultimately, acquire the judicial virtues. Different stages of professional self-development call for different models of legal decision-making, that is to say, there should be a match between the stage of self-development of the judge and the model of judicial decision-making that is to be applied. Thus, in Stępień's view, no single model of legal decision-making best serves the goals of adjudication, but any normative (as well as descriptive) theory of adjudication should make room for all three approaches.

Part III of this book, 'Virtue Theory and Criminal Law', applies virtue theory to various issues in criminal law. According to an aretaic theory of punishment, the determination of criminal fault consists of an assessment of the quality of the defendant's practical reasoning. Against this theory, it has been objected that the commission of a criminal offence provides too little information for an assessment of the quality of the defendant's practical reasoning for the purpose of determining criminal fault and moral desert for legal punishment. In his chapter, Kyron Huigens develops two responses to the 'inadequate basis' objection. The first reply is that intentional actions reflect a wide range of motivating intentions, beyond the simple intention that corresponds to intentional action – wide enough to facilitate an evaluation of the quality of the defendant's practical reasoning that is sufficient to find legal punishment morally justified. The second reply draws on the idea of specification: an assessment of the quality of the defendant's practical reasoning requires an inquiry into the defendant's deliberation about ends and this may be done by tracing the courses of reciprocal specification of conflicting ends. This explanation of intentions and ends shows that the adjudication of offences entails an evaluation of the defendant's practical reasoning broad enough to justify the imposition of legal punishment.

The second chapter of this Part of the book, by Ekow Yankah, is devoted to examining one example where ignoring virtue-based intuitions hinders our ability to make progress on important legal questions, namely, the prohibition of prostitution. According to Yankah, current decriminalisation arguments have not succeeded in promoting legal reform because they disregard core intuitions about the moral wrongness of prostitution that are central to its prohibition. Indeed, argues Yankah, there are good reasons, whether one accepts a Kantian or an Aristotelian moral theory, which support the commonly held intuition that prostitution is morally wrong. From this, however, it does not follow that the law ought to prohibit it. Though both Kantian and Aristotelian philosophical traditions view prostitution as morally wrong, these traditions are cautious about translating this moral wrong into a legal prohibition. This philosophical agreement does not mean, however, that there should be a complete absence of regulation; rather it provides valuable guidance as to the kind of regulation that is justified. Critically, this agreement shows that arguments in favour of decriminalisation and regulation do not need to assume either that prostitution is morally harmless or the commands of liberalism: one may support legal reform, from a wide range of philosophical positions – including virtue theory – despite viewing prostitution as morally wrong.

Antony Duff's chapter provides a commentary to both Huigens' and Yankah's essays. These chapters, argues Duff, exemplify two kinds of role that ideas of virtue and vice might play in criminal law: first, a view of the further goods that criminal law should aim to achieve and, second, a view of the proper objects of criminal liability. While Yankah's chapter illustrates the former role, Huigens' illustrates the latter. Duff's commentary on Yankah's chapter focuses on the suggestion, which is presupposed in his discussion, that a virtue theorist will or should see reason to criminalise conduct (eg, prostitution) on the grounds that it hinders virtue. A virtue theorist, argues Duff, need not make such an unqualified claim, but she can instead embrace a liberal distinction between the public and the private realm and hold that the state, and thus criminal law, has an interest only in the subset of virtues or vices that properly count as civic. Duff's discussion of Huigens' chapter is concerned with his general claim that a court's retrospective assessment of criminal fault consists of a particularist evaluation of the defendant's practical reasoning. According to Duff, while we can typically infer some deficiency in an agent's practical reasoning from the commission of a criminal offence, and some legal excuses can be most plausibly interpreted in virtue terms, that is not true of justificatory defences, and this undermines the claim that criminal liability is grounded on vice.

Part IV ('Legal Fact-Finding: Aretaic Perspectives') begins with a chapter by Hendrik Kaptein on lawyer-client confidentiality.[70] Legal adjudication typically involves the 'undoing' of '*past* wrongful harm' as broadly conceived. For example, where the defendant has committed a tort (a 'wrongful harm') against the plaintiff, the award of damages for the loss she has suffered aims to 'undo' the harm through 'restoration of the plaintiff's original position.'[71] Client confidentiality prevents a past wrongful harm from being undone in this sense when it keeps away from the court evidence that is necessary for the proof of the plaintiff's case. Kaptein suggests that the '"undoing" of a harmful past is analogous to preventing harm in the future . . . [P]ast and future are symmetrical from a legal point of view.'[72] There is 'broad consensus' that the lawyer's duty of confidentiality should not apply to '*future* wrongful harm'; disclosure may be permitted or obligatory where the client is about to wrongfully harm someone. According to Kaptein, just as we accept that confidentiality should give way in order to prevent a 'future harm', we should not extend confidentiality to a 'past wrongful harm' when 'the main facts of the case leading to justice [can] come to light in no other way.'[73] However, the virtuous lawyer will not necessarily make disclosure in such cases. 'Professional silence' can be virtuous in the circumstances, as where 'openness on facts' will produce even greater injustice, or where one is faced with 'mala fide opponents', 'incompetent courts' or 'wrongful law and legal procedure'. The virtuous lawyer will exercise practical wisdom in determining whether, all things considered, 'secrecy [will lead] to better realisation of material law and right'.[74]

Whereas Kaptein examines the virtues of the lawyer, Ho Hock Lai explores the virtues of the fact-finder. He contends that how well deliberation is conducted can be evaluated independently of the truth in the finding of fact that is made. Legal fact-finding invariably involves judgement and the exercise of discretion, and Ho shows how epistemic virtues provide standards of excellence for the conduct of deliberation. The chapter discusses in detail a selection of those intellectual virtues and vices that are or partake of a moral character. First, the author examines the connected virtues of 'justice as humanity' and 'empathic care' for the accused person (and for others who stand to be affected by the court's judgment); these virtues give the trial its humane quality and bear on the way that the fact-finder approaches the evidence and reaches the criminal verdict.[75] The chapter then moves on to discuss the vice of 'prejudice' and its virtuous counterparts. Drawing on the work of Miranda Fricker, Ho highlights instances of testimonial injustice and hermeneutical injustice in the trial setting. Epistemic virtues such as intellectual humility and open-mindedness are needed to prevent these kinds of injustice. Lastly, the chapter addresses the virtue of

[70] For another valuable virtue-ethical analysis of lawyer-client confidentiality, see Hursthouse (2008).
[71] This volume, at 228.
[72] ibid.
[73] ibid at 237.
[74] ibid at 236.
[75] See also Ho (2008: 78–84).

'practical wisdom' and the various important roles it plays in virtuous verdict deliberation.

Frederick Schauer offers a commentary on Ho's chapter. He addresses a question that he finds 'almost entirely absent in the entire virtue ethics literature': is it possible to be virtuous without being particularistic? Schauer suggests that 'the virtuous legal deliberator may not only not be required to be particularistic, but may also, at times, be required not to be particularistic'.[76] Schauer disputes Ho's (descriptive) claim that fact-finding deliberation is inescapably discretionary and non-rule-based. The 'process of finding the defendant guilty' and the application of 'legal rules to individual conduct' are sometimes 'mechanical and algorithmic.' According to Schauer, Ho is best understood to be making the different claim that particularism is desirable in criminal law and, on Schauer's reading, Ho makes the mistake of moving from the premise that some generalisations are objectionable to the conclusion that verdict deliberation should not be based on any generalisations at all. Although generalisations may be imperfect, not all of them are objectionable. The law, including the law of evidence, is 'replete with generalisations and it is hard to imagine how it could be otherwise'.[77] While it is indeed wrong to base a legal judgment or rule on a bad stereotype, the 'wrong lies in the content of the generalisation and not in the very idea of generalisation'.[78] In the context of verdict deliberation, the virtue of humility may require the decision-maker to follow rules (laid down by others) rather than make an all-things-considered particularistic judgement.

Finally, Part V of this book is devoted to a discussion of the relationship between 'Law, Empathy and Justice'. In the opening essay, Michael Slote sets out his views on the subject. This is followed by commentaries from John Deigh and Susan Brison. In the closing chapter, Slote replies to both of them.

Slote is the proponent of a distinctive sentimentalist version of care ethics that he considers to be a form of virtue ethics.[79] Care ethics is 'not based on rational consideration or arguments'. It measures morality according to how caringly one treats others. The disposition to care altruistically for others is driven by empathy. One acts wrongly if the act reflects or exhibits a lack of fully developed empathic caringness. In his essay, Slote focuses on extending his theory of moral sentimentalism beyond matters of personal morality to the realms of legal and political justice.[80] He claims that 'empathy and empathic concern for others can function as . . . the entire basis . . . for a plausible understanding of legal and social justice (as . . . they do for personal morality).'[81] This expansion into the public/political sphere rests on the recognition that morally decent people will not only care about

[76] This volume, at 226.
[77] ibid at 271–2.
[78] ibid at 272.
[79] *cf* Held (2006: 550). She differs from Slote: 'Virtue ethics focuses especially on the states of character of individuals, whereas the ethics of care concerns itself especially with caring relations. It is caring relations that have primary value.'
[80] See further Slote (2007).
[81] This volume, at 280.

family and friends but will also be capable of having some (generally lesser) measure of empathic concern for people they are not personally acquainted with. We can think of the laws, institutions and customs of a society as like the actions of those members who are responsible for making or sustaining the same.[82] Slote argues that 'laws, institutions and social customs are just (and consistent with our basic rights) only if they don't manifest a lack of fully empathic concern for (groups of) other people on the part of those who promulgate, maintain, or participate in them.'[83] He then proceeds to apply his theory to issues of religious freedom, political rights, distributive justice and legal adjudication.[84]

In his commentary on Slote's chapter, John Deigh draws a distinction between empathy as a cognitive state and empathy as a vicarious affective state. Unlike Slote who (according to Deigh) uses empathy in the affective sense and as a term of ethics, Deigh relies on the cognitive meaning of empathy and treats it as a term of positive psychology. He contends that moral judgements of the kind Kant identified as categorical imperatives require the exercise of (cognitive) empathy. Using the case of *Ledbetter v Goodyear Tire & Rubber Co*[85] as an example, Deigh shows how such empathy is also essential to sound legal judgments.[86] He points out that, in this respect, sentimentalist ethics and rationalist ethics are not as different as Slote seems to think they are. Deigh also questions Slote's thesis that his ethics of care has reintroduced into ethics a powerful version of Hume's moral sense theory. On Hume's subjectivism, 'a personal trait is a virtue or vice because one who regards its exercise from a general view takes a certain pleasure or displeasure in it and not the other way around'.[87] As Deigh sees it, there is no need to incorporate this position in an ethics of care and doing so saddles it unnecessarily with all the difficulties Humean subjectivism faces. Caring for others cannot have value merely because 'a sober judge of moral matters feels a certain way about these acts or about the kindheartedness and responsiveness they manifest'.[88] For Slote's theory to be persuasive, some explanation of normativity must be offered.

In his reply, Slote refers to a number of misunderstandings. First, while the kind of empathy on which his theory rests involves affect or feeling, it is not entirely or simply an affective state. Secondly, his position is different from the standard reading of Hume's; for Slote, sentiment fixes the reference of moral claims but is not their subject matter, and his theory supports rather than denies the objective validity of morality. Thirdly, on the point of normativity, Slote's

[82] On the attribution of virtues to social collectives and institutions, see Beggs (2003); Lahroodi (2007); and Fricker (2010).

[83] This volume, at 282.

[84] For an ethics of care approach to criminal punishment that relies on Slote's work, see Gelfand (2004).

[85] 550 US 618, 127 S Ct 2162 (2007).

[86] More fully see Deigh (2011). On the role of empathy in legal decision-making, see also Henderson (1987); Bandes (2009) and (2011), the latter is published with responses by Hasnas (2011), Leben (2011) and Franks (2011); Abrams (2010); Rollert (2010); Wardlaw (2010); Merriam (2011); and West (forthcoming).

[87] This volume, at 298.

[88] ibid at 299.

answer is that 'empathy enters into our moral concepts' and that 'empathy is essential to normative morality through being essential to meta-ethics'.[89]

In the second commentary, Susan Brison agrees with Slote that empathy is necessary for justice but is doubtful that it is sufficient for justice. On her analysis of Slote's account of empathy, X's empathising with Y's pain involves three stages: (1) X feels pain as a result of X's awareness that Y is feeling pain; (2) X judges that Y views feeling the pain as desirable or undesirable; and (3) X's feeling Y's pain prompts a moral sentiment that (typically) is (or leads to) a correct moral judgement (provided X has a sufficiently developed and appropriately exercised capacity for empathy). Brison points out that it is possible for error to occur at each of these three stages: (1) Y may not in fact be feeling pain; (2) Y may, contrary to what X thinks, desire (or not) the pain; and (3) X may arrive at the wrong moral judgement. On the last point, Brison cites a situation where women in a particular region have their assessment of well-being distorted by adaptive preference formation and have higher levels of satisfaction with their lives even though they are worse off than men in the region. Here, '[e]mpathy with what [these women] are feeling is not an adequate guide to what justice requires in our treatment of them.'[90] Another difficulty is that the development of empathy varies among different people and can be thwarted; we therefore 'need an independent standard to determine when empathy is sufficiently developed' for the purposes of Slote's theory.[91] Even if our empathy is fully developed, empathy for different groups of people may pull us in different directions. A judge who let her decision be influenced by 'greater empathy for members of her own ethnic group than for other similarly-situated persons of different ethnicities would not be acting justly'.[92]

In his reply, Slote accepts that our empathy can be misleading. But 'the non-culpable ignorance that is involved [in such cases] doesn't affect our moral judgement'.[93] Slote finds Brison too uncritical of the idea of adaptive preference formation and contentment. Many women who become preferentially adaptive have been treated with lack of empathy (for their aspirations and desires) and hence treated unjustly; further, it is doubtful that such women are really contented. Slote is not persuaded that a theory of objective welfare is needed to supplement empathy as a criterion for acting morally and justly. While he agrees that empathy can lead us astray, his criterion for morally acceptable action is a 'fully-empathic' concern for others and it is this 'fuller, wider, deeper empathy' that is a sufficient condition for acting morally. Brison is right that (fully developed) empathy can tug us in different directions. But this is a problem only if there is a definite moral obligation in one specific direction. For Slote, more than one course of action may be morally acceptable in such situations.

[89] ibid at 312. Elaborated in Slote (2010).
[90] This volume, at 306.
[91] ibid at 307.
[92] ibid.
[93] ibid at 313.

REFERENCES

Abrams, K (2010) 'Empathy and Experience in the Sotomayor Hearings' 36 *Ohio Northern University Law Review* 263.
Alexander, GS (2009) 'The Social-Obligation Norm in American Property Law' 94 *Cornell Law Review* 745.
Alexander, GS and Peñalver, EM (2012) *An Introduction to Property Theory* (New York, Cambridge University Press).
Amaya, A (2008) 'Justification, Coherence, and Epistemic Responsibility in Legal Fact-Finding' 5 *Episteme – Journal of Social Epistemology* 306.
——(2011) 'Virtue and Reason in Law' in Maksymillian del Mar (ed), *New Waves in the Philosophy of Law* (New York, Palgrave-MacMillan).
Annas, J (2006) 'Virtue Ethics' in Coop (2006) 515.
——(2011) *Intelligent Virtue* (Oxford, Oxford University Press).
Anon (2010) 'Uncommon Goods: On Environmental Virtues and Voluntary Carbon Offsets' 123 *Harvard Law Review* 2065.
Anscombe, E (1958) 'Modern Moral Philosophy' 33 *Philosophy* 1.
Arpaly, N (2003) *Unprincipled Virtue: An Inquiry into Moral Agency* (New York, Oxford University Press).
Axtell, G (1997) 'Recent Work on Virtue Epistemology' 34 (1) *American Philosophical Quarterly* 1.
——(2000) *Knowledge, Belief, and Character* (Lanham, Rowman and Littlefield).
Baehr, J (2008) 'Four Varieties of Character-Based Virtue Epistemology' XLVI *The Southern Journal of Philosophy* 469.
——(2010) 'Epistemic Malevolence' 41 *Metaphilosophy* 189.
——(2011) *The Inquiring Mind: On Intellectual Virtues and Virtue Epistemology* (New York, Oxford University Press).
Bandes, S (2009) 'Empathetic Judging and the Rule of Law' *Cardozo Law Review de novo* 133 available at www.cardozolawreview.com/content/denovo/BANDES_2009_133.pdf
——(2011) 'Moral Imagination in Judging' 51 *Washburn Law Journal* 1.
Bankowski, Z and MacLean, J (eds) (2006) *The Universal and the Particular in Legal Reasoning* (Aldershot, Ashgate).
Baron, M 'Virtue Ethics in relation to Kantian Ethics: An Opinionated Overview and Commentary' in Jost and Wuerth (2011) 8.
Barzun, CL (2010) 'Jerome Frank and the Modern Mind' 58 *Buffalo Law Review* 1127.
Battaly, H (2008) 'Virtue Epistemology' 3/4 *Philosophy Compass* 639.
——(2010a) 'Epistemic Self-Indulgence' 41 (1–2) *Metaphilosophy* 241.
——(ed) (2010b) Virtue and Vice, Moral and Epistemic 41 (1–2) *Metaphilosophy. Special Issue.*
Benkler, Y and Nissenbaum, H (2006) 'Commons-based Peer Production and Virtue' 14 *Journal of Political Philosophy* 394.
Beggs, D (2003) 'The Idea of Group Moral Virtue' 34 *Journal of Social Philosophy* 457.
Berges, S (2009) *Plato on Virtue and the Law* (London, Continuum).
——(2007) 'Virtue Ethics, Politics, and the Function of Laws: The Parent Analogy in Plato's Menexenus' 46 (2) *Dialogue* 211.
Blasi, V (1988) 'The First Amendment and the Ideal of Civic Courage: The Brandeis Opinion in Whitney v California' 29 *William and Mary Law Review* 653.

Bowers, J (2010) 'Legal Guilt, Normative Innocence, and the Equitable Decision Not to Prosecute' 110 *Columbia Law Review* 1655.
Brady, M (2010) 'Virtue, Emotion, and Attention' in Battaly (2010b) 115.
Brady, M and Pritchard, D (eds) (2003) *Moral and Epistemic Virtues* (Malden, Blackwell).
Brewer, T (2009) *The Retrieval of Ethics* (New York, Oxford University Press).
Brun, G, Doğuoğlu, U and Kuenzle, K (2008) *Epistemology and Emotions* (Aldershot, Ashgate).
Brooks RO and Murphy JB (eds) (2003) *Aristotle and Modern Law* (Aldershot, Ashgate).
Carr, D and Steutel, J (eds) (1999) *Virtue Ethics and Moral Education* (London and New York, Routledge).
Cassidy, RM (2006) 'Character and Context: What Virtue Theory can Teach us about a Prosecutor's Ethical Duty to "Seek Justice"' 82 *Notre Dame Law Review* 635.
Chapman, JW and Galston, WA (eds) (1992) *Virtue*, NOMOS XXXIV (New York, New York University Press).
Chappell, T (2006) *Values and Virtues* (Oxford, Clarendon Press).
Cimino, CF (2009) 'Virtue and Contract Law' 88 *Oregon Law Review* 703.
Claeys, ER (2009) 'Virtue and Rights in American Property Law' 94 *Cornell Law Review* 889.
Clark, SJ (1999) 'The Courage of Our Convictions' 97 *Michigan Law Review* 2381.
——(2004) 'The Character of Direct Democracy' 13 *Journal of Contemporary Legal Issues* 341.
——(2005) 'Law as Communtarian Virtue Ethics' 53 *Buffalo Law Review* 757.
——(2006) '"Who do you Think you Are?" The Criminal Trial and Community Character' in Antony Duff, Lindsay Farmer, Sandra Marshall and Victor Tadros (eds), *The Trial on Trial volume 2 – Judgment and Calling to Account* (Oxford, Hart Publishing) 83.
Code, L (1987) *Epistemic Responsibility* (Hanover and London, University Press of New England).
Colombo, RJ (2012) 'Towards a Nexus of Virtue' (forthcoming) 69 *Washington and Lee Law Review*.
Coop, D (ed) (2006) *The Oxford Handbook of Ethical Theory* (New York, Oxford University Press).
Cordell, S (2011) 'Virtuous Persons and Social Roles' 42 *Journal of Social Philosophy* 254.
Crisp, R (ed) (1996) *How Should One Live?* (Oxford, Oxford University Press).
Crisp, R and Slote, M (eds) (1997) *Virtue Ethics* (Oxford, Oxford University Press).
Dagger, R (1997) *Civic Virtues (New York, Oxford University Press).*
Dare, T (2009) 'Virtue Ethics, Legal Ethics and Harper Lee's *To Kill a Mockingbird*' in Tim Dare, *The Counsel of Rogues? – A Defence of the Standard Conception of the Lawyer's Role* (Farnham, Surrey, Ashgate) 101.
Darwall, S (ed) (2002) *Virtue Ethics* (Malden and Carlton, Blackwell).
Deigh, J (2011) 'Empathy, Justice, and Jurisprudence' 49 *Southern Journal of Philosophy* 73.
DePaul, M and Zagzebski, L (eds) (2003) *Intellectual Virtue: Perspectives from Ethics and Epistemology* (Oxford, Clarendon Press).
Doris, J (2002) *Lack of Character: Personality and Moral Behavior* (Cambridge, Cambridge University Press).
Douglass, R, Mara, G and Richardson, H (eds) (1990) *Liberalism and the Good* (New York, Routledge).
Driver, J (2001) *Uneasy Virtue* (Cambridge, Cambridge University Press).
Duff, RA (2003) 'The Limits of Virtue Jurisprudence' in Brady and Pritchard (2003) 199.
——(2006) 'The Virtues and Vices of Virtue Jurisprudence' in Timothy Chappell (ed), *Values and Virtues – Aristotelianism in Contemporary Ethics* (Oxford, Oxford University Press) 90.

——(2008) 'Virtue, Vice, and Criminal Liability' in Farrelly and Solum (2008) 193.

Edmundson, WA (2006) 'The Virtue of Law-Abidance' 6 *Philosophers' Imprint*, available at www.quod.lib.umich.edu/cgi/p/pod/dod-idx?c=phimp;idno=3521354.0006.004

Engstrom, S and Whiting, J (eds) (1996) *Aristotle, Kant, and the Stoics: Rethinking Happiness and Duty* (Cambridge, Cambridge University Press).

Failinger, MA (2004) 'Virtuous Judges and Electoral Politics' 67 *Albany Law Review* 769.

——(2005) 'Can a Good Judge Be a Good Politician? Judicial Elections from a Virtue Ethics Approach' 70 *Missouri Law Review* 433.

Fairweather, A and Zagzebski, L (2001) *Virtue Epistemology: Essays on Epistemic Virtue and Responsibility* (Oxford, Oxford University Press).

Farrelly, C (2008) 'Civic Liberalism and the "Dialogical Model" of Judicial Review' in Farrelly and Solum (2008) 107.

Farrelly, C and Solum, LB (eds) (2008) *Virtue Jurisprudence* (Basingstoke, Palgrave MacMillan).

Feldman, HL (2000) 'Prudence, Benevolence, and Negligence: Virtue Ethics and Tort Law' 74 *Chicago-Kent Law Review* 1431.

Foot, P (1978) *Virtues and Vices and Other Essays in Moral Philosophy* (Oxford, Blackwell).

——(2001) *Natural Goodness* (Oxford, Clarendon Press).

Franks, MA (2011) 'Lies, Damned Lies, and Judicial Empathy' 61 *Washburn Law Journal* 61.

French, PA, Uehling, T and Wettstein, H (eds) (1988) *Midwest Studies in Philosophy Vol. XIII Ethical Theory: Character and Virtue* (Notre Dame, University of Notre Dame Press).

Fricker, M (2007) *Epistemic Injustice: Power and the Ethics of Knowing* (New York, Oxford University Press).

——(2010) 'Can There Be Institutional Virtues?' in Tamar Szabó Gendler and John Hawthorne (eds), *Oxford Studies in Epistemology*, vol 3 (Oxford, Oxford University Press).

Gaebler, RF (2011) 'On the Incompatibility of Political Virtue and Judicial Review: A Neo-Aristotelian Perspective' 34 *Hamline Law Review* 263.

Galston, WA (1991) *Liberal Purposes: Goods, Virtues, and Diversity in the Liberal State* (New York, Oxford University Press).

Gardiner, S (2005) *Virtue Ethics, Old and New* (Ithaca, Cornell University Press).

Gaskarth, J (forthcoming) 'The Virtues in International Society' *European Journal of International Relations*.

Gelfand, SD (2004) 'The Ethics of Care and (Capital?) Punishment' 23 *Law and Philosophy* 593.

George, RP (2008) 'The Central Tradition – Its Value and Limits' in Farrelly and Solum (2008) 24.

Gill, C (ed) (2005) *Virtue, Norms, and Objectivity: Issues in Ancient and Modern Ethics* (Oxford, Clarendon Press).

Graham, L M (1995–96) 'Aristotle's Ethics and the Virtuous Lawyer: Part One of a Study on Legal Ethics and Clinical Legal Education' 20 *Journal of the Legal Profession* 5.

Greco, J (2000) *Putting Skeptics in their Place* (Cambridge, Cambridge University Press).

——(2002) 'Virtues in Epistemology' in Moser (2002) 287.

——(2010) *Achieving Knowledge* (Cambridge, Cambridge University Press).

Greco, J and Turri, J (2011) 'Virtue Epistemology', *The Stanford Encyclopedia of Philosophy (Spring 2011 Edition)*, Edward N Zalta (ed), www.plato.stanford.edu/archives/spr2011/entries/epistemology-virtue/

Greer, S and Lim, TP (1998) 'Confucianism: Natural Law Chinese Style?' 11 *Ratio Juris* 80.

Haddock, A, Millar, A and Pritchard, D (eds) (2009) *Epistemic Value* (New York, Oxford University Press).

——(2010) *The Nature and Value of Knowledge* (New York, Oxford University Press).

Hasnas, J (2011) 'Is Moral Imagination the Cure for Misapplied Judicial Empathy? Bandes, Bastiat, and the Quest for Justice' 51 *Washburn Law Journal* 25.

Held, Virginia (2006) 'The Ethics of Care' in Coop (2006) 536.

Henderson, L (1987) 'Legality and Empathy' *Michigan Law Review* 1574.

Hendricks, V and Pritchard, D (eds) (2006) *New Waves in Epistemology* (New York, Palgrave-MacMillan).

Herman, B (1993) *The Practice of Moral Judgment* (Cambridge, Harvard University Press).

Ho, HL (2008) *A Philosophy of Evidence Law – Justice in the Search for Truth* (Oxford, Oxford University Press).

Hookway, C (1994) 'Cognitive Virtues and Epistemic Evaluations' 2 *International Journal of Philosophical Studies* 211.

——(2003) 'How to be a Virtue Epistemologist' in DePaul and Zagzebski (2003) 287.

Horwitz, P (2009) 'Judicial Character (and does it Matter)' 26 *Constitutional Commentary* 97.

Huigens, K (1995) 'Virtue and Inculpation' 7 *Harvard Law Review* 1423.

——(1998) 'Virtue and Criminal Negligence' 1 *Buffalo Criminal Law Review* 431.

——(2002) 'Homicide in Aretaic Terms' 6 *Buffalo Criminal Law Review* 97.

——(2003) 'Nietzsche and Aretaic Legal Theory' 24 *Cardozo Law Review* 563.

——(2008) 'On Aristotelian Criminal Law: A Reply to Duff' in Farrelly and Solum (2008) 214.

——(2009) 'The Continuity of Justification Defenses' *University of Illinois Law Review* 627.

Hurka, T (2003) *Virtue, Vice and Value* (Oxford, Oxford University Press).

Hursthouse, R (1990–91) 'After Hume's Justice' 91 *Proceedings of the Aristotelian Society* 229.

——(1999) *On Virtue Ethics* (Oxford, Oxford University Press).

——(2008) 'Two Ways of Doing the Right Thing' in Farrelly and Solum (2008) 236.

——(2010) 'Virtue Ethics', *The Stanford Encyclopedia of Philosophy (Winter 2010 Edition)*, Edward N Zalta (ed), www.plato.stanford.edu/archives/win2010/entries/ethics-virtue/

Hutton, E (2002) 'Moral Reasoning in Aristotle and Xunzi' 29 *Journal of Chinese Philosophy* 355.

Jost, L and Wuerth, J (2011) *Perfecting Virtue: New Essays on Kantian Ethics and Virtue Ethics* (Cambridge, Cambridge University Press).

Katz A (forthcoming) 'Virtue Ethics and Efficient Breach', *Suffolk University Law Review.*

Koller, Peter (2007) 'Law, Morality and Virtue' in Rebecca L Walker and Philip J Ivanhoe (eds), *Working Virtue – Virtue Ethics and Contemporary Moral Problems* (Oxford, Oxford University Press) 191.

Kronman, AT (1993) *The Lost Lawyer – Failing Ideals of the Legal Profession* (Cambridge, Massachusetts, Harvard University Press).

Kvanvig, JL (1992) *The Intellectual Virtues and the Life of the Mind* (Savage, Rowman and Littlefield).

——(2003) *The Value of Knowledge and the Pursuit of Understanding* (Cambridge, Cambridge University Press).

——(2010) 'Virtue Epistemology' in Pritchard and Bernecker (2010).

Lahroodi, R (2007) 'Collective Epistemic Virtues' 21 *Social Epistemology* 281.

Lametti, D (2003) 'The (Virtue) Ethics of Private Property: A Framework and Implications' in A Hudson (ed), *New Perspectives on Property Law, Obligations and Restitution* (London, Cavendish Press) 39.

Lametti, D (2010a) 'How Virtue Ethics Might Help Erase C-32's Conceptual Incoherence' in M Geist (ed), *From 'Radical Extremism' to 'Balanced Copyright': Canadian Copyright and the Digital Agenda* (Toronto, Irwin Law) 327.
——(2010b) 'The Objects of Virtue' in G Alexander and E Peñalver (eds), *Property and Community* (New York, Oxford University Press) 1.
——(forthcoming) 'The Virtuous P(eer) – Reflections on the Ethics of File Sharing' in Lever, A Lever (ed), *New Frontiers in the Philosophy of Intellectual Property* (Cambridge, Cambridge University Press).
Leben, S (2011) 'An Expectation of Empathy' 51 *Washburn Law Journal* 49.
Louden, R (1984) 'On Some Vices of Virtue Ethics' 21 *American Philosophical Quarterly* 227. Reprinted in Crisp and Slote (1997) 201 and Statman (1997) 165.
Luban, D (1992) 'Justice Holmes and Judicial Virtue' in Chapman and Galston (1992) 235.
Lund, N (2012) 'Judicial Independence, Judicial Virtue, and the Political Economy of the Constitution', 35 *Harvard Journal of Law and Public Policy* 37.
Macedo, S (1991) *Liberal Virtues: Citizenship, Virtue, and Community in Liberal Constitutionalism* (New York, Oxford University Press).
MacIntyre, A (1984) *After Virtue* (Notre Dame, University of Notre Dame Press).
Maclean, A (2008), *Autonomy, Informed Consent and Medical Law* (Cambridge, Cambridge University Press).
Markovits, D (2008) *A Modern Legal Ethics* (Princeton, Princeton University Press).
McConvill, J (2005) 'Positive Corporate Governance and its Implications for Executive Compensation' 6 *German Law Journal* 1777.
McDowell, J (1998) *Mind, Value, and Reality* (Cambridge, Harvard University Press).
Merriam, J (2011) 'The Stoics and Legal Conservatives: Strange Bedfellows or Just Strange Fellows?' 30 *Law and Philosophy* 201.
Mescher, B and Howieson, B (2005) 'Beyond Compliance: Promoting Ethical Conduct by Directors and Corporations' 1 *Corporate Governance Law Review* 93.
Michelon, C (2006) 'Practical Reason and Character Traits: Remarks on MacCormick's Sentimentalist Theory of Moral Perception' in Bankowski and MacLean (2006) 115.
Milde, M (2002) 'Legal Ethics: Why Aristotle Might Be Helpful' 33 *Journal of Social Philosophy* 45.
Miller C (2009) 'Social Psychology, Mood and Helping: Mixed Results for Virtue Ethics' 13 *Journal of Ethics* 145.
Modak-Truran, MC (2000) 'Corrective Justice and the Revival of Judicial Virtue' 12 *Yale Journal of Law and the Humanities* 249.
Montmarquet, J (1993) *Epistemic Virtue and Doxastic Responsibility* (Lanham, Rowman and Littlefield Publishers).
Moser, P (ed) (2002) *The Oxford Handbook of Epistemology* (New York, Oxford University Press).
Nadler, J (2012) 'Blaming as a Social Process: The Influence of Character and Moral Emotion on Blame' 75 *Law and Contemporary Problems* 3.
Nussbaum, M (1990) 'Aristotelian Social Democracy' in Douglass et al (1990) 203.
——(1999) 'Virtue Ethics: A Misleading Category?' 3 *The Journal of Ethics* 163.
——(2006) *Frontiers of Justice* (Cambridge, Harvard University Press).
O'Neill, O (1989) *Constructions of Reason* (Cambridge, Cambridge University Press).
Oakley, J (1996) 'Varieties of Virtue Ethics' IX *Ratio (New Series)* 128.
——and Cocking, D (2007) *Virtue Ethics and Professional Roles* (Cambridge, Cambridge University Press).

Opderbeck, DW (2007) 'A Virtue-Centred Approach to the Biotechnology Commons (or, the Virtuous Penguin) 59 *Maine Law Review* 315.
Pattinson, SD (2011) *Medical Law and Ethics* (London, Sweet and Maxwell).
Peñalver, EM (2009) 'Land Virtues' 94 *Cornell Law Review* 821.
Pence, G (1993) 'Virtue Theory' in Singer (1993) 249.
Pritchard, D and Bernecker, S (eds) *The Routledge Companion to Epistemology* (New York, Routledge).
Proceedings of 'Aristotle and the Philosophy of Law' IVR Special Workshop (2007), 3 *Revista da Facultade de Direito de Conselheiro Lafaiete*.
Riggs, W (2006) 'The Value Turn in Epistemology' in Hendricks and Pritchard (2006).
——(2010) 'Open-Mindedness' 41 *Metaphilosophy* 172.
Roberts, R and Wood, J (2007) *Intellectual Virtues: An Essay in Regulative Epistemology* (Oxford, Oxford University Press).
Rollert, J P (2010) 'Reversed on Appeal: The Uncertain Future of President Obama's "Empathy Standard"' 120 *Yale Law Journal Online* 89, http://yalelawjournal.org/images/pdfs/903.pdf.
Saguil, RM (2006) 'A Virtuous Profession: Re-Conceptualizing Legal Ethics from a Virtue-Based Moral Philosophy' 22 *Windsor Review of Legal and Social Issues* 1.
Schaeffer, M (2010) 'Virtue Ethics and the Justification of Punishment' 6 *International Journal of Punishment and Sentencing* 36.
Scharffs, B (1998) 'The Role of Humility in Exercising Practical Wisdom' 32 *University of California Davis Law Review* 127.
Sreenivasan, G *Emotion and Virtue* (forthcoming) (Princeton, Princeton University Press).
Sherman, N (1997) *Making Necessity a Virtue: Aristotle and Kant on Virtue* (Cambridge, Cambridge University Press).
Sherry, S (2003) 'Judges of Character' 38 *Wake Forest Law Review* 793.
Shiner, RA (1994) 'Aristotle's Theory of Equity' 27 *Loyola of Los Angeles Law Review* 1245.
Shklar, JN (1992) 'Justice without Virtue' in Chapman and Galston (1992) 283.
Siegel, NS (2008) 'The Virtue of Judicial Statesmanship' 86 *Texas Law Review* 959.
Sim, M (2007) *Remastering Morals with Aristotle and Confucius* (Cambridge, Cambridge University Press).
——(2011) 'Rethinking Virtue Ethics and Social Justice with Aristotle and Confucius' 20 (2) *Asian Philosophy* 195.
Singer, P (1993) *A Companion to Ethics* (Oxford and Malden, Blackwell).
Slote, M (1993) 'Virtue Ethics and Democratic Values' 24 *Journal of Social Philosophy* 5.
——(1995) *From Morality to Virtue* (New York, Oxford University Press).
——(2001) *Morals from Motives* (New York, Oxford University Press).
——(2007) *The Ethics of Care and Empathy* (London, Routledge).
——(2010) *Moral Sentimentalism* (New York, Oxford University Press).
Soeharno, J (2009) *The Integrity of the Judge – A Philosophical Inquiry* (Surrey and Burlington, Ashgate).
Solomon, D (2003) 'Virtue Ethics: Radical or Routine?' in DePaul and Zagzbeski (2003) 58.
Solum, LB (1988) 'The Virtues and Vices of a Judge: An Aristotelian Guide to Judicial Selection' 61 *California Law Review* 1735.
——(1994) 'Equity and the Rule of Law' in I Shapiro (ed), *The Rule of Law: NOMOS XXXVI* (New York, New York University Press).
——(2003) 'Virtue Jurisprudence: A Virtue-Centred Theory of Judging' in Brady and Pritchard (2003) 163.

Solum, LB (2005a) 'The Aretaic Turn in Constitutional Theory' 70 *Brooklyn Law Review* 475.
——(2005b) 'A Tournament of Virtue' 32 *Florida State University Law Review* 1365.
——(2005c) 'Judicial Selection: Ideology versus Character' 26 *Cardozo Law Review* 659.
——(2006) 'Natural Justice' 51 *American Journal of Jurisprudence* 65.
Sosa, E (1980) 'The Raft and the Pyramid: Coherence versus Foundations in the Theory of Knowledge' 5 *Midwest Studies in Philosophy* 3.
——(1991) *Knowledge in Perspective* (Cambridge, Cambridge University Press).
——(2007) *A Virtue Epistemology I: Apt Belief and Reflective Knowledge* (New York, Oxford University Press).
Statman, D (1997) *Virtue Ethics: A Critical Reader* (Washington DC, Georgetown University Press).
Steup, M (2001) *Knowledge, Truth, and Duty: Essays on Epistemic Justification, Responsibility, and Virtue* (New York, Oxford University Press).
Strang, LJ (2012), 'Originalism and the Aristotelian Tradition: Virtue's Home in Originalism' 80 *Fordham Law Review* 1997.
Swanton, C (2003) *Virtue Ethics: A Pluralistic View* (New York, Oxford University Press).
Tan SH (2005) 'Imagining Confucious: Paradigmatic Characters and Virtue Ethics' 32 (3) *Journal of Chinese Philosophy* 409.
Tessman, L (2005) *Burdened Virtues: Virtue Ethics for Liberatory Struggles* (New York, Oxford University Press).
Tiwald, J (2010) 'Confucianism and Virtue Ethics: Still A Fledgling in Chinese and Comparative Philosophy' 1 (2) *Comparative Philosophy* 55.
Trianosky, G (1990) 'What is Virtue Ethics All About?' 27 (4) *American Philosophical Quarterly* 355.
van Norden, B (2007) *Virtue Ethics and Consquentialism in Early Chinese Philosophy* (Cambridge, Cambridge University Press).
Walker, R and Ivanhoe, P (eds) (2007) *Working Virtue: Virtue Ethics and Contemporary Ethical Problems* (Oxford, Oxford University Press).
Wardlaw, KM (2010) 'Umpires, Empathy, and Activisim: Lessons from Judge Cardozo' 85 *Notre Dame Law Review* 1629.
Watson, G (2007) 'On the Primacy of Character' in Statman (1997) 56.
West, R (forthcoming) 'The Anti-Empathic Turn' in LIII *NOMOS*, James Fleming (eds) *Passions and Emotions.*
Woolley, A and Wendel, WB (2010) 'Legal Ethics and Moral Character' 23 *Georgetown Journal of Legal Ethics* 1065.
Wyman, KM (2009) 'Should Property Scholars Embrace Virtue Ethics? A Skeptical Comment' 94 *Cornell Law Review* 991.
Yankah, EN (2004) 'Good Guys and Bad Guys: Punishing Character, Equality and the Irrelevance of Moral Character to Criminal Punishment' 25 *Cardozo Law Review* 1019.
——(2009) 'Virtue's Domain' *University of Illinois Law Review* 1167.
——(2011) 'A Paradox of Overcriminalization' 14 *New Criminal Law Review* 1.
Yu, J (2007) *The Ethics of Confucius and Aristotle: Mirrors of Virtue* (New York and London, Routledge).
——(2010) 'The Practicality of Ancient Virtue Ethics: Greece and China' 9 (3) *Dao: A Journal of Comparative Philosophy* 289.
Zagzebski, L (1996) *Virtues of the Mind: An Inquiry into the Nature of Virtue and the Ethical Foundations of Knowledge* (Cambridge, Cambridge University Press).

——(2001) 'Recovering Understanding' in Steup (2001) 235.
Zahnd, ER (1996) 'The Application of Universal Laws to Particular Cases: A Defense of Equity in Aristotelianism and Anglo-American Law' 59 *Law and Contemporary Problems* 263.

1.

Law, Virtue and Legal Reasoning

2

Practical Wisdom in Legal Decision-Making[*]

CLAUDIO MICHELON

MY OBJECTIVE IN what follows is to try to understand certain aspects of a relationship between, on the one hand, moral and intellectual virtues and, on the other hand, the phenomenon of law-application. What will occupy me is not so much the relationship between a general conception of ethics (ie virtue ethics)[1] and law, as the relationship of certain traits of character, in particular certain aspects of practical wisdom, and the process of legal decision-making. In short, I would like to present a plausible picture of subjectively possessed virtue, and in particular of practical wisdom, that is able to play a role in legal decision-making. Although I cannot provide anything like a complete account of legal decision-making here, I would also like to outline the way in which the theory of virtue and practical wisdom presented here might offer an alternative to the dominant conceptions of legal reasoning and decision-making.

To explain more precisely what the subject of this chapter is, let me start by outlining three (conceptually independent) ways in which virtues might be said to relate to law. First, the development of virtue in the citizenry might be thought to be the reason that justifies the existence of law (in general) or of particular legal institutions.[2] Opponents to that view would not necessarily oppose the idea that developing virtue is a good thing, but would often object to doing it through law and politics rather than, say, education by the family or some religious organisation. According to those opponents, accepting that virtue-training is the central goal of a political community would undermine politics' main business, which is to provide a fertile ground for autonomous choice. As far as actual institutional design is concerned, those opposing views do not necessarily lead to completely

* The author is indebted to Zenon Bankowski, Luis Fernando Barzotto, Andrew Halpin and Neil Walker for their generosity in commenting on an early draft.

[1] As distinct from deontological and utilitarian conceptions of ethics, in R Hurthouse's helpful typology. See Hurthouse (1999: 1–8).

[2] A paradigmatic defence of that is given by Aristotle, for whom politics' main business is the happiness of the citizens (for instance in *Politics* VII 1324a23-25 in Aristotle (1984: 2101)), while happiness cannot be attained without virtue (among many other passages, see *Politics* VII 1323b21-23, in Aristotle (1984: 2101)).

different arrangements. Aristotle, for instance, thought that the exercise of choice was a central component of the development of virtue and, more generally, of leading a good life[3] and that means that political institutions would need to be arranged in such a way as to allow the citizenry to exercise choice (although he would also be willing to accept many different restrictions on choice).

Secondly, virtues might be said to provide the content of legal norms or directives: it is because being, say, truthful is good, that we should keep our promises and contracts. Law and virtues would, in this view, have a (totally or partially) homologous content. That is certainly not the view of many Aristotelians and, in particular, of Aquinas, who famously believed that not all virtues should be prescribed or vices proscribed.[4]

Thirdly, the possession of certain virtues by certain people might be conceived as a necessary condition for the appropriate working of a political community and of its legal system. This is a very complex question that branches out into many different possible sub-themes along the axes of 'who' (should display the virtues), 'which' (virtues) and 'why' (they should be displayed). Should citizens possess civic friendship for a society to be possible? What does 'civic friendship' mean? Should political officials be truthful? Should all kinds of political officials have the same virtues?

In this chapter, I would like to contribute to the plausibility of the thesis that legal decision-making by public officials (paradigmatically judges) can only be carried out appropriately if those officials possess certain virtues. In other words, only a certain kind of *person* would be able to carry out proper legal decision-making. This suggestion runs against the deep suspicion in legal and political theory against the influence of subjectivity on those wielding political power for, in modern western societies, we have come to believe that we should all be ruled by law and not by men. Epistemologically, the modern empire of method promised to purify, at least partially, our scientific conclusions from subjectivity and methodologies presented themselves to the jurist as auspicious strategies to tame the legal decision-maker's subjectivity. The aspiration of controlling subjectivity through method reached its apex in nineteenth-century legal formalism, but later theorists, who were keen on admitting that subjectivity plays a role in legal decision-making, were also careful to explain that legal justification (as opposed to the 'discovery' of the right answer) would not be merely subjective.[5] I believe this suspicion to be deeply rooted in an oversimplified conception of the relation between objectivity and subjectivity and, more importantly, I believe it to be detrimental to the ethical understanding of legal decision-making.

The full defence of this thesis is, of course, a larger project than I could fit into this chapter, but the arguments presented here are a key part of it. What I intend

[3] Although Aristotle did not consider liberty the most important political value, his theory of virtue supposes free choice. For a summary of the arguments see Miller Jr (1995: 356).

[4] Which is the subject of *Summa Theologiae* 1a2ae question 96, articles 2 and 3.

[5] Wasserstrom (1961:25–30, 65–66); MacCormick (1978:15 ff).

to provide here is a conception of the subjective/objective divide that would allow for a theory of practical wisdom as a form of relationship between subjectivity and objectivity.

In what follows I will start by making some preliminary clarifications on what I take to be the most fundamental connection between virtues and legal decision-making (section I). With that in place, I start to address the greatest obstacle in assigning virtues (in particular practical wisdom) a major role in legal decision-making: the fear of subjectivity in decisions taken by public officials. The first step in that argument is to object to an oversimplified conception of the subjective/objective divide that clouds our judgement, and to replace this flawed picture with an alternative (and less threatening) picture. I try to do all that in section II. Section III is where the main elements of my principal argument are displayed and defended. There I discuss practical wisdom, and in particular its 'perceptive' aspect at some length, in a way that will, hopefully, complete the work started in section II and deliver an acceptable account of how the decision-maker's subjectivity could (indeed must) come into play in all forms of practical decision-making. Section IV complicates matters further by arguing that certain moral virtues are necessary conditions for the possession of intellectual virtues (or at the very least of one intellectual virtue, namely, practical wisdom). In section V, I move back to the specific context of legal reasoning to contrast my picture of legal decision-making against a rival picture and conclude by indicating a few peculiarities of the use of practical wisdom in contexts of legal decision-making.

I. VIRTUES, MERE SKILLS AND LEGAL REASONING

Let me start by clarifying what I mean by 'virtue': virtue is a settled disposition or *habitus* that allows you to do, perceive or think certain things effortlessly and intelligently.[6] As such, virtues are (a) subjective traits that include (b) a motivational element, since they are inclinations to react to certain stimuli, and (c) a perceptive element, that is to say, a capacity to see something as something, or as Wittgenstein would put it, a capacity for aspect-seeing.[7] This perception should not be necessarily taken to be a moment of moral clarity or insight (a divination of the right answer), but could take the form of, for instance, a puzzlement that leads to further investigation on the matter. In that case, the 'act' that I am motivated to perform by the perception is to investigate beyond appearances, to leave my intellectual comfort zone. That perceptive element, present in all moral virtues is, of course, a virtue in its own right, namely the intellectual virtue of practical wisdom (*phronesis*, *prudentia*).[8] Certain feelings will also be connected to virtues,[9] such as

[6] McCabe (2008: 56).

[7] Discussed at length in section xi of part II of Wittgenstein (1967: 193–229).

[8] Aristotle (1984: 1748 and 1862), ie *Nicomachean Ethics* 1106b36 and 1178a18. For further explanation see Aubenque (1963: 39–40).

[9] MacIntyre (1985: 149).

pleasure, regret or guilt. Finally, virtues enable their possessor to achieve a good life, not simply as means, but as integral parts of that good life.[10]

Let me just add the caveat that this analysis of virtue should not be taken to imply that the motivational, perceptive and emotional aspects of virtue can be understood in isolation. Quite the contrary: what makes them part of a single virtue (say, courage) is the ways in which they interact and contribute to a final result.

The definition presented above is not completely innocent, in the sense that the aspects of virtue brought to the fore by it will play a role in my account of the particular virtues of legal decision-makers. But there is something missing in it, at least as far as classical accounts of what a virtue is are concerned. In my brief explanation of virtue, I have not discussed its *causa finalis*. The reason for that omission is the fact that I need to provide a more extensive explanation of it. Classical virtue ethics often distinguishes between technique and virtue on the ground that a mere technique is directed towards the excellence of the thing produced (in the way blacksmithing excellence is realised in a sword or a fine piece of jewellery), while virtue is directed towards the excellence of the producer. In McCabe's words:

> So while a skill or a technique is directed to the excellence of the thing produced, a virtue is directed to the excellence of the producer (the development of good or bad dispositions of this kind, virtues or vices, is the development of a self).[11]

In apparent contradiction to that, my main contention in this chapter is that virtues are necessary conditions to achieve excellence not in the decision-maker, but in the world beyond the self. What is relevant in relation to them, from the point of view of my argument, is that they allow the world to be transformed in a particular way (through the decision taken by the legal decision-maker), not simply that the decision-maker becomes a better person.

This apparent contradiction could be explained away by arguing that although virtues are focused on self-improvement, they can also be, in a way that is accidental to their own nature, a necessary condition for appropriate legal decision-making. However, some problems raised by the technique/virtue distinction still persist. For starters, it would appear that, in certain situations, the value of self-improvement would be at odds with the external benefit that might be generated by the action. I have argued elsewhere that public agents have less room for the exercise (and hence, for the development) of certain virtues when compared with agents who are not bound by public office.[12] Think also of a doctor who allows herself to be deeply affected by the suffering of her patients. She might find herself unable to make certain decisions or to perform certain procedures.

[10] ibid 148–49.

[11] McCabe (2008: 57).

[12] In virtue of a more stringent requirement on impartiality that imposes itself to public agents, they are morally obliged to reason their way into their decisions (if that is at all possible in the concrete circumstances) in a way that might preclude them from developing the appropriate degree of spontaneity. For a complete argument see Michelon (2006a: 59–83).

The way out of this tension is to add another element to the conception of virtue exposed above. Many, if not all, virtues are essentially other-regarding. What that means is that all those forms of perception, motivation and feeling that constitute a virtue are aspects of the way in which the self relates to others. They do not simply express, but truly constitute forms of recognition of those others *as* possessing a particular sort of value. If what the self is, she is in relation to others, it follows that her self-perfection is a *relational* perfection. Incidentally, this is an essential part of what is meant by saying that humans are *political*. Now, that relationship finds its objective expression in many forms of communal living, first and foremost of which is a community's law. So, it is not just a happy coincidence that certain virtues might help a person to achieve excellence while also being essential for the appropriate discharge of that person's role as a legal decision-maker. There is an essential connection between the two 'roles' that virtue plays in this case: it is only a perfection of the self because it helps the decision-maker to relate appropriately to another member of the community.[13] Granted, this does not eliminate the tension between self-improvement and appropriate exercise of a public role: it might still be the case that my ability to relate to others through law prevents me from developing other character traits that would be desirable to develop. However, because there is a direct self-improvement gain in learning to relate legally to others, I am not simply sacrificing my self-improvement to the benefit of others when I exercise the virtues necessary to relate to them in such a way.

A second problem arises from the technique/virtue distinction in the context of legal decision-making: if legal decision-making made virtuously improves the self that makes it, wouldn't other people who are not public officials directly in charge of legal decision-making miss out on a key form of self-development and improvement? I believe not. We do not relate to each other legally only through judges. There is probably more legal interaction in one day of someone's life (most of which are just a result of settled dispositions) than there are cases decided in court every year. Although judges are indeed the paradigmatic legal decision-makers, they are obviously not the only ones and, arguably, those virtues I am going to discuss in sections III and IV are also part of the engagement of other members of the community with each other through law.

To conclude: virtues are subjective dispositions to perceive and act, which are accompanied by feelings and are intrinsically connected to the way in which we relate to (recognise) each other. Most, if not all of them, are other-regarding and are directly connected to our recognition of alterity.

[13] Indeed, in Aristotle's *Nicomachean Ethics*, the key to understanding justice (and law) is to locate it in a relation with others (eg in 1130b1, Aristotle (1984: 1784)).

II. THE FRONTIERS BETWEEN SUBJECTIVE AND OBJECTIVE

Defending the theses that the possession of a certain moral character is a necessary condition for success in legal reasoning and legal decision-making and that, consequently, the latter are not simply techniques that can be mastered with sufficient intellectual effort by almost anyone with the appropriate intellectual investment, raises an immediate problem. It would seem that appropriate legal decision-making is subjective in a strong sense. Nowadays, most theorists would agree that legal decision-making is subjective in a weak sense. They might do so by employing a distinction between 'discovery' and 'justification'. As Wasserstrom put it:

> One kind of question asks about the manner in which a decision or conclusion was reached; the other inquires whether a given decision or conclusion is justifiable. That is to say, a person who examines a decision process may want to know about the factors that led to or produced the conclusion; he may also be interested in the manner in which the conclusion was to be justified.[14]

That distinction allows the theorist to admit that decisions reached by legal decision-makers are subjective, while also claiming that the justification process can be understood objectively.[15] In that way, objectivity is preserved and subjectivity in legal decision-making is explained away. It is even possible to accept, in this way, that it is an asset to have virtuous judges; after all, the 'discovery' of the right legal decision would be made easier if we have judges gifted with a certain moral perception. But discovery is accidental to legal reasoning, while justification is not. What I want to put forward here is an account of how the possession of certain virtues might be plausibly conceived as a necessary condition for justification to be carried out appropriately.

Another way to accept subjectivity in a weak sense into legal decision-making is defended by Dworkin, who claims that subjectivity in the assessment of constitutional matters is unavoidable.[16] However, what Dworkin considers to be the unavoidable subjectivity of legal decision-making is very narrow: it comprises only principled positions on matters that judges hold on issues of political morality.[17] Nevertheless, there is much more to subjectivity in legal decision-making than the use of personal moral conviction on matters of political morality by judges. In order to understand how possessing certain character traits, and not only upholding certain moral opinions, is of central importance to legal decision-making, let me first identify the conception of subjectivity that I believe is at the roots of our discomfort with accepting a greater role for subjectivity in legal decision-making.

[14] Wasserstrom (1961: 25).

[15] See MacCormick (1978: 15), where he defends that '[t]he process which is worth studying is the process of argumentation as a process of justification'.

[16] Dworkin (2003: 8).

[17] ibid 11.

There are two radically different ways of conceiving what differentiates subjectivity and objectivity, namely the 'topological' and 'relational' conceptions. According to the topological conception, subjectivity is identified as a stage where events occur.[18] Feelings, thoughts, sensations, the will and other 'mental events' happen in the inner world, which is opposed to the external world, where objective happenings take place. In the topological conception, the total world branches out into two separate worlds, which are partially insulated from one another: the subjective and objective worlds. The separation is carried out by means of a simple procedure: first, one identifies certain kinds of events and, second, following certain criteria, those events are assigned to one of those two worlds.

This brief presentation of the topological concepts of 'mind' and 'external world' glosses over the many different, and sometimes opposing, conceptions of those concepts defended (and sometimes assumed) by philosophers. As an example, think of how Descartes and Galileo would separate internal from external events on the basis that external events could be thoroughly described in terms of the so-called 'primary qualities', while internal events would have to be described in terms of 'secondary qualities'.[19] However, for Descartes, primary qualities are identified by the joint application of three criteria (detectability by more than one sense, possibility of being imagined clearly and distinctively, and measurability), while Galileo only offers one criterion (impossibility of conceiving a material substance without the particular quality).[20] In the standard interpretation of Kant, his take on the issue of the objective/subjective divide was also constructed along the lines of a difference between primary and secondary qualities.[21] While the noumenal world is unknowable, we can use our reason to make sense of the phenomena that we register always in terms of secondary qualities. Our knowledge of the noumenal world is, for the most part, precluded.[22]

However, what matters to me here is not so much what separates Descartes, Galileo and Kant, but what unites them: the mind is a place where events occur, as much as the external world is a place where other sorts of events occur (for Descartes and Galileo, physical events; for Kant, for the most part, unknowable events).

For our purposes, the most important feature attached to this topological separation of the internal (subjective) realm and external (objective) realm is the ensuing thesis that the mind is better known than the external world (in its paradigmatic Cartesian formulation, 'the mind is better known than the body').[23] That

[18] Kenny (1966: 352–53).

[19] The terminology of primary and secondary qualities is not Cartesian (*cf* Hacker (1991: 10)), but it was already in use in the 17th century (eg by Boyle) and it was philosophically current in Locke and Hume. The expressions then gained a philosophical course that lasts until now (eg Hacker (1991) and Putnam (1992: 82 ff)).

[20] For Galileo, see Galileo (1960: 28); for Descartes see summary in Hacker (1991: 11).

[21] This standard interpretation of Kant's critical philosophy is sketched by Henry Alison, who proceeds to attack it. See Alison (1983: 3–10).

[22] Although not in relation to moral and legal issues, as it is explicitly stated, for instance, in the *Groundwork of the Metaphysics of Morals*, 4:451–54 in Kant (1996: 98–100).

[23] Which is, of course, the subject of the second meditation, see Descartes (1973: 23).

makes one's mind immediately known to oneself, while making it completely opaque to everyone else. All subjective events, ranging from emotions to perceptions, from sensations to beliefs (including moral beliefs), are inscrutable to everyone else. It is impossible to know whether someone is acting on moral principle or in self-interest, if one's correct action was just a lucky guess or a result of considered judgement. If that is the conception of subjectivity that dominates one's landscape, it is easy to see why the *rule of men* would strike so much horror both on the political philosopher and on the citizen: if there is no possibility of knowing what happens in other minds, there is no possibility of trusting them. A proper understanding of the constructive (indeed indispensable) role that subjectivity and, in particular, virtues, might play in legal decision-making is dependent on the viability of another conception of subjectivity and of its relation to the objective world. I believe that the relational conception of subjectivity can provide just that.

A relational conception of subjectivity would see it not as referring to a place (with a specific epistemological status) where certain kinds of events occur, but as referring collectively to a number of ways in which a person might relate to the world. If we compare the Cartesian concept of 'mind' with the classical concepts of *dianoia*[24] or *cogitatio*,[25] it becomes clear that the latter express an ability to understand, that is to say, to engage in a particular way with the world, while the former, as I said above, is a stage where emotions, the will, mental images, sensation and thought happen.[26]

If subjectivity is a generic name for ways in which we can relate to the world, whether or not reliance on certain subjective features of the public decision-maker is a good thing might depend on which sorts of ways of relating to the world we are talking about. In a topological conception of subjectivity, the primary relationship between the internal world and the external world would have to be conceived as a causal connection between the internal event (the decision-maker's will, or prejudice, or personal interest, or moral ideal) and the external action. And that relationship might seem to describe appropriately situations in which, for instance, one's personal interest motivates her to do something. Indeed, this seems to be the kind of scenario that the ideal of the rule of law primarily opposes. Also, the idea that public agents are subject to a heightened requirement of impartiality is at its most convincing when placed in such contexts.

What a relational conception of subjectivity brings to this picture is a charge of oversimplification: besides the situation described above, there are also other forms of relationship between the person and the world that cannot be described as a causal connection between an inscrutable internal event and an action. A more complex view of the relationship between subjectivity and objectivity would

[24] An example of this is the Stoic use of *dianoia* to refer to the part of the soul that apprehends objects in the world, *cf* Pereira (1994: 152–53).

[25] A brief comparison between the scholastic and the Cartesian uses of the word *cogitatio* can be found in Kenny (1968: 352 ff).

[26] ibid 352–53.

help us to understand the different ways in which subjectivity can come into play in legal decision-making.[27]

III. PRACTICAL WISDOM AND PERCEPTION

Let me start by stating my next claim in brief: practical wisdom (*phronesis*, *prudentia*) is the way practical decision-makers can face up to the difficulties presented above by providing a blueprint of an appropriate relationship between subjectivity and objectivity in contexts of decision-making, including legal decision-making. Before unpacking this claim, let me just acknowledge how irritating is the all too common strategy of appealing to practical wisdom as an explanation every time the theorist encounters an apparently insurmountable difficulty in explaining practical reason. Appeals to practical wisdom often take the form of appeals to a mysterious form of insight that allows the decision-maker to divine the answer to a difficult practical quandary. Certain features of classical accounts of practical wisdom might add to the confusion, if they are stated outside the context in which they make sense. Indeed, Aristotle's opinion that the *phronimos'* decision is the *criterion* for correctness,[28] if put outside its proper context, seems to be a confirmation of the worst fears of those who are afraid of accepting subjectivity in public decision-making.

I would like to think that my use of practical wisdom would not leave the after-taste of an appeal to something that is beyond all rational accounts. Indeed, it seems to me that we can have a fairly straightforward and informative account of practical wisdom and of its role in legal decision-making. Moreover, I believe that such an account would not necessarily lead to a normative procedure that would (in my view) explain away the very point of needing to appeal to it. That, I believe, is the insufficiency of methodological accounts of practical wisdom such as those provided by Klaus Günther and Neil MacCormick.[29]

The first element of an informative account of practical wisdom is the fact that it is not a single faculty, skill, ability or form of perception, but a bundle of those. The second is the understanding that what holds this bundle together in a complex division of labour is the task of acquiring knowledge (in a qualified sense) about particulars. With that in mind, I move on to try to explain how this objective might be achieved, what the constitutive parts of practical wisdom's complex bundle are, and how the division of labour between those constitutive parts is structured.

In the philosophical tradition to which practical wisdom is a central concept, there has always been an apparent uneasiness between two aspects of it. On the

[27] This conception of subjectivity is part of a philosophical anthropology in which the subject transcends itself by coming into contact with the world and then returning to itself, which might be called an anthropology of exodus (thanks to LF Barzotto for that metaphor).

[28] In the above-mentioned passage of the *Nicomachean Ethics* (1106b36), Aristotle affirms that the just mean is determined by the right reason which is, in turn, defined by reference to the *phronimos* (Aristotle (1984: 1748)). For an enlightening discussion of the *phronimos* as criterion, see Aubenque (1963: 33–41).

[29] See the discussion below in section V.

one hand, practical wisdom is often said to be the ability to choose the right means to a particular end.[30] This aspect of practical wisdom is often related to its intrinsic connection with deliberation. On the other hand, practical wisdom is said to be a form of perception, a capacity to see things in a particular way. But why would the perceptive side of prudence be restricted to the search for the appropriate means? Why can't it also be about ends? Is not the relationship between means and ends too messy to ground any clear distinctions between kinds of intellectual virtue? More generally, what is the relationship between the two aspects of practical wisdom? Is there an internal connection between them, or are they loosely connected features of a makeshift concept designed to explain too much? Those questions stem from a misunderstanding of practical wisdom that can be easily dispelled by explaining what it means in a theory of deliberation.

The best way to start to explain this is to flesh out what is meant by the means-end aspect of practical wisdom. The 'ends' to which practical wisdom finds the means are not established by a whim or temporary fluctuation of the will. They are directly connected with what the agent cares deeply about, that is to say, to the settled dispositions that make up one's character, that are constitutive of her identity. Those ends are both subjectively possessed and relatively stable and they point towards a division of labour between practical wisdom, as an intellectual virtue, and the agent's moral virtues. Practical wisdom is conceptually connected to moral virtue in such a way that, if the particular skills/abilities/forms of perception that would normally constitute practical wisdom are used to help implement a vicious preference by the agent, those skills would simply form part of the intellectual vice of cunning. For reasons I shall present later, I believe this distinction not to be ad hoc.[31]

In order to understand how deliberation connects that conception of practical wisdom as providing means with practical wisdom as perception, let me also make a few clarifications on the latter. Practical wisdom is not just any form of perception, but a perception of something *as something*. For both Aristotle and Aquinas (with whom I wholeheartedly agree in this matter), sense data does not come to us as streams of raw data to be organised by our reasoning capacities. Our senses see the data streams *as something* already. When we look at a tiger we do not see a certain amount of orangeness and blackness, but a tiger. For Aquinas, that is because we have inner senses that organise data streams into *gestalts*, totalities of meaning.[32] Those four inner senses (*communis, imaginatio, aestimativus*[33] and sense-memory) are an integral part of our sensibility and are conditions for us to be able to relate to the particularities of the world. Our reasoning capacities, being linguistic in

[30] See *Nicomachean Ethics* at 1144a8 (Aristotle (1984: 1807)); also, *Summa Theologiae* 2a2ae question 47, article 6 (Aquinas (1974: 23)).

[31] See eg MacIntyre (1985: 154–55).

[32] McCabe (2008: 123–27).

[33] In humans, the *aestimativa* is called by Aquinas *cogitativa*, in order to emphasise the capacity that humans have to acquire their *aestimativa* by comparisons (and not only by instinct, as it occurs in other animals).

nature, are necessarily universalistic and have an intrinsic limitation in dealing with particulars. We learn about particulars through our senses (including, and crucially, through our inner senses), which allow us to recognise in a particular data stream something (or things).

Now, one of the crucial aspects of those inner senses is that they are partly innate and partly acquired. In order to make the interplay between innate and acquired sensibility clearer, let me briefly sketch how the inner senses work according to Aquinas.[34] The first inner sense is *sensus communis*, which refers to our ability to form gestalts from sense data. When I see the tiger and not only patches of colour, that is the working of my *sensus communis*, which is partly shared by ourselves and other animals, and which is partly innate. That coordination of all the data streams flowing in from our senses into a common totality is the work of this particular inner sense. This capacity is not entirely passive, for the subject seeks sense in the data stream and in seeking sense (ie to see the data input *as something*) we need to rely on a basic inherited structure. We are not restricted to it, though. Through habit and experience, including the reflexive experience of language and reasoning, we can build on that inherited basis by using and contributing to the resources of the culture we are immersed in. However, this reasoning would not be possible if we could not retain our gestalts. Neither would story-telling, lying, telling jokes and other activities in which those gestalts feature in the absence of direct sense data. According to Aquinas, the job of retaining those gestalts formed by the *sensus communis* is performed by another inner sense, that of *imaginatio*. Part of that sense of the totality of an object is a certain preliminary idea of how that object relates to the subject herself. Both humans and other superior animals assess the meaning of the gestalt formed by the *sensus communis* for them. This sort of preliminary assessment is an integral part of our experience of the object, not of any reasoning. To use a common example, the lamb that runs away from the wolf is not making the assessment as a result of any reasoning, but simply because it perceives the wolf *as dangerous*. This again might be either hardwired in our biological existence (as my perfectly normal fear of heights seems to be) or acquired. If I stick my hand in the fire, fire might come to mean 'dangerous to touch' for me. This evaluation is performed by my third inner sense, the *aestimativus*. Our fourth inner sense is analogous to our *imaginatio* and refers to our capacity to retain these assessments for future use. For lack of a better name, let us call it, following McCabe, sense-memory.

What the structure of these four inner senses brings out is a more complex theory of perception (than, say, Hume's) which gives a convincing explanation of how our perceptive capacities can evolve by means of an interaction between agent and environment. In this account, our senses learn as much as our reasoning capacities. Indeed, they can even store certain achievements of our reasoning capacities.

[34] What follows is a sketch of the relatively brief discussion in *Summa Theologiae* 1a, question 78, article 4 (Aquinas (1970: 134–43)).

This perceptive capacity to see data streams *as something* is directly connected to what Wittgenstein called a form of life. The concept is used by Wittgenstein to explain the embeddedness of our linguistic criteria in certain complex forms of interaction between individuals. As Cavell puts it:

> That on the whole we do [project words we have learned in some contexts into further contexts] is a matter of our sharing routes of interest and feeling, modes of response, senses of humour and of significance and of fulfilment, of what is outrageous, of what is similar to what else, what is a rebuke, what forgiveness, of when an utterance is an assertion, when an appeal, when an explanation – all the whirl of organism Wittgenstein calls 'forms of life'.[35]

Now, an important part of that form of life is a capacity for appropriate aspect-seeing. The fact that we concur in seeing tigers and wolves when the appropriate sense data hits our inner senses means we share a way of relating to the world. Participation in the form of life that is a condition for *logos* (discourse) comprehends a biological element and an ethnological element.[36] The ethnological element (which is very salient in Wittgenstein's own work) might help with relatively simple operations like recognising certain sorts of objects as part of a social practice (think of the Lilliputians trying to describe Gulliver's watch without partaking in the western conventions of time-mapping), but it might also help to identify morally relevant aspects of reality such as certain forms of human need and suffering. The latter are the most relevant in our quest to provide a workable conception of practical wisdom for legal decision-makers. How we acquire the ability of perceiving those aspects of the social reality (aspects that might be sometimes hidden even from the agents) is a complex matter. Aristotle famously thought that virtue is acquired through experience, through embedding oneself in the world (including the social world) or, in Wittgenstein's jargon, inserting oneself in a form of life. But experience is a vague word that needs specification and I shall come back to that later on in this chapter. For now, let me try to pull the strings together and explain how the 'sense-perception' aspect of practical wisdom might fit with its 'selection of means' aspect.

The key to understanding this is in a crucial difference between practical syllogism and logical syllogism. If a logical syllogism is valid, the conclusion flows *necessarily* from the premises. By 'necessarily', I mean that no new piece of information could possibly upset the flow from major premise to conclusion. Conversely, a perfectly acceptable practical syllogism is vulnerable to new information and, indeed, the practice of identifying relevant information and pitching it against an acceptable practical syllogism is a central feature of deliberation. Think of the following example:

Major premise: It is good to punish people who kill others as a result of their negligent behaviour.

[35] Cavell (1969: 52).
[36] ibid 158.

Minor premise: By imprisoning X for three years, I will be punishing him for behaving negligently and, as a result, having killed Y.
Conclusion: X should be imprisoned.

In this particular argument, the end is set by the major premise, the one that, as we said above, shows the kind of person I am. The minor premise introduces a means to achieve the end established in the major premise and the conclusion points to an action that should be performed. The conclusion seems to be perfectly acceptable, given the premises. But let me add a further element: let us suppose that X happens to be Y's father. Now other factors come into play for the decision-maker: the understanding of the pain of losing a child; the pain caused by the knowledge that the child was killed by one's own fault. The perception of that pain, that most humans would understand upon being told about the relationship between X and Y, would be very likely to bring considerations of appropriate proportional punishment to bear on the case and might show that three years' imprisonment is too harsh a punishment and that the father either should have a shorter period of incarceration or simply be let free (as would happen, I believe, in most contemporary legal systems). The perception of the father's pain is a key factor in determining the right means to achieve the putative end.

In this simple picture (which I am going to make slightly more complex below), it is clear how the means-end and the perceptive aspects of prudence might intersect. Perception of relevant factors that are not already factored into the practical syllogism can potentially destabilise the argument and conduct to the opposite conclusion (which, in the practical syllogism, is always an action).

Now let me complicate matters further. Think of the following argument:

Major premise: An equal distribution of resources available in a particular social group among the citizenry is a good.
Minor premise: In this particular society, taxation on those who have more than their equal share of the resources and allocation of that revenue to individuals in the form of a monetary compensation proportional to each individual's claim to be given an equal share is a way to get to an equal distribution of the available resources.
Conclusion: It is good to institute in this particular society forms of taxation on those who have more than their equal share of the resources and to allocate that revenue to individuals in the form of a monetary compensation proportional to each individual's claim to be given an equal share.

This sort of argument can be challenged in two different ways. On the one hand, one might attack the major premise by arguing that equal social distribution of resources is not a worthy objective or it is a worthy objective only under certain conditions. That sort of challenge is theoretical, in the sense that it attacks the universal conception of the good that the decision-maker is using to ground the argument. If the challenge is successful, the end of the decision-maker would change and, consequently, the decision-maker herself would be partly transformed. Another way in which the argument could be challenged would be to point out that the system of money transfers from individual to individual is not as good at bringing about equality of distribution of resources as a system of public provision of services to all the citizenry (say, a universal health service system). It might be argued that universal provision of services reinforces the sense that all citizens are in the same boat, that they should care about the suffering of others, at least to some extent, and that, in turn, would make equality in the distribution of resources more likely to be achieved. If this challenge is successful, the decision-maker is enlightened as to how the world works and about how to bring about the ends she so much believes in, but there is no further (necessary) transformation of the self.

However, the dynamics of rational decision-making and deliberation are not that neat. Even if we accept a conceptual separation between arguments about ends and means, actual processes of decision-making are messier in two related senses. First, sometimes arguments about means trigger a need for theoretical reflection. In my example above, the decision-maker's deliberation might lead her to consider whether social solidarity is not an end in itself that she should strive for. This consideration, in turn, would call into question the end she initially thought important to pursue (equality) and how it might relate to the end of reinforcing social solidarity. Secondly, it is also a means to bring about other ends that might already be part of the decision-maker's subjectivity, but that were lurking in the background. As Aristotle and Aquinas were deeply aware, human good is rather complex and being able to perceive which aspects of the situation call into question each good is a considerable deliberative achievement.

In such contexts the sort of perception of totalities needed is rather complex and depends on our ability to stock considerable numbers of complex and interlocking gestalts in our *imaginatio* and sense-memory. That aspect of our subjectivity is built up in a number of different ways, all of which are often brought together within a slightly vague conception of experience. Although I do not have the space to provide a comprehensive account of *phronesis*-building experience here, it is important for my argument to identify at least a few of its main sources. In the first place, one acquires certain relevant categories by relating in a particular way to the events in one's life. Losing a loved child will bring deep understanding of the suffering afflicting the killer in my first syllogism above. But, as Martha Nussbaum and others have pointed out, there are other ways to acquire a certain degree of understanding such as being exposed (and relating in a particular way) to human artefacts, in particular stories.[37] Martha Nussbaum rightly points out that the novel's narrative structure and ordinariness of theme makes it a particularly effective way to acquire the relevant subjective tools. But one should not underestimate other forms of storytelling. Fairy tales, and the stereotypes that go with them, make up for the lack of subtlety and character construction by their somehow wider (perhaps sweeping) unities of meaning. Beside personally experienced events and stories stand practices of reasoning and arguing. Aristotle's

[37] Nussbaum (1995: 4–10).

claim that virtue is a creature of habit and not of argument does not mean that the latter has no role whatsoever to play in the acquisition of practical wisdom, but only that it must build on other forms of experience. Although reasoning cannot do all the work, it might usefully influence the configuration of our inner senses.

So, at least one aspect of our subjectivity, our sense-perception, is a key element in practical decision-making and, by implication, in legal decision-making. But that subjectivity is neither mysterious nor static. It grows with experience, that is to say, with particular forms of engagement between the subject and certain aspects of the world, such as events that happen in one's own life and the narration of stories both fictional and real. Living through those events and being exposed to those stories and arguments cannot, *by itself*, bring any growth in moral perception. The subject needs to engage with those events and stories in a particular way. In other words, the subject must possess a particular set of virtues that allow her to engage appropriately with them.

In the next section, I discuss virtues that allow appropriate (ie *phronesis*-enhancing) engagement by the subject. Those might be called epistemic virtues since they allow for the development of an intellectual virtue (practical wisdom), but that should not obscure the fact that they might be aspects of more general moral virtues. The discussion is not meant to be exhaustive and, indeed, I believe that there might well be many epistemic virtues which either allow or at least facilitate *phronesis*-building. But a brief explanation of the mechanism through which they contribute to the development of practical wisdom is in order.

IV. VIRTUES AS CONDITIONS TO PRACTICAL WISDOM

In the past 30 years, epistemology's struggle with its inner demons has produced an unexpected upshot. From Ernest Sosa's seminal articles of the 1970s and 1980s to Roberts and Wood's recent *Intellectual Virtues*, epistemologists have been essaying with the idea that subjective features (including certain virtues) hold at least one of the keys for a correct account of human knowledge.[38] Now, practical wisdom, and the perceptual schemes outlined above that I take to be an important part of it, is itself a virtue. It is an epistemic virtue, not a moral virtue, but it is a virtue nevertheless. Moreover, as I have mentioned in my definition of virtue, it is an integral part of the possession of any virtue. However, that should not blind us to the fact that practical wisdom is complex and is more adequately described as a bundle of virtues, which might even include some moral virtues, or aspects thereof.

For all the novelty of the ways in which contemporary virtue epistemology fleshes out those connections between virtue and knowledge, it must be acknowledged that the idea of specific virtues that are integral parts of broader intellectual virtues, in

[38] Although many virtue epistemologists use the word 'virtue' in a broader sense than the one used in this chapter. Some use it to refer to any sort of subjective perceptive perfection, including the accuracy of external senses (eg good eyesight).

particular of practical wisdom, is not entirely new. Aquinas not only put forward a list of the constitutive elements of *prudentia*, amongst which feature openness to be taught and caution,[39] but he also offered clear evidence of previous work attempting to identify those constitutive parts.

I cannot offer a complete account of the constitutive parts of prudence here, but I would like to provide some clarification as to the mechanics of interaction between practical wisdom and those more specific 'epistemic' virtues.[40] I am not interested here in the relationship of those virtues to our ability to reason matters through or to build theories. My focus in practical wisdom leads me to focus on the relationship between the subject and the particularities of a given situation. The first and foremost role of epistemic virtues in relation to practical wisdom is to prevent what Roberts and Wood called 'perceptual rigidity'.[41]

By 'perceptual rigidity', I mean a failure of a subject's perceptual framework to react appropriately to certain stimuli, that is to say, a kind of aspect-blindness. The result of this failure is at best the creation of an obstacle for a perceptual framework to change appropriately; at worst it makes this change impossible. It is worth keeping in sight what the stakes are here, to wit: the possibility of the subject improving the way in which she relates to the objective world.

Each of our perceptual frameworks generates for us a zone of conceptual clarity, within which stimuli are disposed along familiar conceptual lines. One should not expect a significant challenge to our conceptual framework from stimuli that sit comfortably within it. One of the ways (perhaps the most important) in which our perceptual framework might be challenged and transformed is to acknowledge that it proves to be useless to understand certain stimuli. Here, the challenge for the subject is, first of all, to be able to perceive the shortcoming of one's own perceptual framework as it stands at a particular moment. The often-cited experiment run by Brunner and Postman serves to illustrate the point: subjects are invited to recognise playing cards shown to them. Anomalous cards (black hearts and red spades) are inserted in the deck with all the other regular cards. Subjects often failed to identify the anomalous cards, and classified them within the four familiar categories (red hearts and diamonds, black clubs and spades).[42] What is interesting for my purposes is that some subjects did recognise the anomalous cards – the irritation in their perceptual framework – even though they had no previous concept of red spades or black hearts.

[39] Although Aquinas includes caution not among the perceptive elements of prudence, but as one of the elements of its preceptive part (*Summa Theologiae* 2a2ae question 48, sole article, reply, in Aquinas (1974: 54–55)).

[40] I use epistemic in quotation marks in order to call attention to the fact that some of those epistemic virtues are specifications of general moral virtues to specific contexts of knowledge acquisition, which are, in turn, conceived very broadly to encompass not only our true justified beliefs, but also the excitement of our perceptual schemes by particulars.

[41] Roberts and Wood (2007: 202–04). Although I borrow their phrase here, the overlap between what I mean by it and what Roberts and Wood mean is only partial, given the fact that there is only partial coincidence between what I call perceptual scheme and what they call perception (or acquaintance).

[42] Bruner and Postman (1949).

I am able to perceive this uneasiness of my perceptual framework to cope with certain features of the particular situation because our perceptual framework does not generate only a comfort zone: it also creates a *zone of peripheral conceptual perception.* We acquire our perceptual framework from experience (which I use here to encompass very basic sense-experience, complex forms of engagement with the world and with others, and everything in between) and we do so by being presented with exemplars of the fact or object. We acquire our perceptual framework *in context.* Our peripheral conceptual perception is the ability to perceive something *relevantly* unusual in a new context on which we project our perceptual framework.

One's openness to be influenced by this peripheral perception varies from subject to subject, and reacting appropriately to it (with neither over-reaction nor blindness) is a matter of possessing certain traits of character. We might call those traits of character 'intellectual virtues'. Roberts and Wood provide a number of good examples of intellectual failure that result from the possession of the wrong character inclinations by the subject. Some of those failures create blind spots in our perceptual framework. Take the example of dogmatism, that is to say, the 'disposition to respond irrationally to oppositions to the belief [held]: anomalies, objections, evidence to the contrary, counterexamples, and the like'.[43] Such persistent disposition of character would lead the subject to discount whatever threatens their perceptual comfort zone as irrelevant and, as a result, the subject would fail to carry out the necessary investigation of the perceptual anomaly.

Dogmatism is, of course, just one of many ways in which one's settled dispositions might thwart the evolution of one's perceptual framework. A subject might lack interest in investing the necessary energy, might lack the courage to pursue a line of inquiry that could potentially jeopardise one's life by implying the need for a certain kind of action, or might fail in a myriad of other ways.

An appropriate use of one's peripheral conceptual perception is, hence, dependent on the possession of certain character traits. If that use is a condition for the evolution of our perceptual framework, which is, in turn, a constitutive part of practical wisdom, we must conclude that practical wisdom is dependent on the possession of certain character traits.

V. PRACTICAL WISDOM IN LEGAL REASONING

There can be little doubt that practical wisdom is a key intellectual virtue for legal decision-makers as well. The alternative to this would be to offer a method in which those forms of subjective perception that are key elements of practical wisdom could be tamed within legal contexts.

In the last few years, legal theorists' attempts to cope with the problem of bridging the gap between universals and particulars (which is, in the account provided,

[43] Roberts and Wood (2007: 195).

the key role of practical wisdom) in legal decision-making have generated theories that push practical wisdom to the periphery of decision-making. None of those theories denies that practical wisdom might be somehow useful, and indeed some of them are attempts to explain in methodological terms what practical wisdom consists of.[44] However, it is not very clear that any of those theories truly engages with practical wisdom and often it seems to be considered simply an intuition, insight or divination of mysterious origin and dubious value. Indeed, the theory of perception that is a key element of a theory of practical wisdom is not thematised in those attempts that, by and large, seem to assume a modern conception of the subjective/objective divide and, consequently, of perception.

The most sophisticated of such attempts are Neil MacCormick's and Klaus Günther's, in arguments that are, at their core, very similar. I have put forward a critique of MacCormick's view elsewhere[45] and I shall not restate that critique here in any detail. Nevertheless, it is worth outlining MacCormick's view in order to show how it fails to capture the perceptive aspect of practical wisdom as a means to bridge the gap between universals and particulars.

MacCormick starts by objecting to what he calls the intuitionist approach, according to which 'we have the capacity to discern (to "intuit") the factors in situations of choice that make a decision right or not wrong'.[46] So MacCormick's intuitionist judge has a capacity to single out the aspects of the case that are relevant. In order for it to make any sense, however, it is necessary to connect this intuition with a sentimentalist theory of moral perception that is heavily dependent on two universalistic criteria, namely, impartiality and full information.

Let me explain this sentimentalist/universalist approach. If intuitions are to be trusted at all, they have to be the expression of sentiments of resentment or contentment that the decision-maker might feel when faced with the particular situation. Those emotions can be felt either directly or sympathetically and, since the latter is an expression of the deep attachment we have to others, it is the key emotion for the perception of morally relevant aspects of particular cases. Now, it is clear that not any sympathetically felt emotions would do. Both MacCormick and Adam Smith (from whom MacCormick draws inspiration) add further requisites for those emotions to help in perceiving relevant particularities. For MacCormick, the right moral sentiments require that the agent be (a) impartial and (b) fully informed about the situation.[47] Here one can perceive the true depth of MacCormick's commitment to a deontological conception of ethics, since impartiality and full information are clearly the necessary conditions for correct norm-application. Indeed, it is not surprising that Günther, another deontologist, arrives at similar conclusions in his attempt to fit the idea of *phronesis* into discourse ethics through the introduction of a 'discourse of application': if the key to success in

[44] Klaus Günther, for instance, starts his section on the discourses of application with an attempt to connect them and the Aristotelian notion of *phronesis* (Günther (1993: 171–201)).

[45] Michelon (2006b).

[46] MacCormick (2005: 84).

[47] ibid 87–88.

discourses of justification is universalisation, the keys to success in discourses of application are impartiality and full-information.[48]

Neither MacCormick nor Günther envisage the need for anything like the theory of practical wisdom outlined in the preceding sections and, insofar as they are willing to accept the need for *phronesis*, they would have it reduced to rational procedures and techniques of information-gathering guided by the idea of impartiality. The active role of the decision-maker's subjectivity and, in particular, of her perceptive framework, are not part of the basic structure of legal and moral decision-making: norms and methodology can cope with the most fundamental problem of decision-making, that is, the connection between universals and particulars.

What I have outlined in the preceding sections is an attempt to show how the 'intuition' of relevance can be conceived as part of the subject's intellectual framework. If the picture presented above is correct, subjectivity is not inscrutably private and, as a result, there are ways of conceiving it that do not lead to the conclusion that *phronesis* is a mysterious form of divination that cannot be rationally understood or, importantly, improved. The understanding of how our inner senses operate and of how our perceptual framework might leave space for a peripheral conceptual perception allows us to understand subjectivity as a way to relate to the objective world, a way on which we can pin our hopes for a more wholesome explanation of how we relate universals and particulars, law and facts.

I cannot here offer a full defence of the superiority of an approach to legal decision-making that is predicated on the possession of a perceptual (and, hence, subjective) conceptual framework that is an integral part of practical wisdom to a methodological-deontological approach to it. My aim was simply to defend the plausibility of the former.

In doing so, I hope to be helping to strengthen the position of a certain approach to legal theory and the theory of legal decision-making that is in tune with the picture I put forward. Zenon Bankowski has, for many years now, insisted on the idea that good legal decision-makers develop something akin to a legal peripheral conceptual perception. According to him, the way in which legal decision-makers acquire that skill to 'jump out of the law' when appropriate is the experience of relentlessly applying the legal categories that frame their perceptual framework to numerous cases.[49] Learning the regular case of concept application would help the decision-maker to perceive an awkward element in the particular case and trigger a need to reflect upon the appropriateness of the conceptual 'drawers' that make up one's conceptual framework. It might be that it turns out to be a false alarm and that our perceptual framework needs no change. But it might be the start of a revision process that would reshape the way in which the subject relates to the world through legal concepts. I believe that the early Hart was onto something similar

[48] Günther (1993) explicitly refers to both requirements. The demand for full information is justified at 229–39, while the general requirement of impartiality for appropriateness discourses is discussed throughout the book and, as a matter of fact, this is one of the book's main theses, as we can see at 203.

[49] eg Bankowski (2001: 104–08; 135).

when he defended the thesis of the defeasibility of legal concepts.[50] If legal concepts are inherently defeasible, that is, if no enumeration of the necessary and sufficient conditions for their application would be able to exclude the possibility of an extraneous, unexpected factor excluding the application of the concept to a situation in which all the necessary and sufficient conditions obtained,[51] it follows that we must need a way to spot that unexpected factor. A theory of legal decision-making as practical wisdom would fit the bill.

It is clear that legal decision-making is not simply to be subsumed under general practical wisdom. Any conception of law and legal decision-making that is of any use to us must acknowledge the fact of positive law. Indeed, positive law heavily influences the perceptual framework of a legal decision-maker and, consequently, her perceptual peripheral zone is first and foremost (although not exclusively) a legal zone. Subjectivity is a form of engagement with the world that is not necessarily opaque to critical scrutiny and to improvement and, therefore, should not be thought of as a threat to the rule of law. If anything, it is a necessary condition to realise it.

REFERENCES

Alison, H (1983) *Kant's Transcendental Idealism* (New Haven, Yale University Press).

Aquinas (Vol XI, 1970; Vol XXXVI, 1974) *Summa Theologiae* (London, Blackfriars).

Aristotle, J Barnes (ed) (1984) *The Complete Works of Aristotle* (Princeton, Princeton University Press).

Atria, F (2002) *On Law and Legal Reasoning* (Oxford, Hart Publishing).

Aubenque, P (1963) *La Prudence chez Aristote*, 2nd edn (1997) (Paris, Quadrige/PUF).

Bankowski, B (2001) *Living Lawfully* (Dordrecht, Kluwer).

Bruner, J and Postman, L (1949) 'On the Perception of Incongruity: A Paradigm' 18 *Journal of Personality* 206.

Cavell, S (1969) *Must we mean what we say?* (Cambridge, Cambridge University Press).

—— (1995) *Philosophical Passages: Wittgenstein, Emerson, Austin, Derrida* (Oxford, Blackwell).

Descartes, R, Adam, C and Taunery, P (eds) (1973) *Oeuvres de Descartes Vol 8* (Paris, Librarie Philosophique J Vrin).

Dworkin, R (2003) 'The judge's new role: should personal convictions count?' 1 *Journal of International Criminal Justice* 4.

Galileo, G (1960) 'Two kinds of properties' in A Danto and S Morgenbesser (eds), *Philosophy of Science* (Cleveland/NY, Meridian Books).

Günther, K, Farrell, J (tr) (1993) *The Sense of Appropriateness: Application Discourses in Morality and Law* (Albany/NY, SUNY Press).

Hacker, PMS (1991) *Appearance and Reality* (Cambridge/Massachusetts, Basil Blackwell).

Hart, H (1948) 'The Ascription of Responsibility and Rights' 49 *Proceedings of the Aristotelian Society*, New Series, 171.

Hurthouse, R (1999) *On Virtue Ethics* (Oxford, Oxford University Press).

[50] Hart (1948: 173 ff).

[51] For an enlightening discussion of Hart's thesis of defeasibility, see Atria 2001 (esp 87–140).

Kant, I (1996) *Practical Philosophy* (Cambridge, Cambridge University Press).
Kenny, A (1966) 'Cartesian Privacy' in Pitcher (ed), *Wittgenstein: The Philosophical Investigations* (Notre Dame, University of Notre Dame Press).
McCabe, H (2008) *On Aquinas* (London, Burns and Oats).
MacCormick, N (1978) *Legal Reasoning and Legal Theory* (Oxford, Clarendon Press).
—— (2005) *Rhetoric and the Rule of Law* (Oxford, Oxford University Press).
McDowell, J (1981) 'Non-Cognitivism and Rule-Following' in SH Holtzman and CM Leich (eds), *Wittgenstein: To Follow a Rule* (London, Routledge).
Michelon, C (2006a) *Being Apart from Reasons* (Dordrecht, Springer).
—— (2006b) 'Practical Reason and Character Traits: remarks on MacCormick's sentimentalist theory of moral perception' in Z Bankowski and J MacLean (eds), *The Universal and the Particular in Legal Reasoning* (Aldershot, Ashgate).
MacIntyre, A (1985) *After Virtue*, 2nd edn (London, Duckworth).
Miller Jr, F (1995) *Nature, Justice and Rights in Aristotle's Politics* (Oxford, Clarendon Press).
Nussbaum, M (1995) *Poetic Justice* (Boston, Beacon Press).
Pereira, OP (1994) *Vida Comum e Ceticismo*, 2nd edn (São Paulo, Brasiliense).
Putnam, H (1992) *Renewing Philosophy* (Cambridge/Massachusetts, Harvard University).
Roberts, R and Wood, WJ (2007) *Intellectual Virtues* (Oxford, Clarendon Press).
Wasserstrom, R (1961) *The Judicial Decision: Toward a Theory of Legal Justification* (Stanford, Stanford University Press).
Wittgenstein, L (1967) *Philosophical Investigations*, 3rd edn (Oxford, Blackwell).

3

The Role of Virtue in Legal Justification[*]

AMALIA AMAYA

THE CONCEPT OF virtue is central in contemporary discussions of the nature of justification. Virtue ethics, which seeks to analyse moral justification in aretaic terms, is nowadays one of the major approaches to normative ethics, and virtue epistemology, which understands the normative properties of beliefs in terms of the epistemic virtues of agents, is one of the most important developments in contemporary epistemology. In law, however, with few exceptions, there has not been a comparable trend towards explaining normativity on the model of virtue theory.[1] The theory of legal justification is dominated by a debate between normativist approaches, that is, approaches that explain legal justification primarily in terms of rule-application, and instrumentalist views, which make consequentialist arguments the clincher of justification. In this chapter, my aim is to explore the possibility of developing a virtue theory of legal justification, which puts a primary emphasis on virtues, rather than on rules or consequences.

The structure of this chapter is as follows. In section I, I shall distinguish different versions of a theory of legal justification by the role that they assign to virtue in the analysis of justification. In section II, I argue that a weak version of a virtue theory of legal justification, according to which legal justification requires a combination of both aretaic and non-aretaic concepts, is problematic. In section III, I argue for a strong aretaic approach to legal justification that says that a legal decision is justified if and only if it is a decision that a virtuous legal decision-maker would have taken in like circumstances. Section IV considers some objections that may be raised to the proposed account of legal justification. I conclude, in section V, by claiming that a virtue theory of legal justification is grounded on an Aristotelian conception of practical reason, which contributes a distinctive perspective to our understanding of reason in law.

* Earlier versions of this chapter were presented at the International Symposium of Philosophy at the National Autonomous University of Mexico; the XIV Iberoamerican Coloquium of Philosophy at the University of Lisbon; and the X International Seminar of Legal Theory at the South National University at Bahia Blanca. I want to thank the participants in these seminars as well as the participants of the Special Workshop on 'Virtues in Law' at the 24th World Congress of Philosophy of Law for helpful comments.

[1] For a pioneering work, see Solum (2003).

I. THREE VERSIONS OF AN ARETAIC THEORY OF LEGAL JUSTIFICATION

There are different roles that a notion of virtue may play in a theory of legal justification. First, one may assign virtue an 'auxiliary role'. In this approach, legal justification is explained without any reference to the virtues. The proper locus of virtue theory is not within a theory of justification, but rather, within a theory of legal ethics. On this view, while virtues are crucial for developing a plausible account of the role of a judge, a lawyer, or a prosecutor, they are, nevertheless, irrelevant when determining whether a judge's decision, a lawyer's decision, or a prosecutor's decision is justified. A virtue theory developed along these lines is compatible with rule-based theories of legal justification as well as with consequentialist approaches to legal justification. Virtue theory, on this view, is not an alternative theory of adjudication, but rather a complement to existing accounts of legal justification. Any adequate theory of adjudication should give an account of the qualities of the agents that make for good legal decision-making. However, neither normativism nor instrumentalism has provided a thorough account of the traits of character needed by legal decision-makers if they are to discharge their responsibilities properly. Virtue theory may then come to the fore to fill in this important gap in current approaches to adjudication.

That virtues ought to play a role in a theory of professional ethics in law is, I believe, a claim that most legal theorists would be ready to accept. To date, most theories of legal ethics are, however, deontological or utilitarian theories. The possible application of virtue theory to legal ethics remains a relatively unexplored topic.[2] A potential advantage of virtue theory over other approaches to legal ethics is that it may give richer accounts of the legal institutional roles. Good decision-making, particularly in hard cases, requires the possession of capacities that go beyond the ability to properly assess relevant consequences and the mere compliance with a number of duties. The possession of some character traits, such as prudence, courage, wisdom, or justice, is arguably conducive to good (justified) decisions as well as constitutive of the conception of a good judge, a good lawyer, or a good prosecutor. Thus, a virtue approach to legal ethics would allow us to provide a thicker conception of professional legal roles than that offered by either consequentialist or deontological accounts. In this sense, either as a supplement to existing theories of legal ethics or as an alternative to them, virtue theory may play an important (albeit, auxiliary) role in a theory of legal justification.

A second role that virtues may play in a theory of justification is an 'epistemic' one. It is, one may argue, by looking at what virtuous legal decision-makers do that we may identify which legal decisions are right. On this view, what virtuous legal decision-makers do is the best criterion for what is legally justified. A theory

[2] For some attempts to study legal ethics from within a virtue perspective, see Saguil (2006); Milde (2002); Graham (2003); Cassidy (2006); and Markovits (2008).

of adjudication that gives virtue an epistemic role does not hold, however, that what is legally justified is a function of what a virtuous legal decision-maker would do. That is to say, an epistemic version of virtue jurisprudence rejects the claim that a legal decision is right *because* it is a decision that a virtuous legal decision-maker would take. To the contrary, on this view, the notion of a justified legal decision is prior to that of a virtuous legal decision-maker. In other words, the status of legal decisions as justified is independent from the evaluation of legal decision-makers. Nonetheless, virtues are exceedingly important in a theory of legal justification, as they play a crucial role in determining which decisions are justified. According to this approach, the notion of a virtuous judge is best viewed as an important heuristic device. It is by thinking about how a virtuous judge would proceed when faced with a particular case, that one may determine what one ought to do. It might even be the case that, in hard cases, it takes virtue to recognise which decision is justified. That is to say, there might be cases in which virtue is not only the best criterion for determining what is legally justified, but also the only criterion we have. But the status of a decision as justified does not depend on whether a virtuous judge would take it. One could interpret Ronald Dworkin's theory of law as integrity as a theory that gives virtue an epistemic role in legal justification. For Hercules, the virtuous judge par excellence, reaches the decision that is justified in the particular case, but what makes the decision justified is not that Hercules would have taken it, but rather, a condition of coherence.[3]

Last, virtue may play a 'constitutive role' in a theory of legal justification. In this view, virtue is not merely a *criterion* of justification, but rather a *condition* of justification. That is to say, it is not merely the case that what a virtuous judge would decide is the best criterion for determining what is right, but rather the claim is that the rightness of the decision itself depends on its being a decision that a virtuous judge might have taken. There are different ways in which one could develop a theory of adjudication that gives virtue a constitutive role. I would like to distinguish between two different aretaic conceptions of legal justification: a 'strong' version and a 'weak' one. According to a 'strong' version, the justificatory status of legal decisions is entirely derivative from the character of legal decision-makers. In contrast, a 'weak' aretaic theory of legal justification denies that one may explain all there is to legal justification in aretaic terms. On this view, while one cannot explain the nature of legal justification without appealing to aretaic concepts, these are not sufficient to give an account of adjudication. I turn now to examine in some detail each of these constitutive versions of a virtue theory of legal justification. I start by discussing the weaker, less controversial, thesis about the connection between virtue and legal justification.

[3] Dworkin explicitly averts us against any interpretation of Hercules' answer to legal problems as defining what law as integrity requires. Hercules merely illustrates how a judge approaching a legal problem as law as integrity demands would proceed, but his judgments are not meant to be constitutive of the truth of the answer at which he arrives. See Dworkin (1986: 33).

II. JUDICIAL WISDOM AND HARD CASES

One could give virtue a constitutive role in a theory of adjudication, but deny that legal justification may be entirely explained in aretaic terms. In this approach, while virtue is a main contributor to legal justification, it is necessary to appeal to non-aretaic concepts in order to give a full account of the conditions under which legal decisions are justified. There are two reasons why – it might be argued – virtues do not suffice to explain the nature of legal justification. First, virtues may play a legitimate role in the justification of decisions in hard cases; however, in easy cases there is no need to appeal to the judicial virtues in order to determine the justificatory status of a legal decision. Decisions in easy cases are fully justified on the grounds of non-aretaic notions. Thus, an aretaic approach to legal justification is at best applicable only to hard cases. Secondly, the aretaic theory of legal justification is insufficient even in those cases where it may be said to apply. In hard cases, as much as in easy cases, legal rules and principles ought to play a role in justification. While virtues are necessary to correctly apply the law in hard cases, this does not dispense with the requirement that legal decisions be grounded on the applicable law. Thus, virtue theory is a crucial supplement to a rule-based conception of adjudication, but it is not a sufficient substitute for this conception.

Neil MacCormick seems to be sympathetic to this mixed account of adjudication.[4] In easy cases, claims MacCormick, the justification of legal decisions can be achieved by simple deduction from clearly established rules and the undisputed facts of the case. However, when the application of law becomes problematic (because of problems of interpretation, relevance, proof, or classification)[5] a judge needs 'Solomon's wisdom', that is, a capacity for practical judgement, a moral sense which allows her to make 'a fresh judgment directed at its very particulars.'[6] In hard cases, where the decision is not tractable as a 'rule case',[7] the judge may take King Solomon as a model to guide her reasoning. In this approach to legal justification, virtues help the decision-maker apply the rules: wisdom will lead the judge to problematise the rule's applicability, and thus to remove it from the category of rule-cases, and decide in a way that is fully responsive to the particularities of the case. This, however, does not mean that in hard cases rules do not play any role. For, according to MacCormick, the particular facts of the case, as detected by the judge endowed with wisdom, may be justifying reasons only if they are subsumable under a relevant principle of action universally stated.[8] Further, such principle has to be shown to be grounded in pre-established law in order to comply with the requirements of the rule of law.[9] Hence, on this view,

[4] See MacCormick (2005: 78–100).
[5] MacCormick (1994: 65–97).
[6] MacCormick (2005: 81).
[7] The term is Detmold's. See Detmold (1984). Quoted in MacCormick (2005: 81).
[8] MacCormick (2005: 88–91).
[9] ibid 99–100.

virtues are essential to legal justification, in that they are necessary to justify decisions in hard cases, but they function as aids to rule-application rather than as substitutes for rules.

This mixed approach to adjudication has some problems. To start with, this approach fails to provide a unitary theory of adjudication for both easy and hard cases. However, it is desirable that one and the same method be shown to apply to all legal cases. In addition, this mixed theory assumes too sharp a distinction between easy cases and hard cases. The distinction between easy cases and hard ones is neither rigid nor stable over time.[10] Moreover, there is often disagreement about whether a case is hard or not. It might take virtue to determine whether the application of a rule to a case is, despite appearances to the contrary, problematic. Hence, the distinction between easy and hard cases cannot be used to determine when a virtue approach is called for and when, to the contrary, a rule-based method of reasoning is appropriate.

Another problem with this mixed approach to adjudication stems from the relationship between theories of legal justification and conceptions of practical reason. The attempt to explain adjudication in terms of both rule-application and virtue notions may be viewed as an effort to fix a main problem of normativist approaches to adjudication, namely, the problem of indeterminacy. Rule-based conceptions of adjudication fail to supply a criterion for choosing among different outcomes of rule application. As a result, they do not give determinate guidance to legal decision-makers as to how they ought to decide in cases in which more than one decision is justifiable under the applicable rules. Virtues solve this problem by providing a further criterion for choosing among several justifiable outcomes. Faced with a case in which more than one decision seems to be equally legitimate, the justified one is the decision that a virtuous judge would have taken. Thus, a mix theory of justification, one that combines aretaic notions with normativist elements, apparently has the resources to address the nagging problem of legal indeterminacy. Doubts may be raised, however, as to whether such a mixed account may be developed into a coherent theory of justification. While a normativist conception of justification is grounded on a rule-based approach to practical reason, generally associated with Kant, an aretaic approach has its roots in an Aristotelian conception of practical reason. Thus, the coherence of a theory of legal justification which coordinates irreducible notions of virtue along with irreducible normative notions will, in the end, depend on the controversial issue of whether the Kantian and the Aristotelian views on practical reason may be satisfactorily reconciled.[11] In light of these problems, it is worth exploring the possibility of providing a unified account of legal justification that explains all there is to legal justification in aretaic terms.

[10] See Dworkin (1986: 350–54). See also MacCormick (1994: 197, 227–28).

[11] For an argument to the effect that it is desirable to seek an integration of an ethics of rules and an ethics of virtue, see Louden (1997: 201). For a thorough examination of the possibilities of bringing Kant and Aristotle together, see Sherman (1997).

III. LEGAL JUSTIFICATION BY VIRTUE

The strong aretaic conception of adjudication defines legal justification by appealing exclusively to aretaic notions. On this view, the justification of legal decisions entirely depends on the character traits of legal decision-makers. There are different forms which a strong aretaic virtue theory might take. Two main versions may be distinguished: a 'causal' version and a 'counterfactual' version. They may be succinctly stated as follows:

- *Counterfactual version.* A legal decision is justified if and only if it is a decision that a virtuous legal decision-maker would have taken in like circumstances.
- *Causal version.* A legal decision is justified if and only if it has been taken by a virtuous legal decision-maker.

According to the counterfactual version, the justification of a legal decision is a function of what an idealised, virtuous, legal decision-maker would have done if she had to decide the case. If the decision is one which a virtuous legal decision-maker would not have taken under the circumstances, then the decision is unjustified. The causal version sets up a more demanding standard for the justification of legal decisions: it is not enough for a legal decision to be justified that it be a decision that a virtuous person might have taken in like circumstances, but the decision itself has to be virtuously motivated. Thus, on this view, the rightness of a legal decision crucially depends on its causal history. A decision is justified if and only if it has its source in virtue. A legal decision that is viciously motivated, for example, a decision which is the product of bias, corruption, partiality, etc is unjustified, even if it is the same decision that a virtuous legal decision-maker would have taken. For example, consider a case of murder in which, in light of the evidence available, a fact-finder possessing the epistemic virtues, such as impartiality, intellectual sobriety, the ability to recognise salient facts, diligence, open-mindedness, etc would have decided that the defendant is guilty.[12] Now, suppose that the fact-finder finds the defendant guilty, but he reaches this verdict out of racial prejudice against the defendant. According to the causal theory, the verdict would be unjustified. In contrast, the counterfactual approach would hold that the verdict is justified, despite the fact that it was not virtuously motivated.

The causal version of a strong aretaic theory of legal justification is, to my mind, untenable. There is a crucial difference between the reasons that support a decision and the reasons that explain why a particular decision was taken that is missing in the casual account. To be sure, an agent may do the right act for the wrong reasons. That he so acted does not make the act wrong, but it prevents us from giving the agent any moral credit for it. That is to say, we should distinguish between the evaluation of an act and the evaluation of an agent for doing an act. So if a person does the right thing (eg, she takes care of an elderly uncle) for the

[12] For an account of the traits of character that mark out virtuous behaviour in the context of legal fact-finding, see Amaya (2008).

wrong reason (eg out of a desire to inherit her uncle's fortune), the act itself is right, but the agent is not morally praiseworthy for doing it.

In law, a distinction between normative and explanatory reasons is crucial as well.[13] Further, because of the institutional nature of legal decision-making, such a distinction is even sharper. For while the fact that a right action was done for the wrong reasons seriously detracts from its moral worth, that a right legal decision was taken for the wrong reasons does not in the least reduce its correctness. For instance, a legal decision to provide compensation for physical injury caused by driving under the influence of alcohol might be correct even if the decision itself was motivated by the judge's disgust at whoever drinks alcohol rather than by a careful assessment of the facts of the case and the applicable rules. Of course, the judge who takes the right decision for the wrong reasons is not praiseworthy for doing it. Indeed, a judge who takes a decision based on revulsion at the defendant deserves criticism. But this does not imply in any way the incorrectness of the decision, which might well be justified, in light of the evidence available and the principles regulating compensation for physical injury.

This is not to say that it is irrelevant whether judges take their decisions for the right reasons. To be sure, there is something amiss in a right legal decision which has been taken for the wrong reasons. We expect legal decision-makers to be properly motivated, and it is certainly desirable that the justifications they offer for their decisions do not constitute a mere rationalisation aimed at making them publicly acceptable. But from this it does not follow that the normative and the explanatory reasons for a legal decision are indistinguishable. The rightness of a legal decision is a function of the former, but not of the latter. The causal version, however, makes the justification of a legal decision (wrongly) depend on the psychological process whereby such a decision was taken.[14] Thus, this theory fails to distinguish the conditions under which a legal decision is justified from the conditions under which a legal decision-maker is justified in taking a decision.

Lawrence Solum seems to endorse a causal version of virtue jurisprudence.[15] Solum distinguishes between a 'virtuous' (or 'just') decision and a 'correct' (or 'lawful') decision.[16] According to Solum, whereas a virtuous decision is one made by a virtuous judge acting from the judicial virtues, a correct decision is a decision that would characteristically be made by a virtuous judge in the circumstances that are relevant to the decision. Thus, it would seem that Solum holds that a legal decision could be justified (ie, correct) even if it was made for the wrong reasons.[17] However, he writes:

[13] See MacCormick (2009: 6–12).

[14] *cf* Duff (2003: 199). In his view, 'the justice or correctness of a judicial decision is in part a matter of the justice of the process by which it was reached.' ibid 205.

[15] See Solum (2003).

[16] The virtuous and the just are made equivalent, but this cannot be right, as there might be just decisions which are not virtuous. Judicial integrity, ie, fidelity to law, is also a virtue, and this might make it the case that the virtuous decision turns out to be different from the decision which best satisfies the demands of justice.

[17] See Solum (2003: 183 fn 66).

> In cases in which the judge was not acting from virtue, but was acting from vicious motives, such as corruption, wilful disregard of the law, or bias, then a discretionary decision may be legally incorrect – even though the very same outcome would have been acceptable if the decision had been made by a virtuous judge.[18]

Hence, according to Solum, in cases in which the law commits decision to the discretion of the judge, the justification of a legal decision depends on the motives of the legal decision-maker. Thus, in these cases there does not seem to be any relevant distinction between the correct decision and the virtuous one: legal justification does not merely demand deciding *in accordance with* virtue, but rather it requires deciding *from* virtue. It is unclear whether Solum would be willing to extend this thesis beyond cases which involve discretion. But given the (quite common) view according to which hard cases involve discretion, the thesis can potentially hold in a significant number of cases (and, in any event, in the most interesting cases). This thesis, as argued, cannot be right. We can certainly criticise a judge who is corrupt, who shows a disregard for the law, and who is biased towards one of the parties. But we need to allow for the possibility that he might have taken a right decision in the case. If a judge who is honest, impartial, and faithful to the law would have taken the very same decision, the vicious judge's decision is correct, even if that judge could hardly be given any credit for it.

In contrast, the counterfactual version holds, more plausibly, that accordance with the requirements of virtue is enough for legal justification. This aretaic theory is very close to views that tie justification to what would be rationally acceptable in ideal conditions, which have been very popular in legal theory.[19] A main problem with these theories is that they involve quite implausible idealisations. These theories abstract away from human cognitive limitations and contexts and make justification an ideal that is far removed from human possibilities. As a result, these theories are not well-suited to play a regulatory role and, thus, to guide the legal practice in an effective way. An aretaic theory which explains legal justification in terms of what a virtuous person might do has an important advantage over these theories in that it posits a normative ideal – that is, a virtuous legal decision-maker – which is, in principle, realisable by flesh and blood legal decision-makers. Thus, such a theory is in a good position to serve as a regulatory standard and, ultimately, ameliorate the legal practice. I turn now to examine some objections that may be raised against this aretaic approach to legal justification.

IV. SOME OBJECTIONS TO A VIRTUE THEORY OF LEGAL JUSTIFICATION

There are some objections that are likely to be raised against the proposal to explain legal justification in terms of what a legal decision-maker might do. In this

[18] ibid 189.

[19] Prominent examples include Perelman's theory of the ideal audience, Habermas' theory of ideal discourse, and Smith's theory of the ideal spectator.

section, I shall address three main objections which might be levelled at this proposal, namely, the 'publicity objection,' the 'authority objection', and the 'disagreement objection'.

A. The Publicity Objection

A basic constraint in a democratic system is that legal decisions ought to be backed by reasons.[20] It might be argued that a virtue approach to legal justification is at odds with the basic requirement that judicial decisions be reasoned. If what the objector has in mind is that a judge cannot justify her decision by appealing to her own virtue, then this is obviously correct.[21] Indeed, it would be unacceptable for a judge to justify a decision on the grounds that she is a virtuous judge. However, that reasons for a legal decision ought to be publicly stated says nothing about what it is that makes legal decisions justified. Justification, as a property of decisions, ought not to be confused with citing reasons. In other words, the justificatory status of a legal decision needs to be distinguished from the activity of publicly justifying the decision. Consider, for example, the case of a jury's decision. While the jury does not engage in the activity of justifying a belief about guilt, to be sure, at least some of the decisions reached by the jury are justified. The importance of the distinction between justification as a property of a decision and the activity of justifying a decision can also be appreciated by considering poorly justified legal decisions. There are decisions which, while correct, are poorly reasoned. That they are justified does not depend on their being publicly defended on the basis of reasons. Thus, the requirement of publicity is a requirement that is over and above the requirement of justification. The reasons for a legal decision ought to be made public, but what makes them reasons for a decision is, precisely, that a virtuous legal decision-maker would recognise them as such.

Another form which the publicity objection might take appeals to a certain intuitionist interpretation of the virtues according to which it is in the nature of a virtuous person that he has a perceptual sensitivity that allows him to see or grasp what would be the right thing to do, without needing to offer any further reason or justification for his decision. In other words, virtuous legal decision-makers are those who have a direct insight into the right which does not admit of discursive justification. But then – the objector might argue – an aretaic approach to legal justification does not seem plausible, as judges are expected – indeed, obliged – to give reasons for their decisions. So stated, the objection also fails to undermine an aretaic theory of legal justification. For a virtue approach to legal justification need not be committed to claiming that the perceptual sensitivity in which virtue consists precludes the provision of reasons. On the contrary, the virtuous legal

20 See Pettit (2001: 168).

21 Duff has argued against Solum's aretaic approach to adjudication on the grounds that it conflicts with the way in which judicial decisions are justified. See Duff (2003: 206–07).

decision-maker has a perceptual sensitivity which, precisely, enables him to discern the reasons for his decision in the particular case and to provide the corresponding justifications. This perceptual sensitivity, as it were, makes visible to the virtuous agent what are the relevant reasons or justifications in the particular case, and hence, what it is that, in the case at hand, virtue requires.[22]

To sum up, I have considered two possible ways in which one may press the publicity objection. On one reading, the objection says that since a legal decision cannot be justified by a judge by pointing to her own judicial virtue, the justification of a legal decision cannot be explained in aretaic terms. I have argued that this objection cannot get off the ground once a distinction is made between a decision being justified and the activity of publicly justifying a decision. On another reading, the objection says that, since virtues are a kind of rational intuition, a virtue approach is incompatible with the requirement that legal decisions be reasoned. However, I have argued that the perceptual sensitivity of the virtuous legal decision-maker need not be construed as an insight which does not admit of discursive justification, but rather as a capacity that enables the virtuous judge to grasp the reasons or justifications in the particular case. Thus, none of these lines of argument undermine the case for a strong aretaic theory of legal justification.

B. The Authority Objection

It is a necessary condition for a legal decision to be justified that it be shown to be grounded in the law. Reasons from authority ought to play a pivotal role in determining how cases ought to be decided. The aretaic theory of legal justification could be objected to on the ground that it does not give to legal sources their due in justification. In the aretaic approach, justified legal decisions are those that might be taken by a virtuous judge. But the reaction of the virtuous to the case might differ from the law's response: what the law requires in a particular case may not be what best accords with the requirements of virtue. Therefore, a virtue approach to legal justification is incompatible with the authoritative nature of law.

The authority objection, while important, does not succeed in undermining the case for an aretaic theory to legal justification. For even though such a theory does not explicitly establish as a condition of justification that legal decisions be grounded on legal reasons, this requirement is implicitly built into the theory. Any plausible account of the judicial virtues ought to include a virtue of 'integrity', namely, a disposition to assess the merits of the case from an 'internal point of view', that is, from the point of view of someone who endorses the rules that structure legal deliberation and is disposed to guide his conduct in accordance to

[22] See Wallace (2006: 242). MacCormick has also argued against a conception of virtue as a capacity that is at odds with the practice of giving reasons. He writes: 'Practically wise people do not only issue delphic assurances as to what is right, they explain why it is. They show the reasons that seem most relevant and why one is valued for more in a given context than another, and so on. . . . They are not infallible oracles but valuable guides.' See MacCormick (2009: 17).

them.[23] Thus, a judge who has the virtue of integrity is committed to deciding a case in a way that shows due respect to the rule of law. In short, a good account of the judicial virtues will ensure that legal reasons play the role that they ought to play in a theory of legal justification. Provided that we have a substantial account of the virtues associated with the role of the various legal decision-makers, an aretaic theory of legal justification will guarantee that the appropriate connection obtains between legally justified decisions and the established law. Thus, a strong version of a virtue theory of justification is consistent with the authoritative character of law.

C. The Disagreement Objection

It might be argued that an aretaic conception of legal justification is ill-suited as a normative model in the conditions of disagreement that characterise modern societies. Virtue conceptions of normativity may be plausible in societies that are remarkably homogeneous, as it was in the case of Ancient Greece. However, in societies such as ours, in which there is a plurality of inconsistent views on moral, religious and political issues, virtue theory fails to provide determinate guidance.[24] Given that there are competing conceptions about political morality, which the law is likely to reflect, a virtue approach to adjudication cannot enable us to determine what the right decision is in the particular case. For there is no shared ideal of what virtue requires upon which judgements about what ought to be done could be grounded.

Two lines of response to this objection may be advanced. First, this objection is based on a misunderstanding of the relevance of disagreement to the rational status of legal judgments. That there is disagreement about what the best legal judgment is in a particular case does not deprive legal decision-making of a rational foundation. Only if disagreement is all-encompassing would it render a normative model incapable of guiding action.[25] But in complex legal systems cases in which each side has an equally strong legal argument are not so common as to make the identification of justified decisions by appeal to the normative ideal of a virtuous judge (who possesses, among others, the virtue of integrity) impossible.[26] Secondly, the disagreement objection relies on a mistaken view about the commitments of virtue theory. A virtue theory of adjudication is not committed to the claim that there is only one right answer.[27] When stating the main tenet of a virtue theory to legal justification, I have claimed that a right decision is what a virtuous decision-maker would make, not what the virtuous decision-maker would make.

[23] Hart (1994: 88–91).

[24] See Wallace (2006: 258–59). See, also, Louden (1997: 213).

[25] See Wallace (2006: 259).

[26] That in complex legal systems it is unlikely that one answer does not provide a better fit than another has been argued by Dworkin. See Dworkin (1977: 75–76, 83–84).

[27] That virtue theory allows for the possibility that different virtuous agents faced with the same decision may act differently has been argued by Hursthouse. See Hursthouse (1999: 68–71).

Thus, a virtue theory allows for the possibility that two virtuous judges faced with the same decision in the same circumstances may disagree. [28] In short, a virtue approach to legal adjudication is perfectly applicable in conditions of value pluralism.

Hence, while the foregoing objections need to be taken seriously, they are not decisive against a strong virtue approach to legal justification. This still does not vindicate the case for such a theory as the reluctance to accept an account of legal justification in purely aretaic terms might come from a rather different front. Ultimately, I would argue, the main obstacle to this aretaic conception of justification may stem from a desire to provide an external validation of legal decisions, that is, a validation external to the legal practice, even to the practice of the virtuous. Perhaps, the main reason for rejecting an aretaic approach to legal justification is an attachment to a strong version of objectivism. In this view, a legal decision is objectively justified if it is supported by reasons the adequacy of which is *independent* of any beliefs we might have. But there seem to be no such reasons: the notion of a reason for a decision which no virtuous decision-maker would recognise as such is hardly a coherent one.[29] Thus, if one rejects such an uncompromisingly objectivist account of justification, there does not seem to be any reason which militates against an aretaic account of legal justification. Furthermore, an aretaic theory of legal justification has some interesting implications about the nature and scope of reason in law, which I now turn to examine.

V. VIRTUE AND REASON IN LAW

In the previous sections, I have argued for a virtue approach to legal justification according to which a legal decision is justified if and only if a virtuous legal deci-

[28] Solum argues that different virtuous judges could reach different decisions in the same case. See Solum (2003: 187).

[29] Consider the following case. Let us think of an exemplar judge who, acting virtuously, decides that in case C, decision D should be taken. What else, one might ask, could be added to D so that it is justified? It would be odd to say that for D to be justified it has to be a decision that a virtuous judge might have taken *and* a decision that is backed up by any of the reasons that obtain in the particular case. The judge, if virtuous, would be able to determine the salient facts, the relevant reasons, and judge accordingly. Thus, it goes without saying that the decisions taken by a virtuous judge would be properly justified on the relevant facts and legal reasons. This does not mean, however, that these facts and legal reasons provide the justifying grounds for the judgment independently of whether a virtuous judge would recognise them as such. Consider an analogy with a wine contest. Suppose that the wine experts determine that, in light of characteristics X and Y, a certain wine is the best one of those in competition. Now, the relevance of these characteristics to assessing the goodness of wine depends on the judgements of the experts. If someone came along and said that another wine is better by virtue of having characteristic Z, but Z were a characteristic that no wine expert would recognise as constitutive of the goodness of a wine, we would dismiss his claim right away (and maybe wonder what he might have intended to say by claiming that Z, despite it being a characteristic that no expert could recognise, should determine the judgement as to which wine is best). Thus, what qualifies as a good reason is relative to what a virtuous person would recognise as such. Distinguishing the 'real' reasons for a decision from what a virtuous judge would take as such is as nonsensical as distinguishing characteristics of a good wine from the characteristics which a wine taster would recognise as constitutive of the goodness of a wine.

sion-maker would have taken it in like circumstances. This conception of justification has important implications for questions concerning the role of reason in law. As stated above, contemporary accounts of adjudication may be divided into two main camps: normativism and instrumentalism. While normativism explains legal justification primarily in terms of rule-application, instrumentalism gives to consequences, rather than rules, a central role in a theory of legal justification.

Normativism and instrumentalism are grounded on different conceptions of practical reason. Normativists assume a Kantian view according to which rational action is rule-governed, that is to say, it is action done in accordance with rational norms and appropriately motivated by them.[30] In contrast, instrumentalists rely on a Humean conception of practical reason that conceives rational action instrumentally, that is to say, as action that has an appropriate causal link to some given ends.[31] This has significant consequences for the way in which legal reasoning is conceived: whereas on a Kantian approach, legal reasoning primarily consists of applying principles or rules, in a Humean view, legal reasoning is of an instrumentalist kind, that is to say, it is a type of means-ends reasoning. As opposed to both normativism and instrumentalism, a virtue approach to legal justification is grounded on an Aristotelian conception of practical reason. To develop an Aristotelian approach to legal reasoning is beyond the scope of this chapter, but I would like to suggest some distinctive features of such an approach.[32]

First, according to an Aristotelian conception of practical reasoning, practical reasoning is not only an instrumentalist kind of reasoning, but deliberation is also of ends. Ends are often too vague to serve as starting points for means-ends reasoning. Thus, practical reasoning must consist at least partly in specifying an agent's ends and norms.[33] Another reason for engaging in deliberation about ends concerns the possibility of value conflict: many of our ends come into conflict and we may remove the conflict by specifying them.[34] Hence, in the Aristotelian view, deliberation is a search for the best specification of ends.[35] Such specification provides, first, the starting point of instrumentalist reasoning and, second, a way to proceed in the face of conflict. This conception of practical reasoning accords a broader scope to reason in law than instrumentalist conceptions which take ends and norms as fixed points that constrain the space of deliberation. From an Aristotelian point of view, reason in law does not merely play a role in choosing means to ends, but also in deliberating about the ends themselves and what specifications of law's ends are best.

Second, according to the Aristotelian approach to practical reasoning, excellence in deliberation (ie, *phronesis* or practical wisdom) cannot be captured in terms of a set of general principles or rules, capable of being formulated in advance to

[30] See Audi (1989: 60–80).

[31] ibid 39–60.

[32] For a development of an Aristotelian theory of legal reasoning, see Amaya (2011) and Michelon (2012).

[33] For this interpretation of Aristotle's views on practical reasoning, see Wiggins (2001).

[34] See Richardson (1994).

[35] Wiggins (2001: 287).

the circumstances of action.[36] In other words, the practical reasoning of the virtuous agent is not susceptible of 'codification'.[37] Thus, the Aristotelian conception rejects the view according to which reasoning about what to do is a matter of applying general principles and following a set of procedures. This rule-based approach underwrites what is one of the most influential models of legal reasoning, namely, the balancing model. On this model, legal reasoning consists first and foremost in the application of legal rules and principles to the particular case. When – as is often the case – conflicting norms bear on a particular case, one should weigh and balance the values involved so as to adjudicate the conflict.[38] The problems of this model of legal reasoning are well-known.[39] Despite efforts to provide guidance as to how one may rationally balance the values in conflict, this model must either assume value commensurability – which is a highly controversial assumption – or fall back on intuition, unduly restricting the scope of reason in law. Insofar as an Aristotelian approach does not take rule-following to be the central notion in an account of legal decision-making, it avoids the problems that face principle-dependent approaches to legal reasoning.

Last, according to the Aristotelian picture of practical reason, practical reasoning critically involves a refined capacity to recognise the salient features of a situation which provide reasons for action.[40] On this view, judgements about what to do in a particular situation are the deliverances of a perceptual sensitivity that allows one to detect the requirements that situations impose on one's behaviour. Practical reason is viewed as a form of 'connoisseurship', that is to say, as an 'ability to appreciate heterogeneous, case-specific reasons for choice or preference by means of informed judgment or perception rather than the application of general principles or procedures.'[41] In this view, legal reasoning involves primarily an ability to apprehend the case-specific reasons for action by means of judgement or perception. This approach to legal reasoning does not need to amount to a kind of intuitionism, for, as argued, this sensitivity is not an ineffable capacity but rather it is best understood as a capacity to discern the reasons which support the decision that virtue requires in the particular case. But, crucially, these reasons are not grasped by appeal to a set of principles and rules, but they are inextricably linked to the perception of the particulars of the case.

Hence, a virtue-based theory of legal justification is of a piece with an approach to legal reasoning that differs in some important aspects from views that place either rules or consequences at the core of a theory of legal reasoning.

[36] Wallace (2006: 250).

[37] See McDowell (1998: 57–58).

[38] A most prominent example of this approach is Alexy's theory. See Alexy (2003).

[39] See MacCormick (2009: 36–38).

[40] This Aristotelian account of practical reason has been most forcefully defended and developed by McDowell, see McDowell (1998). For an extremely instructive discussion of McDowell's views, see Wallace (2006: 242–62).

[41] Wallace (2006: 257).

VI. CONCLUSION

Virtues, I have argued, are central in a theory of legal justification. This chapter has provided an aretaic approach to legal justification according to which a legal decision is justified if and only if it is a decision that a virtuous judge similarly circumstanced might have taken. Unlike current approaches to legal justification, which assume either a rule-based or a consequentialist conception of practical reason, this approach to legal justification is grounded on an Aristotelian conception of practical reason. From an Aristotelian perspective, legal reasoning is of ends; it is not principle-based, and it is best understood on the basis of a 'connoisseurship' model, which gives a crucial role to judgement and perception in legal decision-making. This conception of legal reasoning significantly departs from both instrumentalist approaches to legal reasoning and normativist views of legal reasoning. Thus, the study of the notion of virtue and its relevance to justification provides a distinctive perspective to our understanding of legal reasoning.

REFERENCES

Alexy, R (2003) 'On Balancing and Subsumption: A Structural Comparison' 16 *Ratio Juris* 433.

Amaya, A (2008) 'Justification, Coherence, and Epistemic Responsibility in Legal Fact-Finding' 5 *Episteme* 306.

—— (2011) 'Virtue and Reason in Law' in M Del Mar (ed), *New Waves in the Philosophy of Law* (New York, Palgrave MacMillan).

Audi, R (1989) *Practical Reasoning* (London, Routledge).

Cassidy, RM (2006) 'Character and Context: What Virtue Theory can Teach us about a Prosecutor's Ethical Duty to "Seek Justice"' 82 *Notre Dame Law Review* 635.

Detmold, MJ (1984) *The Unity of Law and Morality: A Refutation of Legal Positivism* (London, Routledge).

Duff, A (2003) 'The Limits of Virtue Jurisprudence' in M Brady and D Pritchard (eds), *Moral and Epistemic Virtues* (Malden, Blackwell Publishing).

Dworkin, R (1977) 'No Right Answer?' in PMS Hacker and J Raz (eds), *Law, Morality, and Society* (Oxford, Clarendon Press).

—— (1986) *Law's Empire* (London, Fontana).

Graham, LM (2003) 'Aristotle's Ethics and the Virtuous Lawyer: Part One of a Study on Legal Ethics and Clinical Legal Education' in R Brooks, JB Murphy and RO Brooks (eds), *Aristotle and Modern Law* (Aldershot, Ashgate).

Hart, HLA (1994) *The Concept of Law* (Oxford, Oxford University Press).

Hursthouse, R (1999) *On Virtue Ethics* (Oxford, Oxford University Press).

Louden, RB (1997) 'On Some Vices of Virtue Ethics' in R Crisp and M Slote (eds), *Virtue Ethics* (Oxford, Oxford University Press).

MacCormick, N (1994) *Legal Reasoning and Legal Theory* (Oxford, Oxford University Press).

—— (2005) *Rhetoric and the Rule of Law* (Oxford, Oxford University Press).

—— (2009) *Practical Reason in Law and Morality* (Oxford, Oxford University Press).

Markovits, D (2008) *A Modern Legal Ethics* (Princeton, Princeton University Press).
McDowell, J (1998) *Mind, Value, and Reality* (Cambridge, Harvard University Press).
Michelon, C (2012) 'Practical Wisdom in Legal Decision-Making' chapter 2 of this volume.
Milde, M (2002) 'Legal Ethics: Why Aristotle Might Be Helpful' 33 *Journal of Social Philosophy* 45.
Pettit, P (2001) *A Theory of Freedom: From the Psychology to the Politics of Agency* (Oxford, Oxford University Press).
Richardson, H (1994) *Practical Reasoning about Final Ends* (Cambridge, Cambridge University Press).
Saguil, RM (2006) 'A Virtuous Profession: Re-Conceptualizing Legal Ethics from a Virtue-Based Moral Philosophy' 22 *Windsor Review of Legal and Social Issues* 1.
Sherman, N (1997) *Making a Necessity of Virtue: Aristotle and Kant on Virtue* (Cambridge, Cambridge University Press).
Solum, L (2003) 'Virtue Jurisprudence: A Virtue-Centred Theory of Judging' in M Brady and D Pritchard (eds), *Moral and Epistemic Virtues* (Malden, Blackwell Publishing).
Wallace, J (2006) *Normativity and the Will: Selected Essays in Moral Psychology and Practical Reason* (Oxford, Clarendon Press).
Wiggins, D (2001) 'Deliberation and Practical Reason' in E Millgram (ed), *Varieties of Practical Reasoning* (Cambridge, MIT Press).

4

Education and Paternalism: Plato on Virtue and the Law

SANDRINE BERGES

I. VIRTUES AND PATERNALISM

THE VIRTUE ETHICS revival that began in the 1950s was at first decidedly Aristotelian. Later it diversified so that now virtue ethicists look at Hume, Hutcheson, Nietzsche, and even the Stoics. But on the whole, Plato is still excluded from extended consideration.[1] This is despite the fact that many of the key theses in virtue ethics, from the theory of habituation to perfectionism, were first formulated by Plato. Habituation, for instance, the theory that natural dispositions become virtues through the habitual performance of the kind of actions that a virtuous person might do, is described at some length in Book II of the *Laws*:

> I call education the initial acquisition of virtue by the child when the feelings of pleasure and affection, pain and hatred, that well up in his soul are channelled in the right courses before he can understand the reason why. Then when he does understand, his reason and his emotions agree in telling him that he has been properly trained by the inculcation of appropriate habits. Virtue is this general concord of reason and emotion. But there is one element you could isolate in any account you give, and this is the correct formation of our feelings of pleasure and pain, which makes us hate what we ought to hate from first to last, and love what we ought to love. Call this 'education' and I, at any rate, think you would be giving it its proper name.[2]

All the features of Aristotle's account of habituation are present in this passage. There should be first unconscious habituation, imposed from the outside (parents, or the state), then this becomes a conscious process, led by reason. The key to success is that our emotions and reason should agree, in other words, that we should not only think that something is the right thing to do, but also that we should desire to do it. It follows that to be virtuous will be in great part to have the right kind of emotions and desires, in the right degree, at the right time.

[1] With a few exceptions such as Slote (1995) who describes Plato's virtue ethics as more radical than Aristotle's, and Annas (2005) whose discussion of 'wickedness' is based on Books 8 and 9 of the *Republic*.

[2] The *Laws* at 653.

Despite this and other examples of Plato's deep insights into virtue ethics, he remains mostly in the background of recent discussion. There are several reasons for this exclusion, the first of which is luck. Philippa Foot, in her seminal paper, 'Virtues and Vices' wrote: 'I have myself found Plato less helpful [than Aristotle] because the individual virtues and vices are not so clearly distinguished in his work.'[3] Of course, a great deal of what differentiates virtue ethics from alternative moral theories is the fine detail of the moral psychology it supports. Aristotle does give very plausible accounts of what it means to exemplify certain virtues or vices, and his theory of what it is not to be quite virtuous but to be trying to become so – *akrasia* and *encrasia* – are both philosophically and intuitively powerful. Aristotle proposes more virtues than Plato – so his picture is richer – and rather than simply attempt to define the virtues, or even use those attempts to display philosophical methods (as it can be argued Plato does in the early dialogues), he really does offer accounts of what it may mean to be courageous, or generous, or to have the corresponding vices of excess (recklessness, prodigality) or deficiency (cowardice, meanness). So it is not surprising that as far as working out the details of a moral psychology for virtue ethics is concerned, Aristotle should be considered a very rich source.

But even if Foot was right, it is important to bear in mind that not all of virtue ethics is about setting out the detail of the moral psychology: some of it must also be concerned with developing the theory behind this psychology. This is particularly true when it comes to applying virtue ethics to new domains, be it political philosophy, or jurisprudence. Even though part of what needs to be done consists in describing relevant virtues, for instance, patriotism in political theory, and the virtues of judging in jurisprudence, there are also more theoretical questions to be asked. In those circumstances, what would be more natural than to turn to a philosopher who has written much on the topic of virtue and the law, namely, Plato?

Unfortunately there is a more substantial reason why Plato is so often cast aside, namely that his political writings have the often deserved reputation of being highly paternalistic and authoritarian. Some of his more outrageous claims include that we owe the laws unconditional obedience, even when they will put us to death unjustly,[4] and that a good ruler should rule without laws, deciding for each individual what he or she deserves without referring to anything other than his or her (the ruler's) own wisdom.[5] So taking these writings as an inspiration risks giving virtue jurisprudence a bad name.[6]

Of course, the worry may not simply be that Plato's virtue jurisprudence is paternalistic, but that any virtue jurisprudence would necessarily be so. If the central claim of a virtue-based theory of the law is that laws should promote and

[3] Foot (1978: 1).

[4] Hamilton (1961: *Crito*).

[5] ibid *Statesman*.

[6] We also need to bear in mind that what the ancients had to say about the law may not be as obviously relevant to problems we are trying to solve as what they had to say on virtue was to contemporary ethical problems. So for these reasons I do not want to suggest that someone interested in virtue jurisprudence ought to become a Platonist (or an Aristotelian for that matter).

protect virtue, then we can see how it might strike one as paternalistic. Laws should tell us what to do, not what to be. They should regulate our behaviour insofar as it affects other people's lives, but they should not regulate our thoughts, or our feelings. So for example, the law should attempt to prevent me from driving faster than the speed limit. But I could nonetheless be the kind of person who would enjoy driving fast, and if I was, there is no reason why I should not be allowed to play video games in which I indulge in virtual fast driving.

This is of course Mill's harm principle: 'That the only purpose for which power can be rightfully exercised over any member of a civilized community, against his will, is to prevent harm to others. His own good, either physical or moral, is not sufficient warrant.'[7]

Driving too fast can certainly harm others, but playing video games in which I drive too fast cannot. So the law should not concern itself with this aspect of my life. Nor should it concern itself with the fact that if I did not know it was illegal, I would probably really enjoy driving too fast. In other words, the law can tell me what I can and cannot do, but it should let me work out for myself what my motivations are for not doing the things I am not allowed to do. I may avoid doing x because I think x is morally wrong, or because I know x is illegal, but that is no one's business but my own.

Plato would of course be deeply dissatisfied with Mill's principle. My being the kind of person who likes to drive fast is in itself a problem, he would say, and it is sheer naivety to distinguish the character trait or disposition from actually being the kind of person who might drive too fast. As to playing video games in which I pretend to do what I should not do, it is quite clear what Plato would have to say about that. The section on censorship in the *Republic* leaves very little doubt as to Plato's thoughts on the effect that art and play can have on our behaviour. If even reading Homer is potentially harmful to society, then playing video games must also be so. By engaging in play activity that develops certain aspects of my personality which are potentially harmful to others, I make myself more likely to harm others – at least this is what Plato would say. And in some cases, we may even be tempted to agree with him. (Do we think it is a good idea for people with paedophiliac tendencies to watch animations in which children are abused? Might it not encourage them to try out some of what they see in the real world? Might it not give them ideas they would not have had otherwise?) The problem with this line of thought is that it does not refute Mill's principle; it merely shows that 'harm to others' can start a long time before the behaviour takes place, and that therefore if we do want to prevent harm to others, we need to do a lot more than simply regulate behaviour.

Maybe a better way of ensuring that laws do not become overly paternalistic is to ask that they respect what Joseph Raz refers to as people's ability to 'shape their life and determine its course' and to be 'creators of their own moral world'.[8] By

[7] Mill (1991: 14).
[8] Raz (1986: 154).

focusing on the positive rather than the negative, that is, autonomy rather than paternalism, Raz does a better job of ensuring that the laws limit their reach to behaviour, and do not invade the development of our minds. This, rather than Mill's harm principle, is what virtue jurisprudence has to contend with.

So things look fairly bleak for the virtue ethicist who wants to do jurisprudence. Of course, she could decide to focus on some aspects of virtue jurisprudence, such as legal ethics, or the virtues of judging (some philosophers have done so very successfully)[9] but in a sense it would be disappointing not to be able to put forward a virtue ethical view on the bigger question of what the ultimate end of laws should be.

II. WISDOM-PROMOTING LAWS

Although things do look bleak, in fact, it seems that Plato himself has an answer to the problem of paternalism in virtue jurisprudence which he formulates in his last dialogue, the *Laws*.

In Book III at 687d–e, a father is reflecting on his child's dreams for the future, and worries lest those dreams should come true. The passage is suggestive, as parents often shudder at their children's ambitions, be they to become a soldier or a princess – equally frightening prospects! But should a parent see his or her role as the destroyer of these ambitions, or the remover of the means by which they may be realised, or should he or she seek to replace these ambitions with more suitable ones? Often none of these is the case, and the parent will simply trust that by growing up, and becoming wiser, the child will naturally come to give up his or her dreams and adopt different ones. What is more, Plato tells us, a parent's wish for his or her child may be as dangerous as the child's own wish if the parent has not much sense. So a parent who loves his or her child should desire not to be the instigator of their dreams but that the child should acquire suitable ambitions which conform to reason. This is just the father's wish in the *Laws*: that his child may acquire enough wisdom so that he may, come the time, make the best choices. So parental intervention limits itself to teaching the child wisdom, or enabling the child to become wise.

Plato, drawing on an analogy between parent and statesman, then transfers his observations to an analysis of what we might expect from laws. It seems that to legislate on the principle that the good life is the virtuous life endangers people's autonomy in that it prevents them from choosing for themselves a moral way of thinking. It is nonetheless true that autonomy requires the capacity to choose, that is, being informed about what choices are available, being able to reflect on the short and long-term consequences they are likely to have, and on whether our several choices are compatible with one another. It follows that one virtue, wisdom, may be promoted without endangering autonomy: on the contrary, pro-

[9] See Solum (2003).

moting wisdom is tantamount to helping people become more autonomous. If the virtue ethicist can limit her claim to the idea that laws should be wisdom-promoting, then the paternalism threat disappears.

This is precisely what Plato suggests in the *Laws*:

> I, for my part, urged that this is an injunction to legislate with a view to one single virtue out of four. He should keep them all in his view, I said, and in the first place that virtue which brings all the rest in its train, that is, judgement, intelligence, and right conviction attended by appropriate passionate desire.[10]

The *Laws*' proposal deflects paternalism without losing any ground for virtue ethics. Either Plato is right that the good life is the virtuous life or he is wrong. If he is wrong then the effect of wisdom-promoting laws will not be to impose the virtuous life as the best life, but merely to put people in a position to choose for themselves which life is the best life (as long as it is not harmful to others). So people will be able to 'create their own moral worlds' and live according to consequentialist, deontological, or other moral norms.

The claim that laws should be wisdom-promoting gives us a minimalist kind of paternalism. The laws do not make it their business to teach all citizens to be virtuous. On the assumption that wise people will know what is best for them and make the right choices, the laws only need to ensure that wisdom prevails. This leaves laws with two main tasks: to educate the young into wisdom, and to preserve a peaceful, stable and prosperous environment in which wisdom may be sustained. This covers laws on education, and laws which prevent harm to others, but it is not obvious that this virtue ethicist account will warrant other laws – it will be expected that citizens who have been properly educated will on the whole know how to make the right choices. If the system fails them and they make choices that threaten others, then they are faced with the laws designed to protect the environment – and these laws will therefore act as deterrents, or failing this, as protection. Thus the account I have described, according to which the function of laws is to promote wisdom in the community, gives us a very minimalist legal system – one which even Mill might find acceptable.

There is one important objection to this line of thought. Do we and Plato mean the same thing when we talk of wisdom, that is, the ability to think about our lives, consider our options, and choose the best one in the most efficient way? Or does Plato mean something very different, namely knowing the truth such as he conceives it? It is hard not to see Plato as dogmatic here. As far as he is concerned, being wise does mean knowing the Forms, and those who know the Forms must agree with him that, for instance, justice is always more beneficial than injustice.

On the other hand, what it means to try and become wise is very different from seeking knowledge about the Forms from those who know them. What is 'needful' is not obtaining this knowledge by whatever means, but conducting philosophical inquiry, examining one's beliefs through the *elenchos*, until one is satisfied that one

[10] The *Laws* at 688a.

has no inconsistent beliefs. To become wise, for Plato, is first and foremost to ask questions, of others, but also of oneself. Socrates in the *Apology* is not wise, he tells us. But because he knows that he is fundamentally ignorant, he is closer to wisdom than anyone in Athens: he does not take any of his beliefs for granted, does not mistake them for knowledge, and forever inquires.

If the aim of wisdom-promoting laws is to encourage citizens to question their beliefs, seek to understand others, and not be too confident that one's own beliefs are closer to the truth than someone else's, then in a sense it does not matter that Plato also believes that those who have achieved wisdom will all share the same beliefs.

In the next section, I want to test this claim in various ways. First, I want to ask whether Plato is himself able to sustain this proposal in the one of his dialogues that has the most to say on the question of virtue-promoting education, the *Republic*.[11] I shall argue that even though Plato seems to have the tools for building the kind of theory of education we might accept, in the *Republic*, he fails to do so quite spectacularly. I will show several of the overly paternalistic aspects of the proposal of the *Republic*, and ask why and where Plato was not able, in that dialogue, to develop a more acceptable version of virtue-promoting education.

III. PATERNALISM AND ELITISM IN THE REPUBLIC

In the *Republic*, Plato argues that laws should be concerned mostly with 'education and nurture'.[12] The principle seems to be that provided children are well educated, they will grow to become lawful citizens who have no need for the imposition of penalties to regulate their behaviour, as they will be regulated from the inside.[13]

Accordingly, the role of the rulers, the philosopher kings, is to legislate for the education of all, and that of the guardians, to ensure that these laws are respected. The first point is made at 590c–591a:

> And it is plain that this is the purpose of the law, which is the ally of all classes in the state, and this is the aim of our control of children, our not leaving them free before we have established, so to speak, a constitutional government within them and, by fostering the best element in them with the aid of the like in ourselves, have set up in its place a similar guardian and ruler in the child, and then, and then only we leave it free.

Thus the law, rather than control the behaviour of citizens, determines what that behaviour is most likely to be by controlling the education of young citizens. But once the citizens have grown up, they are no longer subject to legislation regarding their everyday or business transactions with each other. They are deemed capable of doing the right thing without fear of retaliation from the state.

[11] For a detailed version of the view that education is a central concern of the *Republic*, see Scholfield (2006: 32–37), and Burnyeat (1999).

[12] The *Republic* at 424a.

[13] ibid 591a.

The second point, that the task of the guardian is mostly the control of education, is made at 423d–424b:

> These are not, my good Adeimantus, as one might suppose, numerous and difficult injunctions that we are imposing upon [the guardians], but they are all easy providing they guard, as the saying is, the one great thing, or instead of great let us call it sufficient.
>
> What is that? He said.
>
> Their education and nurture, I replied. For if a right education makes of them reasonable men they will easily discover everything of this kind and other principles that we pass over now.

The key point of the passage is the appeal to sufficiency: Plato does appear to believe that if the children of the state are brought up in the right manner, they will be lawful citizens and require none of the squabbling legal threats and disputes that he sees democratic states as suffering from. This ties in nicely with the proposal that a platonic virtue-jurisprudence might limit its reach to wisdom, and that this would entail virtue-promoting laws being focused on education of the young citizens, that is, both on the curriculum and on the safety of the infrastructure which makes this education possible.

In the *Republic*, Plato does spend some time dealing with the minutiae of a suitable curriculum for the citizens of the just city. This is because he believes firmly that what children are taught will determine whether they can become just citizens:

> And so we may reason that when children in their earliest play are imbued with the spirit of law and order through their music, the opposite of the former supposition happens – this spirit waits upon them in all times and fosters their growth, and restores and sets up again whatever was overthrown in the other type of state.[14]

As we examine whether what Plato suggests in the *Republic* does indeed fail to avoid the pitfalls of paternalism, we must ask whether his intention matches his practical proposals, that is, whether he does indeed believe that all children can receive an education such that they will not need to be ruled by laws in the detail of their adult lives. There are two points in particular which might lead us to question Plato's intentions. First, is it the case that all citizens will receive sufficient education for his intentions to be realised? And secondly, should we assume that simply because the laws concern education, they are wisdom-promoting rather than generally virtue-promoting?

It is fairly clear that Plato does not believe all citizens can be educated to the point where they may rule themselves. At 590d he writes:

> It is better for everyone to be governed by the divine and the intelligent, preferably indwelling, and his own, but in default of that imposed from without, in order that we all so far as possible may be akin and friendly because our governance and guidance are the same.

[14] ibid 425a.

This means that for some citizens, their education will not suffice to render them wise enough that they can do without laws. This makes some sense of Plato's claim at 425b that '[i]t would not be fitting . . . to dictate to good and honourable men'. This sentence is strongly reminiscent of Jane Austen's Darcy when he says that as a gentleman, he expects his actions to be trusted without having to explain or justify them. There is arrogance in this claim, a belief in the superiority of a certain class of people so that they do not have to abide by universal rules. Those who are virtuous, the philosopher-kings, simply do not need laws. For the rest, who are unfortunately not to be termed 'good and honourable', they will need laws regulating their everyday interactions and dealings. These laws will presumably ensure that whatever happens, nobody behaves in ways that are not virtuous. They will therefore be as paternalistic as it is possible for laws to be.

It follows that we need to investigate Plato's educational system, and in particular, the differences between the types of education offered to each of the three classes.

In spite of the fact that Plato does deal with the education of the citizens in great detail (even to the extent of going through some of the texts they may or may not be taught) he is not clear on who will benefit from what education. For instance, although there are sections of the text dealing with the education of the guardians and of the philosophers, there is none to deal with the education of the third and the largest class. Are we to assume that they receive none, and that they will therefore, throughout their lives, be guided by laws that they cannot anticipate and that regulate their behaviour down to the last detail? Plato does not tell us that specifically. Indeed, some of what he says in his discussion of the education of the guardians may lead us to believe that he intends at least part of this education to apply to the third class as well.

At 389d–e while discussing the censoring of texts depicting the gods as intemperate, he says that this type of censorship is especially important because of the effect it will have on the multitude. The role of the third and the largest class is the first and the foremost to obey: they must obey their rulers, and to do this they must develop the kind of gentleness that is present in the temperate agent, so it is crucial that they should be taught self-control. Thus it does seem as though the third class will benefit from some kind of education. But it is clear that this education will concern itself first and foremost with promoting temperance, not wisdom. In fact, it is clear from Plato's description of the souls of this section of society that he does not indeed believe them capable of becoming wise. Wisdom requires that one's soul is ruled by one's own reason.[15] But in the *Republic* Plato describes the class of the producers as one of people whose reason is too weak and whose appetites are too strong for this to be possible.

What is also not clear is the extent to which the education of the auxiliary guardians and that of the philosophers is separate. Although they are detailed in different parts of the book (that of the guardians at 376e–412b and of the philosophers at 521c–541b), it seems they must be connected. At 521e Plato describes the

[15] ibid 442c.

early part of the philosophers' education as music and gymnastic, and implies that he is referring to that which has already been described in the earlier discussion of the education of the guardians.

What one might conclude from all this is that all the citizens follow one educational programme and that they stop, earlier or later, depending on their class or ability (as Plato does recommend that a member of one class who shows abilities that are characteristic of another should move up or down in the system).[16] But this would not entail, presumably, that the classes are educated together, as Plato seems to believe that it is important that members of different classes do not mix.[17]

It does seem that the educational programme proposed in the *Republic* is largely unequal, with only the smallest portion of the society receiving a complete education, and the possibility that the largest part receives none at all. In that sense, whatever Plato's beliefs about the role of education in promoting virtue, what he has to offer in the *Republic* will certainly not be enough to render all citizens virtuous and to make laws outside of the domain of education redundant. But another way in which Plato's proposal in the *Republic* fails to implement the solution to the paternalism problem discussed here is that the education he proposes is not merely wisdom-promoting, but is concerned at least as much, and in some cases exclusively, with promoting temperance and courage.

The later stage of the philosophers' education is indeed wisdom-promoting in that it is concerned with pulling the soul away from 'the world of becoming' and towards 'the world of being'.[18] But the first part of their education, and therefore the entire education of the guardians, is concerned with something different, namely the promotion of temperance and courage. It follows that the educational system promoted by the *Republic* is not, for the most part, the kind that we would expect to solve the paternalism problem.

IV. CONCLUSION

I argued that there are at least two ways in which the *Republic*, which is the dialogue in which Plato discusses laws concerning education in the greatest detail, fails to implement the solution to the paternalism problem we discussed in section II. First, although Plato seems to believe that the point of education is to help citizens develop sufficient wisdom that they may rule themselves, without appealing to laws, he only proposes that one small portion of the population should receive the necessary education. For the rest, they will have to make do with what Plato apparently considers second best, that is, being told what to do by those who are wiser than they. Secondly, although Plato insists that wisdom be part of the philosophers' education, it is not the only virtue that they are taught. In fact, it is not till they have become temperate and courageous that they are taught to be wise.

16 ibid 423d.
17 ibid 459a–460b.
18 ibid 521d.

Worse, the auxiliary guardians are only taught to be temperate and courageous: if we believe that what is paternalistic about virtue jurisprudence is that it programmes citizens to want to act as the state wants them to, then the laws concerning the education of the auxiliaries are extremely paternalistic. Add to that that the auxiliaries are basically the police and the army, and the overall picture is a very frightening one indeed!

That the auxiliaries should be taught temperance and courage but not wisdom is one thing, but should we object as seriously to the teaching of these same virtues in cases where wisdom is also taught? In the *Laws*, we saw that Plato suggests that it is best to teach only wisdom – this will allow the learner to make up his or her own mind as to what the good life is, and how best to achieve it. And if Plato is right that it is not possible to have one virtue without the others also, then by promoting wisdom, the other virtues will automatically be learned. But if temperance and courage are actively taught, indeed, if the teaching of them is a precondition for the teaching of wisdom, then the legislator does not for one moment allow that wise citizens may decide for themselves whether a good life is a virtuous life, rather than say, a life led by strong principles, or by a desire to maximise happiness for oneself or for others.

It is conceivable, of course, that an individual who has acquired sufficient wisdom may decide that virtues are a hindrance to the good life, and attempt to dishabituate him or herself. For instance, he or she may find that temperance prevents one from experiencing life at its richest and deepest levels, or that it restricts one's participation in the life of one's society, and therefore prevents one from fully relating to peers. Such an individual may then teach himself or herself to 'let go' of the virtue of temperance, and to indulge in excess every now and again. So clearly, the teaching of temperance and courage alongside wisdom is not as objectionable as the teaching of these virtues without wisdom.

Furthermore, one may argue that for the same reasons as wisdom is necessary for the ability to make up one's own mind about the good life, to some extent, so are the other virtues. How does one become wise? The process is that of habituation, doing tasks again and again, until one masters them, and until eventually they are effortless, and later, enjoyable. But what kind of person is best able to go through such a disciplined and lengthy education as that of the philosopher kings? Arguably, they would have to be courageous – it takes courage to face, again and again, tasks one is not very good at, tasks which are arduous, and little rewarding in the short term. It also takes courage to stick to doing what one believes to be the right thing even though one is not yet wise enough to know that it is right. A teenager who decides to work hard at school in order to go to university rather than leave to get work experience and earn cash is courageous: she is facing the prospect of long years of hard work and little money for a very uncertain future. A future without a degree may be bleaker, but it is also more familiar – it may be what her parents, her friends, her sisters have experienced, and as such, it is less frightening.

Temperance also has a clear place in the teaching of wisdom – how successfully can one train to become a philosopher ruler if one is constantly swayed by temptation? How likely are we to practise wisdom if we are recovering from a reckless night of drinking? Might we not want to give up studying altogether if we had expensive habits that required more money than a wise person could make?

On the whole, it seems that the students of wisdom have a much greater chance to succeed if they are also taught to be courageous and temperate. But it could also be argued, more straightforwardly, that courage and temperance are part of what it takes to be autonomous. One needs to be courageous to stick to the decisions that one has wisely decided are the right ones. It takes courage especially not to do the wrong thing because of peer pressure, or not to give in to threats from people one depends on professionally. Temperance also is necessary if we are to weigh the pros and cons of a life choice without being swayed by temptation of short-term enjoyment.

At the end of the day, it is not clear that anyone would seriously object to educational laws recommending that children be taught to be courageous and temperate as well as wise. Though Plato is right to insist in the *Laws* that the emphasis must be placed on wisdom, this is because it is harder to make mistakes when teaching children to think for themselves than it is when teaching them to be courageous or temperate. Temperance has too often been interpreted as the complete abandonment of pleasurable things – sometimes simply as chastity. Courage can turn into blind patriotism, soldier-like obedience to those who are older or socially superior, or even simply bodily violence. Plato is right that teaching these may be dangerous, because the teacher may not clearly understand what these virtues mean, or how to transmit them. Teaching children to think for themselves, to ask questions, and to look for answers is somehow less dangerous – maybe because, as Plato says, the danger lies in one's conception of a desirable trait not being derived from sober judgement but rather from passion. Desiring children to become wise, on the other hand, can only be derived from the recognition that we should be ruled by reason. It is harder, therefore, to make mistakes as to what constitutes proper training on that count.

REFERENCES

Annas, J (2005) 'Wickedness as Psychological Breakdown' 43 *Southern Journal of Philosophy* (supp) 513.

Burnyeat, MF (1999) *Culture and Society in Plato's Republic* (Cambridge, Massachusetts, Harvard University).

Foot, P (1978) *Virtues and Vices* (Oxford, Blackwell).

Hamilton, E and Cairn, H (eds) (1961) *Plato: Complete Dialogues* (Princeton, Princeton University Press).

Mill, JS (1991) *On Liberty and Other Essays* (Oxford, Oxford University Press).

Raz, J (1986) *The Morality of Freedom* (Oxford, Oxford University Press).

Scholfield, M (2006) *Plato: Political Philosophy* (Oxford, Oxford University Press).

Slote, M (1995) 'Agent-based Virtue Ethics' 20 *Midwest Studies in Philosophy* 83.

Solum, L (2003) 'Virtue Jurisprudence: a Virtue-centred Theory of Judging' 34 *Metaphilosophy* 178.

II.

Law, Virtue and Character

5

Neoclassical Public Virtues: Towards an Aretaic Theory of Law-Making (and Law Teaching)

SHERMAN J CLARK

I. INTRODUCTION

IN PRIOR WORKS, I have argued for attention to the connections between law and character and human thriving.[1] Here, I try to identify particular traits of character arguably crucial to human thriving in a democratic free market society. The virtues I describe are analogues to or versions of the classical virtues of courage, temperance and wisdom. In addition, and central to this account, I argue for the importance of preserving a particular trait or attitude, analogous to the classical virtue of piety, for which I use the term 'aspiration'.

I use the phrase '*towards* an aretaic theory' because I do not claim to offer anything like a full account of the connections between law, character and thriving. Rather, my aim is twofold: first, to suggest the features or elements that any such account would seem to require; and second, to begin to give content to one possible version of such an approach.

It may be helpful to situate the argument. Under the heading of virtue ethics, philosophers have rediscovered ancient ways of thinking rooted in ideas of human excellence and thriving – *aretaic*, as opposed to deontological or consequentialist, approaches to the question of how one ought to live.[2] The central insight of virtue ethics, old or new, is that if we want to live rich and full lives, we ought to pay attention to what sort of people we are. The ancient tradition was to think broadly about what ways of being, character traits, or attitudes would lead to or constitute a full and excellent life. That necessarily involved arguments over and attempts to describe necessary or valuable particular virtues or forms of excellence, as well as

[1] Clark (2007), (2005), (2003) and (1999).
[2] Useful collections of contemporary work on virtue ethics include: Gardiner (2005); Darwall (2003); Statman (1997); Crisp and Slote (1997); and Crisp (1996).

conversations about how those qualities were or could be engendered. Thus Socrates is said to have talked of, Plato wrote dialogues about, and Aristotle lectured on different virtues and their possible connection to or place within a rich and excellent and happy human life. The current academic incarnation of virtue ethics is more narrow and theoretical; but the underlying impulse remains the same – to think about how to live in terms of character, rather than rules or preferences.

Some legal scholars have recently tried to apply these ways of thinking to the law. As reflected in the contributions to this collection, some of this work is in the vein of virtue ethics in philosophy – unpacking the theory, asking, for example, whether or to what extent a 'virtue jurisprudence' is really distinct from deontological approaches. More often, efforts have focused on framing virtue-based ways of evaluating the operation of the law or the actions of legal actors, producing theories of virtuous judging, or virtue-based theories of criminal responsibility.[3] My approach is different. Instead of using ideas of virtue and character as tools within the law – ways of *doing* law, I see them as potential *consequences* of law. Rather than using virtue to judge or justify conduct, I see virtue as itself a crucial consideration. Much of the current virtue jurisprudence might be described as deontological in flavour – seeking virtue-based ways of framing or addressing essentially normative principles such as justice or responsibility. If so, my approach could be described as consequentialist in inclination – seeing character as a crucial way to pursue, even as an essential component of, full and happy lives.

Any character-based account of law will need to address two questions: first, how does law impact on or influence the kind of people we become; and second, what sort of people should we try to become if we hope to thrive. This essay sketches briefly the outlines of an answer to the first of these questions, then turns to the second, albeit in still tentative terms. What virtues ought we to ask our law and politics to help us develop or retain? Underlying any such effort will be the Aristotelian premise that our aim ought to be to live full and satisfying lives – to thrive as human beings. And beneath this will necessarily lie the belief, or at least the hope, that we can say something coherent and of more than individual applicability about what it means to thrive.

None of this will be easy. Character traits are not subject to precise definition – unless through an impoverishing reductionism – and thus will forever frustrate analytic philosophy. Unlike health or wealth or preferences, character cannot be measured or quantified, and thus will not yield to empirical tools. Because character is impacted by so many things in addition to law – things like education, genes, experiences, popular culture, religion, even luck, all of which overlap and influence each other and us in a million ways – it will never be possible to regress our way to certainty or even confidence about the ways in which law might make us who we are. Because we will never be sure of or agree on what it means to live a

[3] See eg Feldman (2000) and Huigens (1998).

rich and full life, we cannot hope to settle or resolve the underlying question of who we ought to be. Instead, we have to construct a vision of thriving even as we pursue it. This necessary imprecision can feel like, indeed can easily devolve into, sloppy thinking or hollow rhetoric. All of this means that crafting a useful aretaic approach to law-making will be difficult. Difficult, but I think necessary. Unless we assume that character has no impact on our capacity to live full lives, we need to think about who we are, as well as what we get or do. And unless we assume that our public life has no impact on our character, we need to think about the ways in which our law and politics make us who we are.

The first part of this essay asserts that law and politics impact character whether we like it or not. This part of my argument here is brief not because I believe the matter to be straightforward or uncontroversial. To the contrary, thinking about the myriad and subtle ways law and politics help shape character is a central aspect of the ongoing project of which this essay forms a part. Here, however, my focus is on the substance of the virtues. Nonetheless, the argument does not make sense without at least a preliminary answer to the question of how and why law and politics have anything to do with the matter. To this end, I highlight six overlapping ways in which law and politics, whether intentionally or inadvertently, may have an influence on the sorts of people we become. They are: by requiring or prohibiting conduct thought to display or evince traits of character; by requiring or prohibiting conduct that might indirectly engender traits; by facilitating (or undercutting) institutions that provide fora for the articulation and construction of traits of character; by providing (or precluding) opportunities for exemplars to thrive; by providing concrete contexts for discussion and argument about what sort of people we are or want to be; and, perhaps most subtly and most crucially, by facilitating (or stifling) public conversation about character and thriving. I illustrate each of these with brief but concrete examples, and argue that we should attend to and be aware of these and similar ways through which our law works to make us who we are.

In the second part, I argue that we should try to develop or retain particular virtues – inward-looking versions of or analogues to the classical virtues. Along these lines, I have argued elsewhere that a certain form of *courage*, understood as internal responsibility-taking – the willingness to see ourselves in what we do – makes possible the self-reflection through which other virtues are developed and is particularly salient in a modern democratic community.[4] Here, I suggest that traits analogous to three other classical virtues are particularly crucial: *temperance*, understood as freedom from slavery to pleasure or praise or prosperity; *wisdom*, understood as love of knowledge or truth; and, most critically, something corresponding to *piety*, for which I use the term *aspiration*, understood as the willingness and ability to reach for better and truer things than we can currently grasp.

That last is the most difficult to define, but also the most central to my argument. The label – 'aspiration' – is imperfect, with its unfortunate connotation of

[4] Clark (2007).

ambition or goal-setting. Terms such as transcendence, divinity, and hope can help triangulate the attitude or trait I hope to describe and defend; but it will remain difficult to nail down. I might simply adopt the classical term 'piety', but the modern connotations of formal religiosity, meek or callow conformity, weak or thoughtless devotion, and the like, are just too powerful. I mean instead a kind of strength – the capacity and courage to keep our eyes off the bottom line, and out of the mud. Psychologists have begun to describe and study an emotion they term elevation,[5] which overlaps with what I am after; but what I argue for is more attitude than affect, more capacity than feeling. It is the ability and willingness to care about and strive for things deeper and beyond those we can define clearly or measure with precision. This is, I argue, an essential vehicle for and element of human thriving; and we should guard against the possibility that our law and politics, including the ways in which we talk about and teach and justify what we do, may be diminishing this crucial capacity by turning us into the sort of people who believe, or behave as though we believe, that more safety, health, prosperity, or prestige will make us happy.

II. LAW AND CHARACTER

One objection to this project will be that this all ought to have little to do with law or politics. Perhaps public life should simply aim to provide physical security, material prosperity and the like – the background conditions for our varied visions of the good life – remaining neutral on deeper questions about character and the nature of human thriving.

Initially, even if it were possible to craft legal and political institutions that have no impact whatsoever on our character or on our capacity to live rich and full lives, it is not at all clear that we should desire to do so. Building capacities may be like building highways or protecting public health – something we can best do by cooperating. More to the point, our public life may be shaping our character whether we like it or not. We ought to ask, rather than assume away, the question of whether and how law and politics influence who we are. If government institutions and practices have potential effects on our bodies, as if a military base were leaking toxins into our water, we want to know about it. The same ought to be true for the impact of law and politics on our souls.

A. Exhortation and Expression

Most obviously, law and politics might be vehicles through which we directly exhort ourselves to certain traits. However, without dismissing the possibility that particularly charismatic leaders might directly inspire virtue, this sort of overt

[5] See eg Haidt (2006: 193–200).

inculcation of character is not my primary concern. Rhetoric matters a great deal to character formation, but indirectly, and as connected to and giving meaning to action; so direct hortatory exhortation is not likely to be the most important way law and politics influence who we are. It is also not the most dangerous. Direct and overt efforts to inculcate character are evident for what they are, and can be embraced, rejected, or ignored as we choose.

An almost equally obvious way in which law may interact with character is where law or policy has expressive content. Law can express substantive norms; but it can also express visions of community identity or character. We might encourage or discourage behaviour in part because of what we understand it to say about who we are. For example, objections to the treatment of prisoners at Guantánamo were rooted in three sorts of inter-related concerns. There were utilitarian or consequentialist concerns – arguments that mistreating prisoners is ineffective foreign policy. And of course there were normative or deontological concerns – arguments that that treatment was wrong or illegal. But it is safe to say that there were also identity and character-based concerns. We do not want to see ourselves as the sort of people who do that sort of thing. Safe to say, but not easy to demonstrate, because such concerns are rarely well or clearly articulated, and are easily dismissed as 'merely symbolic'.

Too easily, I think. Implicit in the dismissal of expressive concerns as merely symbolic is the unspoken claim or assumption that such matters should be reserved for circumstances under which there are few or no real consequences – as though attention to character were a luxury to be indulged in only after we have attended to more important matters.

This is an unfortunate stance for two reasons. First, and most essentially, character does matter. If our aim is to thrive, we have no warrant for saying that what sort of people we become through our conduct is less important than the more easily measurable consequences or more clearly definable normative status of our conduct. Second, if we are to use our actions to define ourselves, we need to use actions with real consequences. If we want to understand ourselves as generous, for example, to construct in ourselves the character trait of generosity, it will not suffice to simply announce that we are a generous people. That would be hollow, unpersuasive and ineffective. We need instead to give something away. An act must have costs to have meaning. If our conduct is to assist us in articulating and developing traits of character, we cannot relegate characterological concerns to circumstances where nothing else is at stake.

When public action is motivated by concerns about its meaning for who we are, we should find ways to talk about, rather than dismiss, those motivations. What also require our particular attention and caution, however, are the less direct and less obvious ways in which law and politics may be constructing our character in ways we do not realise, and thus influencing our capacity to thrive in ways we do not recognise.

B. Cultivation

A more subtle way law can influence character is indirectly, by encouraging or discouraging conduct that might indirectly cultivate traits of character. Someone trying to lose weight and get in shape might intentionally park farther from his or her workplace – not merely to express a commitment to fitness, but because it necessitates a longer walk each day, thus burning more calories, thus indirectly helping him or her lose weight. Or, a baseball player might avoid playing slow-pitch softball out of concern that adjusting his swing to hit lobbed softball pitches will throw off his mechanics. We recognise, and thus can either make use of or guard against, the possibility that the demands we put on ourselves physically may have indirect consequences, good or bad, for our bodies. We can and should do the same thing for our souls. We should be aware of the indirect consequences for our character of what we allow or require ourselves to do – of how we regulate our lives.

One obvious example would be integration or anti-discrimination law. We might hope that integrated and diverse institutions will allow or require us to interact with others from different backgrounds and thus indirectly help us to develop desirable traits of tolerance or open-mindedness – or that requiring ourselves to work with others with varying viewpoints will help us to develop the wisdom that comes through seeing things from different perspectives. Similarly, we might regulate pornography and/or prostitution not just to protect from harm those directly impacted, and not just to express our disdain, but also to avoid engendering in ourselves the trait of misogyny, which we think might come about through participation in or exposure to the systematic exploitation of women and girls.

But the indirect effects can be more subtle. Consider the constitutional prohibition of cruel and unusual punishment. Most obviously, eschewing cruelty might say something about who we are, and thus help us construct an identity; but there may be less obvious indirect characterological consequences as well. Engaging in behaviour we feel to be cruel and unusual may, for example, encourage or even require us to distance ourselves from our actions – to reduce our willingness to see ourselves in what we do. If so, it may indirectly undercut the capacity for self-reflection arguably critical to the development of other virtues – a capacity or trait I have described as a form of the classical virtue of courage.

C. Seedbeds

Yet another way in which law and politics can influence character development is by encouraging or facilitating the development of other institutions through which traits are articulated or developed. For example, law can facilitate, or inhibit, the development of philanthropic, fraternal, or religious institutions through which individuals and groups construct and pursue visions of themselves. More subtly, zoning regulations and land use policies can influence the shape of our communities, thus making it easier or more difficult for people to live and work together in ways conducive to the development of character traits such as cooperation and a sense of shared responsibility, as opposed to isolated individualism or a gated us-versus-them way of conceiving of public life.

But civic virtue or public-spiritedness is of course not the only character trait that might be articulated or constructed through institutions which law or politics might or might not in turn encourage or facilitate. Military organisations might help people construct and aspire to courage and loyalty. Religious organisations might help articulate and provide an arena for the development of temperance or spirituality. Sporting organisations may offer vehicles through which people understand and develop traits of persistence, toughness or teamwork. Fraternal organisations often self-consciously define themselves as instruments for the construction of visions of manhood, responsibility and/or charity. Nor, however, is it all necessarily for good. Military and sporting organisations can under some circumstances become arenas for the development of traits of violence or misogyny. Religious and fraternal organisations can foster intolerance or provincialism.

My point, therefore, is not to advocate support of any particular institution, but rather to suggest that when we decide what public policy choices to make, we should do so with an awareness of how those choices will influence our character. In particular we should think about whether those choices will facilitate or undercut the institutions through which we articulate or develop our sense of who we are. If, for example, we decide how to regulate or tax fraternal organisations, or how to control land use, or whether to fund sports leagues or stadiums, based entirely on the measurable economic consequences, or in terms of aggregating preferences, we will be missing much of what matters. The institutions we build or encourage do not just help us get what we want; they are also the arenas in which we learn how to be.

D. Heroes

Law and politics are not merely vehicles through which we pursue pre-defined or agreed-upon characterological aims. Again the nature and desirability of character traits is not something about which we can expect precise definition or agreement. For this reason, law is not merely a means through which we pursue ways of being. It is a forum through which we understand and construct them. Our law and politics do not merely help or hinder us from being the sort of people we want to be; they help us figure out who we want to be.

It is possible, of course, to engage in theoretical discussion of the virtues – to analyse and argue about what forms of what virtues are desirable and why, given various views of what it means to thrive. But that is like trying to choose or design clothes by imagining them on hangers. We need someone to put them on and model them for us if we want to know what they really look like. So, rather than merely defining virtues in the abstract, we construct them in part through moulds and models. A person says to himself or herself, 'I want to be brave like my father, wise like my teacher, tough like my coach.' Or, alternatively, 'I do not want to be weak or foolish or irresponsible like X, and Y and Z.' We also use famous people, or what we think we know of them, to embody traits to which we aspire or which we hope to eschew. The point here is not just that these people *represent* traits of character in our imagination. More than that, they are also the vessels through which we construct those traits. We do not have some agreed-upon and clear idea of courage or wisdom, which a father or teacher then comes to stand for in our minds, or an unambiguous picture of greed or materialism, for which a particular villain, real or fictional, becomes a shorthand. Those people are the ways in which we come to conceive of those ways of being.

So, what does law have to do with this process? Directly, not much; but indirectly, perhaps a great deal, by providing, or undercutting, conditions under which those who might exemplify character traits can thrive and inspire emulation. While law and politics can overtly and intentionally create opportunities for, and/or celebrate role models and heroes – such as in the context of military or other public service – their more subtle effects are again likely to be equally significant.

Consider Title IX of the Education Amendments of 1972 in the United States, for example, as applied to college athletics. On its face, Title IX is a straightforward anti-discrimination statute, modelled after Title VI and Title VII of the Civil Rights Act 1964, prohibiting discrimination in education on the basis of sex. I suggest that there is something missing from the debate over Title IX. Title IX is also, albeit indirectly, about character. Most obviously, again, anti-discrimination law can express a commitment to a particular vision of fairness; and Title IX may do that. But that is not my point here. Here, I am looking to Title IX as one of the ways in which law can facilitate the flourishing of exemplars though which we can understand and aspire to traits of character. Title IX does not just help the women and girls who gain opportunities thereby. It helps us all. By encouraging and allowing women and girls to excel in sports at the highest (and highest profile) levels, it provides us with more and better heroes.

We do not look for every virtue in or through athletes. Wisdom and temperance, for example, are not necessarily traits we associate with or look for in young athletic heroes. We do, however, look to them to help us imagine a set of traits including perseverance, toughness, teamwork and the like. But we can do that well or poorly. Given a limited set of models, we might, for example, come to see the virtues of endurance, perseverance, strength and the like as associated with, even inevitably tied to other, less desirable traits such as a tendency to violence or disrespect for women. Boys will be boys, as we say, but only if they are always boys. We associate these sorry traits with the admirable ones, and thus have a lesser picture of what it is possible to be, in part because we see the relevant virtues always or often modelled by a particular and narrow set of exemplars – men and boys. If we had more women and girls among our athletic heroes, perhaps we could see these traits better, develop a richer conception of them, imagine ways in which they need not be understood as tied to other less desirable traits often found in men. Our very conception of virtues can be richer or more impoverished depending on the vessels through which we conceive of them.

Nor is Title IX the only possible example. Many areas of law are likely to have some impact, direct or indirect, on whether those who might embody and help us construct richer versions of virtues can thrive and do so. Intellectual property law, for example, does not merely encourage invention and creative works, but can also nurture exemplars of ingenuity and creativity. Tax and antitrust and corporate law help determine the extent to which small business people can thrive and inspire emulation of entrepreneurial virtues. Immigration law can broaden or narrow our sense of possible ways of being by allowing for or inhibiting the flourishing of those who might help us see or construct those ways.

E. Proxies

Legal and political issues also provide concrete contexts for defining and discussing character. Consider guns, for example. As Dan Kahan and Donald Braman have shown, Americans' views over gun control are determined largely by what Kahan and Braman call 'cultural values'.[6] People make arguments about safety, or the text of the Second Amendment; and they are not necessarily disingenuous in doing so; but what seems really to drive views on the issue is a deeper and perhaps unexamined set of ideals about what guns mean, and what it would mean to regulate them.

But what Kahan and Braman describe are not merely competing views of what is right, but also accounts of arguably admirable character traits – self-reliance and courage and independence on the part of gun rights advocates competing with non-violence and shared community responsibility on the part of gun control advocates, for example. Nor is it merely that views on the issue are informed by competing visions of community character. Rather, community character *is* the issue, with gun control serving as a vehicle or proxy for a conversation we could not have, or not have as well, in the abstract. If so, we should help people articulate those concerns, flesh them out, and think well about the connections between various accounts of identity and character and various visions of individual or collective thriving. The concrete issue can provide the grounding and context necessary for a richer conversation about what kind of people we want to be.

[6] Kahan and Braman (2006).

F. Rhetoric and Reasons

More subtly still, we become who we are not just through what we do, but also through how we understand and justify our conduct. As James Boyd White has highlighted, we become who we are in part through the ways in which we speak.[7] An obvious example would be the use of dehumanising rhetoric in war. But other, less obviously problematic ways of talking and thinking also can be constitutive, and potentially corrupting. Well-intentioned, seemingly uncontroversial, and ostensibly neutral ways of talking and thinking about law and politics potentially undercut the very thriving law and politics are presumably intended to make possible. As I suggest below, this may be the most important if least obvious way in which certain essential traits are developed or stunted.

III. NEOCLASSICAL VIRTUES

So far, I have simply tried to highlight some of the ways in which law may construct various traits. But the conversation cannot continue at that level indefinitely. We need to be willing to make, and listen to, arguments about the particular ways of being to which we ought to aspire if we hope to thrive. This will be difficult, because it requires that we ground our claims in some at least tentative and general account of thriving. In this part, I make such an effort. I hope to show that it is possible to talk about character and thriving in ways that are open enough to respect the freedom we each must have to craft our own visions of a full and satisfying life, but focused and specific enough to provide a basis for shared conversation and action.

I suggest that to preserve our ability to search for, and develop our capacity to find, the thriving we seek, we should strive to develop a particular, although broadly defined, set of capacities or traits of character. Elsewhere I have described and argued for the importance of a particular form of *courage*, understood as the willingness to confront one's own agency in and responsibility for one's actions. Here, following classical philosophy, and Plato's *Republic* in particular, I further suggest that we should try to develop or retain particular modern versions of other central classical virtues. I argue that versions of or analogues to three of the classical virtues are particularly crucial: *temperance*, understood as freedom from slavery to pleasure and praise; *wisdom*, understood as love of knowledge or truth; and *piety*, understood as the capacity for aspiration, and not merely or necessarily on religious terms. Despite our various and even competing visions of what it might mean to thrive as human beings, we can perhaps agree that these traits or capacities are valuable, even vital, to our capacity to thrive in a modern democratic society. Although law cannot ensure that we develop or retain these crucial traits,

[7] White (2006) and (1973).

the ways in which lawyers and legal academics argue about law and policy, conduct our research, represent our clients, and teach our students can either bolster or undercut these crucial capacities.

A. *The Republic*

In thinking about the relationships between politics, law, character and human thriving, we do not have to start from scratch. The arguably seminal work of western philosophy revolves around just these questions. Plato's *Republic*, nominally an extensive dialogue on the particular virtue of justice, actually offers a broader theory of character and human thriving. It does so, moreover, through the lens of community life, and thus provides a template for thinking about not only which traits we might hope to cultivate, but as well about the role law and politics might play in cultivating them.

The first and crucial step in looking to Plato's *Republic* to think about law and politics is to recognise that *The Republic* is *not* essentially a book about law and politics. It is a book about the soul – about individual character and happiness. *The Republic* uses the construction of a highly artificial and impracticable (even undesirable) city/state as a lens through which to think about the individual. Socrates describes three elements of the community, defined by what they each desire, and corresponding to aspects within each individual. This Socratic geography of the soul is not meant to be a literal psychology. It is a way of defining character – useful because it focuses our thinking not on what we do but what we seek. Specifically, it asks us to think about who we are in terms of our aspirations – by thinking carefully about where we set our sights.

In Socrates' imagined city, the most numerous and naturally powerful segment of the community is made up of those who desire and seek pleasure – whether in the form of physical gratification or material goods. If that element is allowed to rule, Socrates argues, the city will not thrive. They provide the energy, the might and the productive force of the community. But they cannot and should not govern the whole. So too for the individual. We each have within us a part of ourselves that desires pleasure and comfort. This, Socrates suggests, is naturally the strongest or at least most forceful element in each of us. This is the part that is prone to fall into the belief that more stuff will make us happy. This part is neither wise nor thoughtful enough to see the way in which things recede, and therefore will, if allowed to govern our souls, have us blindly chasing one pleasure after another, one possession after the next.

The second element of the city described by Socrates is made up of those who desire and seek honour. Fewer in number but strong, they provide protection and security. Placing honour above comfort or safety, they can be brought to place the city's safety above their own. This class is essential – necessary to protect the city from both outside threats and from the restless, thoughtless hunger of the pleasure-seeking masses. But they cannot govern the whole any more than can the pleasure-seeking many. So too, Socrates suggests, do we each have within us, at least potentially, a part which loves honour. We should cultivate this part, and train it to our use. Like a good and loyal dog, this part of the soul can protect us – both from others and from ourselves. It can enable us to rise above pleasure and fear. But neither can this part be permitted to govern the soul, because honour is ultimately no more capable of bringing us sustained well-being than is pleasure. Should this part be permitted to govern, we would simply trade the fruitless pursuit of acquisition for the equally fruitless hunger for praise.

Socrates famously concludes that the city will not thrive – will see no end of evils – unless governed by the third and least numerous element – philosophers. By philosophers, however, he does not mean professional theorists, nor even merely those who possess prudence. He means *philosophia* – the love of knowledge and truth. Those who ultimately govern, those whose aspirations set the course of the city, must be those who love not pleasure or praise but knowledge – who seek truth and comprehension. Again, the analogy to the soul is clear. If we hope to thrive as human beings, we need to find within ourselves that part which loves knowledge. We need somehow to cultivate that part, educate it, protect it. And above all we need to find a way to put that part of ourselves in charge.

How should we understand and to what extent should we embrace the Socratic claim that wisdom, understood in this way as the love of truth, is central to thriving? That is the core of the thing, really. For now, it is enough to say that the upshot of my argument is manifestly *not* that philosophers should make our laws. Rather, we should look to our laws to help us retain, or at least not undercut, our capacity to be true philosophers – to love something like knowledge and truth more than pleasure or praise.

I say 'something like' knowledge and truth because in a pluralist free society, the Socratic love of knowledge must at best serve as a place-holder for an entire range of higher aspirations. Obviously, if any useful talk about human thriving were to require us first to agree on a precise account of the ultimate good, we would be stuck.

Fortunately, a place-holder will suffice. We need not nail down the precise nature of the good we should seek before we can begin thinking about how to help ourselves and one another to seek it. Leaving Los Angeles for New York on a cross-country car trip, fellow-travellers can cover a lot of ground before having to agree on whether Brooklyn or The Bronx will be the ultimate destination. The varied accounts of the higher and better good similarly seem to lie in the same direction. In particular, we can agree that neither pleasure nor praise will suffice. That alone is enough to get us headed in the right direction. Couple that with the tentative corollary that the something more we need is something analogous to or at least intimated by ideas such as love of knowledge, truth and beauty, and we have enough to get us well along the road.

B. Temperance

One way to describe a soul fortified against the tendency to love and desire pleasure or prosperity or material well-being is to describe it as 'temperate'. The virtue of temperance had any number of meanings in classical philosophy, but often referred to the avoidance of excess in the enjoyment of physical pleasures. A more internal aspect of the traditional virtue may be particularly crucial in modern life. A temperate person, on this account, is one who can enjoy but is not enslaved to pleasure or prestige. Unfortunately, our world can make this form of temperance a hard thing to acquire. No thoughtful person really believes that creating and satisfying preferences constitutes human thriving; but the relentless and pervasive selling which inevitably characterises a market-based economy can cause even the most thoughtful people to confuse the means for the ends. If we hope to find the better, more lasting goods that may bring us real thriving, we need to find ways of thinking and talking about material well-being which allow us to resist this inclination.

This will be difficult, and presents something of a catch-22, because we have become dependent on creating and fulfilling desires and preferences to fuel our economy. In our current economic crisis, we are forced to try and stimulate demand and spending, without regard to whether the things we are encouraging people to want and buy will bring them any lasting satisfaction. More to the point, we are doing this without regard to the cost for our souls of continuing to behave as though having more stuff will make us happier. Democracy makes this difficult as well, by encouraging if not requiring public conversation to hinge on least common denominators. This is perhaps inevitable, even a good thing. Cooperation in a pluralist society must rest on common ground. But common ground, while perhaps solid, is often low; and what we can all agree on is not necessarily what any of us do or ought to consider most important.

This is not an attack on the market, let alone on democracy. Grant that the former is the best way to keep ourselves fed and safe and prosperous, and that the latter is the only way to keep us free, even a necessary precondition to thriving, even a normative requirement. Grant that we need the market and democracy. Still, we ought to be aware of what they may be doing to us. Farmers pray for rain; but they also roof their barns, or else the very thing that nourishes their crops will rot their harvest.

It is possible to talk about economic prosperity and basic needs in terms that recognise and remind us that they are vehicles for thriving rather than ends in themselves. Amartya Sen and Martha Nussbaum, for example, have described a capabilities approach to evaluating freedom and economic progress.[8] Rather than look to the average or total, we should look to get as many people as possible to the point where they have the basics necessary to thrive. This is a good and right way to think about economic needs in their appropriate relation to human

[8] Nussbaum and Sen (1993).

thriving. Collectively, rather than do what we *know* will not make people any happier, by seeking marginal increases in the well-being of the great middle, we should think about what is required to thrive, and get as many folks as possible to that level.

But even a capacities approach begs the question. Granted that above some threshold, more prosperity is not all of what we need, what *do* we need? Absent some at least general response to that question, we will perhaps inevitably be prone to keep looking for more of the same. As long as all we know how to talk about – all we make room for in our public conversation – are health, wealth, safety and the like, we will find it hard to keep in mind that those things will never bring us what we need to thrive.

C. Wisdom

Again, the Socratic answer is wisdom – understood as love of knowledge and truth, which we ought to distinguish from mere 'prudence' or knowledge in the service of lesser aims. It is not *phronesis* (for which the Latin *prudentia*, from which our 'prudence'), but rather *sophia*, or *philosophia*, which elevates us from slavery to the material things and honours which we must transcend.

Adam Smith made the distinction:

> Prudence, in short, when directed merely to the care of the health, of the fortune, and of the rank and reputation of the individual, though it is regarded as a most respectable and even, in some degree, as an amiable and agreeable quality, yet it never is considered as one, either of the most endearing, or of the most ennobling of the virtues. It commands a certain cold esteem, but seems not entitled to any very ardent love or admiration.[9]

Smith goes on to argue that this mere prudence can be ennobled by being directed outward, rather than selfishly, as in the case of the great general, statesman, or legislator. I would suggest, however, that while caring for the health, fortune, rank and reputation of the community is no doubt a nobler thing than caring for one's self alone, it is still insufficient, so long as it remains attention to health, fortune, rank and reputation merely. Those, recall, are the very things we have determined to be inadequate to our happiness; and while seeking them for others is better than seeking them selfishly, we need more.

As acknowledged, the Socratic love of knowledge and truth can serve only as a place-holder for a range of higher ideals. It would be hubris to think we can say with confidence and precision just what higher goods people ought to pursue, foolish to think we can reach agreement on the question, and oppressive to try and enforce on others a particular answer. We need, therefore, to retain the capacity to aspire to what we cannot agree on or define.

[9] Smith (1976: Part IV, s I).

D. Aspiration/Piety

This is crucial. We need to be willing to strive for what we cannot nail down. Otherwise, we risk being trapped in cynical, shallow ways of thinking, which we may want to describe as 'realist' or 'practical' but which are in fact just small and low. It is one thing to be realistic, even pragmatic; it is another thing entirely to be narrow souls, incapable of looking for or believing in anything more than what we are currently capable of defining with precision. Whatever the higher truths we might see, and through which we might truly thrive, we will not find them if we insist on, much less pride ourselves on, looking only to and for the bottom line.

Drawing again on the language of classical virtues, we can describe what we need as a form of piety. The virtue of piety, which in the classical tradition was concerned with matters such as making proper sacrifices to the gods, and which in current usage has a strong religious connotation, might seem poorly suited to serve as a goal or guide for modern life. Understood more broadly, however, it may be just what we most need. We can redefine piety as the capacity for aspiration – the willingness to look for and desire higher, better things than we can precisely define. We need somehow to resist the tendency to become narrow souls – lacking the ability to articulate and listen to appeals to higher goods without scoffing or rolling our eyes.

To see how this form of piety, the capacity for aspiration, need not imply weakness or soft-headedness, consider what was perhaps the strongest and most demanding manifestation of classical philosophy – Roman Stoicism. *The Meditations* of Marcus Aurelius, alongside Plato's *Republic*, can help us think about how it is possible to aspire to that which we cannot define with precision. Like *The Republic*, a book Aurelius knew and considered central to his own brand of Roman Stoicism, *The Meditations* offers us a way to think about character and thriving which is rock-solid without being low, capacious without being hollow, and capable of guiding us to a richer life while leaving us free to define that life for ourselves. *The Meditations*, however, is also like Plato's *Republic* in that it is often and easily fundamentally misread.

Marcus Aurelius counselled and consoled himself with a brand of Stoic philosophy drawn most directly from the works of Epictetus, a former Roman slave turned philosopher/teacher. Epictetus in turn had drawn elements not just from the Greek Stoics – Zeno, Cleanthes, and Chrysippus – but also, if not equally, from Socrates as described by Plato. The core teaching of the Roman Stoic philosophy of Epictetus and Marcus Aurelius was freedom from slavery to the illusory and unreliable things of the world. We should not allow our happiness to depend on things we cannot fully control – health, prosperity, honour or fame, for example. So far so good. This is the aspect of Stoic philosophy from which emerges our current usage of the term 'Stoicism', understood as the ability firmly to deal with pain or misfortune.

Where Epictetus and Marcus Aurelius are misread, however, is in regard to both the reason for and the method of developing this firmness – this freedom. It can seem as though the Stoic reason to avoid dependence on the things of the world is that because we cannot control them, it is futile and inevitably frustrating to depend on them. Caring about health or wealth or honour, we are constantly subject to the risk of unhappiness in the event of illness, misfortune, or loss of place. While this may be part of the reason for not allowing our happiness to depend on external things, it is only a small part. First of all, we *can* control to at least some extent the way our lives go as to these external things; and there is no harm in doing the best we can in those areas – as long as we do not depend on them for our happiness. The reason we should not depend on them for our happiness is not merely that they are unreliable and transient, but more fundamentally that they are simply incapable of bringing us the happiness we seek.

That in turn illuminates the method through which Roman Stoics advocate achieving freedom from slavery to these lesser and unreliable things. It is easy to assume that Stoicism must mean joylessness – that the only way to inure yourself to pain is to inure yourself to happiness. If the only way to avoid pain were to become unable to feel anything, most would find it a sorry bargain. But that is not how Epictetus or Marcus Aurelius teach that we should overcome dependence on things incapable of bringing us happiness – by anaesthetising ourselves to *everything*. Rather, the method is to find something better – something that is capable of bringing us lasting well-being.

To the Stoics, that something was usually described as the *logos* – meaning something like the order and unity and beauty underlying the world. Seeing that, even a glimpse of it, will bring us more satisfaction than all the health and wealth and honour we could imagine. That is what we should pursue – what we should love. And, having gotten even an intimation of it, we will no longer need the transient things. We will not need to steel ourselves daily against the temptation to value things unworthy of us, and on which we cannot depend.

It may seem as though the Stoics specified more clearly than did Plato's Socrates the nature of the higher good we should seek and love in place of pleasure or praise. They did not, and intentionally and wisely so. The term *logos* is as broad a term as one could imagine – meaning not just order but reason and story and word and logic and knowledge and even truth. In some places Epictetus and Marcus Aurelius each use the term nature in place of *logos*, and in some places even personify it as God (singular). *Logos* too is a place-holder – a way of pointing to what we cannot define.[10] But, like the Socratic love of knowledge and truth, the Stoic *logos* does point in a particular direction. In fact, both point in the same direction. What we need is to replace our desire to get and do with a desire to see and learn – to believe in and strive to see the deeper truth and order underlying our world.

Could Socrates or Marcus Aurelius prove that such order exists, or that it has such beauty as to free us from the things that would otherwise enslave us? No. We

[10] See eg John 1:1 'In the beginning was the Word (*logos*), and the Word (*logos*) was with God, and the Word (*logos*) was God.'

do have intimations – ample hints that our world is not without meaning. Socrates would point to mathematics, and indeed advocates the study of mathematics not for its usefulness but because of the way it hints at and attunes the mind to the possibility of underlying order. Marcus Aurelius, belying efforts to paint the Stoic as soulless, suggests that even the most mundane things can give us a hint of the beauty of the *logos*:

> [A]nyone with a feeling for nature – a deeper sensitivity – will find it all gives pleasure. Even what seems inadvertent. He'll find the jaws of live animals as beautiful as painted ones or sculptures. He'll look calmly at the distinct beauty of old age in men, women, and at the loveliness of children. And other things like that will call out to him constantly – things unnoticed by others. Things seen only by those at home with Nature and its works.[11]

Granted, intimations are not proof. I cannot prove that the *logos* is as Marcus Aurelius hoped. It is possible that there is nothing more – that all we have are the material things we know to be inadequate to our happiness.

I do not mean to be glib about this question; but neither am I going to try to prove the existence of God or universal order. Instead, a version of Pascal's wager will suffice, albeit not with reference to a particular vision of an active or even personified God, but rather as to the existence of some deep and beautiful underlying order. If there is a deeper truth – something worth pursuing under the heading of *logos* or truth – and we ignore it because we cannot measure it or nail it down with precision, we have lost the opportunity to thrive. If on the other hand there is no deeper order or beauty in our world – just more or less safety and health and prosperity and the like – we lose nothing by sacrificing some of them at the margins while we search for more. First, those things are inadequate anyway, so we lose little by aspiring to something higher. More to the point, we stand to gain much even if we are wrong about, or fail to find, that deeper truth and order, for the striving itself is arguably a form of thriving – a more noble and potentially more satisfying way of being.

Thus the need for something like the virtue of piety, with its unsettling but appropriate connotation of faith. Not in this doctrine or that, in this or the other way of naming the *logos*; but in the existence of a truth and beauty worth searching for – worth making our aim in place of the material things and honours we know to be inadequate.

This broader and internalised understanding of piety or aspiration bears the same relation to the traditional classical virtue of piety as the neoclassical versions of temperance and wisdom described above bear to their classical counterparts. Temperance, understood in its classical sense as moderation, demonstrates and helps develop the more essential freedom from slavery to pleasure. Wisdom, even understood merely as prudence or knowledge, is evidence of and can lead to a love of truth. Similarly, piety, understood in the classical or common way as the doing of correct religious practices – paying due respect to God or the gods – is

[11] Aurelius (2004: Book 3, s 2).

both the external manifestation of and a way of developing the more essential internal trait. By giving appropriate sacrifices, or keeping Kosher, or going to Mass, or praying toward Mecca – manifestations of piety in its classical form – we not only satisfy the external dictates of a particular tradition, but also remind and teach ourselves that it is possible and appropriate and necessary to regard highly and strive for what we cannot measure or count.

E. The Laws

So, what does law have to do with it? In particular, how can lawyers and legal academics help us develop or retain this set of virtues, this capacity for aspiration? Here, I think what matters most is the last of the several phenomena described in the first part of this essay as rhetoric. We can perhaps make the most difference to our fellow citizens' capacity to aspire, and thus to thrive, not by advocating this policy or that, but rather through how we talk about and justify our law and politics.

We can facilitate, rather than disregard, efforts to think and talk about the characterological implications of law and public policy. We can resist the temptation to reduce issues to the easy but inadequate language of measurable costs and benefits or preference satisfaction. As pretentious as it may sound to say so, we are keepers and voices of the law, which in the ways described above helps make us who we are, and thus more or less capable of thriving. And while we cannot and should not try to impose a particular view of thriving on others, we can and should at least avoid using our bully pulpit to narrow their souls.

We too often convey, if indirectly, the message that narrow instrumental concerns or deontological arguments are what really ought to count; and thus forego the opportunity to help people think about the aspects of law and politics that might really matter to their thriving. People want to think and talk about who they are; but we implicitly and inadvertently tell them they should just care about how safe they are, or how rich. By learning to talk and think, and helping others learn to talk and think, about the ways in which law and policy reveal or construct our character, and thus impact our capacity to thrive, we could not only have better conversations about particular issues, we also help ourselves and others develop and retain the capacity to think about better things. As suggested, we can do this in at least three ways: through our public policy advocacy, through our scholarship, and through our teaching.

One particularly salient and somewhat ironic example is public debate over education policy. The great bulk of public discourse, even coming from those who advocate greater attention to and spending on education, takes the form of arguments about the importance of education for economic opportunity. When President Obama spoke to schoolchildren about the value of education, he devoted the entire talk to instrumental arguments. You should stay in school and study, he told our children, because it will help you get a good job, a career. All well and good; but these ways of talking cannot help but reinforce the confusion of means and ends. If we accept the Socratic account of thriving, on which the love of truth must supplant the desire for material goods if we are to thrive, we should find ways of saying that learning is itself worthwhile – that we earn so we can learn, rather than vice versa.

In the context of politics more broadly, there is a common refrain. Candidates, we say, should focus on 'the issues'. When Obama (or before him Clinton or Reagan) talked during campaigns about hope, or spoke in other aspirational terms about the sort of people we as Americans are or ought to want to be, there was the usual tendency on the part of academics and policy experts to dismiss the talk as mere rhetoric – inspiring, perhaps, and perhaps necessary to get elected – but ultimately besides the point. Although the masses might be moved by talk of character or identity, we often behave as though our job as sophisticated legal and political thinkers should be to keep people focused on the 'real' issues. And so we dismiss, or at least fail to assist, people in using elections and issues to think and talk about public character. But once we realise that character has as much to do with thriving as do consequences, we should recognise that there is nothing 'mere' about aspirational rhetoric. What sort of people we are or want to be as impacted by our law and politics is a real issue; and it is hardly helpful to insist that people set that aside and focus instead on marginal increases in health, prosperity or prestige.

I cannot demonstrate empirically the extent to which our modes of policy argument undercut people's ability and willingness to aspire to higher things. There are certainly other institutions through which that capacity can be developed, and perhaps people will not listen to us when we explicitly or implicitly counsel them to set aside concerns of identity and character. There would still be opportunity costs, however. We who are experts at articulating reasons and arguments, and knowledgeable about law and public policy, are choosing not to help people argue about and articulate much of what matters most about the law and policy. It would be ironic, moreover, if our best hope regarding our contribution to the real thriving of our fellow citizens were to be the hope that they continue to ignore us.

As for our scholarship, the raw weight of research and writing speaks louder than any particular issue or argument. Mountains of scholarly ink – indeed entire organisations, academic programmes, endowed fellowships, and specialised publications – are devoted to tracing the consequences of law for our material wellbeing. Whole branches of legal and political theory are devoted to various rights-based or other deontological statuses of law and politics. At the same time, however, little attention is paid to the impact of law and politics on our character. Even setting aside occasional efforts to argue explicitly for a narrowing of legal discourse, it is clear that we as a community communicate, through our relative silence and lack of attention, a disregard for character-based arguments.

More than that, we can be tempted to intentionally ignore concerns of thriving from our scholarship in an effort to make social or legal problems amenable to our methodologies. The most obvious example is the necessity faced by empirical scholarship and law and economics to focus on things that can be counted and measured. You cannot regress courage, meaning, or the narrowing of a soul. Or consider analytic philosophy, which requires precise definition, and thus can call for the radical oversimplification of rich characterological ideas. This need not be fatal, as long as we are clear that we are choosing to look at what we can best measure, rather than what most matters. We can study the economics of family life without assuming or meaning to communicate that families are merely economic entities. The risk is that we can be tempted to define problems in terms of what our methodologies can best handle. We describe and construct our social life and self-understanding in reductionist terms to make problems tractable, perhaps without regard to the possibility that our self-understanding can be, thereby, reduced. Meanwhile, little explicit attention is paid by legal academics to the consequences of our law and politics for the kind of people we become, and thus on our capacity to thrive.

I understand why. Lacking a contemporary language for this kind of conversation, it is difficult to articulate characterological concerns. Given the impossibility of pinning down these matters with precision, it is hard not to seem flakey when discussing them – flakey and preachy. Eye-rolling is a reflex response to talk about character and virtue. But that response is a symptom of the problem, not an excuse for ignoring it. The narrower our souls get, the harder it is to make space for what matters, but the harder we need to try. There will always be good reason to be suspicious of arguments couched in terms of character or identity. Are they merely unsophisticated ways of getting at what could be better framed in more grounded terms? Are they serving as cover for some hidden agenda? Again, however, the answer cannot be to ignore character, but rather to learn to talk about it well rather than poorly.

As teachers of law, we can also help the next generation of lawyers and legal scholars be better at this than we are – more open to and capable of thinking well about the connections between politics and law and character and thriving. For example, in teaching our students how to make and respond to legal arguments – what might be seen as our core pedagogical task – we do them and ourselves an injustice if we teach them that concerns about who we are should be ignored or at best reframed in consequentialist or deontological terms.

We can teach this unfortunate lesson in any number of ways. Most obviously, we can give bad or thoughtless or narrow accounts and explanations of what it means to think like a lawyer. More subtly, we can simply fail to help our students make or realise the potential legitimacy of character-based arguments and concerns.

For example, if a student were to say that something about a given case or policy seems 'stupid' or 'crooked', we would appropriately understand it as part of our job to help or require the student to clarify that inchoate response – make an argument. But we could do that well or poorly. Perhaps the student means to make what is at bottom a consequentialist argument about the costs and benefits of the rule in question. If so, we should press him to clarify that argument, identify the costs and benefits, and sharpen the analysis. Or, perhaps the student means to make what is essentially a normative argument rooted in some implicit set of principles or some view of rights. If so, again, we should help and encourage him to identify the principles, tighten his logic, and respond to objections. But perhaps the student has in mind a different or overlapping sort of concern – one rooted in what it would say about us to behave in the way in question, or about what sort of people we will become if encouraged or permitted to behave in that way. Lay terms like 'stupid' and 'crooked' are at least as likely to stand for and point towards unarticulated characterological concerns as to under-developed utilitarian or normative arguments. If so, we should do as we do with any sort of argument – help and demand the student sharpen the point and make it well. What sorts of traits does he feel the law or practice in question would express or engender? Why does he think those would be bad traits? How might the other aims of the law or practice be accomplished without these consequences for our character?

These will be difficult questions for the student to answer – indeed difficult for us to ask – because we lack a habit of a language for them. But once we recognise that law has consequences for character, and that character has consequences for our capacity to thrive, we have no warrant for treating those arguments as foolish or irrelevant. I realise we do not *intend* to be ignoring or dismissing students' efforts at argumentation merely because they do not fit into narrow categories. We do it because we ourselves are not attuned to or in the habit of making and responding to characterological concerns. But we do it and, in the process, not only narrow the thinking of our students, but also potentially narrow the soul of the society for whom and about whom we are purportedly teaching them to speak.

Granted, it is not clear how much students listen to or accept of what we teach them about good lawyering; but again, it would be ironic if our best hope for our students were to be that they may not pay much attention to what we say to or model for them.

IV. CONCLUSION

The emphasis in this characterological account of public life, as in virtue ethics more broadly, is on the self-regarding significance of public action – on what it does to or says about us to act or speak in certain ways through law and politics. This obviously cannot replace relational concerns. We still must attend to what is generally assumed to be the central concern of law – how we treat each other. But self-regarding need not mean selfish; and a regard for the impact of public life on our own character need not mean a disregard for its impact on others.

Initially, once we acknowledge that character is central to thriving, and that law impacts on character, concern for the effect of law on our fellow citizens implies a concern for its impact on who they/we become as well as on their/our economic welfare or the like. Character-based thinking is no more inherently selfish than is cost-benefit analysis.

The question of how an emphasis on character and thriving might or ought to impact on our treatment of others can be framed differently, in terms of the classical virtue so far missing an analogue in the account offered here. Specifically, where does justice fit into this virtue-based account of law and politics? Recall that an effort to define justice is the question with which Plato's *Republic* begins, and around which it ostensibly revolves. Socrates answers that question in part by reframing it. He defines justice as a certain right relation of other traits, which will produce the sort of external conduct meeting the traditional definition of the virtue.

Similarly, we can, without denying the necessity to judge and evaluate our conduct, describe justice as in part a manifestation of a certain set of internal traits. Put simply, people who have developed the habit of facing their own conduct (courage), and who have found ways to temper their desire for pleasure and prestige (temperance), and who have tried to cultivate instead a love of truth and beauty (wisdom), and who retain the capacity to aspire (piety), will have less need or desire to treat others poorly.

Unfortunately, it is still possible that an emphasis on our own character development might cause us to treat others poorly if we get it wrong. Developing the base line traits essential to aspiration is not likely to require or lead us to treat others unjustly. As I suggest, however, the value and necessity of an emphasis on character extends to thinking about the connection between law and more specific and contingent traits, the pursuit of which could have that consequence. For example, an uncritical effort to develop or display a particular form of courage, understood in its traditional external sense as the willingness to take risks, might lead us to violence, even war. Or, a poorly developed vision of manliness could manifest itself in discrimination against or the mistreatment of women.

This has two implications. First, it means that a character ethics can augment but never completely replace a relational ethics. Nothing about virtue ethics generally or the communitarian form outlined here suggests that we can abandon or avoid an ongoing obligation to think about morality and justice.

More fundamentally, the risk that a focus on internal character traits might come at a cost to relational concerns or external justice suggests that we need to think about character well, rather than poorly. We need to attend to how we define ourselves and whether the traits to which we aspire will lead us to mistreat others. But the answer to this risk cannot be to ignore character or the effect of law and politics on character. We are going to be some sort of people or another; and law and politics are fora through which we build and display competing visions of who we are. The only question is whether we ignore that process, allowing ourselves to become whoever we happen to become – with whatever costs that process might impose on others – or whether we think carefully about the matter.

Finally, an emphasis on what I have called 'aspiration' can seem, even if not inherently selfish, as something of an indulgence or distraction, particularly in times of pressing need. Can we really afford to worry about abstract higher goals when people need jobs?

The only good response to this objection will sound cold-hearted: 'The poor will always be with you'. Reported in three of the four Gospels,[12] this is perhaps the meanest thing Jesus is reported to have said. Recall the context. An unnamed woman has washed and anointed Jesus' feet with expensive oil, and Judas argues that it is foolish to use resources that way. The oil could be sold and the proceeds given to the poor. Jesus tells Judas to leave the woman be, '[f]or you will have the poor always with you, but me you have not always.' Considering the source, this cannot mean we should disregard crucial needs. The best reading, I think, is that material needs – real and constant – are insatiable. We need to care for them, and as justly as possible, but if we devote all our time and energy to what is most basic, and only learn to talk and think about what is most urgent, we will never get to what is best and most deeply needful.

REFERENCES

Aurelius, Hays G (tr) (2004) *The Meditations* (New York, Random House).

Bible, *New King James Version*.

Clark, S (1999) 'The Courage of Our Convictions' 97 *Michigan Law Review* 2381.

—— (2003) 'The Character of Persuasion' 1 *Ave Maria Law Review* 61.

—— (2005) 'Law as Communitarian Virtue Ethics' 53 *Buffalo Law Review* 753.

—— (2007) 'Ennobling Direct Democracy' 78 *University of Colorado Law Review* 1341.

Crisp, R (ed) (1996) *How Should One Live: Essays on The Virtues* (Oxford, Oxford University Press).

Crisp, R and Slote, M (1997) *Virtue Ethics* (Oxford Readings in Philosophy) (Oxford, Oxford University Press).

Darwall, S (2003) *Virtue Ethics* (Blackwell Readings in Philosophy) (Malden, MA, Blackwell Publishing).

Epictetus, PE Matheson (tr) (2004) *Discourses* (New York, Dover Publications).

Feldman, H (2000) 'Prudence, Benevolence and Negligence: Virtue Ethics and Tort Law' 74 *Chicago-Kent Law Review* 1431.

Gardiner, S (ed) (2005) *Virtue Ethics Old and New* (Ithaca, New York, Cornell University Press).

Haidt, J (2006) *The Happiness Hypothesis* (Cambridge, MA, Basic Books).

Huigens, K (1998) 'Virtue and Criminal Negligence' 1 *Buffalo Criminal Law Review* 431.

Kahan, D and Braman, D (2006) 'Overcoming the Fear of Guns, the Fear of Gun Control, and the Fear of Cultural Politics: Constructing a Better Gun Debate' 55 *Emory Law Journal* 569.

Nussbaum, M and Sen, A (1993) *The Quality of Life* (Oxford, Clarendon Press).

Plato, Bloom, A (tr) (1968) *Republic* (New York, Basic Books).

Smith, A (1976) *The Theory of Moral Sentiments* (Oxford, Oxford University Press).

Statman, D (1997) *Virtue Ethics: A Critical Reader* (Edinburgh, Edinburgh University Press).

White, JB (2006) *Living Speech: Resisting the Empire of Force* (Princeton, NJ, Princeton University Press).

—— (1973) *The Legal Imagination* (Chicago, University of Chicago Press).

[12] Matthew 26:11; Mark 14:7; and John 12:8.

6

Confucian Virtue Jurisprudence

LINGHAO WANG AND LAWRENCE B SOLUM

I. INTRODUCTION

THIS ESSAY SKETCHES a position in general jurisprudence that is distinctive in two ways. First, it is rooted in the traditions of Confucian (or Ruist,儒家) thought. Second, the view of law offered in the theory is aretaic (virtue centred). We have dubbed our theory, *Confucian virtue jurisprudence*, with the understanding that our version of a contemporary aretaic theory of law with roots in Confucian thought is not the only possible member of a family of theories that could accurately bear that name.[1] More broadly, Confucian virtue jurisprudence is a member of a larger family of aretaic legal theories, including Neo-Aristotelian versions of virtue jurisprudence.[2]

The tradition of Confucian thought centres on the writings of an historical figure, Confucius (Kongzi, Master Kong, or 孔子). Our focus will be on ancient thought, with an emphasis on Confucius' *Analects* supplemented by the views of other thinkers in the Confucian tradition. At various points, we will be concerned with issues of translation, but our main purpose is to develop a contemporary theory of law that builds on ancient foundations.

What are the elements of a general jurisprudence? Legal theorists generally take two positions in searching for answers to this meta-theoretical question. One group believes that legal theory should investigate normative questions and that the fundamental purpose of legal theory is to support prescriptive legal scholarship. A second group claims that the primary aim is description. Some members of this second group believe that this involves analysis of the concept of 'law'; others would describe the project as the development of a theoretical account of the essential or necessary features of law or legal institutions. From a Confucian perspective, however, the fundamental question in legal theory is the aim and proper

[1] The most sophisticated interpretation (or reconstruction) of the classical Confucian texts from a modern jurisprudential perspective can be found in Chang (1990: chs 2, 6 and 7). Our work is inspired and influenced by his excellent scholarship on Confucian jurisprudence.

[2] See Farrelly and Solum (2007).

function of law.[3] In this short essay, we sketch some of the central elements of Confucian virtue jurisprudence. We begin with an overview of Confucian thought.

II. AN INTRODUCTION TO CONFUCIAN SOCIAL AND ETHICAL THOUGHT

Just as Neo-Aristotelian virtue jurisprudence is developed from Aristotelian virtue ethics,[4] Confucian virtue jurisprudence draws on Confucian thought.

A. The Basic Structure of Confucian Moral Theory

In Confucius' time, China's feudal system was in its final stage of collapse, causing social chaos and disorder. The old social system was fading and the new one had not yet been established, so it 'was up to the thinkers of the first millennium BC to come up with answers, solve the puzzle and restore peace.'[5] Confucianism is one of the schools of thought that undertook this task.

There are three main figures in early Confucianism. The first, Confucius, lived between 551 and 479 BC. Confucius' words and deeds are recorded in the *Analects*, a book edited by later disciples. The second figure is the 'second sage', Mencius (372–289 BC), who is famous for his positive (or optimistic) view of human nature. His moral theory has an inward-out character; he believed that self-cultivation is sufficient to lead a moral life and thus his theory focuses on the virtues. Unlike Mencius, the third thinker, Xunzi (479–221 BC), has views that could be called outward-in; he claimed that biological needs and desires are central to human nature. Xunzi believed that external habituation and deliberative correction are the only ways to rectify man's selfish nature. There are differences among the three main thinkers in early Confucianism, but we will pass them over and attempt to interpret their texts so as to reconstruct a consistent and plausible theory.

Confucian theory provides an overall account of both conduct rules and character traits. The conduct rules are *Li*, normally translated as *rules of propriety* or *ritual*, which refers to ceremonial rituals, proper manners in social interactions, conventional customs and even civil law (in the modern sense). The most important character traits are *Ren* and *Yi*, fundamental virtues in Confucian ethical theory. *Ren* (translated as *humanity* in the broad sense) is the cardinal virtue that unifies the particular moral excellences; *Ren* also has a narrow sense (translated as *benevolence*) that identifies a particular virtue related to the affective capacity con-

[3] The move beyond the necessary or essential features of law is in sympathy with a view expressed by Frederick Schauer (2010).

[4] Solum (2006: 75–76).

[5] Chang (1990: 20).

cerning caring for others. The virtue of *Yi*, translated as *rightness* or *appropriateness*, is a character trait related to the motivational attitude to abide by *Li* (social norms).

On the Confucian account of the relationship between rules and virtues, rule-following actions should be properly motivated in order to achieve a harmonious society – a well-ordered flourishing society governed by virtuous political leaders with limited use of coercion or punishment. Ideally, both citizens and rulers possess the virtues of *Ren* and *Yi*, enabling them to act according to *Li* for the right reasons and with the proper emotions.

Many scholars have argued that Confucian moral theory can be seen as a Chinese version of virtue ethics. For other scholars, however, the deontological notion of *Li* has been seen as the core ideal in Confucian moral theory: *Confucian Ritualism* is the theory articulated by some historians to emphasise the significant importance of *Li* in traditional Confucian society of China.[6]

We will interpret Confucian thought as a particular version of virtue ethics in the sense specified by Michael Slote; a virtue ethics that (1) takes aretaic notions rather than deontological notions as primary and (2) emphasises moral evaluation of agents and their motives and character traits.[7] Early Confucian ethical thought is a virtue ethics in Slote's sense.[8]

The aretaic character of Confucian thought is consistent with the role played by *Li* (or social norms that provide comprehensive governance of social life). Confucian thought posits that ideal moral agents (in the conditions of traditional Chinese society) should strictly observe *Li*. In the *Analects*, we read, 'Do not look unless it is in accordance with *Li*; do not listen unless it is in accordance with *Li*; do not speak unless it is in accordance with *Li*; do not move unless it is in accordance with *Li*'.[9]

So on the one hand, we have a deontological notion *Li*, which functions as a set of external rules specifying right action. But on the other hand, we have *Ren* and *Yi*, which are virtues or character traits. *Ren* is more fundamental than *Li*; as Confucius once said, 'A man who is not *Ren* – what has he to do with *Li*?'[10] The virtue of *Yi* is related to the proper motivational attitudes of abiding by *Li*. In another place in the *Analects*, Confucius stated that *Li* is the form and *Yi* is the essence in virtuous agents' moral lives.[11] So, virtues are more fundamental than rules[12] and moral evaluation of agents' characters is primary.

[6] See Chow (1994).

[7] See Slote (1992: 89).

[8] Wai-Ying Wong has an excellent discussion of the distinctive features of virtue ethics and its relationship to Confucian moral theory. See Wong (2001: 286–89). A lot of important works in Chinese philosophy have been devoted to an aretaic reading of Confucian ethics. See eg Gier (2001: 280–305); Slingerland (2001: 97–125); van Norden (2007); and Yu (1998: 323–47).

[9] Confucius (2001: 32), with some modifications to the translation.

[10] ibid 7, with some modifications to the translation.

[11] ibid 41.

[12] By claiming 'more fundamental', we are not arguing that *Li* loses its independent value or that *Li* can be deduced from virtues.

Confucian ethics incorporates both aretaic notions and deontological notions, postulating a harmonious unity of the external rules and internal virtues. The deontic and aretaic elements are unified by the social roles of agents; those roles govern relationships between members of the community. The same agent might occupy different roles in connection with different relationships. For example, a woman might be a mother with regard to the relationship between her and her children and simultaneously a disciple with regard to the relationship between her and her teacher.

Thus, we can summarise as follows: *Li* prescribes rules attached to roles. *Ren* is the cardinal virtue of humanity and the particular virtue of benevolence. *Yi* can be seen as an intermediate between the deontological notion *Li* and aretaic notion *Ren* by specifying the motivational attitude appropriate to the fulfilment of responsibilities and duties attached to social roles. Thus, Confucian moral thought is a role-based virtue ethics. It is role-based because 'it is based on the roles that make an agent the person he or she is';[13] it is a virtue ethics because the ultimate concern of early Confucian thinkers was the inner characters of moral agents. The diagram below roughly shows the structure of Confucian ethics:

Li (Social norms) Role

⇩

Yi (Properly motivated to fulfill the responsibilities and duties set by *Li*)

⇧

Ren (Fundamental virtue)

Agents who possesses all the virtues are *Junzi* (君子), commonly translated as *gentleman* or *superior man* in English. A *Junzi* possesses all the virtues, and thus he or she is able to autonomously abide by the external rules specified by *Li* in accord with his or her own dispositions. Someone who is a *Junzi* and lives under favourable conditions could be said to live a flourishing life. We might call this view of human flourishing *the harmony conception of human flourishing*. The life of a *Junzi* is harmonious because in such a life the aims or values of the individual are consistent with the social norms of the community in which the agent lives.

With the overview complete, we now provide a fuller description of the fundamental concepts in Confucian ethical and social thought; these concepts are the building blocks of the Confucian virtue jurisprudence we sketch in the next part.

[13] Nuyen (2009).

B. Four Concepts: *Li*, Correcting Names, *Yi*, and *Ren*

i. Li

There was no word precisely corresponding to *positive law* in ancient China. Nonetheless, there were traditional norms governing human conduct and coordinating social interactions; these norms formed the normative domain called *Li* (禮) – a crucial ideal in Confucian practical philosophy. However, since this Chinese word has undergone a long history of linguistic evolution, the meaning and scope of *Li* has changed over time. The conventional view is that *Li* originated from the practice of sacrifice; *Li* was constituted by the rules specifying rituals governing sacrifices performed by individuals or groups in honour of their common ancestors.[14] Later, the scope of *Li* was extended to include etiquette and proper manners in social interaction. Our view is that the scope of *Li* in the Confucian context refers to the whole normative system in the society, including the rituals and rites in the sacrifice ceremony, etiquette, moral rules and political institutions, and even some rules we would not call *laws*.[15]

But our conception of *Li* is not an idea limited to a purely external standard of conduct. Confucius made this point explicit in his comparison between governing people by government regulations backed by punishments and guiding people by virtues and *Li*:

> The Master said, 'If the people be led by governmental regulations, and uniformity sought to be given them by punishments, they will try to avoid the punishment, but have no sense of shame. If they be led by virtue, and uniformity sought to be given them by *Li*, they will have the sense of shame, and moreover will reform themselves.'[16]

From this comparison, we know that *Li* has an internal aspect and is necessarily connected with the emotion of shame and the virtue of *Yi*.[17]

Why was *Li* necessary for social order? Confucian philosophers answered this question by developing several functional arguments. For Xunzi, the primary function of *Li* is the coordination of social interactions and the creation of social order: we call this the *social coordinative function*. Xunzi claims that human beings have natural desires while the good is insufficient for the fulfilment of people's desires. If these desires are left unregulated, 'there will be chaos' and people 'will be impoverished'.[18] *Li* can provide a proper common ground for social interactions and overcome the problem of chaos produced by unregulated natural desires. Moreover, by regulating resource distribution, *Li* can produce prosperity.[19]

[14] Chang (1983: 37).
[15] It was common in the history of Imperial China for *Li* to be codified and enacted by political authority.
[16] Confucius (1971: 146), with some modifications to the translation.
[17] The relationship between the emotion of shame and *Li* will be discussed more thoroughly in our investigation of the virtue *Yi*.
[18] Xunzi (2001: 265).
[19] ibid.

In Confucian role-based virtue ethics, *Li* provides information about social rules to which moral responsibilities are attached. These ethical roles are closely connected with five crucial ethical relationships (君子), which are (1) that between parents and children; (2) that between ruler and subject; (3) that between husband and wife; (4) that between elder and younger brother; and (5) that between friends.[20] *Li* can be described as a sort of social grammar, which 'provides each member with a defined place and status within the family, community, and polity'.[21]

Li also has an expressive function; it enables the expression of sentiments and dispositions. There are two typical ways in which *Li* performs this expressive function: first, the rules of *Li* set up uniform standards in circumstances and regulate the agents' feeling of certain emotions; and, second, the rules of *Li* provide agents a proper way to successfully express their emotions.[22]

Since Confucian theory is a role-based virtue ethics, 'a moral agent must aim not only at the cultivation of right feelings, but also at the right expression of these feelings in proper context'.[23] For Confucius, *Li* has a fundamental role in the practice of some virtues.[24] *Li* sets standards for the proper manner and right feeling of emotions in particular contexts of social interactions. As Confucius put it, without agents' observance of *Li*, some virtues will become vices.

Finally, *Li* has a constitutive role for human beings as social creatures. This theme can be seen as a further development of the coordinative function and the expressive function. *Li* incorporates rules of propriety, rituals, customs and law. From the social perspective, *Li*'s coordinative function establishes the foundation of social life. From the personal perspective, the expressive function of *Li* provides agents with a means and standard for the expression of their interior dispositions. Thus, we say that *Li* has a constitutive role. *Li* is like 'the cement of the entire normative sociopolitical order', [25] which binds 'human beings and the spirits together in networks of interacting roles within the family, within the human society, and with the numinous realms beyond.'[26]

ii. Correcting Names

The next idea that we examine is the doctrine of *correcting names* and the associated concept of *name* (名). Confucian philosophers developed an account of the use of names (ie characters in writing and by words and phrases in speech) in moral language and recommended a doctrine of correcting names (正名) as the principle

[20] Mengzi (2001: 127).

[21] Ames and Rosemont (1988: 51).

[22] See *Li Ji*: *Tan Gong* (《礼记·檀弓》). Also see Chang (1990: 12).

[23] Cua (1971: 134).

[24] eg he claims that '[r]espectfulness, without *Li*, becomes laborious bustle; prudence, without *Li*, becomes timidity; courage, without *Li*, becomes insubordination; straightforwardness, without *Li*, becomes rudeness.' Confucius (1971: 162), with some modifications to the translation.

[25] Schwartz (1985: 67).

[26] ibid.

for the proper use of moral language. In this part of the essay, we interpret *names* as *thick ethical concepts*; this account of names is then used to illuminate the nature of the practice of correcting names.

The phrase *correcting names* appears only once in the *Analects*.[27] For Confucius, the correction of names is crucial to the establishment of a stable social order. Confucius offered a chain of arguments, within which the notion of correcting names operates as the most fundamental premise.

> If names be not correct, language is not in accordance with actuality. If language be not in accordance with actuality, affairs cannot be carried on to success. When affairs cannot be carried on to success, *Li* and music will not flourish. When *Li* and music do not flourish, punishments will miss the mark. When punishments miss the mark, the people do not know how to move hand or foot. Therefore a superior man considers it necessary that the names he uses may be spoken appropriately and also that what he speaks may be carried out appropriately.[28]

In other words, this passage suggests that Confucius viewed the proper use of names as a precondition of social practice that functions well.

Ethical names have two functions: one is descriptive and the other is prescriptive. On the one hand, names have a descriptive function that enables us to make reference to different things or describe different properties of things in the world. In this regard, correcting names 'constructs a model of the proper function of language on the basis of the claim that the role of "names" (generally, substance words) is to distinguish differences in "realities".'[29] With the use of names, we can understand one another's beliefs about the world and communicate with each other. For example, the names of *lord*, *minister*, *father* and *son* refer to different people who possess these social roles.

On the other hand, names have a prescriptive function that is deeply connected with the traditional norms of *Li*. For example, the meaning of *lord* should be understood in its connection to the virtues, duties and proper ways of behaviour of a morally ideal lord. In ancient China, someone who properly understood the name of *lord* would have applied *lord* to express their normative expectations of the men who were actually in charge of political affairs.

Understood literally, the process of correcting names seems to be the re-establishment of the proper correspondence between names and the actual state of ethical practice. However, this understanding does not specify the object of correction, which could be either ethical practice or linguistic practice. From the descriptive perspective, the actuality of ethical practice is prior to the description, thus the object of correction (in the practice of correcting names) is current usage of the relevant names.[30] But from the prescriptive perspective, names imply the standards of actions, thus the objects of correction should be the actual states of affairs or actions that are connected with the prescriptive content of the names.

[27] Confucius (1971: 263–64).
[28] ibid, with some modifications to the translation.
[29] Eno (1990: 146).
[30] Fung (1952: 60).

So what is the nature of the Confucian idea of 'names'? Descriptive, prescriptive, or both? Bernard Williams' account of what he called 'thick ethical concepts' gives us a clearer picture of the descriptive and prescriptive features of names as well as the relationship between these two features.

The notion of thick ethical terms was introduced by Williams in his influential work *Ethics and the Limits of Philosophy*, where he famously distinguished thick ethical concepts from thin ones. Thick ethical concepts include words like *brutality* or *courage*, which carry more factual or descriptive content than thin ethical concepts like *right* or *wrong*. Thin ethical concepts do not contain substantive information about states of affairs: from an assertion that a situation is good or an action is right, we can infer very little about the nature of the situation or action. But thick ethical concepts are different. For example, if an action is described as *courageous*, then we know that the agent faced the danger in an appropriate way.

Because thick ethical concepts are world-guided, they can facilitate moral convergence among the members of a particular community and serve as the basis for social coordination. By way of contrast, thin concepts (like *right* or *good*) lack this close connection to facts about the world, and for this reason, thin concepts cannot facilitate agreement by providing a basis for agreement in judgements about particular cases.

We can characterise thick and thin ethical concepts as follows. Thin ethical concepts are concepts that only have general and abstract evaluative or prescriptive content. Thick ethical concepts are ethical concepts that have both descriptive content and prescriptive content. For Williams, thick ethical concepts may have another crucial feature; they imply 'a union of fact and value': 'The way these notions are applied is determined by what the world is like (for instance, by how someone has behaved), and yet, at the same time, their application usually involves a certain valuation of the situation, of persons or actions.'[31] Thus, thick ethical terms are both 'world-guided' and 'action-guiding' at the same time.

Thick ethical concepts are world-guided because the application of a thick ethical term is guided by facts about the world. These concepts are also action-guiding, in the sense that thick ethical concepts provide standards that give reasons for action and can be used to evaluate actions.[32] For example, if someone describes an action as 'cruel', she has a reason not to do that action: the cruelty of the action provides her with a reason to refrain from engaging in the action.

The third feature, and also the most important one, is what we call the *amalgam nature* of thick concepts. A thick concept represents an indissolubly united amalgam of description and evaluation.[33] This amalgam nature has two dimensions, which we theorise as nondetachability and underdeterminacy.

On the one hand, thick concepts convey an evaluative attitude directed at a specific feature of a person, action or circumstance. Or, we might say that the

[31] Williams (2006: 129).
[32] ibid 140.
[33] See Payne (2005: 96).

evaluative attitude is expressed *in the light of* the description.[34] When we say that an action is cruel, we are not making an all-things-considered assessment of that action but an assessment of a specific descriptive property of that action. This feature of thick concepts could be conceptualised as the *Nondetachability Thesis*.[35] The evaluative content of a thick concept is always the evaluation of one or more descriptive elements of that concept that cannot be fully detached from the concept's descriptive content.

On the other hand, users of thick concepts specify descriptive content from an evaluative point of view that is constructed by shared human needs, interests and concerns.[36] For example, the evaluative point in the application of *rudeness* might be constructed by a particular concern of politeness or good manners in social interaction; so the thick concept *rudeness* might cover a wide range of actions.[37] To apply thick concepts correctly, people always need to resort to the evaluative point underneath the concept. This aspect of thick concepts is described by the *Underdeterminacy Thesis*:[38] the descriptive content of a concept alone cannot adequately determine the application of that concept. The implication of the *Underdeterminacy Thesis* is that a thick concept may lack a natural shape,[39] a shape that is defined solely by its descriptive elements. Instead, such concepts have a normative shape or evaluative shape that is organised by their evaluative point.

William's notion of thick ethical concepts and the amalgam account of their nature help to provide a much clearer understanding of the Confucian idea of names and the related practice of correcting names. In the traditional understanding of Chinese scholars, there is some tension between the descriptive and the prescriptive view of names. Williams' notion captures the nature of Confucian names and provides us with a new perspective on the superficial tension between the descriptive function and prescriptive function.

Confucian names, *qua* thick ethical concepts, are indissolubly united ethical concepts combining descriptive and prescriptive elements. They can both serve the function of categories distinguishing like from unlike and have ethical implications indicating what is particularly right and morally wrong. The use of names of this sort can be improper for either one of two reasons: (1) inability to track the world or (2) inability to provide appropriate guidance for actions. If we understand the doctrine of correcting names in this way, then the objects of correction turn out to be the mistaken application of names to actions or persons. Whether to change the name to capture the genuine features of the world – as Mencius did when he rectified the name of *lord* – or to reveal the true moral implications of existing names – as Confucius did when he emphasised the importance of fulfilment of duties connected to social roles – depends on the particular circumstances. Improper use

[34] See Blackburn (1992: 289).
[35] A more complete account is provided in Wang (2010).
[36] See Feldman (1994: 1195, 1196).
[37] See Goldie (2008: 97).
[38] See Wang (2010).
[39] For discussions of the naturally shapeless nature of thick concepts, see Dancy (1996: 263).

of a thick ethical concept can prompt either one of two responses: we can change the way we talk (apply the correct name) or we can change the way we act (act in accord with the correct name).

Since names are concepts with rich ethical meaning, they provide ethical guidance for actions. Confucian philosophers' ultimate goal in emphasising the correction of names is to give people ethical guidance through the application of names in the correct way and to the correct persons and actions. For example, the spontaneous application of the name *regicide* by an agent provides a reason not to kill.[40] Similarly, the application of the word *cruel* to a type of punishment gives us a reason not to use that kind of punishment.

iii. Yi

Yi is normally translated as *rightness*, *righteousness*, *appropriateness*, or *dutifulness*. Since *Yi* functions as an intermediary between *Ren* and *Li*, that is, between an aretaic notion and a deontological notion, there might be some confusion about the nature of *Yi*. In the *Analects, Yi* refers to the quality of actions[41] and thus it might be understood as a deontological term. But *Yi* sometimes refers to the attribute of persons[42] and thus it might be understood as an aretaic concept.

The key to answering the question of whether *Yi* is aretaic or deontological lies in the relationship between *Yi* and *Li*. Another paragraph in the *Analects* sheds some light on this relationship:

> The Master said, 'The *Junzi* takes *Yi* as essential. He performs it according to *Li*, gives it expression through modesty, and perfects it with sincerity. This is indeed a *Junzi*.'[43]

This remark implies that *Li* cannot be reduced to external rightness. To perform the right action in the particular circumstances, one must have the right feelings and express these feelings rightly.[44] This is why Confucius asked, 'A man who is not *Ren* – what has he to do with *Li*?'[45] Since *Ren* is a fundamental virtue – with content that is too abstract to connect directly with *Li* – *Yi* can be conceived as a virtue that mediates between *Ren* and *Li*. On this account, *Yi* harmonises external rightness (*Li*) with internal rightness (*Ren*).

Because *Yi* mainly deals with the social norms that constitute *Li*,[46] *Yi* can be seen as a virtue concerning the motivational attitudes of actors who observe these social norms. A person possessing *Yi* is motivated in the right way to fulfil the responsibilities and duties of *Li*. Confucius did not elaborate on what exactly the appropriate motivation is, but he ruled out the motivations based on personal

[40] Of course, the reason might not be an exclusive or decisive one, as Williams pointed out. See Williams (2006: 140). In other words, these reasons are defensible.

[41] See Shun (1997: 25).

[42] See ibid 26.

[43] Confucius (1971: 299), with some modifications to the translation.

[44] See Cua (1971: 134).

[45] Confucius (2001: 7).

[46] See Cua (2007: 134).

gain.[47] This distinction between *Yi* and profit is one of the central theses in the Confucian tradition of ethical and political thought.[48]

Yi is connected with the emotions of shame (羞) and aversion (惡). Mencius famously claimed that 'the heart of shame and aversion is *Yi*.'[49] As Mencius explains, the core of shame involves a negative emotion triggered by failure to conform to *Li*.[50] In the western tradition, we can distinguish conventional shame from ethical shame. Conventional shame 'is a sort of unpleasant feeling we have when we believe those whose views matter to us look down on us (or on those with whom we identify) on the basis of a standard of appearance we share'.[51] Ethical shame 'is a sort of unpleasant feeling we have when we believe that we (or those with whom we identify) have significant character flaws.'[52]

What kind of shame was the concern of early Confucianists? On the one hand, they emphasised the importance of self-cultivation, so ethical shame would be of the right kind. This view is supported by Mencius' recognition that the sense of shame is a crucial element in ethical self-cultivation.[53] On the other hand, *Li* has an independent and irreducible role in the whole theoretical structure, and conventional shame will support agents in their attempts to abide by social norms. When Confucius emphasised the crucial role of the sense of shame in the political contexts,[54] his views seem to involve conventional shame as the mechanism that creates social pressure and thus maintains the social order.

We conclude that the emotions connected to *Yi* include both conventional shame and ethical shame. Both forms of shame motivate agents to act according to the rules in *Li*. From another perspective, we might say that *Li* is internalised by agents with the help of *Yi*. *Li* provides the concrete, formal way of the expression of *Ren* (in the general sense) and *Yi* sets the appropriate internal attitudes and emotions in the process of expression. *Yi* provides harmony between external standards and internal virtues.

iv. Ren

Now we come to the most fundamental virtue, *Ren*, which has both a broad and a narrow sense.[55] *Ren* in the narrow sense is translated as *benevolence*, which is connected with the natural affective capacity of humans; in this context, *benevolence* means caring for or loving others. The broad sense of *Ren* is more ambiguous; it is

[47] The Master said, 'The *Junzi* understands what is *Yi*, the petty person understands what is profit.' Confucius (2001: 11).

[48] See eg Mengzi (2001: 113).

[49] Mengzi (2001: 143), with some modifications to the translation.

[50] See Shun (1997: 58). See also van Norden (2007: 262).

[51] van Norden (2007: 259).

[52] ibid 260.

[53] Mencius said, 'A sense of dishonor is indeed important for people. Those who are crafty in their contrivances and schemes have no use for dishonor. If one is not ashamed of not being as good as others, how will one ever be as good as others?' Mengzi (2001: 148), with some modifications to the translation.

[54] See Confucius (1971: 146).

[55] See Shun (1997: 23–24).

translated as *perfect virtue*, *goodness*, *humaneness*, or *humanity*. *Ren* in the broad sense is regarded as the unity of all the virtues including *Ren* in the narrow sense.

The broad sense of *Ren* was not elaborated on in the *Analects*, but we can characterise *Ren* in the broad sense by examining more particular virtues such as filiality. The virtue of filiality (or filial loyalty and respect, 孝) is regarded as the root of the development of *Ren*. In the *Analects*, we read at the opening of the text that, 'The *Junzi* applies himself to the roots. That being established, all practical courses naturally grow up. Filial piety and brotherly respect! – are they not the root of all benevolent actions?'[56]

Though *Ren* in the broad sense is an abstract notion concerned with interpersonal relations, the cultivation of *Ren* occurs within the family and with the people to whom we are most closely connected. So filiality is the preliminary form of *Ren*. An agent who fully extends the virtue of filiality to all social relations is a *Ren* agent. But extension of filiality to other social relationships is context-sensitive: the kind of respect that is due to members of one's family will not be identical to the kind of respect that is due to a friend, co-worker, or official.

Another virtue involved in the development of the broad sense of *Ren* is courage. Confucius once remarked that, 'men possessing *Ren* are sure to be courageous, but those who are courageous may not always be men possessing *Ren*.'[57] Joining filiality and courage are several other virtues that are united in the broad sense of *Ren*: these particular virtues are reverence, respectfulness, loyalty,[58] tolerance, trustworthiness, quickness and generosity.[59]

The general notion of *Ren* represents the highest human achievement in ethical self-cultivation, hence the common translation as *humanity*. In addition, *Ren* involves action conforming to social norms and therefore *Ren* constrains action on the basis of unrestricted desires and impulses:

> Yan Hui asked about *Ren*. The Master said, 'Restraining yourself and returning to *Li* constitutes *Ren*. If for one day you managed to restrain yourself and return to *Li*, in this way you could lead the entire world back to *Ren*.'[60]

Human beings have natural desires and impulses, but given the social nature of human beings the expression of these desires can and should be regulated by *Li*. *Ren* is the virtue that endows 'these feelings, impulses, and desires with a signifi-

[56] Confucius (1971: 139), with some modifications to the translation.

[57] ibid 276, with some modifications to the translation.

[58] Fan Chi asked about *Ren*. The Master said, 'While at home hold yourself in a respectful attitude; when serving in an official capacity be reverent; when dealing with others be loyal. These are qualities that cannot be put aside, even when you go and live among the barbarians.' Confucius (1979: 121).

[59] Zizhang asked Confucius about *Ren*. Confucius said, 'There are five things and whoever is capable of putting them into practice in the world is certainly *Ren*.' When asked for details, he went on, 'They are respectfulness, tolerance, trustworthiness, quickness, and generosity. If a man is respectful he will not be treated with insolence. If he is tolerant he will win the multitude. If he is trustworthy in word his fellow men will entrust him with responsibility. If he is quick he will achieve results. If he is generous, he will be good enough to be put in a position over his fellow men.' Confucius (1979: 144), with some modifications to the translation.

[60] Confucius (2001: 32), with some modifications to the translation.

cance beyond their *de facto* character'.[61] The general notion of *Ren* was articulated by Cua as 'moral life at its best' and the 'thematic unity of Confucian discourse'.[62] Although these characterisations of *Ren* are very abstract, they point to the unifying character of *Ren*: particular virtues are unified by and constitutive of the general virtue of *Ren*.

The narrow sense of *Ren* mainly concerns empathetic affections in the ethical life. It is illustrated in Mencius' claim that '[t]he heart of compassion is benevolence.'[63] Confucius' thin definition of this narrow sense of *Ren* is loving people.[64] However, in Confucius' understanding of *Ren*, there might be two aspects expressed in two formulas, related to *Ren* as the practice of loving or caring for persons. The positive formula is as follows:

> Desiring to take his stand, one who is *Ren* helps others to take their stand; wanting to realize himself, he helps others to realize themselves. [65]

And the passive formula is this: 'Do not impose upon others what you yourself do not desire.'[66]

These formulas emphasise the empathetic nature of *Ren*. The two formulas require the virtuous agent to examine the impact of her decisions from the perspective of the persons who are affected by her actions. However, since *Ren* is supposed to be a virtue,[67] these formulas should be understood as a requirement of empathy (as a disposition of character) rather than a requirement that agents engage in a particular procedure of practical reasoning: hence, *Ren* differs from Kant's notion of the categorical imperative understood as a decision procedure for ethics.

On Mencius' account, each virtue is connected with an emotion. According to Mencius, the emotion connected with *Ren* is sympathy or compassion; his account of the connection is based on his conception of human nature. Mencius argued for his positive conception via a thought experiment, which he described as follows:

> The reason why I say that humans all have hearts that are not unfeeling toward others is this. Suppose someone suddenly saw a child about to fall into a well: everyone in such a situation would have a feeling of alarm and compassion – not because one sought to get in good with the child's parents, not because one wanted fame among their neighbors and friends, and not because one would dislike the sound of the child's cries.[68]

Mencius' thought experiment is designed to elicit the natural moral reactions of human beings towards the accident. The baby is going to fall into the well! It happens suddenly, and for this reason, it tests the gut reactions of human beings and

[61] Cua (1971: 132).
[62] ibid 127.
[63] Mengzi (2001: 143).
[64] See Confucius (1979: 116–17).
[65] Confucius (2001: 19), with some modifications to the translation.
[66] ibid 42.
[67] The contexts in which *Ren* is used in the *Analects* do imply that *Ren* is primarily a quality of the agents.
[68] Mengzi (2001: 129).

is designed to exclude the possibility of extended deliberation that might conceal the natural human reaction to the situation described in the thought experiment. Moreover, Mencius imposed several restrictions upon other possible relative factors that might motivate the observer's reaction.

Using this thought experiment, Mencius argued that the natural emotional reaction of a human being is alarm and compassion. Seeing this intuitive sympathetic reaction helps us to distil those human character traits that distinguish human beings from other animals. Mencius explicitly claimed, 'From this we can see that if one is without the heart of compassion, one is not a human'.[69] He then connected this emotional reaction with the narrow sense of *Ren*: 'The heart of compassion is the sprout of *Ren*.'[70]

For Mencius, human nature is characterised by the natural course of human ethical development:

> In general, having these four sprouts within oneself, if one knows to fill them all out, it will be like a fire starting up, a spring breaking through! If one can merely fill them out, they will be sufficient to care for all within the Four Seas. If one merely fails to fill them out, they will be insufficient to serve one's parents.[71]

Mencius's claim in this paragraph is that given the proper circumstances and what he calls the *four sprouts*, human virtues will naturally begin to grow or emerge and subsequently will achieve completeness or full development.

In the case of the development of virtues, according to Mencius, human moral agents themselves create the natural circumstances for development. This is why he claimed, 'To have these four sprouts but to say of oneself that one is unable to be virtuous is to steal from oneself'.[72] The possession of the natural potential for virtue is sufficient to enable humans to acquire the virtues and hence to lead a virtuous life.[73] This account can be characterised as a naturalistic developmental view of human nature. It is naturalistic, since good human nature is the normal expression of human nature, given the tendency of the development of particular species and the normal circumstances they live in. It is developmental, because it takes account of the process of the development instead of, say, stable functions of the complete or end state of the species.

This explanation of Mencius' conception of human nature lays the ground for a better understanding of the relationship between the broad sense and the narrow sense of *Ren*. Since the narrow sense of *Ren* is the ethical capacity of sympathy or caring for others, it defines genuine human nature. While the broad sense of *Ren* concerns the whole unity of human excellences or the complete humanity, it could be seen as the highest ethical achievement of human beings. Then, we

69 ibid.

70 ibid 130, with some modifications to the translation.

71 ibid. The 'four sprouts' here are the emotions that function as the foundation of Mencius' four virtues. They are compassion, shame, deference, approval and disapproval.

72 ibid.

73 Confucius has a similar remark. The Master said, 'Is *Ren* really so far away? If I merely desire Ren, I will find that Ren is already here.' Confucius (2001: 22), with some modifications to the translation.

might claim that the broad sense of *Ren* is the final development of the narrow sense of *Ren*.

III. A SKETCH OF A CONTEMPORARY CONFUCIAN VIRTUE JURISPRUDENCE

The task in this section is the application of Confucian thought in the context of modern legal theory. This section deals with the basic structure of Confucian legal theory.

A. Conceptual Clarification

When we turn to the Confucian legal theory, the enterprise of reconstructing Confucian views runs into a significant obstacle: the three great Confucian figures of antiquity did not articulate well-developed or elaborate theoretical views about law in the modern sense. The reason for their failure to pay theoretical attention to law may be connected to the fact that law in ancient China did not play the central role that it does in contemporary western societies.

The relatively minor role of law in ancient China has at least two aspects. First, *Li* governed most of the social conduct in the Pre-Qin dynasty that modern societies regulate through formal positive law. Second, laws were enacted by rulers in particular states (of which there were many within the territory that constituted the larger social, cultural and linguistic community), and the application of law was limited by the geographical boundaries of those states. By way of contrast, *Li* had universal application (within the relevant social world): thus *Li* constituted 'the common norms of the ancient world' in ancient China.[74]

Given that *Li* was the dominant normative system in ancient China, our inquiry may be illuminated by a conceptual comparison between *Li* and law. But there is a potential confusion because of the linguistic dislocation of modern and ancient Chinese. The Chinese character *Fa* (法) is used as the parallel of *law* in translation between modern Chinese and English, but the ancient Chinese character *Fa* referred only to the rules governing punishment.[75] So it is plausible to conclude that the main body of *Fa* in early Chinese history is limited as a subset of criminal law – essentially instructions to officials regarding criminal punishments.[76]

While *Fa* had a very limited scope, *Li* and modern positive law overlap to a significant degree. The first area of commonality occurs in those instances in which *Li* is codified and enacted by a political authority. *Li* (and not *Fa*) governed the basic political institutions and governmental procedures and hence the behaviour

[74] Chang (1990: 9).

[75] According to *Shang Shu* (《尚書》), an ancient script, '(these) five kinds of punishment are called law'. *Shang Shu: Lv Xin* (《尚書·呂刑》).

[76] Hansen (undated).

of officials.[77] Most contemporary legal theorists believe that for a norm to count as positive law it must be enacted or practised by officials. So some parts of *Li* share this crucial characteristic (governing official behaviour) with positive law. *Li* also included some norms or rules that would be classified as civil law in modern western legal systems. For example, marriage was regulated by *Li*. Sometimes, *Li* functioned as an authoritative standard in dispute resolution.[78] For these reasons, some historians claim that *Li* was actually the ancient Chinese equivalent of the modern concept of law.[79]

In sum, we are dealing with three conceptions, corresponding to the phrase positive law and the ancient Chinese words *Fa* and *Li*. *Fa* in ancient China referred only to the rules governing the imposition of punishment; these rules did not create legal obligations for legal subjects. *Li* is a specific kind of social norm, including propriety, ritual, custom, etiquette and both customary and positive law: even when *Li* was uncodified, it performed most of the social functions that law performs in contemporary western cultures. That is, *Li* overlaps with the modern conception of positive law, but is not identical to it, encompassing some social norms that would not be classified as positive law on contemporary views of the nature of law.

B. The End of Law

Confucian philosophers did not take *Fa* as their central concern, but they addressed the ancient practices that roughly correspond to modern positive law. The traditional view of Confucius' attitude towards law is characterised in his injunction to 'eliminate litigation'. The Master said, 'In hearing litigations, I am as the others. The point is to eliminate litigation.'[80] Is 'eliminate litigation' a strong claim about all possible circumstances or is it a moderate claim limited to ideal circumstances? We believe that the moderate version provides both the best historical interpretation and the best contemporary reconstruction of the Confucian view.

Borrowing the distinction between first best and second best from economics illuminates our case for the moderate interpretation. Consider the first-best world of Confucian theory: in that world, the preconditions for an optimal harmonious Confucian society would be satisfied. These preconditions include the following: (1) each and every member of society would possess sufficient virtue; (2) the content of *Li* would have been framed by the Sage Kings – who themselves would be fully virtuous, possessing *Ren* and *Yi*; (3) *Li* would be properly observed by the members of society, including those aspects of *Li* that regulate or govern conduct

[77] See *Li Ji: Wang Zhi* (《禮記·王制》).
[78] See *Li Ji: Qu Li* (《禮記·曲禮》).
[79] See Mei (1975: 137).
[80] See de Montesquieu (1981: 3).

(apologies, voluntary restitution, etc) after social conflict (to the extent it is unavoidable) has occurred. If these conditions (and perhaps others) were satisfied, then we would have the first-best state of society: in this state, the best policy for judicial activity is to eliminate litigation, or if that is not possible, to constrain litigation so that its occurrence is rare and exceptional.[81]

Suppose, however, that one of the preconditions for an optimal harmonious Confucian ideal society could not be fulfilled. For example, if some members of society do not possess the minimal amount of virtue required, then the public policy of 'eliminate litigation' may actually result in less harmony. Under these circumstances, some litigation should be encouraged to produce the best possible results given non-ideal conditions. Thus, we contend that the most reasonable interpretation of Confucius' remark, 'eliminate litigation', construes his injunction as a description of the first-best state.

Confucius' opinion about litigation leads us to our account of the ends of law. We begin with *Li*, because *Li* played an essential role in the social and political life of ancient Chinese. We read in the *Analects* that '[i]n practicing *Li*, harmony is to be prized'.[82] This conception of harmony has two aspects: harmony of society and harmony of the individual.

The first aspect of harmony is the social coordinative function of *Li*. This function of *Li* is directed at the harmony of society; everyone has a proper position in the community regulated and guided by *Li*. We might call this aspect of harmony *coordinative harmony*. Given the similar coordinative functions of *Li* in the ancient world of China on the one hand, and of law[83] in modern society on the other, we conclude that coordinative harmony is an important end of law. In modern society, law creates a formal and relatively determinate guidance for social interaction as well as an ultimate standard of dispute resolution. In an ideal society, the dispute-resolution function of law is displaced by the law's action-guiding role.

The second aspect of the harmony-creating function of law is based on the premise that societies will function better if the rules of law are the object of voluntary compliance by individuals. Achieving voluntary compliance creates associated requirements for the inner dispositions possessed by the subjects of law. We might call this kind of harmony *autonomous harmony*. Autonomous harmony is related to the expressive function of *Li*. Individuals can express their emotions or exercise their virtues smoothly with the help of *Li* and follow their own sentiments and desires without creating a breach of *Li*. Since the natural tendency of moral development of human beings is defined by their affective and empathetic capacities, Confucian thinkers believe that given the external proper social circumstances and the natural development of affective capacity without disruption, humans can experience an inner harmony between their emotional state and the requirements of virtue.

[81] For a more complete account of the role of litigation, see Solum (2004: 181, 186–89).

[82] Confucius (1971: 143), with some modifications to the translation.

[83] Raz provides us with an insightful modern perspective of the coordination value of law. See Raz (1986: 57–62).

Our notion of autonomous harmony depends on the constituent notion of autonomy. For our purposes, *autonomy* can be defined abstractly; Gerald Dworkin defines autonomy as 'a second-order capacity of persons to reflect critically upon their first-order preferences, desires, wishes, and so forth and the capacity to accept or attempt to change these in light of higher-order preferences and values'.[84] With this abstract concept of autonomy in mind, we can see how autonomous harmony works. Although the virtue of *Ren* is based on natural intuitive emotional reactions, possession of this virtue enables self-cultivating agents to, first, reflect on the natural de facto feelings, desires and impulses and, secondly, to reshape their behaviour without external direction. This satisfies the two elements required by the general concept of autonomy proposed by Gerald Dworkin: (1) the ability to perform, based on higher-order evaluation, critical reflection and (2) the freedom to lead a good life without direction from others.

Ren (or virtues) and *Li* (or social norms) are mutually supportive. In the context of traditional Chinese society, the relationship between internal dispositions and external norms is harmonised by the expressive function of *Li*. Because *Li* embraced the highly uniform cultural values of ancient Chinese society, members of that society could successfully express their virtues autonomously. The autonomous harmony between conduct rules *Li* and internal virtues *Ren* could be archived by the fully virtuous *Junzi*. This harmonious state is conveyed in Confucius' remark on his own experiences of self-cultivation: at 70, he could follow what his heart desired without disobeying the rules.[85]

But in modern societies, this might not be the case. On the one hand, there are differing and sometimes inconsistent values in modern societies characterised by value pluralism. On the other hand, law in modern society regulates behaviour rather than mental states, but virtue is constituted by inner dispositions. Law might have some expressive function, even if there might be an overlap in the content of law and the deeply held conventional norms in a given society, but the expressive function of law is quite limited given the fact of value pluralism.

Given these two factors, autonomous harmony cannot be fully achieved under contemporary conditions in the same way that Confucian thinkers believed it could in ancient China. For this reason, the development of contemporary Confucian virtue jurisprudence requires us to re-examine the relationship between law and virtue. When an agent performs actions in accord with external norms, she is fully autonomous if and only if she has critically reflected upon the norms and decided for herself to abide by the norms without any coercion, deception, or other forms of autonomy-nullifying interference. However, since humans have the potential to become fully virtuous, law can play a formative role that is consistent with autonomy during the process of moral development. During the time when an agent is developing the capacity to reflect on her own values, she must follow conduct rules which have not yet been thoroughly reflected upon and

[84] Dworkin (1988: 20).

[85] See Confucius (2001: 5).

endorsed autonomously. Absent such rules, the developing moral agent might injure others or invade their rights or act in ways that destroy her own capacity for critical self-reflection. The development of both virtue and autonomy is enabled by the developmental exercises that involve actions guided by the rules. Rules are necessary in the process of self-cultivation and habituation that enables individuals to develop the capacities and dispositions that constitute virtue and enable autonomy.

Autonomous harmony can be achieved by observing two moderate requirements for the content of law. The first requirement is that the range of legally permissible and legally required conduct should (a) permit a sufficient range of virtuous conduct and (b) not require vicious conduct. This requirement ensures that people can develop their natural capacities and maintain autonomy without violating the law. On the one hand, virtuous humans would then be enabled to lead virtuous lives according to their own conception of human flourishing without being subjected to compulsory interference. On the other hand, persons who do not possess the full measure of virtue are not forced to act in accord with values that they have not chosen autonomously.

The second requirement is that law should create conditions that can facilitate individuals in the development of virtue without offending the rights of others. In some situations, law may be able to create conditions that can gradually change people's moral preference. One of the well-known examples in the Anglo-American tradition is provided by good Samaritan laws. The concrete content of good Samaritan laws varies from one jurisdiction to another, but the basic idea is that law exempts rescuers from certain kinds of legal liability and hence encourages rescue. To the extent that citizens learn the content and purposes of the law, laws of this kind can alter the moral preference of legal actors and help them in the development of virtues (and therefore, in Confucian terms, *Ren*).

In sum, the highest value of Confucian ethical, political theory is the harmony of society and individual. At the social dimension, we have *coordinative harmony*, which is related to the coordinative function of *Li*. At the individual dimension, we have *autonomous harmony*, which is connected with the expressive function of *Li*. Because *Li* and law do not share the function of expression of dispositions and emotions, our claim is that law's ability to foster 'autonomous harmony' is limited in scope: whereas *Li* can play a pervasive role in shaping values and virtues, the educative and developmental function of law is restricted. Of course, law can indirectly create the conditions for the development of autonomous harmony in other ways – by enabling, supporting and protecting the institutions that directly engage in moral education and development – primarily the family, schools and other institutions (such as religious institutions or voluntary social associations).[86]

[86] See also Clark (2012).

C. Names and Confucian Theories of Legislation and Adjudication

Given coordinative harmony and autonomous harmony as ends of law, we need to provide an account of how the legal norms are internalised by legal actors. The Confucian doctrine of correcting names might give us an explanation of the mechanism of internalisation in terms of the relationship among social norms, law and names. Given the end of law as the coordination of social interactions and harmonious autonomy, we claim that there are important normative requirements regarding the usage of names in legislative and judicial proceedings.

We have already seen that names (thick ethical concepts) provide guidance for actions. *Regicide* and *cruelty* were provided as examples in our introduction of the doctrine of correcting names above. But *regicide* is thinner than *cruel*. The application of *regicide* requires a deep and complex evaluation of whether the person claiming to be a lord is virtuous and whether he fulfils the political obligations attached to his political role.[87] But in the case of *cruel*, we frequently do not need to engage in deep and complex evaluations prior to the application of the concept. Usually, we are able to *see* cruelty: we are able to perceive cruelty in the situation. In the case of *regicide*, more than perception is required. For this reason, we believe that *regicide* is thinner than *cruel*. Our view of the doctrine of correcting names explicitly adopts the idea that what we call the *thickness* of ethical concepts is scalar – although the scale may be coarse-grained rather than continuous.

We have already discussed the fact that in ancient Chinese society, *Li* was the basic normative system 'involving rite, ceremony, manners or general deportment that bind human beings and the spirit together in networks of interacting roles'.[88] Social interactions were coordinated by *Li* and an individual's virtues were expressed with the help of *Li*. But it seems plausible that both *Li* and names (thick ethical concepts) perform an action-guiding function. This common function leads naturally to the next question: what is the relationship between *Li* and names? There are two perspectives on this question.

From the first perspective, some thick ethical concepts in a given community are dependent on the normative system of that community. Consider *regicide*. The proper application of this term requires evaluation of the actions performed and character traits possessed by the political leader. In other words, the true ethical meaning of this name, as Mencius recovered it, makes reference to the normative requirement for the role of lord as specified by *Li*, the normative system of the community.

From the second perspective, however, it turns out that stable linguistic practice of thicker names is one of the necessary conditions for the action-guiding

[87] These two kinds of evaluation are normally connected with each other since many political norms binding the ruler or subjects are so called v-rules. V-rules in ancient political morality can be expressed like this: Given a political virtue X, the v-rule related to this virtue is 'perform actions in accordance with what an X agent would characteristically do in the circumstances'. A sophisticated discussion of V-rules can be found in Hursthouse (1999: 26–42).

[88] Schwartz (1985: 67).

function of a normative system. Consider *cruel*. The proper application of *cruel* can (in normal circumstances, if not all circumstances) be accomplished without deliberation about or reliance on related social norms. But *cruel* plays a role in the system of norms. One can imagine a case in which the proper application of *regicide* would depend on whether someone was not properly described as a lord because of systematic acts of cruelty. Hence, the system of norms that provides the conditions for the correct application of the thinner name *regicide* includes thicker names such as *cruelty*.

These two perspectives on the relationship between *Li* and names suggest that there might be a multi-layered structure concerning the thickness of the Confucian names. Thicker names like *cruel* or *courageous* are in the lower layers, layers that are tightly entangled with the non-ethical qualities of the world. Thinner names like *regicide* or *thief*, whose application may involve moral norms or other thicker names, are in the upper layers[89] – where the entanglement of fact with value is mediated by the system of social norms. Due to their thinness, the layer of thinner names is tied more closely to *Li*. Expressed from a different angle, the world-guidedness of thinner names is dependent on the normative system of particular communities.

This brings us to the relationship between thick ethical terms and legal terms. Williams discusses thick terms that are ethical, but for our discussion there is no reason to stick to this moral sense. We call the general notion *thick evaluative concepts* (or simply *names*) and the legal notion *thick legal concepts* (or *legal names*).

The paradigm cases of thick legal concepts, in Xunzi's discussion, are the names for punishments. In the contemporary legal context, the categories of different crimes provide good examples of legal names; these include robbery, theft, murder, rape, and so on.[90] On the one hand, we have legal names like *robbery* or *murder*, which have a technical meaning in the legal context, but on the other hand, we use *robbery* or *murder* in the sense of general evaluative thick ethical concepts in our ordinary moral discourse. To avoid ambiguity, we might call the moral notion *thick extralegal concepts* and the legal notion *thick legal concepts*.[91]

Given that law is a normative system, the most fundamental function of law should be action guiding. What role do thick legal concepts play in law's action-guiding function? To answer this question, we need an account of the action-guidance function of law in general. We begin by observing that there are two

[89] Williams was criticised by Samuel Scheffler on the ground that he did not give us a well-defined notion of thick ethical concepts. Scheffler is worried that some concepts, such as 'justice' and 'equality', might not be confidently classified as either thick or thin concepts. See Scheffler (1987: 417).

In our interpretation of Confucian names, they can be located on the upper levels. Since they are at the very top level and hence lose most of the world-guidedness character, they might be viewed as thin ethical terms as well. Concepts of this sort cannot be classified as thicker or thinner according to their relation to norms.

[90] Antony Duff, in his discussion on the relationship between thick legal concepts and thick extralegal concepts, took the various kinds of crime as examples of thick concepts involved in the law. See Duff (2001: 191).

[91] ibid.

patterns for the action-guiding role of law: following Shapiro, we will call the first pattern *epistemic guidance* and the second pattern *motivational guidance.*[92]

The first pattern is epistemic guidance. To ensure that legal rules actually guide behaviour, individuals must know what is required by law. In the mode of epistemic guidance, legal subjects learn what is required by legal rule and perform actions required by law because of their knowledge of the rule. Their motives may or may not involve the aim of complying with the law; for example, knowledge of the law plus fear of punishment might produce compliance by agents who have no regard for the law itself.

The second pattern is motivational guidance, which can be seen as a subset of epistemic guidance. In the pattern of motivational guidance, legal subjects are successfully motivated by the legal content to actually perform law-abiding actions. For example, if an agent were moved by a desire to comply with the law, we would have a clear case of motivational guidance.

How do thick legal concepts contribute to the guidance function of law? First, consider the epistemic guidance role of rules and thick legal concepts. Suppose that a legal rule R employs a thick legal concept T to describe one of the essential premises for the application of that rule and/or the attribution of certain legal consequences. By incorporating a thick concept in that rule, legislators and judges could regulate a specific type of behaviour that might not be accomplished by employing merely descriptive concepts. Legal rules are designed to reflect practical concerns or interests. Thick concepts are perfectly suited to the task of formulating rules that capture these concerns and interests. The scope of the application of thick concepts is limited by the concerns or interests behind them and thus can precisely express the intention of legislators or judges. In this scenario, we might say that *fraud* is not just illegal and deceitful but it is illegal *in the light of* its deceitfulness. A citizen who grasps *fraud* would grasp the content of a legal rule using that term and understand which actions are within the scope of the rule.

Thick legal concepts also have motivational value for those who embrace them. For instance, if someone fully embraces the concept of cruelty and describes an action as *cruel*, she has a reason not to do that action. Suppose that a legal rule forbids parents from inflicting cruel punishment on their children and a particular parent fully embraces the concept of *cruel*, then that parent will be motivated to refrain from punishing her child in a cruel way.

Now consider the relationship between thick legal concepts and their raw form – thick extralegal concepts in ordinary moral or normative language. Some of the categories of crimes are the representatives of thick legal concepts, such as robbery, theft, murder and rape. On the one hand, we have thick legal concepts like robbery or murder, which have a technical legal meaning, but on the other, we use thick extralegal concepts like robbery or murder in our ordinary moral discourse. The fact that thick terms can have this dual role leads to the well-known

[92] See Shapiro (1998: 490). We will return to this point and have a more extended discussion in the next section.

phenomenon of the same word having two different senses – a technical legal sense (the thick legal concept) in which the full content of the concept is specified by a system of legal norms and an ordinary sense (the thick extralegal concept) in which the content is based on the system of social norms. The two senses of the concept and the two systems of norms may interact with each other in complex ways – with the law both shaping and responding to the social norm system. Does the content of a thick extralegal concept in some way determine, shape, or constrain the content of a thick legal concept that shares the same name (eg 'murder' in ordinary discourse and 'murder' in the technical legal sense)?

One way to answer this question is to imagine an acoustic separation (as Dan-Cohen has famously done in his account of conduct rules and decision rules)[93] between thick extralegal concepts understood by general citizens and thick legal concepts understood by legal experts. We can imagine that a society is divided into two separate discourse groups: in one discourse group we would have the general citizens and in the other group we would have legal experts, lawyers and legal officials. Suppose these two groups are acoustically separate from each other and they have the same legal text. And, let us further suppose that these two groups' understanding of the extensions of thick concepts does not have substantial overlap. If the law is to fulfil its crucial epistemic action-guiding function, the thick legal concepts and their extralegal versions have to share a similar normative shape.

Another argument in support of this conclusion is based on the motivational role of thick normative concepts. Thick concepts can reinforce the motivational force of law only when there is an overlap between the legal meaning of the concept and the ordinary meaning which is shaped by the values embedded in a specific cultural community conveyed through daily linguistic practice. If the legal technical meaning of thick ethical concepts becomes totally disconnected with their ordinary meaning, a linguistic barrier will be built between the legal elites and the lay citizens and the law will be in danger of losing its motivational power. From the perspective of ordinary citizens, the law will no longer make normative sense – the disconnected legal concept will seem arbitrary or unreasonable.

Confucian virtue jurisprudence holds that for law to guide conduct optimally, it must be capable of being internalised and thereby capable of generating motives for conformity by legal subjects. The correct use of names can help citizens to internalise legal norms and become naturally motivated to obey the law. Moreover, convergence between thick legal concepts and thick ethical concepts enables law to produce both coordinative harmony and autonomous harmony. Thus, the doctrine of correcting names explains how internalisation occurs and, at the same time, prescribes a normative requirement for the use of thick ethical concepts in legislation and by the judiciary.

[93] See Dan-Cohen (1984: 630–34).

D. The Nature of Law

Some scholars have argued that Confucian theory of law, as it was developed in the classical literature without any further articulation, can be seen as a Chinese version of natural law,[94] while others ascribe to it a Dworkinian coherentist reading.[95] In this part of the essay, we address these arguments and take a step towards the development of a theory of the nature of law.

Informally, we might say that legal positivism claims that the question of whether a given rule is law can only be answered by consulting things like statute books, court decisions and patterns of behaviour by officials, whereas natural law theory asserts that the justice (or injustice) of a rule factors into the answer to that question.[96] More technically, contemporary legal positivism asserts that it is necessarily the case that legal content is determined by social facts. Exclusive legal positivism claims that only social facts determine legal content, while inclusive legal positivism allows that moral facts may determine legal content, but only if social facts establish this role for moral facts.[97] Natural law theory, on the other hand, claims that moral facts necessarily determine legal content.

Now consider our Confucian account of the nature of law. Our theory is both a positive as well as a normative theory of law. As a positive theory, it describes and explains how law functions in the society; as a normative theory of law, it sets up normative standards for the content of law and legal practice. Our positive theory is an explanatory functional conception of law, rather than a direct answer to the metaphysical or conceptual question 'What is law?' That is, in this essay, we adopt an agnostic stance on the debate between natural lawyers and legal positivists.

As we have seen earlier, Confucius believed that pre-Qin ancient Chinese law (*Fa*) could not serve as a normative system sufficient to provide guidance for actions; instead, he contended that only *Li* (social norms already internalised by community members) could fulfil this function. As we have discussed in last section, the action-guiding function of law is also the central theme in contemporary western analytic jurisprudence. A good place to start with is Hart's conceptual analysis of law. Hart took the guidance function as one of the basic functions that law serves.[98]

[94] See Needham (1956: 544). See also Greer and Lim (1998: 80–89).

[95] See Peerenboom (1990:12–39).

[96] See Hart (1994). We choose Hart's theory of law as a point of comparison for two reasons. First, Hart's work is key to the evolution of modern positivist theory, representing the bridge between the positivism of Bentham and Austin and contemporary analytic positivism. Second, Hart's theory is the best-known version of contemporary positivism among legal theorists generally. Other important forms of legal positivism include those developed in the work of Coleman (2001); Kelsen (1945); Raz (1979); and Shapiro (2000: 127–70).

[97] Inclusive legal positivism accepts the view that legal contents and moral facts can be indirectly connected with each other.

[98] Hart writes (1994: 249): 'In fact I think it quite vain to seek any more specific purpose which law as such serves beyond providing guides to human conduct and standard of criticism of such conduct.'

The primary aim of Hart's theory is a conceptual account of the nature of law, and hence an account of what counts as law and what does not. In this regard, this guidance function is a necessary but not sufficient condition for a normative system to qualify as a legal system. Hart added that this guidance function 'will not of course serve to distinguish laws from other rules or principles with same general aims' and 'the distinctive features of law are the provision it makes by secondary rules for the identification, change, and enforcement of its standards and the general claim it makes to priority over other standards.'[99] So, Hart's positivist account of the nature of law has two elements. The first is a second-order binding rule (a rule of recognition) that is applied by legal officials, including judges, administrative officials and legislators, as a standard of validity of law. The second element is acceptance by most individuals of the first-order rules (primary rules) validated by the rule of recognition. These two elements give rise to ontological criteria for the existence of a legal system in a given community. In a legal system, according to Hart, the binding second-order rule of recognition is a fundamental social norm, but valid first-order rules are not necessarily social norms because their validity is derived from the rule of recognition. What kind of guidance function, associated with the fundamental social norm and the rules that are derived from it, is involved here? Hart's answer to this question rested on his notion of internal point of view. An internal point of view is an evaluative perspective adopted by community members from which they see rules of law as their own reasons for actions and criticise others' behaviour when others disobey the law.[100]

By incorporating the idea of internal perspective, Hart presented two ontological standards for the existence of a rule: (1) a standard of the state of mind (internal point of view) and (2) a standard of behaviour (stable pattern of behaviour). According to this ontological standard, a rule exists in a community if and only if the relevant actors in that community take this rule as a reason for their action and their behaviour actually fits the pattern that is prescribed by that rule. By reading Hart in functionalist terms, Shapiro showed that there might be two patterns of rule guidance with regard to secondary social norms and primary conduct rules.[101] Shapiro distinguished motivational guidance from epistemic guidance – along the lines we discussed above. On Shapiro's interpretation of Hart's account of legal guidance, lay citizens need not be motivationally guided by the content of law in order to obey the law, because epistemic guidance is sufficient.

Confucian virtue jurisprudence gives emphasis to the motivational process when legal subjects are guided by the law. Based on the distinction between epistemic and motivational guidance, we can articulate the general motivating process in legal domains like this:

[99] ibid.
[100] ibid 55–57.
[101] See Shapiro (1998: 490).

> A legal subject S will perform rule-governed action A if and only if she learns that it would be required by rule R (epistemic judgement) and she is motivated by motivational factors Fs, which possibly (but not necessarily) include normative judgements and emotional reactions.

Thus, our theory takes a normative stance on the legal subjects' motives in law's guidance process. In a well-functioning rule-of-law society, according to Confucian thinkers, a sufficient number of citizens possess the virtue *Yi*. These virtuous citizens perform law-governed actions for the right reasons and with the right motivational attitudes; shame plays a crucial role in their motivational attitudes. Shame can be divided into two subcategories, conventional shame and ethical shame. A person with a sense of conventional shame only conforms to the rules because she is afraid of the social pressure generated by rule-breaking behaviour and not because she really thinks it is wrong to break that rule. Someone with a sense of ethical shame (or possessing the virtue of *Yi*) abides by the rule because she thinks it is wrong to break the rule. For these people, the feeling of shame is raised from their own reflection on what they have done with regard to what kind of person they expect themselves to be.

Using Hart's terminology, the Confucian notion of an attitude towards rules that incorporates ethical shame as a focal motivation can be seen as a strong version of internal point of view. It is not clear, however, whether Hart would accept this Confucian account of the internal point of view. Hart explicitly claims that understanding his conception of internal point of view as internal feelings of compulsion or being bound and the externally observable physical behaviour is a misrepresentation of his account.[102] Translating Hart's claim into Confucian language, it seems conventional shame cannot be a necessary part of the internal aspect of rules. Later on, Hart acknowledges that the internal point of view may display itself in self-criticism,[103] but in legal contexts this self-criticism is not necessarily connected with a sense of shame because Hart classifies rules that give rise to shame when disobeyed as moral rules.[104] So, Hart does not seem to endorse the strong Confucian claim that a well-functioning social order requires that subjects of the law must take this strong version of internal point of view towards legal rules. As we have discussed earlier, this strong version of internal point of view is at the centre of our Confucian theory of law.

This view of the internal aspect of law can be generalised as what we have called the *Internalisation Thesis*. In the original context, Confucius' internalisation thesis concerns *Li*, which is situated between morality and positive law (as those notions are understood in contemporary legal theory). Let's recall what Confucius has said:

> The Master said, 'If the people be led by governmental regulations, and uniformity sought to be given them by punishments, they will try to avoid the punishment, but

[102] Hart (1994: 57).
[103] ibid.
[104] ibid 86.

> have no sense of shame. If they be led by virtue, and uniformity sought to be given them by *Li*, they will have the sense of shame, and moreover will reform themselves.'[105]

This leads to a possible objection to our account of the internalisation thesis: modern law (or *positive law*) does not necessarily share this expressive function with ancient *Li*. By definition, the content of *Li* is internalised by social members. In the case of positive law in modern societies, however, the content of legal norms is frequently not internalised (or in some cases even known) by citizens.

This possible objection is illuminated by considering the Confucian attitude towards positive law. That attitude is based on the premise that a normative system, be it morality, social norms or positive law, functions well if and only if it is able to guide the behaviour of citizens. Confucian theory assigns the emotions of the subjects of the law a central role in determining the ability of norms to guide action. For Confucian virtue jurisprudence, in a well-functioning rule-of-law society most legal subjects must be motivated in the following way when they perform law-governed actions:

> A legal subject S performs law governed action A if she learns that it would be required by legal rule R (epistemic judgement) and she is motivated by motivational factors Fs, which includes normative judgements and emotional reactions.

Since we have already shown the value of thick legal concepts in legal contexts, the *normative judgement* here could either be an intuitive, thick judgement (with the help of thick concepts) or a reflective, overall judgement (about the all-things-considered rightness or wrongness of an action). The presumption under this formulation of law-guided action is that the epistemic apprehension of a legal requirement cannot guarantee the motivational state. For Confucius, in a well-functioning society, legal actors' motivational states and their knowledge of law should be in a harmonious relationship. If the content of a legal rule is fully understood by a legal actor with a proper motivational state in place, then we would say that this rule is internalised by that legal actor.

Since we are dealing with a Confucian account of the nature of law, a question naturally arises as to what kind of law can be internalised by virtuous legal subjects. Before we answer this question directly, consider a dialogue in the *Analects*:

> The Duke of She told Confucius. 'There is an upright man among my people. His father stole a sheep, and he testified against him.'
>
> Confucius replied, 'Among my people, those we consider "upright" are different from this: fathers cover up for their sons, and sons cover up for their fathers. This is what it means to be "upright."'[106]

At first glance, the issue concerned in this dialogue has the character of a moral dilemma. Testifying against a criminal is a civic duty required by political morality, but the crime to be reported is performed by one's father. The virtue of filial

[105] Confucius (1971: 146), with some modifications to the translation.
[106] Confucius (2001: 36), with some modifications to the translation.

piety and the rules in *Li* require that one should love one's father and thus should cover up this crime to protect him from serious punishment. Confucius' resolution of the dilemma seems to suggest that in this specific circumstance, the virtuous agent should not report the crime. Given Confucius' particularism, his resolution should not be interpreted as a universal claim about all cases that share the basic structure described in the dialogue.[107]

The reason for Confucius' resolution of the dilemma is not clear in the dialogue.[108] Our interpretation is that the strong emotions of love and affection that a good son has towards his father override the civic duty to report a trivial case of theft. One of the basic presumptions of Confucian virtue ethics lies in its role-based character, so moral requirements differ according to the roles an agent possesses in her ethical relations. Because the son is in this special relation to his father, he should care more deeply for his father than should ordinary community members.

What then is the implication of this dialogue? Suppose that in the state where this dialogue happened, there was a general legal rule that requires citizens to report every crime, including crimes committed by one's close family members. From a Confucian point of view, this rule should neither have been enacted nor be enforced, because the rule goes against the natural sentiments of legal subjects and thus could not be fully internalised by virtuous actors.

This claim can be seen as a normative account of the content of law. As characterised from a Confucian perspective, we can make a normative claim about the content of law based on the internalisation thesis:

> The content of law should be such that the law can be internalised by legal actors to the extent required for law to perform its essential function of action guidance.

Two further points clarify this claim. First, this claim about the content of law should be restricted to those legal rules that have morally significant content. Rules concerning purely coordination or the efficiency of social interactions have nothing to do with this internalisation thesis; and technical rules which are not directly related to the citizen's ordinary life are excluded as well. In this regard, there is no requirement of the capability of internalisation for the content of regulations requiring all traffic to keep either to the left or the right side of the road or for legal rules governing the use of the radio spectrum.

Second, intuitive emotional reactions are essential elements of social norms (*Li*), but social norms also reinforce or weaken emotional reactions. In a society like that of ancient China, which highly values family relations, one's intuitive emotional reaction of filial piety might be stronger than that in modern societies. If

[107] eg consequence matters here. Let's imagine that his father has conducted a crime of manslaughter, then what would Confucius say about this? We do not know, but Confucius would probably not suggest that the son cover up the father's crime in this case.

[108] Some commentators provide us with a nepotistic, as well as consequentialist, reading. They suggest that Confucius saw filial piety as the foundation of the development of any other virtues, or, family relation as the most fundamental social relation for human beings, without which the society will collapse. See Chen (1990: 925).

this is the case, then social norms and law do share some content with regard to the very deep moral intuitions of human beings, but that content might be slightly different depending on the fundamental values embedded in different communities' social norms. Take the mutual concealment of father and son as an example. Similar principles of the concealment between close family members are found in several legal cultures, be it modern or ancient, east or west. But the specific content of this principle in a legal culture varies depending on the fundamental values embedded in the social norms in that culture.

This brings us back to the relationship of Confucian virtue jurisprudence to legal positivism and natural law theory. Because our theory offers a normative and functionalist account of law, its relationship to contemporary debates over the nature of law is oblique. Our theory does not take a direct stand on the question of whether social facts (or moral facts) determine legal content. So it seems, on the surface at least, that Confucian virtue jurisprudence might be consistent with either natural law or legal positivism.

At this point, a legal positivist might offer the following objection. Our theory seems to require a substantial overlap between thick legal concepts and thick moral concepts. So the legal concept of cruelty would have to have substantially the same content as the thick moral concepts. This might seem to lead to the conclusion that legal content is determined by moral facts, but legal positivists deny that this can be the case – while natural lawyers affirm that it must be.

But this objection would be based on a misunderstanding of our theory. We do not claim that thick legal concepts must substantially overlap with thick ethical concepts as a matter of legal ontology. That is, we are not claiming that a thick legal concept like cruelty would not be positive law if it were detached from the thick ethical concept whose name it shares. Our claim is simply that detachment would prevent the legal concept from guiding behaviour in the way that it should.

This point about the limited nature of our claim becomes clear in the extreme case of detachment – acoustic separation. Suppose that the system of adjudication were to employ a legal concept of cruelty that was radically different than the ordinary moral concept – and that ordinary citizens were completely unaware of the technical legal notion of cruelty. In those circumstances, the legal concept could still be called *law*, because it would provide the standard for authoritative legal resolution of disputes, but the legal concept could not properly fulfil the action-guiding function of law, since citizens would be unaware (or only partially aware) of the technical legal concept.

IV. CONCLUSION

We have offered a sketch of Confucian virtue jurisprudence, a distinctive position in the general theory of law that has its ancient roots in classical Confucian thought in China. We interpreted Confucian ethical and social thought as a version of virtue ethics. That interpretation served as the basis for developing a contemporary legal theory. The core of our theory is our account of law's proper function, which we can summarise as the creation of a social order on the basis of coordinative harmony and autonomous harmony. That is, we believe that the aim of law is to provide a social order that rests on norms that can be internalised by autonomous agents who possess certain virtues. In other words, our view of law reconciles individual freedom and social order via the fundamental Confucian notion of harmony.

REFERENCES

Ames, RT and Rosemont, H (1988) The Analects of Confucius: A Philosophical Translation (New York, Ballantine Books).

Blackburn, S (1992) 'Through Thick and Thin' 66 *Proceedings of the Aristotelian Society*, Supplementary Volumes 285.

Chang, KC (1983) *Art, Myth, and Ritual: the Path to Political Authority in Ancient China* (Cambridge, MA, Harvard University Press).

Chang, W (1990) *Traditional Chinese Jurisprudence: Legal Thought of Pre-Qin Thinkers* (unpublished manuscript).

Chen, S (1990) *Lun Yu Ji Shi* (《論語集釋》) (Beijing, Commercial Press).

Chow, KW (1994) *The Rise of Confucian Ritualism in Late Imperial China: Ethics, Classics, and Lineage Discourse* (Stanford, Stanford University Press).

Clark, SJ (2012) 'Neoclassical Public Virtues: Towards an Aretaic Theory of Law-Making (and Law Teaching)' chapter 5 of this volume.

Coleman, J (2001) *The Practice of Principle* (New York, Oxford University Press).

Confucius (2001) 'Analects' in EG Slingerland (tr), PJ Ivanhoe BW and van Norden (eds), *Readings in Classical Chinese Philosophy* (New York, Seven Bridges).

——(1979) 'Analects' in DC Lau (tr), *The Analects* (New York, Penguin Books).

——(1971) 'Analects' in J Legge (tr), *Confucian Analects, The Great Learning, and The Doctrine of the Mean* (New York, Dover Publications).

Cua, AS (1971) 'Reflections on the Structure of Confucian Ethics' 21 *Philosophy East and West* 125.

——(2007) 'Virtues of Junzi' 34 *Journal of Chinese Philosophy* 125.

Dan-Cohen, M (1984) 'Decision Rules and Conduct Rules: On Acoustic Separation in Criminal Law' 97 *Harvard Law Review* 625.

Dancy, J (1996) 'In Defence of Thick Concepts' 20 *Midwest Studies in Philosophy* 263.

de Montesquieu, C, Fu, Y (tr) (1981) *The Spirit of Laws* (Beijing, Commercial Press).

Duff, RA (2001) *Punishment, Communication, and Community* (New York, Oxford University Press).

Dworkin, G (1988) *The Theory and Practice of Autonomy* (New York, Cambridge University Press).

Eno, R (1990) *The Confucian Creation of Heaven: Philosophy and the Defense of Ritual Mastery* (Albany, State University of New York Press).

Farrelly, C and Solum, LB (eds) (2007) *Virtue Jurisprudence* (Basingstoke, Palgrave Macmillan).

Feldman, H (1994) 'Objectivity in Legal Judgment' 92 *Michigan Law Review* 1187.

Fung, YL (1952) *A History of Chinese Philosophy: The Period of the Philosophers*, Volume I (Princeton, Princeton University Press).

Gier, N (2001) 'The Dancing Ru: A Confucian Aesthetics of Virtue' 51 *Philosophy East and West* 280.

Goldie, P (2008) 'Thick Concepts and Emotion' in D Callcut (ed), *Reading Bernard Williams* (London, Routledge).

Greer, S and Lim, TP (1998) 'Confucianism: Natural Law Chinese Style?' 11 *Ratio Juris* 80.

Hansen, C *Rule of Law in Ancient China: Chinese Substance or Western Function?* (Available at: www.hku.hk/philodep/ch/Substance-Function.htm, visited 4 May 2009).

Hart, HLA (1994) *The Concept of Law* (Oxford, Clarendon Press).

Hursthouse, R (1999) *On Virtue Ethics* (Oxford, Oxford University Press).

Kelsen, H (I945) *General Theory of Law and State* (Cambridge, MA, Harvard University Press).

Mencius (2001) 'Mengzi' in BW van Norden (tr), PJ Ivanhoe and BW van Norden (eds), Readings in Classical Chinese Philosophy (New York, Seven Bridges).

Mei, Z (1975) 'Li and Fa' in D Xu (ed), Essays on Chinese Legal History (《中國法制史論集》) (Taipei, Zhiwen Press).

Needham, J (1956) *Science and Civilization in China* vol 2 (Cambridge, Cambridge University Press).

Nuyen, A (2009) 'Moral Obligation and Moral Motivation in Confucian Role-Based Ethics' 8 *Dao: A Journal of Comparative Philospophy* 1.

Payne, A (2005) 'A New Account of Thick Concepts' 39 *Journal of Value Inquiry* 89.

Peerenboom, R (1990) 'Confucian Jurisprudence: Beyond Natural Law' 18 *Asian Culture Quarterly* 12.

Raz, J (1979) *The Authority of Law: Essays on Law and Morality* (Oxford, Clarendon Press).

—— (1986) *The Morality of Freedom* (Oxford, Oxford University Press).

Schauer, F (2010) 'Necessity, Importance, and the Nature of Law' *Virginia Public Law and Legal Theory Research Paper No 2010-19* (Available at www.ssrn.com/abstract=1594930).

Scheffler, S (1987) 'Morality Through Thick and Thin: A Critical Notice of Ethics and the Limits of Philosophy' 96 *Philosophical Review* 411.

Schwartz, BI (1985) *The World of Thought in Ancient China* (Cambridge, MA, Harvard University Press).

Shapiro, SJ (2000) 'Law, Morality and the Guidance of Conduct' 6 *Legal Theory* 127.

—— (1998) 'On Hart's Way Out' 4 *Legal Theory* 469.

Shun, WL (1997) *Mencius and Early Chinese Thought* (Stanford, Stanford University Press).

Slingerland, E (2001) 'Virtue Ethics, the Analects, and the Problem of Commensurability' 29 *Journal of Religious Ethics* 97.

Slote, MA (1992) *From Morality to Virtue* (New York, Oxford University Press).

Solum, LB (2004) 'Procedural Justice' 78 *Southern California Law Review* 181.

—— (2006) 'Natural Justice' 51 *American Journal of Jurisprudence* 65.

van Norden, B (2007) *Virtue Ethics and Consequentialism in Early Chinese Philosophy* (New York, Cambridge University Press).

Wang, L (2010) *Living by Thick Legal Concepts: A Confucian Account of How Law Guides People's Actions* (Unpublished manuscript: Presented at University of Illinois).

Williams, B (2006) *Ethics and the Limits of Philosophy* (London, Routledge).

Wong, WY (2001) 'Confucian Ethics and Virtue Ethics' 28 *The Journal of Chinese Philosophy* 285.

Xun Zi (2001) 'Xunzi' in EL Hutton (tr), PJ Ivanhoe and BW van Norden (eds), *Readings in Classical Chinese Philosophy* (New York, Seven Bridges).

Yu, J (1998) 'Virtue: Confucius and Aristotle' 48 *Philosophy East and West* 323.

7

The Three Stages of Judges' Self-Development

MATEUSZ STĘPIEŃ

I. INTRODUCTION

IN *THUS SPOKE Zarathustra*, Friedrich Nietzsche sketched the postulated direction of change in the (over)man's soul as a metamorphosis from 'the spirit that would bear much, and kneels down like a camel wanting to be well loaded' through 'a lion who could conquer his freedom and be master in his own desert' to a child who 'is innocent and forgetting, a new beginning, a game, a self-propelled wheel, a first movement, sacred "Yes"'.[1] With regard to this vision of personal gradual development, I would like to pose a question regarding the desirable 'spiritual' transformation route of the judge. I will analyse the process of the judge's professional self-cultivation in a manner similar to the Nietzschean transition, that is, by postulating stages of the judge's metamorphosis distinguishable by specific styles of judicial decision-making characteristic of each of them. In other words, I am interested in the judge's professional self-development examined in the context of prescriptive (normative) models of judicial decision-making.

By referring to the three-step metaphor (camel-lion-child) of the Nietzschean transformation of a person willing to reach perfection, I am going to analyse the three consecutive stages in the judge's 'spiritual' metamorphosis, analytically differentiated by varying models of judicial decision-making characteristic of each of them. The differences between the presented models lie in the range of decision-making factors taken into account. During the first stage the judge should act as an administrator of legal procedures and a guardian of the legal status quo. The judge's goal here would be to become proficient in applying legal norms and to develop an attitude of abidance with the letter of law. He should consciously overcome the willingness to incorporate his own sense of justice into judicial decisions. At the second stage, an analysis of the consequences of various alternative decisions would take place according to the established criteria of evaluation. At this point, the judge is not only expected to decide by referring to the literally interpreted legal texts, but also to consider the consequences of a particular judgment for the parties involved, for the society and for the legal system. During the third

[1] Nietzsche (1883/1988: 137–40).

stage the judge, apart from the legal norms and the ability to anticipate the consequences of his decision, would also need to ground his judgment in the normative content that stems from his own virtues as developed in the course of the practice of judicial decision-making in a self-reflective way. The judge should consider the influences of the decision-making process on his own personality and cherish the predispositions necessary to perform his profession. My claim is that one may describe the prescriptive route of the 'judge's spiritual' metamorphosis as a transition of decision-making models, from the formal-positivist, through a responsive, and towards an aretaic model. Therefore, I will analyse the relationship between two variables: the self-cultivation stage of a given judge and the model of judicial decision-making.

The chapter is organised as follows: I shall begin by sketching the basic features and the most frequently mentioned advantages and disadvantages of the three prescriptive (normative) models of judicial decision-making treated as consecutive stages of a judge's self-development (section II). Then, I shall examine more closely the most important problems of the aretaic model and investigate if the main objections against this model may be met (section III). Next, drawing on the Confucian idea of life as an ongoing self-development Way (*Dao* 道), I will seek to improve on the aretaic model of judicial decision-making by searching for guidance on how to develop traits essential for a perfect judge (section IV). Finally, I intend to make some general comments concerning the proposed situational approach to judicial decision-making, which aims at unifying three dominant normative legal theories (section V). At the end, I will make some concluding remarks concerning the concept of the three stages of a judge's self-cultivation (section VI).

II. THREE NORMATIVE MODELS OF JUDICIAL DECISION-MAKING

Court adjudication, like any other process of decision-making, is a process based on non-random, deliberate choices. However, the classical rational choice theory is not the best tool for analysing judicial decisions. It is inadequate not only because of the fact that basic purposes of adjudication are often in conflict with each other (eg, flexibility versus stability, efficiency and timeliness versus the search for objective truth). The basic structural limitations of judging derive from the unique position of judicial power and the way it is connected with other public institutions. Judges make decisions in an institutionally guaranteed and axiologically justified situation of 'bounded rationality'.[2] This is the main reason why the kinds and number of factors influencing a judgment are enumerated and established to a large degree before the decision-making process occurs. But obviously in practice, because of the 'open

[2] Here, I draw on an analogy to Simon's well-known theory of bounded rationality. This theory says that cognitive processing limitations force humans to construct simplified mental models of the world. As Simon observed, 'a person behaves rationally with respect to this model . . . (although) such behavior is not even approximately optimal' (1957: 198).

texture' character of law (or legal language) and the complex axiological dimensions of law, it is impossible to determine definitely the set of premises that accounts for the content of a particular decision.[3] The general indeterminacy of law suggests that in the process of judicial decision-making, the situation of the completeness of premises necessary for attaining a judgment almost never exists. That is why prescriptive (normative) models of adjudication might specify different sets of factors that ought to determine a judgment. From the perspective of decision premises one may distinguish three postulative models of judicial decision-making: formal-positivist, responsive and aretaic.[4]

A. The Formal-positivist Model

According to the formal-positivist model, the judge arrives at a decision guided solely by legally binding norms (and judicial precedents in common law systems).[5] The ruling is supposed to be the result of subsumption, and it should not be in any way influenced by any factors other than legal ones. The judge plays the role of the 'mouth of the statute' and only applies positive norms, which are given as axioms of the system, to concrete cases. This model of searching for factors determining the judgment resembles a deontological perspective where norms are the sources of the 'ought' content.

The most frequently mentioned aspect of this model is that it is the least arbitrary and discretionary way of judicial decision-making. It minimises the impact of the decision-maker's individual preferences, values and emotions on court rulings and guarantees the autonomy of law. In addition, it insulates judicial decisions against outside influences, especially the political subsystem and public pressure. The marginalisation of the 'personal' element undoubtedly serves the most important, intrinsic legal value, which is the rule of law. The formal-positivist model fulfils the principle of equality before law and ensures that the same precise criteria and standards are used to determine rights and obligations of various subjects. Moreover, while deciding in accordance with this method the judge mirrors the '*sovereign's will*' expressed in legal acts, passed by democratically elected representatives of society. This model of decision-making is time-efficient because the premises behind the decision are defined to a large extent. The requirement to take legal factors into account only makes the *external control* of the decision-making process possible. This is the reason why you do not need a judge with Herculean powers; all you need is a meticulous craftsman.[6]

[3] Pałecki (2004: 17, 21–22).

[4] Of course, there are different classifications of the judicial decision-making theories. eg Eskridge and Frickey distinguish 'three grand theories': formalism, intentionalism and a result-based approach (1990: 321, 323).

[5] There is a large amount of literature about the formal-positivist or the formalist model of judicial decision-making. It is not possible to discuss in detail all the pros and cons of the formal-positivist model (see eg Schauer (1988: 511); Scalia (1989: 1175); and Eskridge and Frickey (1990: 656)).

[6] See Dworkin (1986: 87–114, 225–75).

Critics of the formal-positivist model emphasise the fact that it provides judges with a cover of formality and creates a situation where the judge can easily avoid personal responsibility for his decisions. The rigid and 'textual' appeal to 'objective' legal norms creates a temptation to hide behind the curtain of 'impartiality' and 'formality'. This model implies the necessity of good law in both the technical and the axiological sense. According to the former requirement, legal texts need to be well-edited, clearly articulated and coherent. According to the latter, legal norms should accurately identify, clarify and balance social values and the means through which these values will be achieved. But given the structural connection between the legislative process and the cyclical elections of political decision-makers, the prerequisite of 'good law' seems unrealistic.[7] Therefore, one should start with more realistic assumptions about the quality of law when one is trying to establish a prescriptive (normative) model of judicial decision-making. Furthermore, the formal-positivist model also becomes difficult to use in more complicated cases where legal norms become ambiguous or where there is a conflict of the values protected by the law. This model does not stimulate judges to develop professional skills or to cultivate the judicial virtues. Rather, it favours a mechanical way of deciding and a ritualised process of law application, which is undesirable if one takes seriously the social functions of law.

B. The Responsive Model

The model of responsive judicial decision-making points to the necessity for the judge to take into consideration not only legally binding rules but also their consequences. More precisely, the responsive ruling may result from an analysis of the future situation of the parties involved in the particular case (individual responsiveness), take into account the anticipated impact of the decision on the whole legal system (intrinsic legal responsiveness) or even involve the consideration of the macro-economic and macro-societal consequences of arriving at the particular decision (social responsiveness). It is easy to notice that all of these different types of responsive judging are oriented towards achieving specific goals that are anticipated, future states of affairs evaluated on the basis of already-established criteria.[8] According to the responsive model one could weigh and anticipate the consequences of a certain choice by considering the level of legitimisation, public trust in the court system, or a specific measure of social prosperity such as increase in satisfaction, social utility, welfare or Gross Domestic Index.[9] Therefore, there are different versions of the responsive model. Nonetheless, they all have

[7] Law is often used as an instrument in the game of remaining in power or reaching political power, so it is not surprising that it is sometimes enacted to achieve, eg a social 'placebo' effect (see Aviram (2005)).

[8] As Richard Posner argues, 'Consequences are facts, and facts have no normative significance in themselves. One cannot derive "ought to" from "is". A value must be placed on each consequence.' (2008: 240).

[9] eg Foxall (2004).

one thing in common, that is, they analyse the outcomes of a given judgment on the basis of certain criteria. Considering such outcomes is a necessary and one of the most important elements of a ruling in this approach.[10] This is a consequentialist position as it puts the emphasis on the evaluation of anticipated outcomes of judgments according to certain criteria.

Responsive adjudication guarantees a larger extent of flexibility and a better adjustment of the decision to the specific circumstances and context. In order to predict the consequences of particular choices accurately, the judge needs to render the decision-making process more inclusive and open to external influences (such as the expert's knowledge), and at the same time he should perform a more in-depth examination of the social predicament of the parties involved. The third-party control of the ruling is possible because one may take into account criteria used by the judge to evaluate the consequences of the decision.

One could argue that this model violates the rule of law. It opens up the possibility of taking arbitrary decisions determined by the judge's axiological preferences and justifying such decisions by 'objective' criteria. One could also ask: who is to select such and not other criteria of evaluating the outcomes and on what basis and why is this selection made? Even if we were to disregard this fundamental problem, this model of judicial decision-making requires much better trained judges than those required by the formal approach. Judges should know the social situation, the society, its problems and aspirations, and they should even be able to anticipate the macro-economic or macro-social effects of certain rulings. You need a judge learned in statistics and economy, the kind of judge that Oliver Wendell Holmes wrote about, a judge capable of foreseeing the outcomes of judicial decision-making, which requires a deep knowledge of sociology, psychology, economics, as well as professional experience.[11] You need a judge with a fair amount of Herculean powers, as the accuracy in foreseeing the results of a particular court ruling depends on the judge's knowledge and abilities.

C. The Aretaic Model

Now, in the aretaic model of judicial decision-making[12] – as a part of virtue jurisprudence[13] – the judge also relies on his own stable dispositions, which he has

[10] In jurisprudence, there has been a very profound and influential tradition of result-oriented theories of judicial decision-making based on utilitarian or pragmatic grounds (see eg Holmes (1897: 468–74); Dewey (1924: 17); Nonet and Selznick (1978: 78-86); and Posner (2008: 13, 119, 238, 243)).

[11] Holmes (1897: 469).

[12] eg Solum (2003).

[13] Even though one cannot really talk of the existence of a cohesive theoretical approach under the banner of virtue jurisprudence (eg Koller (2007) and Farrelly and Solum (2008)), it would be hard not to notice common elements and inspirations in Lawrence Solum's (1988; 2003; 2005a; 2005b; 2006; 2009); Suzanna Sherry's (2003); Heidi Li Feldman's (1996; 1999; 2000); or Kyron Huigen's (2002; 2007) works. These authors agree that the increased interest in ethical virtues does not translate into a sufficient analysis of law from the aretaic point of view. They also stand against the hegemony of deontology and consequentialism in legal discourse.

developed in practice and that are based on an understanding of the objectives of particular legal provisions (more precisely, on the values safeguarded by legal norms and precedents) and assumptions about the general functions and role that the court is supposed to perform in society. The judge is not only guided by the legal norms and the analysis of the effects of their application. The difference lies in the fact that now the judge should extend the set of premises that are supposed to determine the judgment to the normative contents that result from the judicial virtues (such as temperance, courage, good temper, impartiality, intelligence, wisdom, and, especially, the virtue of justice) that he has developed through practice.

According to the aretaic model, the process of judicial decision-making is a mechanism of learning that helps judges to flourish and acquire the necessary judicial virtues, so that one of the goals of court proceedings (not the most important goal, of course) is to form the judge's character, that is, the traits important to achieve excellence in future decisions. As a result, judges are not just Nietzschean 'camels of justice' (obediently 'bearing' and unconditionally applying legal norms) but are sensitive subjects who can approach every situation in a unique way and who try to combine the rigid rules and arguments of law with the requirements derived from the analysis of given circumstances (the parties' situation, the status of the juridical branch, the legal system as a whole, as well as political and economic factors). But the satisfactory functioning of this model requires that judges should be very experienced and self-developed, that they have a vast knowledge of law, psychology, sociology and economics, and, at the same time, that they be aware of many different issues connected with performing the task of judging. One needs a judge who can become a Hercules or is already one.

Many features of the aretaic model open a new and fruitful perspective for normative studies of adjudication. Generally, the vision of judging in the context of self-development of a professional judge is a relatively new and inspiring perspective. In this view, judicial decision-making resembles the process of mastering such trades as medicine, navigation or archery. Moreover, the aretaic approach draws our attention to issues marginalised in jurisprudence. Because legal norms are not self-applicable directives, this approach rightly puts emphasis on the personal element in adjudication by laying stress on the role of individual virtues. The aretaic approach differs considerably from certain inspiring but excessively radical statements of some of the American realists who have analysed the negative side of a judge's personal (and unconscious) impact on the decision content.[14] Stressing the personal element in judicial decision-making does not necessarily trigger the end of the rule of law and the triumph of desires over rationality. Moreover, structural changes concerning the process of applying law, such as turning towards the argumentative, holistically interpretive or pragmatic model of judicial decision-making, require of judges the development of very specific predispositions, abilities and personality traits. That is why a 'thin' concept of the aretaic judicial decision-making model is required if some set of personality attri-

[14] eg Frank (1949/1973: 111, 119); and Michelon (2012).

butes of the judge is really necessary to put the specific model of adjudication into practice.[15]

The preliminary analysis of the aretaic model raises some questions. Is it not too time-consuming to come to decisions in this manner if one needs to take into account the legal norms and the consequences of their application, and at the same time include contextual inferences? Is there any risk of becoming arbitrary in the final ruling while using this model? May even a very experienced judge adjudicating with the best intentions treat his personal axiological choices as the real grounds of his decision? Could the application of the aretaic model violate the principle of stability of law? Finally, does the aretaic model of judicial decision-making give specific guidelines on how to cultivate judicial virtues in practice?

III. PROBLEMS AND LIMITATIONS OF THE ARETAIC MODEL

Without evaluating the entire movement of virtue jurisprudence,[16] I will examine only the aforementioned objections to the aretaic judicial decision-making model. At first glance, the aretaic model might look more time-consuming than other models of adjudication. On the one hand, the judicial virtues stimulate numerous examinations and analyses; they introduce additional normative requirements into the process of judging. However, on the other hand, the judicial virtues are skills and proficiencies which expedite the process of deciding. Thus, sometimes it is quicker rather than slower to make a decision by invoking the judicial virtues.

The fear of arbitrary and discretionary decisions is not justified either, because justice (understood as lawfulness) alongside impartiality are fundamental judicial virtues. These virtues induce judicial self-restraint rather than unbounded judicial activism. Moreover, when it comes to the possibility of axiological interferences in the judgment, the aretaic model expects the judge to articulate clearly his private axiology and become aware of it. These steps are necessary to prevent the judge from transferring his own sense of justice into the decision content. We should remember that achieving perfection enables judges to become fully aware of how both legal and extra-legal factors determine the process of adjudication and lead them to reach thoughtful decisions, of which factors should be considered and which can be dismissed. A good judge certainly does not hide the determining premises but tries to articulate the factors at play in the most precise way so that the independence of the judicature is respected. This explicit articulation also allows the evaluation of the decision by higher courts, which does not begin and end with arguments concerning the textual meaning of legal norms.

Moreover, proficiency in applying the rules, using functional, value-based interpretation and argumentative skills, makes it possible to harmonise and reconcile – to the extent that this is possible – the stability and flexibility of law. While a

[15] Duff (2003: 217).
[16] eg Duff (2003), (2006).

perfect judge, who possesses the virtue of justice as lawfulness[17] makes decisions on the basis of and within the boundaries of literally interpreted legal texts, the virtue of justice understood as fairness requires a sensitive and contextual in-depth investigation of the details of each situation and involves the correction of short-comings stemming from the generality of legal norms.[18] The virtuous judge will do what the spirit of the law demands in each particular case when reliance on the 'plain meaning' of a legal text fails to provide a satisfactory answer. He will explore the most important axiological layers of law, without incorporating his own opinions and values into the decision. Thus, it seems that the aretaic model indeed allows for both the stability and flexibility of law if the judge possesses certain judicial virtues.

So the aforementioned objections to the aretaic theory of adjudication are not entirely justified. Only the lack of direct guidelines as to how to cultivate the judicial virtues in practice constitutes an important limitation of the aretaic model. There is still an open question. How shall we transform the virtue-centered model of judging into a clear set of practical directives? The virtue perspective in jurisprudence should be supplemented by attempts to propose a set of direct guidance or developmental programmes about how to cultivate the judicial virtues in practice.

IV. A CONFUCIAN GUIDE ON HOW TO CULTIVATE THE JUDICIAL VIRTUES

Now, I would like to consider the last objection to the aretaic theory (ie the lack of guidance on how to develop the judicial virtues) by appealing to the longstanding and well-established Confucian version of virtue theory.[19] At first sight, it is easy to notice that the process-oriented vision of a judge's quest for self-improvement closely resembles the transgressive vision of the human being which is common to all Asian cultures.[20] The Confucian philosophy advances a dynamic vision of the man as a ripening subject, potentially capable of developing his natural abilities.[21] The human being is seen as a 'self-creative process rather than accidental qualities happening to a core unchanging essence, where all value lies either by nature

[17] eg Solum (2005c: 678, 681).

[18] eg Solum (2006: 86)

[19] Wang (2001) and van Norden (2007).

[20] The classic Hindu Vedic tradition, which is closer to substantial thinking, is also based on a belief in the possibility and necessity of pursuing perfection through rigorous and disciplined practice. Each person has both the freedom and responsibility to work out his or her own path to perfection. As Coward writes, 'all of the Indian philosophies, traditional psychologies, and religious traditions are simply different paths to perfection' (2008: 164).

[21] The Confucian tradition often uses 'the stage of development' metaphor. As Wang Wai-Ying puts it, 'The ultimate state of achievement, as Confucius describes it, is "to follow one's desires without any deviation from the norm". An agent can reach a certain stage toward this state during his or her lifetime and his or her ethical achievement can thus be assessed by judging which stage he or she is at.' (2001: 291). Nietzsche's metaphor of the three-stage transformation of a man who wants to reach perfectibility (camel-lion-child) drew direct inspiration from the East-Asian philosophical tradition.

or by the creation of God'.[22] Everybody possesses the ability to transgress from a less developed to a more mature form. On this view, to live as a true human is to experience continuous growth, as emphasised by the metaphor of the Way (*Dao* 道), which is fundamental to Chinese culture. Fulfilling the Way consists of the cultivation of one's own virtue – the pictograph 德 contains five elements: the shape of a walking man, 10, one, eye and heart/mind. The digit, 10, indicates the need to repeat a particular activity many times. The shape of a walking man refers to a long-term process of self-cultivation which results in the acquisition of some skills based on the unity ('one') of heart/mind with actions. Confucianism stresses the never-ending flourishing process as something fundamental. As the Confucian classic *Zhongyong* says, everybody 'must consider their self development as the root, the basis'.[23]

But if we look closely at Confucian writings, we will not find any specific instructions concerning the self-cultivation related to social roles. Needless to say, there are no direct guidelines for judges either. We should also remember that according to classical Confucianism, law and the whole set of law-related institutions and professions are means of social control appropriate for barbarians rather than for civilised people who can respect rituals and cultivate their own character by emulating the noble examples of virtuous Sages. However, Confucianism describes the process of self-cultivation as applicable to everybody, regardless of their social position or profession. In other words, I think that some structural features of the process of self-development are common to all professions (or social roles) and thus that it is possible to extend and adopt to some extent the Confucian general guidance to the judicial field.

First, Confucianists (in contrast to Zen Buddhists) stress the necessity of a long and persistent, joyful, progress on the never-ending Way of self-improvement. This is a slow process and cannot be artificially accelerated. In *Lunyu* (14:47), we can find an interesting conversation about a messenger boy. Somebody asks the Master: 'Is he growing up?', to which Confucius responds that he spends his entire time with adults only and is not seeking his own self-development: 'He is trying to grow up too fast'. One goal of the process of educating judges in the virtues is to make the future judge aware of the fact that self-cultivation takes a long time, is incremental in nature and is a never-ending process. He needs to know that the judicial virtues may be developed only as a result of a slow process of making hundreds of decisions, struggling with many legal and moral dilemmas, and slowly acquiring experience in weighing legally protected values in a self-reflective way. The cultivation of virtues necessary to become a perfect judge may be described as learning by doing in a conscious manner.

Second, the way to reaching perfection resembles a long journey which one needs to set upon now and here, from the closest possible point of entry, and persevere in its pursuit (*Zhongyong* 15). The judge should be sensitive to the necessity

[22] Gier (2004: 174).

[23] All translations of the cited Confucian classics (*Doctrine of the Mean – Zhongyong, Analects – Lunyu, Book of Mencius – Mengzi*) come from Wing-Tsit Chan's collection (1969).

to enter the path to self-development here and now, and not to put it aside. One deviates from the Way when saying: 'I will do my best in the next case; I will try to look more closely at conflicting values or complicated facts of the case on another occasion'.

Third, direct contact with virtuous people is most helpful in the development of one's own character: 'Calipers and right angles are the basic pattern for circles and squares, the Sages are the best example to follow in interpersonal relationships' (*Mengzi* 4A:2). The communities and associations of lawyers are responsible for assuring the noble examples of virtuous judges, law professors, etc. In order to create a suitable environment for the judge's professional self-development, there should exist not only appropriate institutional conditions, but also noble examples of temperate, courageous, impartial, intelligent and wise judges.

Fourth, despite the example of the great Masters, the process of growth should be *self*-development. Mechanical travesty in copying the way of the masters is only an illusion of progress. Everything needs to be achieved by one's own effort, discipline, self-control and focus (*Lunyu* 12:1). Judges should become aware that their accepted style of professional work, their choices and motivations will form their characters. The great examples of virtuous judges give us only a general vision and outline the route of flourishing.

Fifth, progress requires a search for explanations of events in one's own features (ie internal attribution). When an archer is trying to hit the target and misses the bull's eye, he turns around and looks for reasons within himself (*Zhongyong* 14). It does not mean that he should find the reason within himself. It only means that he must first check if it is not there. Despite the influence of many complex factors (the hierarchical structure of courts, the jury system, the economic situation, etc), when a judge is looking for the causes of a bad decision, first of all he needs to look at himself. He should critically examine his methodology, knowledge, involvement and motivations in a particular case. The flourishing judge is not the judge who does not make mistakes, but the one who can find their causes and work for improvement.

To sum up, the Confucian philosophical tradition gives us subtle advice and only some general indications as to how to enter and follow the self-cultivation Way. The Great Masters showed only the boundary conditions for the flourishing process, which every man should fulfil on their own while consciously passing over the specific means of self-cultivation. I have shown that it is possible to extend and adopt the general guidelines and principles concerning the process of self-development to the specific juridical field where judges operate. Improving on the aretaic model of judicial decision-making by searching for direct guidance on how to develop traits essential for a perfect judge and how to organise an institutional framework which is conducive for the judge's professional self-development should be the main aim of the emerging so-called Confucian jurisprudence.[24] The success of such an enterprise and even a description of its limitations would

[24] Wang and Solum (2012).

significantly improve on the aretaic model of judicial decision-making as well as the entire virtue jurisprudence movement.

V. A SITUATIONAL APPROACH TO THE PROCESS OF JUDICIAL DECISION-MAKING

Thus far I have considered three main models of judicial decision-making. Instead of endorsing one of these three models, I claim that they may be treated as consecutive stages in the judge's professional self-development. I propose a situational (contingency) approach – that is, that there should be correspondence between the model of judicial adjudication and the self-cultivation stage of a judge. Each stage requires a different decision-making style and each style stimulates the judge to develop and foster a distinct set of skills necessary for correct judging. According to this perspective, the question of whether there is a universal style of judicial decision-making suitable to all situations must be replaced by the question of which is the proper model in relation to the particular stage of a judge's self-development.[25]

Each one of the judicial decision-making models has its strengths and weaknesses, relies on numerous presuppositions and fulfils the court's systematic goals only if the preliminary criteria are fulfilled. For example, the formal-positivist model needs good law, the responsive one requires clear and accepted criteria for evaluating consequences, and the aretaic one needs self-developed and well-formed judges. I claim that the functions of the judicial system are achieved by different means in each of these three stages (positivist-responsive-aretaic). At the first stage, when judges are inexperienced and do not possess judicial virtues, the appropriate proceedings and rulings are generated by formality and adherence to the letter of law. At the second stage, when they become fluent in working on the legal texts, there is an emphasis on the evaluation of alternative decisions. At the third stage, once judges have developed the necessary skills and proficiencies, the focus is placed on perfecting the judicial virtues. The aretaic model serves the objectives of court proceedings to the full only when judges have already reached the two earlier stages of self-development. Not all judges have reached the final stage (ie the aretaic one), and when they have not, they should apply less demanding models of judicial decision-making. In consequence, I do not defend an aretaic model of judging as an approach to adjudication which can be of universal character in its application; each stage should be treated as a consecutive element in the judge's self-cultivation process.

I fully realise that there are some fundamental problems concerning the depicted vision of the three stages of a judge's self-cultivation. This model obviously suits better the legal systems which have a career-based judiciary, that is,

[25] According to the situational theories developed in organisational sciences, there is no single best approach to managing and organisational decision-making that could be universal in its application (see Vroom and Jago (1988)).

'systems manned by lawyers who make an entire career of being judge' and form a 'part of a nation's civil service'.[26] The new, more developed, and comprehensive aretaic model should cope with this restriction. Moreover, one may also claim that it violates the (formal) principle of equality before the law because the 'justice' that a party receives would depend on what stage the judge represents. However, the formal-positivist model of judicial decision-making, which is the first stage of a judge's self-cultivation, guarantees the minimum scope of realisation of the principle of equality. Despite the fact that the application of all three models would lead in most cases to the same 'legal' outcome, they would affect the decision-maker's professional abilities and personality in quite distinct ways. The judgment might be different in a few cases, but this does not violate the principle of equality and the basic requirements of due process of law, because the courts' agendas are not based on the stage of judge's self-development criterion.

The proposed approach differs from the thesis that aretaic elements take primacy over consequentialist and deontological ones. Even though the aretaic approach stresses some important issues which are missing in the dominant legal discourse, it does not resolve all judging-related problems and need to be supplemented by both the deontological and the consequentialist dimensions. I do not – as Solum puts it[27] – 'reject the dominant traditions in contemporary theorizing about the ends of law'. Rather, I argue that an axiological perspective enables the perception of interconnections between legal norms, their consequences and judicial virtues. Let me explain why.

If one treats legal norms not as axiomatic values, but as means for implementing multiple social values (both substantive and formal), then legal norms, the analyses of the consequences of particular decision alternatives, and the judicial virtues should not be treated as mutually exclusive factors affecting the final judgment. The values authorised and protected by law need to be taken into consideration by the judge who analyses the most probable effects of a given judgment. He should make an alternative choice whenever it maximises the scope of realisation of the legally protected values.[28] Moreover, one cannot understand correctly the role of the judicial virtues without locating them in such an axiological context. In the self-reflective, longstanding process of acquiring traits necessary to excel in the judicial profession, a deep understanding of the complex, dynamic and axiological dimension of law is the most important and the most stimulating element. Indeed, the main significance of balancing and weighing values proceeded by law for developing judicial virtues should be maintained. The judges must anticipate and deal with the problem emerging from a possible incoherency between (a) complex social values aggregated in the democratic elections and transformed into public policy; (b) values protected explicitly by legal norms and precedents; (c) dynamics of social values at the time of particular judicial decision-making; and (d) the judge's personal set of values. The last factor is very important because,

[26] Posner (2008: 129).
[27] Solum (2009: 122).
[28] Barak (2008: 125–53) and Feteris (2005: 459–70).

according to an aretaic model, the judge should clarify his axiological attitudes in the particular case in order to avoid possible influences of his preferences, stereotypes and prejudices on the ruling. Even Judge Jerome Frank, who acknowledged that personal values can influence a judge's decision, nonetheless asserted that '[t]he conscientious judge will, as far as possible, make himself aware of his biases of this character, and, by that very self-knowledge, nullify their effect'.[29] In short, I argue that an axiological perspective enables the perception of interconnections between legal norms, their consequences and the judicial virtues.

VI. CONCLUSIONS

With a slight simplification, one may notice that the dominant theoretical approach in Western jurisprudence – with the exception of the virtue jurisprudence movement – marginalises judges' professional self-improvement and the importance of aretaic elements in judging. In contrast, in the East-Asian cultural tradition, the concept of human growth and self-cultivation is stressed, but discussion on the structural (institutional) factors constraining judgments is marginalised.[30] Any comprehensive normative model of adjudication should integrate both elements.

I have conducted a preliminary analysis of professional judges' self-development based on a transition that goes from the formal-positivist model, through the responsive model, to the aretaic model of judicial decision-making. The situational approach presented in this chapter explores the interconnections between the deontological, consequentialist and aretaic elements in judging and provides a good starting point for developing a unified and situational normative theory of judicial decision-making under an 'aretaic umbrella', avoiding false boundaries and antagonisms. Similarly, in the discussion about virtue ethics, Martha Nussbaum writes that 'both Utilitarianism and Kantianism contain treatments on virtues, so virtue ethics cannot possibly be a separate approach contrasted with those approaches'; and 'lots of people are, and have long been, writing and thinking about virtue within the Kantian and Utilitarian traditions'.[31] According to Nussbaum, the three grand theories have much in common and a situation where all ethical theories are divided into three camps is a 'misleading story about the current situation in contemporary moral philosophy'.[32]

Finally, the 'idealistic' portrayal of a judge's self-transformation process presented above does not negate the fact that the three models of judicial decision-making discussed above coexist simultaneously with varying degrees of intensity and in different proportions at the various levels of the hierarchy of court-related

[29] Frank (1949/1973: 414).
[30] Wang (2001) and Coward (2008).
[31] Nussbaum (1999: 163, 121).
[32] Nussbaum (1999: 164).

institutions through different legal cultures.[33] I have presented a prescriptive (normative) analysis concerning the problem of how judges should decide, but, at the same time, one should examine how judges indeed decide cases. Even without referring to empirical data, I think that, quite undoubtedly, we could not accurately describe and explicate the process of judicial decision-making without mentioning all three models.

REFERENCES

Aviram, A (2005) 'The Placebo Effect of Law' *University of Illinois Law and Economics Working Papers* 36.

Barak, A (2008) *The Judge in a Democracy* (Princeton, Princeton University Press).

Chan, WT (1969) *A Sources Book of Chinese Philosophy* (Princeton, Princeton University Press).

Coward, H (2008) *The Perfectibility of Human Nature in Eastern and Western Thought* (Albany, State University of New York Press).

Dewey, J (1924) 'Logical Method and Law' 10 *Cornell Law Review* 17.

Duff, RA (2003) 'The Limits of Virtue Jurisprudence' 34 *Metaphilosophy* 214.

—— (2006) 'The Virtues and Vices of Virtue Jurisprudence' in T Chappell (ed), *Values and Virtues: Aristotelianism in Contemporary Ethics* (Oxford, Clarendon Press).

Dworkin, RM (1986) *Law's Empire* (Cambridge, MA, Belknap Press).

Eskridge, WN and Frickey, PF (1990) 'Statutory Interpretation as Practical Reasoning' 42 *Stanford Law Review* 321.

Farrelly, C and Solum, LB (eds) (2008) *Virtue Jurisprudence* (Basingstoke, Palgrave MacMillan).

Feldman, HL (1996) 'Codes and Virtues: Can Good Lawyers Be Good Ethical Deliberators?' 69 *South California Law Review* 885.

—— (1999) 'Beyond the Model Rules: The Place of Examples in Legal Ethics' 12 *Georgetown Journal of Legal Ethics* 409.

—— (2000) 'Prudence, Benevolence, and Negligence: Virtue Ethics and Tort Law' 74 *Chicago-Kent Law Review* 1431.

Feteris, ET (2005) 'The Rational Reconstruction of Argumentation Referring to Consequences and Purpose in the Application of Legal Rules: A Pragma-Dialectical Perspective' 19 *Argumentation* 459.

Foxall, GR (2004) 'What Judges Maximize: Toward an Economic Psychology of the Judicial Utility Function' 25 *Liverpool Law Review* 177.

Frank, J (1949/1973) *Courts on Trial: Myth and Reality in American Justice* (New Jersey, Princeton University Press).

Gier, NF (2004) 'Whitehead, Confucius, and the Aesthetics of Virtue' 14 *Asian Philosophy* 171.

Holmes, OW (1897) 'The Path of Law' 10 *Harvard Law Review* 457.

Huigen, K (2002) 'Homicide in Aretaic Terms' 6 *Buffalo Criminal Law Review* 97.

—— (2007) 'Law and Morality: Criminal Law: The Jurisprudence of Punishment' 48 *William and Mary Law Review* 1793.

Koller, P (2007) 'Law, Virtue and Morality' in RL Walker and PJ Ivanhoe (eds), *Working Virtue: Virtue Ethics and Contemporary Moral Problems* (Oxford, Clarendon Press).

[33] Posner (2006: 1054).

Michelon, C (2012) 'Practical Wisdom in Legal Decision-Making' chapter 2 of this volume.
Nietzsche, F, Kaufmann, W (tr) (1885/1988) *The Portable Nietzsche* (Harmondsworth, Penguin).
Nonet, P and Selznick, P (1978) *Law and Society in Transition: Toward Responsive Law* (New York, Harper).
Nussbaum, MC (1999) 'Virtue Ethnics: A Misleading Category?' 3 *The Journal of Ethics* 163.
Pałecki, K (2004) 'Stressing Legal Decisions. Basics Assumptions' in Stressing Legal Decisions, IVR Twenty-first World Congress (Cracow, Polpress).
Posner, R (2006) 'The Role of the Judge in the Twenty-first Century' 86 *Boston University Law Review* 1049.
—— (2008) *How Judges Think* (Cambridge, Massachusetts, Harvard University Press).
Scalia, A (1989) 'The Rule of Law as a Law of Rules' 56 *University of Chicago Law Review* 1175.
Schauer, F (1988) 'Formalism' 97 *Yale Law Review* 509.
Sherry, S (2003) 'Judges of Character' 38 *Wake Forest Law Review* 793.
Simon, HA (1957) *Models of Man* (New York, Wiley).
Solum, LB (1988) 'The Virtues and Vices of a Judge: An Aristotelian Guide to Judicial Selection' 61 *South California Law Review* 1735.
—— (2003) 'Virtue Jurisprudence: A Virtue-Centered Theory of Judging' 34 *Metaphilosophy* 178.
—— (2005a) 'A Tournament of Virtue' 32 *Florida State University Law Review* 1365.
—— (2005b) 'The Aretaic Turn in Constitutional Theory' 70 *Brooklyn Law Review* 475.
—— (2005c) 'Judicial Selection: Ideology Versus Character' 26 *Cardozo Law Review* 659.
—— (2006) 'Natural Justice' 51 *The American Journal of Jurisprudence* 65.
—— (2009) 'The Aretaic Turn in American Philosophy of Law' in FJ Mootz and WS Boyd (eds), *On Philosophy in American Law* (Cambridge, Cambridge University Press).
van Norden, B (2007) *Virtue Ethics and Consequentialism in Early Chinese Philosophy* (New York, Cambridge University Press).
Vroom, VH and Jago, AG (1988) *The New Leadership: Managing Participation in Organizations* (New Jersey, Prentice Hall).
Wang, L and Solum, LB (2012) 'Confucian Virtue Jurisprudence' chapter 6 of this volume.
Wang, W (2001) 'Confucian Ethics and Virtue Ethics' 28 *The Journal of Chinese Philosophy* 285.

III.

Virtue Theory and Criminal Law

8

Motivating Intentions, Reciprocal Specification of Ends and the Assessment of Responsibility

KYRON HUIGENS

I. INTRODUCTION

ACCORDING TO AN Aristotelian conception of legal responsibility, the attribution of responsibility turns on the capacity for practical reasoning, and the assessment of degrees of responsibility turns on the quality of one's practical reasoning. For example, John Gardner explains excuses in criminal law in 'broadly Aristotelian' terms with the idea of meeting normative expectations.[1] A more overtly Aristotelian punishment theory articulates these expectations in terms of what is owed to others in a society of inherently social beings whose defining end is rational action. The expectation is that one will deliberate well on one's own ends, because the actions that issue from these deliberations and that serve these ends are partly constitutive of such a society.[2] A reasonable mistake of fact excuses because even though the actor has violated a prohibition, his practical reasoning is nevertheless of good quality. He has met our normative expectations for practical reasoning. Similarly, we excuse for duress, not because the defendant has acted out of character, but instead because she has acted in character. The fortitude she displays in, regrettably, violating a criminal prohibition shows sound practical reasoning over the longer term.

One of the principal objections to this theory of criminal inculpation is that the commission of a criminal offence provides too little information for an assessment of the quality of the defendant's practical reasoning – an assessment that must be fairly comprehensive if it is to morally justify legal punishment. The problem arises not only with respect to the breadth of the required assessment, but also with respect to the requisite level of detail. The law of *mens rea*, culpability, or, as I prefer to call it, criminal fault, demonstrates the problem. According to Aristotelian ethics, sound practical reasoning is necessarily particularistic.[3] This fine-grainedness, however, is

[1] Gardner (1998: 577–78).
[2] Huigens (1995: 1449–56).
[3] Aristotle (1962: 157–58).

hard to find in criminal law. First, criminal law evaluates a defendant's conduct in terms of rules. Given that criminal prohibitions are rules, that violations of criminal law are violations of rules, and that the adjudication of these violations is strongly rule-bound, there is no means or occasion for the assessment of fine-grained practical reasoning posited by an aretaic theory of legal punishment. Second, Aristotelian punishment theory is undercut by the predominance of subjective states fault criteria. Standards such as criminal negligence can facilitate a fairly wide and detailed inquiry into the defendant's practical reasoning, but objective fault criteria such as negligence are generally disfavoured in the definition of criminal offences, in favour of a limited palette of subjective mental states. These discrete states of mind can tell us little about the overall quality of the defendant's practical reasoning.

Neither of these problems is insurmountable. First, criminal law is not as rule-bound as it might seem. Criminal prohibitions are rules, it is true, but rules originate in practical reasoning, which in individual cases issue in particular choices and actions. The offences defined in a criminal code are authoritative normative generalisations of unsound individual choices and actions, and the rules represent deficient practical reasoning in the situations from which criminal behaviour arises. These generalisations are returned to the level of particulars – carrying the legal authority of the prohibition with them – by the judge or jury that determines whether the facts of a particular case constitute a violation of the prohibition.[4] Whatever might be true of the offence definition as a guide to action, retrospective assessments of criminal fault in adjudication are particularistic evaluations of the quality of the defendant's practical reasoning.

As for the second part of the 'inadequate basis' objection, one way to explain the predominance of subjective states of mind in offence definitions and adjudication is to put it down to the rule of law, and not to the nature of criminal fault.[5] Objective fault criteria can involve the legal decision-maker in making raw normative determinations about 'depravity' and 'malice'. Because the exercise of such broad discretion by the legal decision-maker cuts against requirements of notice, specificity and legislative primacy in criminal law, the determination of criminal fault has to be framed in terms of fact-finding about the defendant's state of mind. Concessions to the rule of law aside, however, criminal fault itself is a particularistic assessment of the quality of the defendant's practical reasoning. One indication of this is our practice in defining offences. We often find ourselves balancing these concessions to the rule of law with objective, non-intentional fault criteria like (but, one hopes, more artfully drawn than) 'depravity' and 'malice'.

This chapter will develop two more responses to the 'inadequate basis' objection. Michael Bratman seems to be among those philosophers who think that assessments of moral responsibility are assessments of the quality of practical reasoning.[6] Bratman's analysis of responsibility is of particular value because it occurs within a broader effort to describe what it is to intend and to act intentionally.

[4] Huigens (2000: 1028–31).
[5] Huigens (2002: 108–12).
[6] Bratman (1999a: 173).

The gist of the first reply is that, while the intentional acts employed in offence definitions are narrow, they are not co-extensive with the intentions that are the basis of criminal fault. Intentional actions reflect a wide range of motivating intentions, beyond the simple intention that corresponds to an intentional action. This wide array of intentions – and not the intentional action described in an offence definition or a single intention corresponding to it – is the subject of the assessment of practical reasoning that constitutes the determination of criminal fault.

The second response to the 'inadequate basis' objection draws on the Aristotelian idea that responsibility for ends turns on how well one's deliberations on ends engage the particulars of the case. These aspects of Aristotelian responsibility show up in the aretaic account of criminal fault in terms of specification. Bratman describes practical reasoning about intentions in these terms. My intentions become more and more particular as I engage in intentional action, and this specification of my intentions generates new intentions. The second response to the 'inadequate basis' objection reformulates this account of practical reasoning as an account of deliberation on ends, instead of deliberation on intentions. We resolve conflicts in ends by a process of the reciprocal specification of ends. This account of deliberations on ends, when it is combined with Bratman's account of intentions and intentional actions, shows that the adjudication of offences entails an evaluation of the practical reasoning of the accused that is sufficiently broad to justify the imposition of legal punishment.

II. BRATMAN ON INTENTIONS

Bratman portrays intentions as components of practical reasoning that are distinguishable from both desires and beliefs. Intentions involve a characteristic commitment to action. If and when I form an intention to go to the library, then I stop weighing my desires as they bear on library-going. The matter is settled, and resists reconsideration. This inertia is a primary feature of intentions. When the time that I have set aside to go to the library comes around, then I go because I have made a commitment to go. Whereas desires are conduct-influencing pro-attitudes, intentions are conduct-controlling pro-attitudes – and this is a second distinguishing mark of intentions. A third distinguishing feature of intentions is the fact that prior intentions give rise to further intentions. Bratman describes this feature in terms of means, ends and the specification of intentions:

> The [third feature] concerns the role my intention normally plays in my further reasoning between now and the time for going to Tanner [Library]. I will frequently reason from such a prior intention to further intentions. I will frequently reason from intended end to intended means or preliminary steps: as when I reason from my intention to go to Tanner to intentions concerning how to get there. And I will frequently reason from more general to more specific intentions: as when I reason from an intention to take a bus to Tanner, and from my reflections on the bus schedule, to an intention to take a particular bus. Further, my prior intention to go to Tanner this afternoon will constrain

> the other intentions I form for the day, since I will seek to make my intentions consistent with one another and with my beliefs.[7]

This third feature of intentions needs to be developed further if the theory of punishment is to take full advantage of Bratman's work, and I will attempt to do so below. But for now, let me complete this sketch of Bratman's analysis.

Even though intentions are distinguishable from beliefs and desires, and in some sense of equal status as components of practical reasoning, intentions operate in a subordinate role, as a filter for options. Desires and beliefs provide reasons for action. Intentions do not do so. Instead, intentions govern deliberations on action. The progress from prior intentions to further intentions produces ends, means and specifications for the actor. These intentions are subject to a requirement of strong consistency if the actor is to behave in a way that is not self-defeating and that will engage his efforts with the efforts of others in a productive way.[8] In addition, the ends, means and specifications will themselves have to be coherent. The upshot of consistent intentions and means-ends coherence is a plan for action. These plans are not static, like blueprints or maps. We have plans for action as we have intentions to act.[9]

The defining mark of intentions, then, is that they are embedded in plans. To see intentions as components of plans opens the way to conceptualising responsibility in terms of the adequacy of practical reasoning. Plans exhibit responsible agency, and the evaluation of responsibility is an evaluation of 'the quality of an agent's will'.[10] Bratman relies on PF Strawson's analysis of responsibility in terms of reactive attitudes.[11] Holding another person responsible involves reacting to her actions with attitudes such as disapprobation and indignation. Holding oneself responsible involves reactive attitudes such as remorse. Bratman writes:

> To hold a person responsible for certain of her actions is to include her and those actions among the targets of one's web of reactive attitudes. As Gary Watson has put it, 'to regard oneself or another as responsible just is the proneness to react to them in these kinds of ways under certain conditions'.[12]

And, quoting Strawson, he continues:

> Both participant and moral reactive attitudes are reactions to 'the qualities of others' wills.' Standard excuses of ignorance, accident, or external compulsion work, when they do work, by showing that the quality of the agent's will does not merit resentment, indignation, or the like.[13]

What is the connection between Strawson's reactive attitudes and Bratman's idea that intentions are embedded in plans? To say that 'the quality of the agent's will'

[7] Bratman (1999b: 17).
[8] ibid 30–32.
[9] ibid 28–29.
[10] Bratman (1999a: 173).
[11] ibid 171–73.
[12] ibid 172 (quoting Watson (1987: 257)).
[13] ibid 173 (quoting Strawson (1974: 70)).

merits resentment, indignation and the like, is presumably to say that the quality of his practical reasoning with respect to plans and intentions is not of good quality. Bratman notes that reactive attitudes do not occur without some form of social cooperation that is dependent on planning and intentions.[14] What prompts reactive emotions is, usually, an intentional action embedded in a plan that fails to take account of others' interests; or acting according to contrary intentions within a plan in which one is a participant.[15] In Gardner's terms, reactive attitudes are prompted by failures to meet normative expectations. In more overtly Aristotelian terms, reactive attitudes are responses to the actor's failure to deliberate well concerning the well-being of the society of which he is, in part, constituted, and also of which he is, in part, constitutive.[16] If Bratman were to take the logic of his argument this far, the idea of reactive attitudes could be left out altogether. Regardless of our emotional reactions to wrongdoing, we can hold others responsible simply because we have a right to expect a certain level of competence in practical reasoning as evinced in others' intentions and plans. Something of this kind must be behind our reactive emotions, or they would be unfounded.

III. INTENDING VERSUS ACTING INTENTIONALLY

Bratman portrays the relationship between acting intentionally and having an intention in a surprising way.[17] We naturally suppose that when an agent acts intentionally he so intends. Bratman dubs this the 'simple view', and rejects it. It is possible to act intentionally to A, but not to intend to A. The intention to A has 'motivating potential' with respect to intentionally A-ing, but one can A intentionally in the absence of an intention to A, in response to other intentions that also have motivating potential for A-ing.

In advancing his view of intentions, Bratman uses the example of playing a video game that involves shooting at two targets.[18] If I hit target one, I win. If I hit target two, I win. It is possible to hit both targets in this game – say they move about randomly but sometimes cross paths, so that to hit one at such a moment is to hit both – but if I do hit both targets, then I lose. If I play the game, then I act intentionally to hit target one now, and I act intentionally to hit target two now. On the simple view, this means that I intend to hit target one now and intend to hit target two now. To have this pair of intentions is irrational, however, because it violates a requirement of consistency in ends. Taken together they constitute an intention to lose the game. After all, this is what happens if I hit both targets 'now' – that is, in the same moment. This means that the simple view is mistaken. If this pair of intentional actions each implied a corresponding intention – as the simple

[14] ibid 171–72.
[15] ibid 172.
[16] Huigens (1995: 1461–62).
[17] Bratman (1999b: 111–13).
[18] ibid 113–16.

view has it – then my intention would be to lose the game, whereas my real intention, we suppose, is to win the game. If this is true, then it does not follow that if I act intentionally then I have an intention so to act. My intentions are subject to a requirement of consistency because, if my intentions are not consistent, then I cannot be sure that I will not act in a way that is self-defeating. So, unless it is practically rational to act in self-defeating ways, the simple view is incorrect.

One can object that if I have the intention to hit either target one or target two, then there is nothing irrational about this at all. This either/or intention, however, is a different intention from the one implied by the simple view, under which intentionally acting to hit target one implies that I intend to hit target one now, not that I intend to hit either one or two; and, likewise, intentionally acting to hit target two implies that I intend to hit target two now, not that I intend to hit either one or two.[19] So the objection does not rebut Bratman's argument against the simple view. It does illustrate an important point, however. Acting intentionally to hit target one does not imply that I intend to hit target one, but this is not to say that an intention to hit target one can never motivate my intentional action to hit target one. It only means that there are other intentions that can motivate me. These are intentions that, as Bratman puts it, have motivating potential for my intentionally hitting target one. Among these intentions is the either/or intention.

The problem with relying on Bratman's conception of intentions in developing a conception of criminal fault is this: acting intentionally is relevant to criminal liability because offence definitions usually require intentional actions; and criminal responsibility, as an aretaic theory understands it, rests on intentions that the agent has; but it does not follow from an agent's acting intentionally that he has an intention so to act. By breaking the connection between intentions and intentional action, Bratman seems to break the connection between the quality of the defendant's practical reasoning and the intentional actions that constitute his crime. An Aristotelian theory of criminal fault seems to depend on there being such a connection, so this threatens to be fatal to that theory. As it turns out, however, Bratman's point is a limited one. Putting it in perspective dispels these worries and shows the larger potential of his account of intentions for the theory of punishment.

IV. INTENTIONAL ACTIONS AND CRIMINAL FAULT

The fact that an intentional action has more than one intention behind it answers one of the principal objections to an aretaic theory of punishment. The objection is that the acts involved in the commission of a crime tell us less about the practical reasoning of the accused than an aretaic theory requires. A crime is only one event in a life, but an evaluation of the quality of one's practical reasoning surely would require us to consider many such events. Given that the inquiry into the

[19] ibid 118.

quality of the defendant's practical reasoning is so narrow, it could not possibly justify legal punishment in the way an aretaic theory contends.

Bratman's analysis of intentions and intentional actions provides an answer to this objection. If an intentional action reflects an array of intentions that have motivating potential for that action, then intentional actions tell us far more about the agent's practical reasoning than we might have expected. The number of intentions that have motivating potential – and therefore explanatory value – for intentional actions might be very large. Notice as well that the intentions with motivating potential for an intentional action naturally cluster around what we might call the 'simple intention' – the intention implied by the (false) simple view. This is why the either/or objection seems persuasive, even though it is misleading. For other intentions with motivating potential, however, the fact that they cluster around the simple intention so to act might be helpful in explaining the intentional action. It is possible to build out, so to speak, from the intentional action to a simple intention, then to a range of motivating intentions, and then to a picture of the defendant's practical reasoning that can be evaluated for quality with the depth and breadth that are required to impose criminal responsibility on that ground.

Suppose an elderly husband kills his gravely suffering and terminally ill wife of 50 years, and that he does so in order to relieve her suffering. Ordinarily, we will say that he intends to kill her, and he will be guilty of murder in any jurisdiction. An aretaic theory of punishment and criminal fault will say that the husband's killing of his wife involves an instance of poor practical reasoning, and that he is at fault because poor practical reasoning such as this fails to give society its due. How can Bratman's analysis help to make sense of this case and of the aretaic theory's treatment of the criminal fault it exhibits? Generally speaking, Bratman's analysis makes sense of our ambivalence about punishing the elderly husband as a murderer, and supports one of the principal recommendations that an aretaic punishment theory makes regarding legal doctrine.

To begin with, the statement that the husband intends to kill his wife is inaccurate because it is incomplete. He has acted intentionally to kill her, but the most we can say is that an intention to kill his wife has motivational potential relative to this intentional action. Other intentions can be inferred from his intentional action because these other intentions also have motivating potential for his intentional act of killing. An intention to kill need not be among these intentions. This sounds odd in the elderly husband's case, because his intentional act of killing clearly has an intention to kill behind it. Bratman, however, argues only that the intention to kill *need not* be behind his intentional act of killing – not that it *cannot* be behind his intentional act of killing. Bratman's concern is only to show the falsity of the simple view of intentional actions and intentions, and it is sufficient for this to show a case in which it is not true. This is the point and purpose of Bratman's video game example. He could not have used the elderly husband's case for this purpose, because the simple view is sufficient to explain the connection between the elderly husband's intentional action to kill and his intention to kill – but from our point of view, so what? Bratman's analysis has far less dire implications for an aretaic theory of punishment than it initially seems to have.

A second point in this regard is more important for punishment theory. Even if we could not infer an intention to kill from the husband's intentional action, Bratman's analysis makes the intentional picture richer, not poorer. Think of the answer I gave to the objection that the video gamer can rationally intend to hit either target one or target two. Bratman does not deny that the gamer can have this 'either/or' intention or that we could infer it from his intentional act to hit target one now and his intentional act to hit target two now. The gamer certainly intends something, and the intentions that we can infer from his intentional act – the group of intentions that have motivational potential for this intentional act – will ordinarily cluster around the simple, conflicting, intentions to hit each target. Likewise, even if the simple intention to kill did not follow from the elderly husband's intentional act of killing, he still intends something, probably many things, that have motivating potential for an intentional act of killing. These other intentions will cluster around the simple intention to kill, but it is important – for our purposes as well as for Bratman's – to distinguish them from the simple intention to kill. The husband intends to relieve his wife's suffering, even at the cost of death; he intends to act lovingly, no matter that love now requires him to kill her; he intends to honour the wish to die instead of to suffer that she made clear when she was still young and healthy; and so on. Even though he must be guilty of murder because he kills with the requisite criminal fault – that is, because he commits the intentional act described in the offence definition – our moral judgement is that the elderly husband does not deserve legal punishment. What accounts for this discrepancy? It is the fact that the other intentions that he has have motivating potential for his intentional act of killing, and that these intentions carry more weight for us than the simple intention to kill that corresponds to his intentional act of killing.

This is a critically important point for the punishment theorist. Bratman's analysis reinforces the aretaic theorist's contention that the underlying nature of criminal fault pushes the law toward the use of objective fault criteria. Objective criteria capture a wider range of intentions that have motivating potential for the intentional actions described in offence definitions. As such, they reflect a wide range of the intentions of the actor – wide enough to facilitate an evaluation of the quality of his practical reasoning that is sufficient to find legal punishment morally justified.

As I noted above, we confine ourselves to a very limited palette of fault criteria in criminal law, consisting mostly of intentional acts. We might convict the elderly husband of murder because of his intention to kill, on proof of an intentional act of killing, using a doctrinal definition of murder that employs a thin description of this intentional action. Often, however, these thin descriptions are not enough to facilitate the requisite inquiry into the quality of the defendant's practical reasoning. In these cases, we will employ objective fault criteria in the inquiry, in order to bring a wider range of motivating intentions to the surface for explicit consideration. If most criminal offences do not employ objective criteria, this is because we deem the thin description of an intentional action to be sufficient with respect to the consideration of the motivating intentions that bear on criminal fault.

One cannot overestimate, however, the importance of using thick descriptions of intentional action in order to capture a wide range of motivating intentions. The judgments of criminal law cannot depart too far from our moral judgements of wrongdoing without losing credibility. As a result, someone such as the elderly husband who commits a mercy killing cannot be treated as one of the worst killers – that is, he cannot be convicted of murder without some further consideration of his fault. In spite of his intention to kill, the elderly husband probably would be convicted of manslaughter under a definition of that offence that reflects the rest of the intentions that motivated him to kill. The definition of this homicide – provocation manslaughter – uses objective fault criteria. The circumstances of the terminally ill wife's killing constitute a reasonable explanation for the mental and emotional disturbance that led him to commit murder.[20]

Bratman's analysis explains and justifies the necessity of resorting to objective fault criteria. It is not only the simple intention to kill that should concern criminal law, because this is not the only intention we can infer from the intentional act of killing. The movement from intentional action to intentions embedded in plans is more complex than this. We can infer a cluster of intentions that all have motivating potential for the intentional act. In fact we do make these inferences, and this is precisely what makes us uneasy (or should do) about letting the elderly husband's liability turn on proof of the simple intentional act of killing. If the elderly husband's intentional killing reveals a cluster of intentions embedded in plans – his intentions to relieve suffering, to act lovingly, to honour a loved one's rational wish to die, and so on – then the quality of this practical reasoning certainly does not imply that he should be convicted of murder. Hence the pressure toward more complex criteria of criminal fault that give these additional intentions legal salience and that move the law toward morally defensible outcomes.

V. INTENTIONAL ACTION AND THE RECIPROCAL SPECIFICATION OF ENDS

We have found a route from the intentional actions and fault criteria that define criminal wrongdoing, to the intentions and plans that we evaluate in order to determine desert for punishment. What are the next steps? What will take us from recognising the intentions and plans of the accused, to an evaluation of these things in terms of practical reasoning, and from this evaluation of practical reasoning to the moral justification of legal punishment in her particular case?

[20] The claim that provocation is not a partial defence, but is instead an alternative definition of manslaughter in which provoking circumstances function as objective fault elements, is defended in Huigens (2011).

Bratman's argument against the simple view of intentional action and intentions depends primarily on the requirement of strong consistency of intentions, but he recognises other constraints on intentions as well. Effective plans also require means-ends coherence. The problem for a theory of responsibility based on intentions embedded in plans is that means-ends coherence is not much of a constraint on the evaluation of the quality of practical reasoning, and neither, for that matter, is the consistency of intentions. The most innocent of actors engages in poor means-ends reasoning and fails to seek, much less achieve, consistency of intentions. This practical ineptitude is blameworthy to some extent, but hardly to the extent required for the imposition of punishment. A more comprehensive account of practical reasoning is required.

Bratman describes a particular kind of means-ends reasoning: the specification of intentions.[21] If I want to go to the library, then I will consult a bus schedule; if I want to take a bus on the schedule, then I will have to get to the bus stop on time; if I want to get to the bus stop on time, then I will have to get up early in the morning; and so on. At first glance, following the trail of specified intentions seems no more illuminating on the question of responsibility than our usual matching of means and ends. On closer examination, however, the idea of specification is more promising than it appears to be. Bratman presents the specification of intentions in a way that suggests it consists solely of the specification of means. In the example of my taking a bus to the library, my going to the library is a fixed end. On the other hand, Bratman describes specification as breeding further intentions, and describes this fecundity as something that drives us to formulate and elaborate plans.[22] This is why tracing the specification of intentions tells us more about the agent's practical reasoning than watching her match means to ends does. Specification tells us more about her ends. Specification could not foster further intentions unless it fostered further ends, and not only further means to given ends.

The specification of intentions as Bratman describes it, however, would generate a limited number of more specific ends, and these would be of limited relevance to responsibility. The specification of my intention to go to the library runs aground after a few steps. Having located a bus on the schedule and having arrived at the bus stop in time, I get on the bus and duly arrive at the library. We could slice my specified intentions finer and finer – in order to get to the library, I will get on the bus; in order to get on the bus, I will climb up its steps; in order to climb up the steps, I will lift my foot, and so on. But these finer slices of intentions are of no interest to an inquiry into responsibility. They do not even count, one would think, as the intentions that Bratman has in mind when he gives specification an important role in developing plans.

In order to bring out the full value of Bratman's notion of specified intentions, we need to see specification as productive of further ends, not only means. In this

[21] Bratman (1999b: 30–32).

[22] ibid 32–35.

regard, conflict is – as it is so often – the source of the new. It should be obvious that ends conflict, and that we resolve conflicts of ends on an ongoing basis. An elaboration of the idea of specification captures this process.

We reconcile conflicts in ends by a process of reciprocal specification. Faced with a conflict of ends G and O, we subordinate G to O, treating G as a means to O. We do this in a particular way: we specify G in light of O, producing $G^{1.0}$. Say I want to be a good parent and I want to succeed at work. I will be a good parent by finding a good child care professional so that I can go to work and succeed there. Now recall that a means to one end is usually the end of some other means. I want to succeed at work in order to satisfy my parents' aspirations for me; I will obtain as much education as I can in order to succeed at work; I will live frugally in order to get as much education as I can; and so on. This suggests that the specification of G in light of O, producing $G^{1.0}$, can be followed by the specification of O in light of $G^{1.0}$, producing $O^{1.0}$. Then we will take $O^{1.0}$ as an end that will produce a newly specified means, $G^{1.1}$. After this, we will take $G^{1.1}$ as an end that will specify $O^{1.0}$, producing end $O^{1.1}$; $O^{1.1}$ as an end that will produce $G^{1.2}$; and so on. This reciprocal process of conflict resolution among competing ends continues but never ends. In fact it can generate further conflict. End $O^{1.0}$ might also require a means other than $G^{1.1}$: P. Once P has taken its turn as an end specifying $O^{1.0}$, producing the means $O^{2.0}$, means $O^{2.0}$ then specifies P, producing $P^{1.0}$; and so on.

Say I have a job at which I excel (G), but that requires late hours, interfering with my ability to be involved in my son's life – specifically, to support his early, precocious efforts to achieve excellence as a violinist (O). I might change jobs ($G^{1.0}$), in order to provide this support (O). This change ($G^{1.0}$) might, in turn, require me to provide this support for those efforts (O) in particular ways. Because of my new job ($G^{1.0}$), I can no longer afford violin lessons. Fortunately I am a superb violinist myself, so I take on the role of violin teacher ($O^{1.0}$). In order to teach my son violin ($O^{1.0}$), I might leave work early on Tuesdays ($G^{1.1}$), so I can fit violin lessons into his busy schedule ($O^{1.1}$). But I will have to work late on Mondays ($G^{1.2}$), which means that I will be able to teach my son six days a week instead of seven ($O^{1.2}$). Teaching my son violin ($O^{1.0}$), however, might also require me to seek treatment for the tendonitis in my shoulder (P). In order to treat the tendonitis in my shoulder (P), I will have to put off starting the violin lessons for a time ($O^{2.0}$). In order to put off lessons for the least amount of time ($O^{2.0}$) – the point, after all, is to promote my son's musical development – I might schedule an appointment with a physical therapist at the earliest possible date ($P^{1.0}$).

These rounds of the reciprocal specification of conflicting ends are enlightening on the subject of an agent's responsibility in a way that tracking her means-ends reasoning or tracing the specification of a single end in increasingly specific intentions is not. Tracing these rounds of reciprocal specification provides information that an aretaic theory of criminal fault requires. Under an aretaic theory, the determination of criminal fault consists of an assessment of the quality of the defendant's practical reasoning. A meaningful assessment of this kind must go beyond the agent's matching of means to ends. The assessment of responsibility requires an inquiry into the ends themselves, and into the defendant's deliberation on ends. The reciprocal specification of conflicting ends is one kind of deliberation on ends, and tracing the courses of this specification is a way to assess the quality of the defendant's practical reasoning. If this continual, comprehensive kind of practical reasoning evinces deliberation on ends of a high order, then the defendant is not at fault, because she has met society's reasonable expectations in acting as those deliberations led her to act.

If the evaluation of motivating intentions beyond simple intentions can be said to broaden the evaluative field, then we might say that the specification of ends deepens the evaluative field. However, unlike the operation of motivating intentions, the reciprocal specification of conflicting ends and our evaluations of this kind of practical reasoning are not visible in criminal law doctrine and practice. But of course to show such operations is not required for an adequate response to the 'inadequate basis' objection. It is sufficient as a theoretical account if it explains what is going on behind the scenes, so to speak.

VI. CONCLUSION

I have attempted to show that we have a sufficient basis for an assessment of the quality of the defendant's practical reasoning for the purpose of determining criminal fault and moral desert for legal punishment. The intentional actions contained in offence definitions reflect more than a simple corresponding intention. They reflect a wide range of motivating intentions, and these are the subject of the law's evaluation of the quality of the defendant's practical reasoning. This aspect of criminal fault is reflected in the fact that criminal law is under constant pressure to expand offence definitions to incorporate objective fault criteria. The second reason to think that we have a sufficient basis for decision is that the deliberations examined in the adjudicative process are wide-ranging and – most important to an Aristotelian conception of responsibility – conducted in minute detail as action unfolds. With this explanation of intentions and ends, I hope to have taken an important step in developing an aretaic theory of legal punishment: describing the relationship between the intentional acts described in criminal prohibitions and the evaluation of practical reasoning that is at the centre of the aretaic theory's account of criminal fault.

REFERENCES

Aristotle, Martin Ostwald (tr) (1962) *Nicomachean Ethics* (Indianapolis, Bobbs-Merrill).
Bratman, M (1999a) 'Responsibility and Planning' in *Faces of Intention: Selected Essays on Intention and Agency* (Cambridge, Cambridge University Press).
——(1999b) *Intentions, Plans, and Practical Reason*, 2nd edn (Stanford, CSLI Publications).

Gardner, J (1998) 'The Gist of Excuses' 1 *Buffalo Criminal Law Review* 575.
Huigens, K (1995) 'Virtue and Inculpation' 108 *Harvard Law Review* 1423.
——(2000) 'The Dead End of Deterrence, and Beyond' 41 *William and Mary Law Review* 943.
——(2002) 'Homicide in Aretaic Terms' 6 *Buffalo Criminal Law Review* 97.
——(2011) 'Provocation at Face Value' 95 *Marquette Law Review* 409.
Strawson, PF (1974) 'Freedom and Resentment' in PF Strawson (ed), *Freedom and Resentment and Other Essays* (London, Methuen).
Watson, G (1987) 'Responsibility and the Limits of Evil' in F Schoenman (ed), *Responsibility, Character, and the Emotions* (Cambridge, Cambridge University Press).

9

Liberal Virtue

EKOW N YANKAH

WITH A FEW notable natural law exceptions, normative legal philosophy has been dominated for a generation by intricate debates between deontological and consequentialist theories. This debate has ignored those holding the quite common view that law guides our ethical well-being. Limiting the conversations to a binary clash between various liberal justifications, Kantian deontology and various consequentialist models, has prevented engagement (except in opposition) with those who believe that nurturing virtue is an important justificatory feature of law. The relatively recent rebirth of virtue ethics – or, as applied to law, virtue jurisprudence – presents an important alternative view of the normative justification of law and, in some ways, fills this gap. Proponents of virtue jurisprudence, particularly neo-Aristotelian variations, argue that a virtue-centred theory of law better justifies and explains important parts of law. Ignoring virtue theory-based intuitions cripples our ability to make progress on pressing legal questions. This is particularly evident in the disconnect between the conversation in the legal academy surrounding vice crimes, where common intuitions about the justified use of law are most viscerally tested. One particularly heartbreaking example is the American prohibition of prostitution which results in the legal isolation of tens of thousands of the most vulnerable women.

Academic work on prostitution is worth noticing for two remarkable features. The first is the breadth and the depth of academic positions advocating the decriminalisation of prostitution. Important intellectuals since John Stuart Mill have persistently argued for the decriminalisation of prostitution. That is not to ignore important voices raised in counter-argument – particularly one facet of modern feminist jurisprudence. Still, the bulk of scholarship highlights the harms of the legal prohibition of prostitution in America.

The second striking feature is the complete lack of effect of this sustained argumentation. In America, less than a handful of jurisdictions legally permit prostitution. The steady stream of urging has left legislatures unmoved. This is even more striking given the profound effect academic writing has had on other fields; the effect of the Law and Economics movement springs to mind. Academics are either wholly unheard or arguments that prostitution is morally harmless or reciting the commands of liberalism are missing something deep. This chapter attempts to find that missing piece, to find a way forward.

The problem with the arguments of liberal reformers, mirrored in the unwillingness of liberal theories to engage with virtue jurisprudence, is that they run counter to the deeply-held moral intuitions of many. What decriminalisation arguments miss is that there are sound moral reasons to believe prostitution is wrong, reasons that speak to me deeply. At home and particularly when travelling to countries where prostitution is public and endemic, I have always felt deeply that it would be flatly immoral to accept the solicitations of sex workers. Indeed, to lay my cards on the table, even in penning this piece, I am occasionally gripped by moments of doubt. Unlike those who have total confidence that philosophical conclusions settle the matter, I find it unsettling to write a piece on decriminalisation of prostitution. In this case, the political is personal. The belief that prostitution is morally wrong is a considered and deeply held one. At best, the current arguments seeking to reform prostitution laws ask people to do the very difficult, to set aside their sense of right and wrong or cabin them from the business of running a society. At worst, such arguments treat deeply held moral criticism dismissively.

Arguments that seek to convince others to discard long held moral commitments are, of course, not only acceptable but often essential scholarly projects. Much academic work pursues and advocates the most powerful arguments to convince others of one's position. Nor could a complex and heterogeneous society last long without boundaries between each person's personal morality and the requirements of law. Still, to the extent that theories of decriminalisation ask others to disregard core intuitions, one is unlikely to convince anyone who did not already agree with the position.

This is not a promising method for generating legal reform in the real world. While such debates generate great philosophical heat, one even hopes advancement, they are unlikely to garner the consensus needed to change the law. The problems surrounding prostitution seem intractable precisely because moral intuitions seem deeply divided. Thus, any progress which requires people to ultimately be convinced of the correctness of a unique set of philosophical views is unpromising, to say the least.

This is not merely a matter of abstract concern, a neat philosophical puzzle to be solved. The power of the state finds its most visceral form in the police bursting through doors, the power of arrest and imprisonment. Put bluntly, our inability to find a way to make progress on prostitution banishes tens of thousands of women from the protection of the law, condemning them to beatings at the hands of pimps and leaving them defenceless in a shadow world of sex slavery.

My claims are, at bottom, simple. Despite the efforts of reformers to persuade us that there is nothing immoral about prostitution, many find it morally repugnant. Indeed, not only do many Americans believe that prostitution represents some sort of moral harm but it is the immorality of prostitution more than anything else that keeps prostitution illegal. Inspecting the commonly offered arguments for the prohibition of prostitution reveals what many already know; these arguments offer little support for a prohibition and, in some cases, actually undermine the current laws. This should lead us to suspect that something else is going on here. What people care about in prohibiting prostitution is that it is wrong or immoral. Arguments which impeach deeply held convictions based on very particular metaphysics appear unconvincing at best and condescending at worst.

Without illustrating that one can support legal reform of our prostitution laws despite its immorality, reform efforts are a non-starter, leaving thousands of women abandoned by the law. Thus, it is critical to see that one can support the decriminalisation and regulation of prostitution despite viewing prostitution as immoral. Even virtue theorists, who are committed to the idea that law fundamentally serves to foster moral virtue in society, can take notice of the damage wrought by the current law and support reform. Again, from a wide range of moral starting points, one can support decriminalisation of prostitution even while convinced that prostitution is immoral.

I. A MORAL PROHIBITION

At first blush, the idea that the legal status of prostitution turns on moral objections to commercial sex seems like a philosopher's conceit. After all, it is rare that arguments surrounding prostitution are explicitly conducted in philosophical terms. Further, there is the constant difficulty of disentangling particular reasons that underlie any individual law. Given these difficulties, one cannot conclusively prove that moral objections are central to our ban on prostitution.

If one cannot prove that moral objections motivate the current criminal prohibition, one can reveal the unconvincing nature of the ostensible empirical justifications. When one inspects the commonly offered rationales for the ban on prostitution, what stands out is the difficulty of gathering precise empirical evidence given the illegality, secrecy and stigma that surrounds prostitution.[1] The problem is further complicated by the difficulty of disentangling the problems inherent in prostitution from those that arise because it is illegal.[2] Because sex workers are placed outside the legal system, their work may be pushed into close proximity with other illegal acts and actors. This uncertainty undermines confidence in justifications premised on particular controversial 'facts' about prostitution. Indeed, if the known research is accurate, it is startling how many of the commonly offered justifications for the ban on prostitution fail.

Let us start from the gravest of issues surrounding prostitution. Across the world, numbers of young women and others are coerced into becoming sex slaves, threatened, tortured and killed.[3] In America, where we too often imagine ourselves immune, numbers of illegal residents and underage girls are held against

[1] Law (2000: 535).
[2] ibid; Constant (1999: 103).
[3] Clements (1996: 52–53, 58).

their will and forced into prostitution.[4] Anyone exposed to these heartbreaking stories of human suffering needs no academic musing to understand their tragedy.

As critical as this is, there is no clear reason to believe that making prostitution illegal reduces instances of human trafficking. It is certainly worrisome that decriminalisation could increase human trafficking.[5] Yet, it is possible that the current model of American prohibition contributes to human trafficking.[6] Indeed, one might believe it increases human trafficking by placing sex workers outside of normal legal channels.[7] This problem is made worse by the widespread sexual abuse of sex workers by police officers.[8] The isolation and frayed trust make it even more difficult to garner information from sex workers on activities of vital importance, such as human trafficking.[9] Further, that prostitution is illegal may force sex workers into close proximity with other criminal behaviour, particularly drug-laden spaces.[10] Lastly, isolating sex workers forces them to find means of private enforcement, creating a vacuum for violent pimps.

The point is not that human trafficking is not a grave concern. Rather it seems unlikely that if one's motivation is to reduce human trafficking, a legal prohibition which isolates sex workers, forces them into the arms of pimps and cuts them off from the help of the police is a productive regime.[11]

A weaker version of the argument that prostitutes are forced into sex work focuses not on the total lack of consent seen in human trafficking but rather indicts the quality of the 'consent' given by prostitutes.[12] Here our aversion to prostitution does not seem to centre simply around the question of ensuring voluntary choice. The law routinely handles difficult issues of ensuring that agreements are voluntary in other contexts such as contract law. This no doubt indicates that much of what makes such bargains 'unconscionable' is that they are viewed as morally impermissible. There is a visceral rejection of the idea that some women might willingly choose prostitution as a livelihood.[13] Put another way, I suspect our current laws on prostitution do not truly take consent seriously.

Some view legal permission as a misguided attempt to permit choice. There are Marxist or Feminist critiques that deny that any choice to submit to prostitution can be considered authentic given the social power imbalance which (de)values women as merely sexual objects.[14] Others might think that given our knowledge

[4] Law (2000: 532–35). Though the numbers are hard to access, COYOTE (Call Off Your Old Tired Ethics), the most visible organisation advocating for the rights of prostitutes, estimates that 15% of women are forced into prostitution: Jenness (1993: 32).

[5] de Marneffe (2010: 37).

[6] ibid 37–38.

[7] Law (2000: 581–85).

[8] Silbert and Pines (1981: 387); Erbe (1984: 618).

[9] de Marneffe (2010: 35, 37–38); Law (2000: 581–85).

[10] Richards (1982: 92).

[11] Law (2000: 584).

[12] de Marneffe (2010: 5–7).

[13] Shrage (1989: 437).

[14] Jagger (1980: 259, 265–69); Shrage (1989: 442). I am also indebted to the clarifying treatment on this point in Havelková (2010).

that a disproportionate number of sex workers suffered sexual abuse in their youth, we should be sceptical of their 'choices'.[15] Still others will be rightfully concerned about economic pressures that leave some women with few options, thus undermining the voluntariness of their decision.

These are serious concerns which deserve more attention than can be afforded here. While I take seriously the point that structural inequalities inevitably inform the character of our choices, I am sceptical of the most extreme of Marxist and Feminist views which would eviscerate the possibility of authentic choice.[16] Indeed, there are powerful arguments that a view which makes women unable to choose what to do with their bodies borders on condescension. I do not attempt to settle this debate here. However, besides doubting the plausibility of the most extreme version of this critique, the fundamental structures of our law and our views of personal agency would have to undergo significant change to incorporate a view of structural inequality so deeply into legal consent.

Similarly, while prior sexual abuse may rightfully cause one to be concerned about the soundness and healthiness of a person's choice, it is harder to describe the choice as inauthentic. To do so is to construct an ideal counter-historical person whose choices stand as proxy. The law certainly does not undo the many unsound choices normal adults make as a result of their inner demons and broken pasts. Nor is the law normally willing to disable consent to engage in less-than-ideal work on the basis of economic circumstances.[17]

A couple of other contentions should be addressed briefly. The first issue is the public health dimension of prostitution. Those who came of age during the AIDS epidemic (and perhaps we all came of age during that fraught time) will not lightly shake the feeling of gravity that accompanies the public health dimension of prostitution. Though it is unclear the extent to which sexually transmitted diseases (STDs) are disproportionately linked to prostitution in America, it would clearly be irresponsible for any government to ignore the serious concern.[18] Yet again, it is hard to believe that legal prohibition which submerges the immense sex trade tackles rather than exacerbates the problem. Indeed, successes in controlling STDs in the domestic pornography industry and the few jurisdictions that permit prostitution are attributable to the rigorous health monitoring of an open industry.[19]

The last issue to which we need to attend is the 'public nuisance' aspects of prostitution. The moral status of these behaviours is controversial, particularly, whether behaviour which simply offends others is properly considered harmful. Additionally, as previously mentioned, some question the extent to which certain public nuisances that attend prostitution are a result, rather than the basis, of its legal prohibition.

[15] Dalla (2000: 348); Matthews (2007: 98); de Marneffe (2010: 98).

[16] Jagger (1980: 265–77).

[17] That is not to say that there can be no legally disabling or coercive circumstance, eg unconscionable bargains struck under duress. Indeed, I have argued elsewhere that in certain circumstances, some offers may be considered coercive. Yankah (2008a: 1229) and Zimmerman (1981: 144–45).

[18] Law (2000: 545–52); Center for Disease Control (1998); and Campbell (1991).

[19] Jordan (2005).

Nonetheless, if the goal of our criminal law is to curtail the public nuisance aspects of prostitution, direct regulation seems far more effective as well as far less costly.

There are other reasons why one might worry about a regime of decriminalised prostitution. Perhaps the availability of commercial sex threatens the integrity of marriages and families. Surely there are other unlisted concerns. However, it is hard to believe that many of these concerns are truly greater dangers in a world of decriminalised commercial sex than in our present world where commercial sex is equally widely available but legally prohibited. Thus we have reason to be sceptical that it is merely the social problems attendant to prostitution that have led to legal prohibition. What then explains the deeply held antipathy towards the decriminalisation of prostitution?

Whenever one encounters deeply held convictions, the strength of which vastly outrun the underlying empirical claims, it is well to search for principle or prejudice. Since the proffered reasons to prohibit prostitution are unconvincing and insufficiently supported by the sketchy empirical data, we are led to the unsurprising conclusion that there is something else at work. Specifically, the criminalisation of prostitution seems based in large part on a social conclusion that prostitution is a morally repugnant choice.

II. MORAL HARM

Others who have drawn attention to the fact that social norms underlie the current legal regime quickly dismiss the moral indictment of prostitution as misplaced, antiquated or parochial. In contrast, I believe the commonly held intuition that prostitution is morally wrong is based on sound moral reasoning. Unlike past authors, I will argue that one can understand the immorality from a range of moral positions; one need not be committed to any particular moral framework to believe prostitution is morally wrong. Nor does the immorality of prostitution simply supervene on the extrinsic problems that surround prostitution. Rather, it is in the very nature of the act itself. The common underlying sentiment that prostitution inflicts an objective moral harm on both the buyer and seller of sex is eminently sound and, more importantly for our purposes, supportable from nearly any philosophical tradition.

While the idea of an objective moral harm is not alien, at first blush it may strike some as perplexing. The intuition behind this puzzlement is this: if someone enjoys doing something which hurts no one else and does not regret it, how can this have harmed the person? Yet I am arguing that some actions constitute objective morally cognisable harm. Though it may be impossible in this brief section to convince those deeply committed to a purely relativist or sceptical view of moral wrongs, I hope the picture will be plausible enough for progress.

A moment for a bit of intramural clarification. In current philosophical discourse, a distinction is often made between moral duties, which govern the duties we owe to each other, and ethical duties, which are often self-regarding standards governing the construction of a good and valuable life. Roughly speaking, one has a moral duty not to unjustifiably kill others. One has an ethical duty to not waste one's life away only watching television.[20] While I often find this distinction valuable, I will not make use of it here. Because the philosophical systems at issue here take varying positions on being able to distinguish these two realms of morality, it is useful to not be distracted. Indeed, it is important to note that the idea of committing an immoral act need not be connected to a straightforward idea of 'harm' at all rather than one's failing a moral duty.[21] Here I will use the term moral harm to describe failing a wide range of moral or ethical duties.

A. Kantian Duties to Self

For Kant, the possibility of inflicting a moral harm on oneself is easy to recognise. In some of Kant's most accessible language, the great philosopher instructs us on the duties we owe to ourselves. This is not the place to begin a full exploration of Kant's sophisticated moral theory of duties. The upshot is that for Kant moral duties are grounded in a priori reasons, that is, reasons that are metaphysically true.[22] These duties are based on the fact that human beings have autonomous wills able to recognise reasons in the world.[23] These moral duties can be distilled into three formulations – categorical imperatives – which Kant assures us are equivalent, and only the second of which attracts our attention at the moment. The second formulation of the categorical imperative is, roughly, that people must be treated as ends in and of themselves and never as mere means. If an easy example is needed, making someone a slave is to treat them as a means – an instrument for your purposes – and not as a person with unique ends.[24] Thus, for Kant, human beings have an innate and inviolable dignity.

With that on the table, Kant argues that moral duties are not only owed to others but they are owed, indeed especially so, to ourselves.[25] Violating our moral duties to ourselves threatens our ability to fulfil our moral duties to others (and of the ability of others to count on our fulfilling our moral duties).[26] More importantly, violations of our self-regarding moral duties rob us of our inherent moral dignity.[27] Where we fail to pay ourselves the inherent dignity we deserve, we lose our self-worth and make ourselves the object of scorn and contempt.[28]

[20] There are, of course, complications to this rough and ready divide. As we will see, Kant conceived of some duties as self-regarding duties: Kant (1996: 149–52).

[21] I am grateful to Michael Moore for pressing this clarification.

[22] Kant (1996: 9–18).

[23] ibid 17–19.

[24] Kant (1998: 36–38).

[25] Kant (1930: 117–19).

[26] ibid 118, 123.

[27] ibid 118, 124.

[28] ibid.

Kant is unsparing in his criticism of prostitution. In fact, for Kant, it is fair to say that the whole topic of sex is challenging. Remember that the second formulation of the categorical imperative forbids using another merely as a means. Kant of course recognises that people in some sense play instrumental roles in our life; for most part the relationship with your plumber centres entirely on his instrumental value in sorting out your sink.[29] Unlike the slave, however, your hiring the plumber does not prevent him from planning a life, building a career and aiming that life at the ends he finds valuable.

So why is sex different? Kant argues that sexual appetite is qualitatively different from other instrumental desires. When you desire someone only sexually you do so apart from any of the other things about their personhood, you objectify them, you desire them only as a thing.[30] I do not wish to make Kant sound overly cynical; Kant of course understood that sex could be mixed with love and other deep emotions.[31] But we should be adult enough to admit that Kant is on to something. All sexually mature persons recognise that in sex and sexual desire, there are moments of sheer and lustful physicality; moments when our partners are very much bodies we simply want – to hold, to press, . . . well you get the idea. And to desire someone only as a body is to use them as a thing and ignore their inherent human dignity.[32] Sexual desire, 'taken by itself and for itself, . . . is nothing more than an appetite' and once sated, the object of desire may be cast aside as 'a lemon sucked dry'.[33]

The deeply sceptical will find all of this old-fashioned. If the contention is that sex is ultimately no different from any other service, it settles nothing to assume from the beginning that sex is different. This is the argument forwarded in a thoughtful article by Martha Nussbaum.[34] Nussbaum argues that in using their body for pay, the prostitute is indistinguishable from a range of other workers, say a philosophy professor or a masseuse.[35] Once these similarities are seen, she argues, there is little left of our stigmatisation of prostitution other than antique prejudices against working for money and cultural anxieties surrounding the female body now fashionably repackaged as commoditisation.[36] The dangers surrounding prostitution – coercion, the use of children and lack of other choices –

[29] ibid 163–68.

[30] ibid. Here Kant uses some of his prettiest language:

> Human love is good-will, affection, promoting the happiness of others and finding joy in their happiness. But it is clear that, when a person loves another purely from sexual desire, none of these factors enter into the love. Far from there being any concern for the happiness of the loved one, the lover, in order to satisfy his desire and still his appetite, may even plunge the loved one into the depths of misery. Sexual love makes of the loved person an Object of appetite; as soon as that appetite has been stilled, the person is cast aside as one casts away a lemon which has been sucked dry. Sexual love can, of course, be combined with human love and so carry with it the characteristics of the latter, but taken by itself and for itself, it is nothing more than appetite.

[31] ibid 166–67.

[32] Russell (1958: 121–22).

[33] Kant (1930: 166–67).

[34] Nussbaum (1998: 693–96, 700–07).

[35] ibid 700–07.

[36] ibid 696–700.

are universally intolerable and should not, by themselves, make us think that the exchange of sex for money is different.[37]

There is no point tiptoeing around it. Kant's argument is that sex is fundamentally different. It is undeniable that sex and sexuality play a large role in human development. One's sexuality is among the core features of one's identity. Physical assault is traumatic but rape is a particular horror because we intuitively perceive the centrality of sexual integrity. Further, sexual desire is complex and can bring in a range of emotions (or not, it is hard to know which is worse), baggage and risks. Sexual desire, like few other desires, runs the risk of objectifying its object. This very point is noticed by none other than Nussbaum herself in an earlier piece.[38] In this sophisticated piece, Nussbaum carefully teases out the many subtle ways in which sexuality can lead to objectification. Nussbaum wonderfully illustrates that not every instance of objectification is harmful, some in fact reaffirm our physicality.[39] Some forms of objectification, however, can ignore our full personhood and be deeply damaging to one's sense of self.[40]

What Nussbaum notices in her earlier piece is that sexual desire is susceptible to objectifying persons in a way that is, if not unique, rare in other areas.[41] One rarely fixates on the plumber. Just as importantly, sexuality is central to our identity in a way comparable to few other things. Work and family are critical to successful lives but few things are as potent a mixture of friendship, romance, attraction, self-esteem, love and desire as captured in sexuality. When sexual desire goes wrong, the damage to a person is unique. It is the moral importance of valuing one's sexual integrity and its susceptibility to objectification that is the foundation of the common moral perception that both prostitutes and 'Johns' debase themselves. It is this insight that is at the heart of the Kant's critical appraisal of sexual desire.[42]

So would Kant have us be celibate our whole lives? Of course not. From where will all the little Kantians come? Kant argues that sexual desire is attached to mutual concern for the person as a whole only through marriage.[43] Quite romantic, in its way. Sadly, how to get desire exactly right is not our topic. For our purposes the important point is that there are moral duties in the world owed to oneself and they include never treating another or allowing oneself to be treated as a means or a thing. This aspect of sexuality, while objectionable in any relationship, is brought into starkest relief in the typical case of prostitution where a client need not exhibit any care for the prostitute's sexual needs, desires, pleasures or well-being.[44]

[37] ibid 721–23.
[38] Nussbaum (1995) and Primoratz (1993).
[39] Nussbaum (1995: 398–404).
[40] ibid 404–05.
[41] ibid 393–94.
[42] ibid 118–19, 162–64.
[43] ibid 166–67.
[44] Nussbaum (1998: 394–96) and Russell (1958); but see Primoratz (1993: 462–66).

This is not some abstract idea. Take an example reported by a woman who worked briefly as a sex worker in Amsterdam. When a client's condom broke and she expressed concern to him about contracting AIDS, he simply laughed at her. 'The worst part of it was that the guy was so fucking unconcerned – he just laughed and said I was a good fuck.'[45] Sexual desire stripped of aspects of other-regarding love or concern can quickly and intensely obliterate our concerns for others – to be cast aside as a lemon sucked dry. The very passionate intensity that makes sexual desire an important facet of human life heightens the danger that concern for the other's well-being is swept away. To submit to another whose passion is empty of regard for your pleasures, well-being and humanity is to violate Kant's duties to self and thus constitutes a moral harm to self. It is happily clear to all who have had rewarding sexual experiences that this need not be the case. The important thing, just for the moment, is not that sexual desire can be done right but that one can get it wrong.

B. Aristotle and Aretaic Theories on Moral Wrongs

The aretaic theory exemplified by Aristotle is a natural one in which to locate a view of moral wrongs to oneself. Unlike Kantian deontological theories concerned with right action, Aristotle begins by asking what the highest achievable human goods are; what ends are the most worthy choices.[46] Aristotle concludes that this highest good is *eudaimonia*, uncomfortably translated as 'happiness', which more precisely translates to a life well-lived or a life of human flourishing.[47] Because humans are unique in being rational, *eudaimonia* consists of reasoning well in accordance with the human excellences over the course of a full life.[48] Such theories are also described as aretaic theories, stemming from the Greek word for good or excellence.

In this framework the many moral virtues are exemplified as a mean between two vices.[49] To be paralysed by fear when lightly threatened is to be cowardly. To be insufficiently cognisant of danger is to be rash. To be courageous is to act in accordance with the appropriate mean between these vices.[50] Because vices impede one's ability to live an excellent life and fulfil human capacity, they are morally harmful. The claim here is not overly abstract. People who explode in anger at the smallest provocation (or never get angry no matter how poorly they are treated) rarely do well overall in life.

[45] Chapkis (1997: 116) and de Marneffe (2010: 20).

[46] Aristotle (1941a: Bk I, ch VII).

[47] I set aside for the moment the long-running intramural debate surrounding Aristotle's shift to contemplation as the ultimate end of persons in Book X of the *Nicomachean Ethics*.

[48] Aristotle (1941a: Bk I, ch VII–X).

[49] Aristotle (1941a: Bk II, ch VII–IX).

[50] Aristotle (1941a: Bk II, ch VII, 1107a27–1107b3). To be sure, the virtues are dispositions rather than defined states. For greater precision on these thoughts, see Yankah (2009: 1174–75).

It is easy to see how this model produces a coherent view of committing a moral wrong unto oneself. The rash mountain climber who embarks on a trip certain to result in grave injuries that prevent her from other productive human pursuits fails to properly respect the place physical integrity has in fulfilling other human capacities.[51]

Given its affinity with natural law doctrines, one might think that Aristotelian virtue-based theories would easily align with viewing prostitution as a moral wrong. Yet there is reason to think Aristotle himself would not have found prostitution greatly objectionable. Various forms of prostitution, from the streetwalkers who occupied the bottom of the hierarchy to young boys of poorer families and higher status courtesans, were well known in ancient Athens.[52] To Aristotle, some poorer people were slated to live as prostitutes because he believed that many were incapable of developing to the same level as the Athenian upper class.[53] If those from the class of prostitutes could not have developed higher level capacities, they lost nothing in living a life of prostitution.

Obviously, this will not do. Without argument, I will set aside the position that the prostitution of poor women is harmless because the poor lack the natural capacity for better lives. We need to rescue the insights of Aristotle, unabashedly updated for our time.[54] Luckily, this is not difficult. We need only inspect Aristotle's ideas for those he believed possessed full human capacity. What then did Aristotle believe of the moral consequences of prostitution for the addressees of the *Nicomachean Ethics*?

On the subject of prostitution Aristotle is, well, demure. Aristotle notes that pleasures of the flesh, in which he includes eating, drinking and sex, are worthwhile in themselves but must be pursued in moderation.[55] Thus, if one's appetite for any particular pleasure is excessive, it becomes a vice; self-indulgence or licentiousness.[56] Assuming, however, that licentiousness is not the only reason one would hire a prostitute – say a man who enjoys the services of a prostitute once in a great while – one hardly shows the sort of incontinence Aristotle argues is a moral vice.

As we noted before, romantic relationships and sex play a deep role in human development. Sex, embedded in deep and meaningful relationships, is an expression of love, caring, sacredness, playfulness and physicality in ways that are missing in other sexual relationships. You need not believe that such sexual relationships are the *only* ones with *any* value to believe that sex with those characteristics fulfils greater parts of human lives. Sex reduced to commercial exchange takes away, distracts or

[51] Aristotle (1941a: Bk IV 1119b20–1120a20).

[52] Aristotle (1941b: Bk II, 1272a22-24); Ellis (1910: 218–54); Bollough (1964: 9–15); and Richards (1982: 88–89).

[53] Aristotle (1941b: Bk I, ch IV–VIII, Bk III, ch IV).

[54] There are those who see such updating as a squeamish inability to accept Aristotle's theory. I have never found such arguments persuasive. Theories need not be frozen in the past, and ideas grow. One can be attendant to the historical nuances of a theory without being saddled with its mistakes.

[55] Aristotle (1941a: Bk III, ch X–XI).

[56] ibid.

lacks that deeper value. It does not engage in the deepest human capacities and thus does not contribute to the richest life of human flourishing.

If engaging in prostitution corrupts one's proper understanding of the value of sex, this detracts from the fullest form of flourishing.[57] There is nothing strange about the contention that prostitution commonly takes away from the lives of those engaged in both sides of the practice. Working as a prostitute commonly injures the formation of psychological fitness and healthy character in just the ways those concerned with the promotion of virtue fear.[58] By its nature, prostitution associates sex with feigning emotions for gain and inculcates emotional manipulation and pretence. Worse, prostitution makes the development of capacities critical to human development more difficult – the formation of deep friendships, intimate and supportive relationships.[59] Lastly, engaging in prostitution often derails sex workers from paths in which one normally develops their capacities through discipline, such as schooling.[60] Similarly, those who purchase sex from prostitutes learn to relate to sex as something to be purchased and enjoyed for their pleasure only. In doing so, 'Johns' harm their ability to appreciate the proper role of sexual intimacy and risk retarding or undermining their ability to form intimate relationships.[61]

It is hard to argue how important a healthy sense of one's sexuality is to the formation of character. Equally, it would be a strange view which did not instantly see that the ability to form important, intimate and loving relationships is essential to a flourishing life. It is one thing to decide to remain single, it is another to be unable to find or sustain a relationship. The retardation of these virtues and excellences of character and the way they detract from a life of flourishing are both intuitively and for Aristotle the crux of self-inflicted moral harm.

Of course, such corruption is not necessarily limited to prostitution. The libertine who comes to regard sexual partners as shallow and interchangeable pleasures risks similar injury.[62] Still, the archetype of this devaluation, this moral injury, finds purest expression in prostitution; even the playboy must charm his affairs, engage with them and treat them as more than mere commodities.[63] The buyer of sexual services almost entirely dispenses with that, disconnecting sex from any other values (flirtation, friendship, mutual caring or love) that it plays in the landscape of a flourishing life. When viewed in conjunction with Aristotle's views regarding the value of friendship, one can see that prostitution constitutes a moral harm-to-self.

[57] This need not be reduced to an extreme picture – one encounter with prostitution leaves one permanently unable to experience genuine romantic well-being (Nussbaum (1998: 713–14)). We need only note that prostitution may distract or corrupt one's views of the value that sex can play in the richest of lives.

[58] de Marneffe (2010: 13–15).

[59] ibid 13–15, 22–26, 120–22.

[60] ibid.

[61] ibid 120–22.

[62] ibid 48.

[63] ibid.

I do not expect to have convinced all of the unassailability of objective moral claims. Important philosophical views – scepticism, relativism and others – and further permutations of the views represented here remain unexplored. Each of these philosophical branches has developed in myriad and sometimes conflicting ways. But in both important philosophical systems explored, one recognises that prostitution constitutes an objective moral harm-to-self. While the agreement is not dispositive, for Kant and Aristotle agreed on much we would no longer affirm, the arguments above do, I hope, make the concept of an objective harm-to-self plausible.

III. MORAL WRONGS AND THE LAW

The next step in our argument is a crucial one. Notwithstanding that Kantian deontology and Aristotelian virtue-based theories consider prostitution morally harmful, it does not follow that the law ought to prohibit it. Plainly, I am not the first to argue for a separation between immoral acts and legal prohibition; many take this to constitute one of the foundational tenets of liberalism. Still, even among liberals, there are some interesting distinctions that the conversation highlights. Most notably, the conversation frames the debate differently from the mainstream justification for liberal tolerance, which turns on uncertainty and pluralism about forms of the good life. Rather, the conversation above presupposes the immorality of prostitution. The claim explored here is in many ways a deeper claim than that which grounds much of modern liberal theory.[64]

More importantly, my claim is not limited to liberal justifications of decriminalisation. One may oppose the legal prohibition of prostitution even though it is a moral wrong, whether one is a Kantian liberal or rejects liberalism entirely and is committed to law's role in promoting virtue. This bears underscoring; it is not only liberals who can agree on the reform of this controversial area of criminal law. Though both Kantian and Aristotelian philosophical traditions viewed prostitution as a moral self-injury, there remain good reasons to be cautious of legal prohibitions.

For some this argument proves much too little. Many reformers argue that the perception that prostitution is immoral is mistaken or antiquated folk superstition. Alternatively, the mainstream of liberal political theory asserts that liberal neutrality requires the separation of many deep moral commitments from law. Why should anyone be attracted to an accommodationist argument that seeks agreement over metaphysical truth or comprehensive political theory?

[64] A less common rationale for legal toleration of moral wrongs focuses on an interesting mix of instrumental goods protected by the securing of legal space. It may be that allowing such space creates a social ethic of toleration which will solidify our tolerance towards genuinely good forms of living (Wall (2003: 242)). Secondly, it may be that 'people must live by their own lights' in order to be happy (Dworkin (1989: 486); Kymlicka (1995: 81); Waldron (1993)). Though these 'instrumental autonomy' views are certainly closer, even they do not fully capture the justification I want to explore.

There are two reasons to prefer the accommodationist model, one, itself, ironically accommodationist in flavour. First, those interested in reforming the current criminal law regime need not agree that prostitution is immoral. For those who believe prostitution is morally innocuous or are committed to a view of liberalism that cabins personal moral judgement from law, it will be enough to agree that we have reasons to reform the current failed legal regime.[65]

The second reason is more meaningful and reverberates in both practical and philosophical reasoning. The practical rationale is quite straightforward. Much ink has been spilled by liberal reform-minded theorists attempting to persuade us that prostitution is morally non-problematic. It is unlikely that much progress on reform will be made by convincing large numbers of those who deeply believe that prostitution is immoral to change their minds and hearts in the short term. And why should they? As we have explored, it is morally sound to believe prostitution is immoral. Requiring others to give up their deeply held and well thought-out convictions in favour of a very particular philosophical framework makes great philosophical and political discourse; it does not, however, make for a promising path to political action.

But if this seems like just a practical problem – a matter of opinion polling and playing to prejudice – it belies a deeper philosophical claim. The fact that the body politic contains a wide range of philosophical and political commitments is not a mere inconvenience. That very fact is the morally relevant landscape with which theories of governance must contend. As Rawls and Waldron, among others, have explored in different ways, a diverse range of fundamental philosophical commitments *is* the problem of politics.[66] Theories that begin with the presumption that all must be committed to particular philosophical starting points may be enlightening political philosophy but they are not theories of governance.

To be clear, I am not decrying the important project of pure philosophical debate. In different moods, I too attempt to marshal arguments to persuade others of my particular metaphysics.[67] Many political advances owe some part to relentless pressing of claims of equality and rigorous inspection and discarding of unsupportable ideas. Nonetheless, any theory of governance, as opposed to pure political philosophy, that does not make space for reasonable disagreement, itself borders on being unreasonable and is certainly doomed to failure.[68] The inability to notice fundamental areas of philosophical consensus when seeking to govern is all too often unreasonableness masquerading as high-minded rigour.

With this in mind, we are in a position to inspect the core argument. Despite the fact that deontologists and virtue theorists have ample reason to view prostitution as immoral, it is remarkable that each theory gives reasons to pause before translating the moral conclusion into law. Inspecting both theories leads us to the

[65] Greenawalt (1984); Sunstein (1995); and Rawls (1985).

[66] Rawls (1993) and Waldron (1999).

[67] For a contrast, see Yankah (2009), arguing for a rigorous commitment to Kantian and Hegelian deontological theories in law.

[68] Rawls (1985).

startling conclusion that nearly all of us, starting from a wide range of fundamental moral theories, can agree on fundamental reform.

A. Kant, Criminal Law and Freedom

For Kant the moral worth of an action turns not only on whether one obeys the moral duties but that one does so with a pure will.[69] Thus, being forced to comply with your moral duties, indeed, doing so out of any prudential reasons, robs an action of moral worth.

For the unfamiliar, the distinctions between Kant's moral and legal theory may seem sharp. As mentioned earlier, Kantian moral duties could be recognised by reasoning from a priori truths. Thus to truly fulfil your moral duty is to act only in light of recognising the reasons that ground your duty. If you act for other reasons, for example, to avoid punishment, you are not acting purely in light of the moral value of your duty. In Kantian language, to act for moral reasons alone is to act autonomously, whereas to act from prudential reason is to act heteronomously.

The nuances between Kantian autonomy and heteronomy could provide a career's worth of exploration. Only the basic distinction is necessary for this project. If moral duties depend on acting with a pureness of will for moral reasons alone, then law, which for Kant is constituted by coercive sanctions, is not the stuff of moral duty.

In Kant's framework law is not a matter of moral duty but concerns itself with violations of the external freedom of others; in Kantian language, law is not a matter of morality but of justice.[70] Criminal conduct is not founded in the purity of will that determines the moral worth of one's acts but rather is centred on external action.[71] The nature and justification of state law is to enforce perfect duties to others, the duties of external performance that interfere with the rights of others.[72] In this way criminal law belongs to the realm of justice which differs from Kantian duties of morality.[73]

Even as Kant highlights the significance of our self-regarding moral duties, he repeatedly reminds us that moral duties, especially those owed to oneself, are not a matter of justice and cannot be proscribed by law.[74] Kant explains, 'My duty to myself cannot be treated juridically; the law touches only our relations with other men; and whatever I do to myself I do to a consenting party; I cannot commit an act of injustice against myself.'[75] He repeats elsewhere, '[j]urisprudence should

[69] Kant (1996: 13–14).

[70] ibid 13–14, 19–21, 139; Kant (1965: 231); and Fletcher (2007: 208).

[71] Kant (1930: 116–17, 157), (1965) and (1996: 13–14). George Fletcher attempted to capture this important distinction as one between the *Wille* and the *Willkür* (Fletcher (1987); Fletcher (2007: 208)).

[72] Kant (1930: 116–17, 157); Murphy (1987: 519); and Binder (2002: 353).

[73] Binder (2002: 355–56).

[74] Kant (1930: 116–17, 157).

[75] ibid.

concern itself only with man's duties to his neighbor, with what is lawful and unlawful, but not with duties towards oneself'.[76]

It is this separation between the legal and moral which has led a generation of legal theorists to build their models of liberal legal rights on Kantian foundations.[77] So it is surprising that Kant causally concludes that prostitution, a violation of a duty to oneself, is appropriately outlawed.[78] How could so many Kantian liberals in the academy have been led so wrong? A closer look at Kant's brief reasoning leaves room to doubt that Kant based a prohibition of prostitution on any deep commitments. To quote, Kant argues, '[i]t is important to provide for public decency, for if the feeling for decency (*sensus decori*) – considered as negative taste – is not benumbed by the prevalence of beggars, excessive street noises, offensive odors, and public prostitution, all of which violate the moral sensibilities, then the business of ruling the people through laws is made considerably easier for the government.'[79]

Only two things need be noticed regarding the separation between law and morality. The first is that prostitution is placed in a list including beggars, excessive noise and offensive odours. This hardly speaks of a deep moral violation. Rather, Kant focuses on the nuisance aspects of crimes familiar to decriminalisation advocates who focus on harm reduction. Secondly, the only justifying feature Kant highlights is maintaining public morals in order to govern more effectively. If these are the only reasons, other regulation that controls public nuisance aspects of prostitution would meet Kant's burden. In any case, it is clear that Kant's argument for the prohibition of prostitution is not deeply founded on a view of moral harm.

Given that the public nuisance of prostitution can be more effectively handled by regulation, we have good reason to mind Kant's contention that the realm of law should concern violations of others' rights and not self-regarding duties.

B. An Aristotelian Theory of Law

Though it would seem that Aristotle's claim that law ought to promote human flourishing through virtuous behaviour would be easy to translate into a prohibition against prostitution, it once again turns out to have important nuances. Legal philosopher Lawrence Solum has recently explored the shape of a legal system built on Aristotle's virtue of justice.[80] Though Aristotle viewed law as having a role in inculcating virtue, he also took into account the special role law serves in secur-

[76] ibid.

[77] Richards (1982: 84–127). Here the word autonomy is used in its lay rather than purely Kantian sense.

[78] Kant (1965: 92).

[79] ibid.

[80] Solum (2006). There are, of course, other strategies one might take to build an aretaic theory. Kyron Huigens, eg, has developed an aretaic theory of punishment over many years which, while originally Aristotelian, parts from Aristotle in many ways. See Huigens (2002).

ing a flourishing human society. Given this goal, it may seem that lawmakers and judges ought to aim at promoting ethical lives. The problem, of course, is that there is persistent and deeply held disagreement about what constitutes an ethical life. Thus, if each lawmaker were to act on her own conception of the good, it would lead to endless clashes, ironically undermining the conditions for human flourishing.

An aretaic system of law then ought not to allow lawmakers to render legal decisions based on their first-order views of what is moral.[81] Rather, Solum proposes that the virtue of justice in an aretaic theory is governed by Aristotle's virtue of lawfulness – a judge's recognition and internalisation of the publicly-reached decisions on public controversies.[82] These public conclusions need not be only law but may include the widely-held stable norms and customs of the society as well. Lawmakers in such a model have deeply internalised the shared norms of the community; in Aristotle's language they are *nomimos*. Further, laws on this model are only truly laws if they comport with the society's norms, the *nomoi*.

For Solum, the aretaic justification is integrated in two ways into his model. First, the *nomos* must themselves be aimed at promoting human flourishing. Thus, to the extent that social norms are directly opposed to human flourishing, they may not qualify as true *nomos*.[83] Moreover, the virtue of justice is only one part of human flourishing. To the extent that lawfulness conflicts with human flourishing, the aretaic lawmaker must re-examine the value of lawfulness in her society. The aretaic lawmaker must, above all, be sensitive to the conditions that allow for human excellence. In Aristotle's language, a virtuous law-giver must display practical wisdom or *phronesis*, he must be *phronimos* as well as *nomimos*.[84]

While the details are complex, the upshot is intuitive. The ultimate question on this picture is not whether each law requires virtuous behaviour. Rather, it is to what extent a legal regime nurtures virtue and a flourishing society. Say alcohol is viewed as detracting from a life of virtue, a claim which if not universally true certainly applies to a significant range of cases. If the prohibition of alcohol leads to generalised disrespect for the law among the public, millions of dollars for criminal syndicates and a reign of widespread violence and terror, then surely prohibition cannot be considered robustly supported by a virtue-centred theory of law. A view that focuses only on the prohibited acts and ignores all other effects of a law on the health, virtue and flourishing of a society is too narrow to be a plausible view of virtue-centered governing.

The question for an aretaic system of law is not simply whether prostitution is a moral wrong that retards virtue in a person – we have reasons to believe it is. The question is whether outlawing prostitution will contribute on the whole to a flourishing society. It is possible that criminalising prostitution prevents people from making important decisions about the role of work and sexuality in their lives,

[81] Solum (2006: 87).
[82] ibid 89–91.
[83] ibid 97–98.
[84] ibid.

something which is necessary for one to develop into a successful person.[85] Perhaps sound practical reasoning requires the ability on occasion to exercise poor reasoning.[86] While this position is plausible it strikes me as inconvenient from Aristotle's point of view. Aristotle, after all, made front and centre the role of law in shaping the ability of citizens to learn virtuous behaviour.[87]

More plausibly, the intrusive methods necessary to criminalise and enforce prostitution laws may be too damaging. Similarly, the effects of criminalisation on the success of a society must be taken into account. The criminalisation of prostitution marginalises commercial sex workers. This marginalisation forces prostitutes into proximity with other illegal behaviour, particularly drug dealing, thus increasing the risk to the workers themselves.[88] Further, prostitutes must secure private enforcement mechanisms, in a word, pimps.[89] This means that the legal regime greatly contributes to the violence visited on sex workers. Adding not just insult but injury to injury, the legal marginalisation of prostitutes leaves them not just feeling outside of the protection of the law but perversely the victims of police violence. Prostitutes often feel, with good reason, that they cannot report instances of sexual violence to the police. Prostitutes report widespread sexual and physical abuse by police officers.[90] Surely the fact that both prostitutes and police perceive sex workers as criminals contributes to this high rate of victimisation.[91] Tragically, the marginalisation and distrust between sex workers and police surely make gathering information to combat the tragedy of human trafficking more difficult.[92]

There are less dramatic effects of the legal prohibition on prostitution which nonetheless undermine a flourishing society. The prohibition on prostitution makes the health monitoring of prostitution difficult, posing a public health risk. Further, because prostitution can neither be regulated nor eradicated, the current regime makes it difficult to control public exposure to sexual solicitations. Those living in major metropolitan areas are familiar with the 'bulge' effect of prostitution; increased policing in one area does little other than to shift streetwalkers to different neighbourhoods.[93]

Lastly, it is worth noting that the illegality of prostitution commits us to a callous social hypocrisy. With no chance that prostitution will come to an end and some doubt as to whether we are willing to dedicate more than a symbolic (yet costly) effort to enforcement, the current legal regime turns a blind eye to the widespread law-breaking and inculcates a casual disregard for the law in much of the public. Prostitution is readily and effortlessly available in any barely sizeable city, yet as the violence and suffering of the legal prohibition is borne by poor and

[85] de Marneffe (2010: 32–35).
[86] ibid; Waldron (1993).
[87] Aristotle (1941a: Bk X, ch IX, 1179b32–1180a4).
[88] de Marneffe (2010: 8, 35) and Richards (1982: 92).
[89] de Marneffe (2010: 41).
[90] Thukral (2005).
[91] ibid 10, 13, 35–36.
[92] de Marneffe (2010: 35, 37–38).
[93] ibid 31.

minority women, we turn a blind eye while congratulating ourselves on our moral commitment.

To put it much too lightly, even given that prostitution is immoral, it is not obvious that the current legal regime contributes to a virtuous society.[94] Thus, there is no need to assume that an aretaic theory would necessarily outlaw prostitution – at least not in its current form.[95] Even those who believe it is the duty of law to nurture virtue, those who reject liberalism, can agree that the current prohibition of prostitution fails to promote a flourishing society.

I have no wish to pretend to have found a way to universal agreement. Theories based on Millian utilitarianism, though I believe they would be in accord, have not been explored here. For those who are committed to a divine theory of law, a belief that God has forbidden prostitution may foreclose any agreement on the grounds above. I have serious doubts that at least Christians, whose example in Christ personified unbounded care for the weak and disenfranchised, including the harlots of his time, can turn their back on the suffering inflicted by the current regime. But beyond my own religious upbringing, I am unqualified to pursue this topic in full. Further, as I have mentioned, there is an important debate among feminists about the status of prostitution, with some feminists contending that the ban against prostitution infantilises women and reflects male ideals of purity.[96] Other feminists powerfully argue that in a society dominated by male power, prostitution is an extension of male domination, a form of violence against women or an inauthentic choice. Those deeply committed to this latter view may be unconvinced by the arguments above.

Still, the arguments above have shown that the idea that prostitution could be legalised is not as controversial as one might initially assume. Despite their very different commitments, Kantian deontological thinkers and Aristotelian virtue theorists all have a concept of self-inflicted moral harm. It is of course important to remember that each system conceives of this harm in different ways; Kant focused on the moral duties owed to oneself in light of human dignity and Aristotle on the ethical demands of living a good life and engaging the human capacities. Nonetheless, the core idea of an objective moral harm-to-self can be located in each system.

Despite agreeing that prostitution results in self-inflicted moral harms, both philosophical systems are cautious about translating this moral wrong into a legal prohibition. Kant actually encouraged the prohibition of prostitution but, as we noted, grouped this prohibition along with public noise and odour. Prostitution was viewed as a public nuisance contributing to disorder. Outside of that concern, Kant reminds us that moral duties owed to oneself are immune from legal enforcement. For

[94] Pearl (1987) and Law (2000: 527, 532–35, 584–85).

[95] As far as I am aware the only time Aristotle seems to allude to prostitution is a quite oblique reference to dancing girls for a festival, implying that the guards should ensure they are paid no more than their contracted salaries. Whether it is best understood as a toleration of a certain unavoidable level of prostitution or an attempt to make sure it does not occur is not entirely clear (though it seems to intimate sexual services as a part of the contract): see Aristotle (1984: 96).

[96] Law (2000: 542–45) and Nussbaum (1998: 708).

Aristotle, the ultimate value of law was the role it played in sustaining a flourishing community. That there is agreement between these vastly different philosophical systems, so often used as foils for each other, is remarkable. Nor should one easily dismiss the separation of law and morality as an old liberal trope. The reason this accord is so remarkable is because it is across the range of philosophical systems. It is not strictly limited to liberalism; even those who reject liberalism can support the reform of the current prostitution laws.

If one is philosophically inclined and finds the preceding arguments convincing, surprise may quickly turn into disappointment. How can these major philosophical systems be in agreement regarding the legal permissibility of prostitution and yet the law be nearly universally opposed? Does no one listen to philosophers?! It is to the problem of translating philosophical commitment to law that we now turn.

IV. AN (IN)DECENT PROPOSITION

What are we to do in light of these conclusions? Put another way, were I king, would I snap my fingers and legalise prostitution? Of course not. Does that make me disingenuous? Well, no. Philosophical conclusions, even if true, do not apply themselves. Though theory necessarily takes facts into account, one of the great benefits in submitting a question to philosophical examination is the ability to stipulate facts in order to arrive at important conclusions (I mean, has any one ever seen a veil of ignorance?). Once reached, however, philosophical tenets must be applied to the unruly world, where facts and complications spill one over another, refusing to behave. Much more would have to be known about the facts of prostitution on the ground before a wise statesman would decide to legalise prostitution. To borrow a phrase, philosophy does not get us all the way down. Or there are more things in heaven and earth than are dreamt of in philosophy, if you prefer. This does not mean, however, that the preceding is academic fancy. If the gravity of the issues counsel the wise to move deliberately, it is important to realise how our philosophical conclusions can guide us.

What then can we learn from the philosophical agreement we have discovered? Each system examined gave good reasons to be wary of criminalising prostitution even given that prostitution is immoral. Just as striking, reviewing the major concerns commonly cited in support of the ban on prostitution reveals that we can find remarkable accord regarding the shape and limits of a policy of decriminalisation.

The gravest issue we explored surrounding prostitution is the tragedy of human trafficking. No one could support lifting a ban on prostitution that resulted in the exacerbation of people being forced into prostitution. Not surprisingly, no one we have examined does. Unjust coercion is paradigmatic of the violation of external freedom that grounded law in Kant's legal model. Similarly, the Aristotelian justification for law was its special role in securing the conditions for human flourishing. No one could argue that a legal regime which abetted in people being forced into sexual slavery was a form of flourishing. Thus, the justification of this regulation remains dependent on its ability to combat coercion in the sex industry.

Another issue that related to prostitution is its public health dimension. Once again, there is a plausible philosophical accord on this issue. A Kantian will view the spreading of disease as an invasion of another's external freedom. This is because the public health threat is in large part that a disease will pass beyond those who knowingly subject themselves to the risk.[97] Similarly, aretaic theories of law, focused on the flourishing of society, will be especially concerned with the unregulated spreading of dangerous and debilitating disease among the population. It takes little argument to understand that serious illness can uniquely harm the ability of persons to live a life of excellence and fulfil their human capacities. As explored, the decriminalisation of the sex industry better allows for health monitoring.

The last issue we need to address is the 'public nuisance' aspects attendant to prostitution. As I mentioned earlier, the moral status of these behaviours is not without controversy. There are questions of whether behaviour which simply offends others, take suggestive dressing, is properly considered harmful, and the extent to which many of the public nuisances surrounding prostitution are a result of rather than a reason for legal prohibition. Nonetheless, there are reasons to believe that the public nuisance aspects of prostitution can threaten important social values.

Here too we see that the philosophical positions explored above are in harmony. Kant is explicit in his concern for the public nuisance facets of prostitution. As earlier explored, Kant placed prostitution with excessive noise and odour, focusing on its public nuisance aspects.[98] The extent to which the public nuisance of prostitution made society harder to govern justified legal regulation. Likewise, aretaic law that focuses on the flourishing of society cannot ignore the unregulated confrontation of sexual information on children who may not yet be ready to understand and contextualise it. Indeed, the moulding of the young so that they could independently choose virtuous behaviour was of particular importance to Aristotle.[99] Additionally, allowing avoidably unruly exchanges surrounding sexual services to create a public nuisance is in tension with an orderly and flourishing community.[100] Again, we have noted that regulation allows for more effective management of public nuisance.

In sum, restraining the translation of moral harms-to-self to legal harms does not mean the complete absence of regulation. Again, vastly different philosophical systems recognise that there are justifiable grounds for legal regulation of a

[97] One can recognise a different level of risk assumed by a person who has multiple sexual partners, including prostitutes, and a person who has a single long-term partner who, unbeknown to them, has had a sexual liaison with a prostitute. The deceptive partner would violate the right of the duped.

[98] Kant (1965: 92).

[99] Aristotle (1941a: Bk X, ch 9, 1179b32–1180a4).

[100] I do not wish to imply that everything that is unruly is opposed to a flourishing community.

self-regarding harm such as prostitution. If prostitution, for example, is inextricably linked with violations of the rights of others, such as in human trafficking and other coercive sexual violence, there is surely reason to regulate it. To the extent that prostitution poses a public health risk, the government may act. Where aspects of commercialised sex result in behaviour which cause a harmful public nuisance, regulation is appropriate.

The philosophical agreement we have noticed does not counsel a society to completely forgo regulation of the moral harm caused by prostitution; rather, it provides guidance as to the kind of regulation that is justified. It is striking that despite the philosophical accord on the basic shape of such regulation, our current legal regime adopts little of this guidance. I fear it is because the legal regime produced, though legitimate and wiser, is initially unattractive in permitting admittedly immoral behaviour.

A. Choosing Moral Harm

As opposed to our current regime of criminalisation, regulation takes consent seriously. Its principal legal distinction is that it permits consenting adults to exchange sexual services for money. It does so despite the firm conviction that doing so is a self-inflicted moral harm. For the multiple reasons that we have explored, people have the right to choose to do wrong. Regulation preserves the choice of a person despite our view that they commit a self-regarding wrong.

It is important to see how our consensus differs from the current run of decriminalisation proposals and more fully addresses broader concerns of virtue theories. Because regulation is not based solely on liberal autonomy, it remains sensitive to the need to secure the conditions of a flourishing society as represented here by Aristotle.

There remains one concern which until now has been discussed only elliptically. The current ban on prostitution, I have argued, turns in large part on the fact that significant numbers rightfully think it is immoral. By the same token, the decriminalisation of prostitution is difficult because politicians and other political actors would face the wrath of those same people as voters were they to advocate such a policy. Individual political actors have much to lose and little to gain for protecting prostitutes, even if such a policy were the right thing to do. There is a high political cost and, tragically, no political gain in attempting to spare tens of thousands of women from rape, violence and fear.

To some extent, this chapter is an attempt to address that political cost. By illustrating that there can be broad overlapping consensus from wide-ranging fundamental philosophical starting points, it is hoped that the conventional assumption that prostitution is simply too controversial to address is exposed as untrue. One cannot claim universal assent – important omissions are the important positions in feminism and divine-will theories of law that cannot be brought into agreement. Yet we have seen that major foundational philosophies under-girding our law agree with the common sense intuition that prostitution is immoral, yet caution against prohibition while converging on sensible regulations of sex work. Highlighting this agreement dissolves the assumption that the tension between liberals and those who reject the most stringent forms of liberalism is intractable. Hopefully, recognising and respecting the common moral intuition that prostitution is immoral while illustrating the tragic dimensions of prostitution arms political actors with the arguments needed to address this grim industry which hides in plain sight.

One last concern deserves some attention. Even if consensus succeeds, it is worth asking if the moral costs to a society are too high. Prostitution is a moral wrong and decriminalising may have the moral cost of legitimising it as a plausible way of life. Secondly, a regulatory regime, if successful, would change the way prostitution currently occurs. In particular, an ancillary goal of the rise in price of sexual services would create a society with a particular unattractive feature; a society where the wealthier are free to purchase the sexual services of another and indulge in expensive immoral behaviour others cannot afford. There is a way in which such a regime makes sin a luxury item.

I admit to not having a knock-down answer for these charges. All things considered, I suppose it comes down to a matter of choosing between suboptimal conditions. Our choice is not prostitution or no prostitution but rather more or less and, most of all, what form of prostitution. On the one hand is a world in which prostitution is an openly acknowledged and regulated field, sparing tens of thousands of vulnerable women from violence, rape and death. On the other, our current world in which commercial sex is equally acknowledged but is winked at while violence is looked away from. I may shake my head in sadness but I choose the first.

V. CONCLUSION

Let me conclude by returning to the philosophical project. In concluding, it is as important to point out what I am not arguing as it is to be persuasive for what I am proposing. Let us begin with what I am not arguing.

I have, like many liberals, argued elsewhere that people have a right to commit certain wrong acts, acts that do not harm others. Prior work has focused on the intersection of analytical jurisprudence and criminal theory, arguing that the shape of law and its inherent coerciveness places certain political restraints on the state.[101] That set of arguments concluded that for reasons grounded in the relationship between autonomy, moral agency and identity, virtue is inappropriate as a basis of legal duty.[102] In this chapter, however, I have steadfastly avoided basing the argument for decriminalising prostitution on any deep commitments

[101] Yankah (2009), (2008b) and (2008a).

[102] Yankah (2009: 1208–11) and (2008a: 1254–55).

to unique philosophical premises. I have not argued, as much of mainstream liberalism does, that decriminalisation should be based on the notion that there are plural forms of the good life which citizens should be free to pursue. Similarly, I have not taken the related and familiar tack of arguing that moral uncertainty means the law cannot appropriately legislate.

Here instead I have adopted an approach which takes exactly the opposite view on two levels. First, eschewing deep commitments to any particular theory, I have argued that the two vastly different philosophical traditions in the western world, traditions typically used as foils to test our moral intuitions, have a surprising degree of agreement on what is often considered a deeply controversial topic – prostitution and moral harm. The foundational thinkers of both traditions had no problem conceptualising certain actions as a purely moral harm. Perhaps others will wish to argue that the moral status of trading sex for money is indeterminate or non-harmful, but that is not my position.

Nor are my arguments based on any particular liberal view of the bounds of the state's legitimate actions. Indeed, the very point argued is that the agreement exists regardless of whether one holds a liberal view of the state or not. I do not wish to overstate this; the reasons each philosopher suggests for restraint are importantly different. Yet it is striking how much accord can be found amidst differences which can be soundly extrapolated even to details. It is remarkable on how much those who take starkly different starting points as to first principles can agree. It is also worth noting that while prostitution has been the focus here, there are other places where philosophical accord can provide powerful guidance to the law. There will surely not be agreement on every problem, even on everything that represents a moral harm-to-self. But rather than consistently prosecuting a body of law rooted in one controversial philosophical view, progress may be made by seeing where there is overlap.

This would seem too obvious to say if it were not so painfully far from our actual circumstances. What is remarkable is that this great accord seems to have so little effect on the actual shape of either our criminal law regime or, in most places, our public discourse. Prostitution, in an uncritical response to a collective moral 'ick', results in our continued prohibition and isolation of tens of thousands of vulnerable women. Given that there is so much to agree on, that we too easily ignore sensible accord and condemn untold numbers to a life of violence and legal banishment is tragic.

REFERENCES

Aristotle, WD Ross (tr) (1941a) 'Nicomachean Ethics' in R McKeon (ed), *The Basic Works of Aristotle* (New York, Random House).

——(1941b) 'Politica' in R McKeon (ed), *The Basic Works of Aristotle* (New York, Random House).

——(1984) PJ Rhodes (tr), *The Athenian Constitution* (New York, Penguin Classics).

Binder, G (2002) 'Punishment Theory: Moral or Political?' 5 *Buffalo Criminal Law Review* 321.
Bullough, BL and Bullough, VL (1964) *The History of Prostitution* (New York, New Hyde Park).
Campbell, CA (1991) 'Prostitution, AIDS, and Preventive Health Behavior' 32 *Social Science and Medicine* 1367.
Chapkis, W (1997) *Live Sex Acts: Women Performing Erotic Labor* (New York, Routledge).
Clements, TM (1996) 'Prostitution and the American Health Care System: Denying Access to a Group of Women in Need' 11 *Berkeley Women's Law Journal* 49.
Center for Disease Control, United States of America, 10 HIV/AIDS Surveillance Report 1 (Dec 1998).
Constant, M (1999) 'Federalism, The Mann Act, and the Imperative to Decriminalize Prostitution' 5 *Cornell Journal of Law & Public Policy* 99.
Dalla, RL (2000) 'Exposing the "Pretty Woman" Myth: A Qualitative Examination of the Lives of Female Streetwalking Prostitutes' 31(4) *Journal of Sex Research* 344.
de Marneffe, P (2010) *Liberalism and Prostitution* (Oxford, Oxford University Press).
Dworkin, R (1989) 'Liberal Community' 77 *California Law Review* 479.
Ellis, H (1910) *Studies in the Psychology of Sex* (Philadelphia, FA Davies Co).
Erbe, N (1984) 'Prostitutes: Victims of Men's Exploitation and Abuse' 2 *Law & Inequality* 609.
Fletcher, GP (2007) *The Grammar of Criminal Law* (Oxford, Oxford University Press).
——(1987) 'Law and Morality: A Kantian Perspective' 87 *Columbia Law Review* 533.
Greenawalt, K (1984) 'The Perplexing Borders of Justification and Excuse' 84 *Columbia Law Review* 1897.
Havelková, B (2010) 'European Gender Equality Under and After State Socialism: Legal Treatment of Prostitution in the Czech Republic' (M.St. Thesis, manuscript on file with the author).
Huigens, K (2002) 'Homicide in Aretaic Terms' 6 *Buffalo Criminal Law Review* 97.
Jagger, A (1980) 'Prostitution' in A Soble (ed), *The Philosophy of Sex: Contemporary Readings*, 2nd edn (Maryland, Rowman & Littlefield Pub Inc).
Jenness, V (1993) *Making It Work: The Prostitutes' Rights Movement in Perspective* (New York, Aldine de Gruyter).
Jordan, C (2005) Note, 'The XXX-Files: CAL/OSHA's Regulatory Response to HIV in the Adult Film Industry' 12 *Cardozo Journal of Law & Gender* 421.
Kant, I, Gregor, M (tr) (1996) *The Metaphysics of Morals* (Cambridge, Cambridge University Press).
——(1998) *Groundwork of the Metaphysics of Morals* (Cambridge, Cambridge University Press).
——(1965) Ladd, J (tr) *Metaphysical Elements of Justice* (Indianapolis, Bobbs-Merrill Co).
——(1930) Infield, L (tr) *Lectures on Ethics* (New York, Harpers & Row).
Kymlicka, W (1995) *Multicultural Citizenship* (Oxford, Oxford University Press).
Law, SA (2000) 'Commercial Sex: Beyond Decriminalization' 73 *Southern California Law Review* 523.
Matthews, R (2007) *Prostitution, Politics and Policy* (New York, Routledge-Cavendish).
Murphy, JG (1987) 'Does Kant have a Theory of Punishment?' 87 *Columbia Law Review* 507.
Nussbaum, M (1995) 'Objectification' in A Soble (2002) (ed), *The Philosophy of Sex: Contemporary Readings*, 4th edn (Maryland, Rowman & Littlefield Pub Inc).

Nussbaum, M (1998) 'Whether from Reason or Prejudice: Taking Money for Bodily Services' 2 *Journal of Legal Studies* 27.
Pearl, J (1987) Note, 'The Highest Paying Customers: America's Cities and the Costs of Prostitution Control' 38 *Hastings Law Journal* 769.
Primoratz, I (1993) 'What's Wrong with Prostitution?' in A Soble (2002) (ed), *The Philosophy of Sex: Contemporary Readings*, 4th edn (Maryland, Rowman & Littlefield Pub Inc).
Rawls, J (1985) 'Justice as Fairness: Political not Metaphysical' 14 *Philosophy & Public Affairs* 223.
—— (1993) *Political Liberalism* (New York, Columbia University Press).
Richards, DAJ (1982) *Sex, Drugs, and the Law: An Essay on Human Rights and Overcriminalization* (New Jersey, Rowman and Littlefield).
Russell, B (1958) *Marriage and Morals* (New York, WW Norton & Co).
Shrage, L (1989) 'Should Feminists Oppose Prostitution?' in A Soble (2002) (ed), *The Philosophy of Sex: Contemporary Readings*, 4th edn (Maryland, Rowman & Littlefield Pub Inc).
Silbert, M and Pines, A (1981) 'Occupational Hazards of Street Prostitutes' 8 *Criminal Justice & Behavior* 387.
Solum, LB (2006) 'Natural Justice' 51 *American Journal of Jurisprudence* 73.
Sunstein, C (1995) 'Incompletely Theorized Agreements' 108 *Harvard Law Review* 1733.
Thukral et al (2005) 'Revolving Door: An Analysis of Street-based Prostitution in New York City' (New York, Urban Justice Center, available at www.urbanjustice.org/pdf/publications/RevolvingDoor.pdf).
Waldron, J (1993) 'A Right to Do Wrong' in *Liberal Rights: Collected Papers 1981–1991* (Cambridge, Cambridge University Press).
—— (1999) *Law and Disagreement* (Oxford, Oxford University Press).
Wall, S (2003) 'The Structure of Perfectionist Toleration' in S Wall and G Klosko (eds), *Perfectionism and Neutrality: Essays in Liberal Theory* (Lanham, Rowman & Littlefield).
Yankah, EN (2008a) 'The Force of Law: The Role of Coercion in Legal Norms' 42 *University of Richmond Law Review* 1195.
—— (2008b) 'The Law of Duty and the Virtue of Justice' 27 *Criminal Justice Ethics* 67.
—— (2009) 'Virtue's Domain' *University of Illinois Review* 1167.
Zimmerman, D (1981) 'Coercive Wage Offers' 10 *Philosophy & Public Affairs* 121.

10

Virtue, Vice and the Criminal Law – A Response to Huigens and Yankah

RA DUFF

I. INTRODUCTION: HOW CRIMINAL LAW COULD BE CONCERNED WITH VIRTUE

IT IS WORTH distinguishing two kinds of role that ideas of virtue and vice might play in the criminal law (or in our theoretical understanding of the criminal law). Each kind admits of a range of variations; each can be more or less ambitious in scope and aim: but although there are of course quite close connections between the two kinds, we can usefully sketch them as two different ways of developing a virtue jurisprudence of criminal law. Both kinds of role are connected to views of the proper aims of a system of criminal law: in the first case, a view of the further goods that criminal law should aim to achieve; in the second case, a view of the proper objects of criminal liability.

The first kind of role flows from the thought that if the state, or the political community of which the state is the formal apparatus, has a proper interest in the moral character of its citizens; if it should aim to promote, encourage or foster virtue, and to prevent, discourage or inhibit vice: perhaps it can use the criminal law as one means towards that end. An ambitious role of this kind would use criminal punishment as an instrument of moral improvement: the, or at least a, proper aim of punishment is to promote virtue or to remedy vice. Conceptions of criminal punishment as moral education belong here,[1] as do more old-fashioned conceptions of punishment as a process of spiritual reform or renewal. This most obviously favours such sentences as probation, but some would argue that imprisonment can also serve this end: the isolation to which prisoners used to be subjected was meant to free them from the corrupting influence of their fellows, and enable them to concentrate on penitential contemplation. (Even capital punishment was, notoriously, supported on these grounds by an English bishop, who opposed its abolition because it could induce some impressive death cell repentances.) Less ambitiously, even if criminal punishment cannot be expected

[1] See eg Morris (1981) and Hampton (1984): for criticism see Shafer-Landau (1991).

positively to foster or develop virtue, criminal law could play an important role in guarding against (the development of) vice, or in protecting some of the preconditions for the development of virtue. We could, for instance, proscribe modes of conduct that are likely to encourage vice (either in the agent or in others),[2] in particular (if we follow Aristotle on the crucial role played by habit),[3] modes of conduct that would foster vice if allowed to become habitual; we could, more ambitiously, prescribe modes of conduct which would, if they became habitual, foster virtue. We could, that is, use criminal law and punishment as ways of directly fostering virtue and preventing vice; or as ways of preventing the conditions that are liable to lead to vice, or of securing the conditions under which virtue might develop.

The second kind of role also concerns the proper aims of criminal law, but it concerns the proper objects of criminal liability rather than the further goods that criminal law might bring. The suggestion now is that vice, or lack of virtue, bears on whether someone should be liable to criminal conviction and punishment. On the most ambitious version of this role, vice is the direct object of criminal liability: what we should be held criminally liable, and punished, for is precisely some moral vice or defect of character; so-called 'character' theories of criminal liability make this claim.[4] A different, and slightly less ambitious, claim would be that vice or lack of virtue is a necessary condition of criminal liability, although not its direct object.[5] On such a view, what we are held liable for, what we are convicted and punished for, is not vice itself as a character trait; we are liable to conviction and punishment for what we do or fail to do – for our actions. But we are liable only on condition that those criminal actions flow from or reveal a vice; or, on an even less ambitious version, we are liable unless our actions can be shown to flow from virtue.[6] The difference between these two kinds of view, between taking vice to be a direct object of liability and taking it to be a condition of liability, matters in part because the latter makes it possible to ward off the familiar objection to virtue theories that, whatever we might say about moral judgements, we should be criminally liable only for what we do, not for what we are: on a 'condition' view, we are indeed liable for what we do, and judgements of virtue or vice become relevant only when we inquire into the further conditions under which we are or are not liable for a criminal action.

It might seem that, although one can analytically distinguish the two kinds of role that I have distinguished here, they must in practice go together: if a proper aim of the criminal law is to promote virtue or inhibit vice, surely it can best do this precisely by holding us liable for our vices (or for those actions in which our

2 Compare Yankah's comments on prostitution in Yankah (2012: section III B).

3 Aristotle, *Nicomachean Ethics*, Bk II.

4 For different versions, see Bayles (1982); Brandt (1985: 165); Lacey (1988) (but see Lacey (2011)); and Huigens (1995).

5 On the distinction between objects and conditions of liability and its significance, see Duff (2007a: ch 4.3).

6 Compare Kahan (1998).

vices are revealed); correlatively, if we ask why it should take vice to be either the object or a condition of criminal liability, the obvious answer is that this is because its proper aim is to promote virtue or inhibit vice.[7] But the connection is not as tight as this. For, first, if our interest is in promoting virtue or inhibiting vice, we might think that the criminal law can best assist that goal by proscribing not (or not only) conduct that itself manifests vice, but (or but also) conduct that might encourage vice or make it more likely that people will become or remain vicious; and such conduct need not itself be vicious or manifest vice. Second, if we ask why the law should make vice an object or a condition of criminal liability, the answer might refer not to any further purpose that the criminal law might have of promoting virtue or inhibiting vice, but to some more retributive notion of desert. It might offer a modern version of Stephen's notorious thesis that criminal law is 'in the nature of a persecution of the grosser forms of vice', in order to gratify 'in a regular public and legal manner' the 'feeling of hatred – call it revenge, resentment or what you will – which the contemplation of such conduct excites in healthily constituted minds'.[8] Or it might appeal instead to the negative retributivist principle that punishment is just only if it is deserved, and that it is deserved only by those who culpably commit crimes – adding that the commission of a crime is culpable only if it flowed from or manifested a vice. Although the two kinds of role can be easily combined, they can therefore be separated; a theorist can assert one without asserting the other.

The two chapters that directly concern us here nicely illustrate these two possible roles for ideas of virtue and vice in the criminal law. We will turn to them shortly, but should deal first with two other preliminary matters.

The first is to note that on any plausible conception of criminal law, virtue is certainly not necessary to the avoidance of criminal liability, nor is vice sufficient for liability; indeed, if our virtue theory is Aristotelian, vice is not necessary for liability. Virtue is not necessary for the avoidance of liability because the criminal law does not, and could not plausibly aim to, take an interest in why we refrain from what it defines as crimes, or do what it requires of us. A person might refrain from theft, or hand a purse that someone has dropped to the police, because she respects others' property and has the virtue of honesty; she might see this not as a matter of obeying the law, but simply as a matter of doing what is morally appropriate (and if she is really honest, it might not occur to her to do anything else). Another person might refrain from theft, or hand in the dropped purse (on this particular occasion, or as a general policy), not from honesty or a concern for others' property, but because he knows that theft is criminal, and that to keep what he knows to be another's property counts in law as theft, and thinks that the prospective benefits of breaking the law are not enough to outweigh the costs of

[7] Compare eg Huigens (1995: 1424–25): the purpose of criminal law is 'to promote the greater good of humanity' by 'promoting virtue', which it does 'by inquiring into the quality of practical judgment displayed by the accused in his actions'; what grounds liability is the offender's 'faulty reasoning'.

[8] Stephen (1973: 152).

being caught and punished.[9] The former is virtuous; the latter is vicious, if he would steal were it not for the prospect of suffering punishment: but both are innocent in the eyes of our existing criminal laws, nor is it plausible to suggest that we should criminalise the latter. The slogan that we incur criminal liability for our actions, for what we do rather than merely for what we are, is neither clear nor clearly true,[10] but any plausible virtue theory will hold that we should be criminally liable only when we manifest our defective character in action (or in an omission) that is discernibly criminal; the law is not going to inquire into our motives for refraining from what it defines as crimes.

Furthermore, whilst some character theorists, in particular those inspired by a Humean conception of culpability,[11] talk in quite general terms about the defective character traits that can ground liability, theorists who talk of virtue and vice in Aristotelian terms should bear in mind Aristotle's distinctions between virtue and self-control (*enkrateia*), and between vice and weakness of will (*akrasia*).[12] If I break someone's car window in order to save the animal or child inside who has clearly been overcome by the heat, I have a defence against a charge of criminal damage even on the most demanding 'reasons' account of justification,[13] since I not only do the right thing, but do it for what the law counts as the right reason. This remains the case even if I have to resist my initial inclination to hurry on by so as to avoid being late for an appointment (or simply to avoid fuss): but in that case I display what must count for an Aristotelian as self-control rather than virtue, and my practical reasoning is not as it should be; I am tempted by, and so have to resist, something that would not have figured at all in the practical reasoning of a truly virtuous person. Even in the context of justificatory defences, virtue is therefore not necessary to avoid liability.[14] Nor is vice necessary for liability, since weakness of will suffices: one who weakly gives in to the temptation to steal might thereby display not the vice of dishonesty (the kind of commitment to wrong ends that Aristotelian vice involves), but *akrasia* – a failure to hold fast to and to act in accordance with appropriate ends that are still in a sense her ends; but she is guilty of theft nonetheless. The distinction between virtue and *enkrateia* seems to have no relevance to criminal law; that between vice and *akrasia* might figure at sentencing, but seems irrelevant at the stage of conviction.

[9] He is the 'bad man' whose perspective Oliver Wendell Holmes notoriously urged us to take if we 'want to know the law and nothing else', 'who cares nothing for an ethical rule which is believed and practised by his neighbors [but] is likely nevertheless to care a good deal to avoid being made to pay money, and will want to keep out of jail if he can': Holmes (1897: 457).

[10] See further Duff (2007a: ch 5).

[11] Hume (1978: III.iii.1): see eg Bayles (1982) and Lacey (1988: ch 3).

[12] Aristotle, *Nicomachean Ethics*, Bk II, Bk VII.1-10.

[13] On the controversy between 'deeds' theorists who argue that justification in criminal law does not depend on the agent's reasons for acting, and 'reasons' theorists who argue that justifications should be available only to those who act for the right reasons, see eg Gardner (2007: 91); Robinson (1997: 95–124); Fletcher (1978: 555–66); and Duff (2007a: ch 11.4).

[14] I will discuss later (at nn 46–50 below) the person who acts in order to help someone in need, but only because he hopes for a financial reward: he too has what the law recognises as a defence, since he acts for the right reason, but in so acting he displays neither virtue nor admirable *enkrateia*, given the further reasons for which he acts.

The second preliminary matter is to declare my own hand: that virtue theory can play at most a modest role in criminal law, one that is significant only in the context of certain kinds of excusatory defence. In general, and for good reason, the criminal law takes no interest in the moral character, the virtue or vice, that underpins and may be expressed in our actions: it is focused on what we do, and sometimes on the relatively immediate intentions with which we do it, as in crimes of so-called 'ulterior intent';[15] but although the criminal or non-criminal character of our actions depends partly on the immediate intentions, beliefs and attitudes with or in which they are done, the law's offence definitions and general criteria of liability need not look deeper than that. Some reference to virtue or vice does plausibly figure in such defences as duress (when it serves as an excuse), since we can best interpret that defence as claiming that the defendant's act was motivated by a reasonable (non-vicious) emotion, and did not display a culpable lack of the modest kind of courage or commitment that citizens properly demand of each other.[16] One could of course then say that when the defendant has no such excusatory defence, he is criminally liable because his action does display a lack of minimal civic virtue, or does manifest some relevant vice or defect of character – that such a defect of character is at least a necessary condition of criminal liability. First, however, that is a long way from saying that such vices or defects of character are the objects of criminal liability, as more ambitious virtue theorists claim. Second, vice is on this view not so much a condition of liability as a defeasible presumption: it is not, that is, something that the prosecution needs to prove as part of its case; rather, proof of the elements of the offence – a proof that need not reach beyond the action and the immediate intentions that structured it – amounts to proof of criminal guilt unless the defence can adduce evidence of an exculpatory defence. If guilt is proved, if no such defence is offered, we can infer that the defendant's act flowed from a defect of character – although we do not yet know, and need not care, whether that defect constituted vice or *akrasia*, or just what kind of defect it was; but that is a matter of what we can infer, if we wish, rather than of what we must establish in order to prove guilt.

To say that virtue and vice are not generally relevant to the law's definitions of offences, or to the general criteria of criminal liability, is not of course to say that they are irrelevant to the whole system of criminal justice: in particular, it is not to say that they must be irrelevant to sentencing. They could bear on sentencing either as conditioning just what the convicted defendant deserves by way of punishment, as mitigating or aggravating factors; or as bearing on what kind of penal treatment is needed if the offender's moral character is to be restored or improved. Here too, however, caution is needed if the criminal law is not to transgress the – admittedly

[15] Including eg such general offences as attempt, such specific offences as assault with intent to kill, and possession 'with intent' offences such as possession of prohibited drugs with intent to supply them. See generally Horder (1996: 153).

[16] See Duff (2002) and (2007b: 90). A similar interpretation can be given of the rightly controversial partial defence of provocation, on which see Horder (1992); for a useful recent discussion see Gardner and Macklem (2001).

far from sharp – boundaries set by a liberal respect for privacy. Someone whose attack on another was unusually cruel, or despicably exploitative of the victim's vulnerability, might receive a heavier sentence than would otherwise have been imposed; someone whose killing of a spouse was motivated by love or compassion might receive a lighter sentence,[17] as might someone whose theft could be attributed to momentary weakness of will rather than to true vice: but the focus is still on the action and on the intentions or practical attitudes that it directly manifested, rather than on any deeper or more lasting character traits from which it might have flowed. Similarly, we might hope that the punishment that an offender undergoes will (depending on the spirit and the context in which it is administered) help him to reform himself, and we must certainly try to ensure that it does not hinder such self-reform: but this is more a matter of providing a context and structure within which offenders can embark on that process than of trying directly to engage with their moral characters – with their souls.[18]

I noted above that the two chapters under discussion here illustrate the two roles that ideas of virtue or vice might play in the criminal law, or in our understanding of its proper aims and principles. Ekow Yankah is concerned with the character and force of the argument that we have Aristotelian reason to criminalise prostitution as 'a moral harm-to-self', which 'corrupts one's proper understanding of the value of sex', and thus 'detracts from the fullest form of flourishing': if 'nurturing virtue is an important justificatory feature of law', we have reason to criminalise something that is so inimical to virtue.[19] Kyron Huigens focuses instead on the role that lack of virtue plays in the constitution of criminal fault: 'retrospective assessments of criminal fault in adjudication are particularist evaluations of the quality of the defendant's practical reasoning'[20] – which implies that ethically defective practical reasoning constitutes not merely a condition of criminal liability, but at least an essential dimension of its object. I will deal with each of their arguments in turn in the following two sections.

II. SHOULD WE CRIMINALISE (WHAT CONDUCES TO) VICE?

Many of the reasons we have for criminalising, if not prostitution itself, some or many of the activities involved in it, concern not the inherent character of selling sexual services, but the ways in which prostitution as actually practised involves the coercive exploitation of the weak and vulnerable. Yankah's focus, however, is on the moral character of prostitution as an activity of selling sex, however voluntary and uncoerced such selling might be: he points out the grounds on which both Kantians and Aristotelians should regard that activity as immoral – as mor-

[17] Compare Huigens' discussion of the husband who kills his wife: Huigens (2012: 161–63); and see further at nn 41–44 below.

[18] See further Duff (2001: chs 3–4).

[19] Yankah (2012: 180–81).

[20] Huigens (2012: 156).

ally harmful to both the seller and the buyer. He does not, however, argue either that prostitution should be criminalised or that Kantians and virtue theorists should recommend its criminalisation: the main point of his chapter is to argue that both Kantians and Aristotelians can recognise prostitution as a moral wrong but oppose its criminalisation. The reasons that he cites for virtue theorists not to criminalise prostitution itself are well taken: it might well not serve the aretaic aim of promoting virtue, and has other clearly harmful effects; there are other ways of achieving our aretaic aims, and other ways of regulating prostitution, that are likely to be more effective at lower moral cost. I want to focus here, however, on what that discussion presupposes: on the suggestion that a virtue theorist will or should see good reason to criminalise prostitution, in virtue of its character as 'a moral wrong that retards virtue in a person';[21] in virtue, that is, of the moral harm that it does to prostitutes and to their clients – and would still do even if their exchanges, and the practice as a whole, were wholly voluntary and free of coercion. As Yankah recognises, this will provoke liberal objections to the effect that even if prostitution is in this way immoral, its immorality belongs to the 'private' realm that is, as a famous English report put it, 'in brief and crude terms, not the law's business'.[22] His concern is to show that we can oppose its criminalisation without settling that dispute; my concern is with whether a virtue theorist who shares Yankah's view of the immorality of prostitution is thereby committed to seeing reason to criminalise it.

The point is an important one, and brings out a crucial difference between a Kantian view and the aretaic view that Yankah offers. For Kant, the inherent wrongfulness of prostitution gives us no reason at all to criminalise it.[23] Criminal law is properly concerned with duties of justice; criminalisable wrongs are those that interfere with the rights of others. But consent, as the slogan has it, negates injustice: *volenti non fit iniuria*.[24] What I voluntarily do to myself cannot therefore constitute injustice, nor can what I do to another with his or her free consent; from which it follows that in genuinely voluntary prostitution neither prostitute nor client can be committing an injustice – unless their actions impinge on the rights of third parties. They might so impinge if they are committed in ways that cause offence, in which case we would have reason to criminalise them, as Kant thought we have;[25] but the inherent wrongfulness of the act itself cannot, from a Kantian perspective, give us any such reason. On the aretaic view that Yankah sketches, by contrast, we do have good reason to criminalise prostitution, since the law has a proper concern with any conduct that either conduces to or impairs virtue; to determine whether we should, all things considered, criminalise it we must thus look further, to the likely effects and costs of doing so.

[21] Yankah (2012: 185).

[22] Wolfenden (1957: para 61).

[23] See the account of Kant's view of criminal law in Yankah (2012: section III.A).

[24] On the role of this slogan in a liberal theory of criminal law, see Feinberg (1984: 115–17) and (1986: ch 19).

[25] Yankah (2012: 184).

This kind of virtue theoretic approach to the criminal law thus shares a central feature of legal moralism – a feature that one does not need to be a card-carrying liberal individualist to find disturbing: we have good reason to criminalise any and every kind of moral wrong, even if we also have other and better countervailing reasons not to criminalise many kinds of moral wrong.[26] Indeed, given the scope of Aristotelian virtue theory, and the way in which it (quite rightly) undermines the orthodox distinction between the moral and the ethical, such a virtue theoretic approach to criminal law stretches its potential bounds even wider than does a more classical legal moralism. If I spend too much of my time watching rubbishy television programmes (and perhaps in this context any time is too much time), I am failing to develop or to exercise my more worthwhile human capacities, which 'detracts from the fullest form of flourishing' that I could otherwise achieve; so we have, it seems, reason to criminalise either the watching, or the making, of such programmes – although we will also, no doubt, then find stronger countervailing reason not to do so. But is it at all plausible, even for those who agree that a polity takes a proper interest in its members' moral character, to suggest that we have any reason at all to wield the force of the criminal law in this context? Must a virtue theorist argue that we do?

There are two ways in which a virtue theorist can try to avoid this position, and thus to be a firmer liberal, at least on this issue, than Yankah's virtue theorist. The less radical of these is to accept that an aretaic polity has a proper interest in promoting any and every virtue and in hindering and eliminating any and every vice, but to deny that the criminal law is even in principle an appropriate way of pursuing such ends. Of course, if we see the criminal law as just one among a range of techniques or instruments that a polity might employ to achieve its aims, we must allow that the criminal law can in principle be used for this aretaic purpose; the question of whether and how it should thus be used becomes the question that Yankah discusses, of whether it would be an efficient way of pursuing such aims. Such an approach, however, fails to take the criminal law seriously as a distinctive kind of institutional practice: we must ask not merely whether criminalisation would be useful as a technique for achieving the polity's aims, but whether and when it is appropriate, given its distinctive character.

What is that distinctive character? The most obvious distinctive feature of criminal law is its focus on wrongs.[27] The point is not just that, as many theorists would agree, only wrongs should be criminalised; it is that criminal law makes the wrongness of that with which it deals salient. It defines certain kinds of conduct as public wrongs that merit condemnation as such, and its integral aim is to give effect to that condemnation. It does this in part by its offence definitions, and in

[26] Compare Moore (1997: chs 1, 16) for a non-aretaic version of legal moralism: the proper function of criminal law is to further retributive justice by punishing 'all and only those who are morally culpable in the doing of some morally wrongful act', although countervailing considerations will in the end rule out criminalising many kinds of wrongdoing. See also Moore (2009).

[27] Some would say that it is focused not just on wrongs but on wrong*doings* (eg Moore (1993)): but that would beg the question against the virtue theorist. But see Duff (2007a: chs 4–6).

part by the punishments that it authorises, if we understand punishment (as distinct from mere 'penalty') as essentially censorial;[28] it also does this through the criminal trial, as a process in which those accused of public wrongs are called to answer to their fellow citizens.[29] Criminal law is thus a formal analogue of moral blame: it involves holding people responsible (calling them to answer) for moral wrongs for which they deserve condemnation by their fellow citizens (unless they can offer an exculpatory defence).

Now suppose we accept that prostitution constitutes 'a moral harm-to-self' that 'detracts from the fullest form of [aretaic] flourishing': if 'nurturing virtue is an important justificatory feature of law',[30] this commits us to being willing to use the law to discourage prostitution. We might do this in various ways – most obviously by authorising social services to try to work with prostitutes and their clients; but are we now committed to being willing to use the criminal law in pursuit of this end – in particular to being willing in principle to criminalise prostitution? Perhaps not. For we might argue that whilst prostitution is morally imprudent, while it both displays and is liable to foster an ethically flawed understanding of the proper role of sexuality in human life, it does not constitute the kind of wrong for which its agents should be called to answer or blamed. For on the kind of Aristotelian view to which Yankah appeals, there are moral or ethical failings or imperfections that do not constitute wrongs, and modes of moral or ethical appraisal and engagement that do not constitute blame. We can see someone's sexual habits and attitudes, for instance, as ethically imprudent, misguided, even as morally self-harming; we can try to persuade him to share this understanding and change his ways: but we need neither blame him for what he is doing (and becoming), nor believe that he is blameworthy.

If we were to pursue this line of thought, we might appeal to a version of the distinction between ethics and morality that Williams made central to his critical discussion of 'morality, the peculiar institution',[31] and develop a fuller account of the difference between blame and other modes of moral or ethical appraisal and engagement;[32] we would also need to discuss the different ways in which different modes of appraisal implicate responsibility as a matter of answerability. I will not pursue this route here, however, since I am not sure that it offers the liberal virtue theorist what she needs. We might argue that our ethically flawed sexual understanding and attitudes are not themselves proper objects of blame, and therefore that they are not themselves proper targets of the criminal law: but it is harder to deny that the kinds of conduct which foster such flaws and failings are blameworthy as wrongdoings; so once we allow that such flaws and failings are of proper concern, in principle, to the polity, it will be hard to deny that we have

[28] See Feinberg (1970: 95). For more recent accounts that emphasise the communicative significance of punishment, see von Hirsch (1993) and Duff (2001).

[29] For this conception of the criminal trial, see Duff, Farmer, Marshall and Tadros (2007).

[30] Yankah (2012: 169).

[31] The title of ch 10 of Williams (1985).

[32] For a useful discussion that bears on this, see Fricker (2010) and Brady (2010). See also Williams (1995: 35).

reason, in principle, to criminalise those wrongdoings that foster them. The liberal virtue theorist will do better to offer a more radical argument, which denies that these aspects of ethical or moral life and character are even in principle the proper business of the polity – and thus that they are, even in principle, the business of the criminal law.

A liberal polity is of course, on this view, properly interested in the virtues and vices of its citizens; it will of course use the law in various ways to promote virtue and to discourage vice; it will see reason to use the criminal law to mark out and to provide for an appropriate, condemnatory response to kinds of conduct that culpably manifest vice. It does not, however, take a legitimate interest in *all* virtues and vices, or in *all* aspects of its citizens' flourishing; it is properly interested only in those aspects of ethical flourishing, only in that subset of virtues and vices, that count as 'public' rather than as 'private'. To explicate this possibility fully we would need to articulate a virtue-theoretic account of the proper aims and scope of a liberal polity – a task on which I cannot embark here; all I can do is indicate the direction that such an account might take.

Virtue-theoretic liberals might most naturally appeal to a version of republicanism which takes seriously the idea of civic virtue.[33] The aspect of republicanism on which individualist liberals are liable to focus is precisely its concern with virtue: those who aspire to a polity or state that is drastically limited in its depth (in the interest that it legitimately takes in the more inward dimensions of its citizens' lives) will object that it is one thing to take an interest in citizens' actions, and in the intentions or choices by which they are immediately informed, but quite another and a less legitimate thing to inquire into the deeper attitudes, motives and character-traits from which those actions, intentions and choices flow (hence the attractions of contractualism). But the aspect that is more relevant here is the focus on civic virtues as a particular category of virtues. A republican polity can operate, as liberals demand that any polity should operate, with a distinction between the public and the private: between those aspects of our lives, of our selves, that properly concern the whole polity simply in virtue of our membership of it, and those that are not the polity's, or the state's, business. As citizens, we are mutually engaged (like it or not) in the civic enterprise of living together in the polity, and the polity takes a proper interest in those aspects of our lives and selves that bear directly on the civic enterprise. But while a radically communitarian polity could take an ambitiously all-embracing view of the civic enterprise, as including all aspects of its members' lives (in the way that, for instance, an enclosed religious community might understand itself and its self-defining enterprise), there is nothing in the idea of a republic, or of the civic enterprise, that makes this necessary; a more liberal republic would recognise that the civic enterprise is one among a number of enterprises that structure its members' lives, and that the polity is just one among a number of communities in which they live – and probably not the most significant or identity-constituting of those communities. It takes an interest in those character traits, those

[33] eg Dagger (1997).

virtues and vices, that concern our civic lives, but only in those; the more private virtues and vices, or the more private aspects of virtues and vices, which do not impinge directly on our participation in the civic enterprise, are not its business.[34]

This leaves open, of course, the question of just what the civic enterprise includes, and what virtues and vices bear on it – what are the peculiarly civic virtues and vices? That is not a question that can be answered a priori, or in advance of the kind of public deliberation in and through which a liberal polity defines itself. All we need note here is, first, that a liberal polity will have a limited rather than an all-embracing conception of the civic enterprise, and thus of the virtues and vices that bear on it, leaving a substantial range of aretaic dimensions in the 'private' realm that is not the polity's business. Second, it is easy enough to imagine a liberal polity that locates the particular kind or aspect of virtue and vice with which Yankah is concerned in the private realm. Such a polity must of course be interested in relationships in which one party is or is liable to be exploited or coerced in ways that fail to respect her or his status as a responsible citizen – which is typically if not universally true of prostitution as it is actually practised: but it could certainly take the view that its citizens' genuinely consensual sexual dealings with each other do not bear on the civic enterprise, or on their relationships as citizens – in which case it would have no reason to take an interest in or to intervene in such dealings, unless and until there is reason to fear that they might be exploitative, coercive, or in other ways less than fully consensual. My sexual conduct, attitudes and understandings are no doubt the proper business of others with whom I live in more intimate relationships: of my family or my friends, perhaps, and certainly of those with whom I have or seek to have sexual relationships; but however ethically flawed or inappropriate they may be, they are not on this view the business of my fellow citizens or of the polity or the state. I do not say that a liberal polity must take this view: only that it plausibly could – in which case it would not see reason to criminalise prostitution in the considerations that Yankah offers. It would still have good reason to regulate prostitution, given the ways in which it is in fact coercive and exploitative: but the 'moral harm-to-self', which 'corrupts one's proper understanding of the value of sex' and thus 'detracts from the fullest form of flourishing', would not constitute such a reason.

I have focused so far on the question of whether we have reason to criminalise conduct simply on the grounds that it hinders or undermines virtue, or fosters vice, arguing that even a committed virtue theorist need make no such unqualifiedly

[34] It is worth emphasising that 'public' and 'private' in this context operate not descriptively, but normatively. What is 'public', in the context of the polity, is not what happens 'in public', but what properly concerns 'the public' – all members of the polity in virtue simply of their membership. What is 'private' is not what happens 'in private', but what does not properly concern the whole polity. Actions committed in private can belong in the relevant sense to the public realm (consider domestic violence), while actions committed in public can still be in the relevant sense private (my conversation with a friend in the street, for instance). It is also worth noting that every kind of community draws a distinction between the public and the private – a distinction between those matters that properly concern all members of the community simply in virtue of their membership, and those that do not. See further Duff (2007a: chs 2, 3, 6.5).

general claim. This was the first of the two ways in which virtue theory might impinge on the criminal law; I turn now to the second.

III. ARE WE CRIMINALLY LIABLE FOR VICE?

On an 'Aristotelian punishment theory', Huigens argues, the 'expectation is that one will deliberate well on one's own ends, because the actions that issue from these deliberations and that serve these ends are partly constitutive of . . . a society' of 'inherently social beings whose defining end is rational action';[35] 'retrospective assessments of criminal fault in adjudication are particularist evaluations of the quality of the defendant's practical reasoning'.[36] Whereas many virtue theorists explain the grounds of criminal liability in terms of a range of specific virtues and vices, Huigens focuses instead on the practical reasoning that is indeed central to an Aristotelian account of virtue and vice: for though *ethike arete*, the excellence of character that is constituted by our well-ordered set of emotions and appetites, is a central element of well-being, it requires completion and guidance by practical wisdom, *phronesis*. My concern here is not with his interesting discussion, which provides the main focus of his chapter, of the way in which practical reasoning involves the 'reciprocal specification of ends', but with this general claim about the target of a court's 'retrospective assessments of criminal fault'.

Now one thing is certainly, if not very interestingly, true: under a well-formed criminal law, anyone who culpably commits an offence – anyone who commits an offence without an exculpatory defence – thereby shows his practical reasoning to have been deficient. For the criminal law in its 'special part' tells or reminds us what we have categorical and normally sufficient reason to do or to refrain from doing: only normally sufficient, because the general part defines a range of justificatory defences, recognising abnormal cases in which we have good enough reason to commit an offence; but categorical, since in non-abnormal cases we are not to weigh the reasons expressed in the law but simply to act in accordance with them.[37] When someone commits what a well-formed law defines as an offence, without what the law recognises as a defence, he therefore acts as, according to the law, he had conclusive reason not to act; from which it necessarily follows that there was some deficiency or failing in the practical reasoning that informed his action.[38] But that is not yet an interesting point, since it tells us nothing about

[35] Huigens (2012: 155).

[36] ibid 156.

[37] I leave open the question of whether the criminal law sometimes creates the reasons that it declares should guide us, or always serves instead to remind us of or to highlight reasons that we already had: whilst the latter view might seem to fit so-called *mala in se*, the former might seem more apt for the so-called *mala prohibita*; but I have argued elsewhere (Duff (2007a: chs 4.4, 7.3)) that the latter is always correct.

[38] This is true only if his action was in the relevant sense 'voluntary', but I take it that if it was not, the agent did not satisfy the conditions of the offence. It is also true only if we take it that weakness of will involves some deficiency in practical reasoning, rather than in acting on the conclusions of practical reasoning; but we should surely follow Aristotle, *Nicomachean Ethics*, Bk VII, at least as far as that.

either the objects or the conditions of criminal liability: for all we have said so far, such a deficiency in practical reasoning could be simply an implication (one that need not concern the criminal court) of the judgment that the defendant is guilty; it need not specify either a condition of criminal liability to which the court should advert in making that judgment, or part of the object of that judgment.

Huigens clearly wants more than this. What he offers is a 'theory of criminal inculpation': we can therefore take it that in his view such deficiency in practical reasoning is not a mere inference from the culpable commission of an offence; it is what renders the commission of the offence culpable. Indeed, if 'assessments of criminal fault in adjudication are particularist evaluations of the quality of the defendant's practical reasoning', we can take it that defective practical reasoning is part of the object, not just a condition, of liability: what we are criminally liable for is not (just) the criminal action specified in the offence definition, but the deficiency in our practical reasoning from which that action flowed. This interpretation is strengthened by the suggestion that 'the subject of the assessment of practical reasoning that constitutes the determination of criminal fault' is the 'wide array of intentions' that are reflected in the more 'simple intention' that typically figures in an offence definition:[39] this 'subject' of assessment is, surely, being portrayed as that for which we are held liable. It need not be the sole object of liability: nothing that Huigens says commits him, for instance, to the view that the criminal conduct that is typically required for liability is only a condition of liability – that we are held liable for our defective practical reasoning on condition that it resulted in criminal action; he could instead say that we are liable for the defective reasoning as displayed in our actions – thus making action and practical reasoning jointly constitutive of the objects of liability. But he seems at least to be committed to making the defective practical reasoning a part or aspect of the object of criminal liability.

That 'wide array of intentions' does not, it is true, typically figure in the definitions of criminal offences, which do not usually reach beyond the 'simple intention' that makes an action, for instance, one of intentional killing or wounding or damaging, plus such conditions of awareness as are also required; nor will this wide array typically figure during the course of the trial, or in the judge's or jury's deliberations. This can be explained by arguing that if the law is well-formed, then in most cases we can unhesitatingly infer a deficiency in that wide array, in the defendant's practical reasoning, from proof of the *mens rea* element of the offence – in the same way as, other kinds of character theorist argue, proof of the commission of the specified offence normally warrants an inference to the defective character trait that is the real focus of criminal liability.[40] To meet the charge that the possibility of making such an inference does not show that such a deficiency in practical reasoning is even a condition, let alone the object, of criminal liability, it would need to be argued that in some cases that wide array

[39] Huigens (2012: 157).
[40] See eg Bayles (1982) and Brandt (1985).

does figure explicitly in the substantive law, in the course of the trial, or in judges' and juries' deliberations (when properly conducted); *and* that what is made explicit in those cases should be taken to be implicit in other cases.

This is where the example of the husband who 'kills his gravely suffering and terminally ill wife of 50 years, . . . in order to relieve her suffering', becomes relevant. His action fits the criminal law's definition of murder, but surely the law should look (as morality does) beyond the surface to his underlying motivations, and find there reasons for leniency: here at least the 'thin descriptions' generated by the standard offence definition 'are not enough to facilitate the requisite inquiry into the quality of the defendant's practical reasoning'.[41] Once we accept this, however, we must surely also accept that the wide array of intentions, the quality of the practical reasoning from which the elements of *mens rea* flow, is always crucial to criminal liability, although in most cases this does not need to be made explicit.

Now it is certainly true that what the law defines as defences typically involve examining the further reasons for which, the further intentions with which, the defendant committed the crime in question. This is true both of justifications and of excuses, but in different ways that bear significantly on the issue under discussion here.[42] In the case of excuses, or so I have argued elsewhere, there is reason to recognise a general (at least partial) defence under the following conditions:

> First, [the] agent is motivated by an emotion (love, compassion) that has a proper role in human life, and is appropriately and strongly aroused on this occasion. . . . Second, such emotions could properly motivate something like what [the] agent actually did. . . . What [he] actually did, we are assuming, was not justified. . . . But, third, he displayed no real vice in being tempted to commit such a crime for the sake of such a good, or to avert such an evil: an appropriate attachment to the goods that [he] sought to foster or to protect could tempt even a moderately (humanly) virtuous person to commit such a crime. Fourth, the emotions that [he] properly felt are, when strongly felt, apt to destabilise – to disturb rational deliberation: their motivational power is liable to exceed their rational authority. In the light of all these factors, we may conclude that in committing his crime, the agent did not display a lack of those modest levels of virtue and self-control, of respect for the interests and rights that the criminal law protects, that citizens can properly demand of each other on pain of public condemnation and punishment.[43]

If we assume that euthanasia, at least of the kind committed by this husband, should not be legally justified, we must believe that this husband's practical reasoning was defective; he either wrongly thought that he had good enough reason to kill his wife, or failed to put into practical effect his recognition that he should

[41] Huigens (2012: 163–63).

[42] I leave aside here defences such as infancy or insanity which do not involve any assessment of the person's further reasons for action, but focus rather on his capacity for reason-guided action: that is why some argue that we should distinguish such defences from (other) excuses, by counting them as 'exemptions' – see eg Gardner (1998); Horder (2004: 8–10, 103–6); Tadros (2005: 124–29); and Duff (2007a: 284–91).

[43] Duff (2007b: 99). See also Keating and Bridgeman (2012).

not kill her. We might also reasonably think, however, that he merits at least a partial excuse (whether by way of sentence mitigation, or by reducing his crime from murder to manslaughter), if not a complete excuse; because, to put it in the way that Huigens would favour, when we look behind his immediate intention to kill his wife we find a structure of practical reasoning that is at least not as seriously defective as that displayed by other, more usual murderers.[44] This is where a virtue theorist is on strongest ground: but even if we accept this kind of account of excuses (or of this type of excuse), this is not yet to say that all determinations of criminal liability involve, even implicitly, such an evaluation of the agent's practical reasoning or character traits. All we can say so far is that, given the availability of this kind of defence, a defendant whose conduct satisfies the offence definition is unqualifiedly guilty *unless* that conduct can be explained in a way that shows his practical reasoning or character not to be relevantly defective; and therefore that the criminal law presumes that anyone who commits what it defines as a crime did so because of a defect in their practical reasoning or their character – a presumption that is defeasible by evidence of a suitable excuse. This would portray the relevant kind of vice not as the object of criminal liability, nor even as a condition that must be proved or adverted to, but as a presumption.

Matters become trickier for a virtue theorist when we turn from excuses to justifications. Suppose that we decide that certain kinds of euthanasia, or of assisted suicide, should now be legally permitted: what conditions should the law specify? The most obvious will of course concern the condition and attitude of the person who is to die: we might require both that he positively requests death (building in suitable safeguards to ensure that such a request is both informed and genuinely voluntary), and that his condition and prospects are such as to make such a request reasonable. But what should the law require of the person who is to assist the death? Here at least a 'reasons' theory of justification seems apt.[45] Anyone who is to claim an acquittal on these grounds must show not only that he knew that the other conditions were satisfied, but that he acted because they were satisfied: that, for instance, he killed someone whom he knew to be terminally and very painfully ill, who had, as he also knew, requested this assistance, in the legally prescribed way; and that he did so *because* the person had asked for this help on this basis. To determine whether the defendant was entitled to the defence we would therefore need to look behind his immediate intention to kill or to assist the death of this person, to the reasons for which he formed that intention – which is

[44] Huigens also argues that, once we look at the 'wide array of intentions' in this case, we will see that 'the statement that the husband intends to kill his wife is inaccurate' (Huigens (2012: 161)). There are of course cases in which an agent who does what he knows will cause another's death might deny an intention to kill – most obviously, those in which a doctor administers painkillers which she knows will also hasten death. But we need not tackle the controversial issue of whether the distinction between (direct) intention and foresight can carry any moral weight in such cases here, since this husband surely does intend to kill his wife as the only means available to him to end her suffering; he calculates, for instance, the dose of the drug that will be sufficient to kill her. 'He intends to kill her' is admittedly an incomplete description of the relevant moral aspects of his action; but it is nonetheless true.

[45] See above n 13.

grist to Huigens' mill. The key question, however, is whether we should look further and deeper than that.

Consider two agents who kill or assist the death of someone who satisfies and whom they know to satisfy the patient-oriented conditions for permissible euthanasia, and each of whom acts as he does because the patient satisfies those conditions. One is motivated by compassion for the patient's suffering – by a spouse's or friend's love, by a doctor's concern. The other is not thus motivated, but acts for the sake of the financial reward promised him by the patient; or perhaps he is the patient's heir, and acts for the sake of the money he will inherit.[46] If we are assessing these agents morally, this difference will be important: we will (if we agree that such euthanasia is morally justified, as well as legally permissible) see the first agent in a morally favourable light; we will pass an adverse judgement on the last, who acts for the sake of his inheritance; and we might take different views of the person who acts for the sake of the promised payment. But should these differences concern the law: should an acquittal on the grounds of legal permissibility require evidence that the agent was motivated in a morally appropriate way? A virtue theorist must surely argue that it should. To put the matter in the terms that Huigens uses, there are obvious, significant differences in the moral quality of the practical reasoning of the two agents, and in the ends for the sake of which they act; to put it in terms preferred by other virtue theorists, it is clear that the first agent displays no vice, or even displays a relevant virtue; that the one who acts for the sake of his inheritance displays serious vice (greed, lack of concern for the sufferer); and that the agent who acts for payment, whether we call him vicious or not, is at least significantly different from the first agent in the moral character he displays. But should the criminal law attend to these kinds of difference in the 'wide array of intentions' that inform their actions, or in the moral characters that those actions display?

In other contexts it does not. One who uses the force necessary to protect a victim against an unlawful attack can claim a defence on a charge of wounding or murder; even if he must claim, as 'reasons' theorists argue, that he acted *in order to* ward off the attack, he need not offer any account of his motives for (his 'wide array of intentions' in) acting thus, or of the further ends for whose sake he acted. He is legally entitled to an acquittal, whether he acted out of compassion for the victim of the attack, or in order to obtain some expected financial reward, or just because he enjoys a fight. Nor, surely, *should* the law require that the agent's motives be morally respectable: it should be enough that he acts for the sake of what the law defines as a proper end, using means appropriate to that end and consistent with other legally relevant ends, even if that end figures, in the structure of his own practical reasoning, only as a subordinate end that he pursues for the sake of a further and much less admirable end. We might not admire him or

[46] We could imagine more bizarre cases, such as the enemy who takes this chance to kill the person he hates, but who acts because the victim satisfies the conditions for euthanasia; he would not otherwise have killed him, because he would then risk being convicted of murder. Such outré cases need not concern us here.

commend his character, but we should not convict him of a criminal offence. Similarly, if I break someone's car window in order to save the animal or child who has been overcome by the heat,[47] I have a defence against a charge of criminal damage even if my action displayed neither virtue nor an admirable *enkrateia*, but was motivated by a hope that I would receive a financial reward, or by malice against the car's owner. Not only does the law not in fact attend to that wide array of intentions, those deeper structures of practical reasoning, in determining the success of a justificatory defence; it should not do so. It should be enough that the agent acted not just in accordance with, but on the basis of, what the law recognises as justificatory reasons.

Should euthanasia be any different? Should a legal definition of permissible euthanasia require not only that the killer act as he does because the specified patient-relative conditions are satisfied, but also that he does so out of a specified kind of motive, such as compassion?[48] One problem is that it is not clear how that motive should be specified, if people other than those close to the patient are to be allowed to kill – doctors, for instance: we surely cannot require the doctor to show that he was motivated by compassion. But, more generally, why should the criminal law look beyond the way in which the defendant's practical reasoning engaged (or failed to engage) with what the law specifies to be relevant reasons for action; and why should it specify those reasons any more deeply than it now does?

Of course, the fact that a killer was motivated by profit rather than compassion might arouse our suspicions: we might wonder whether he really did act because the patient-relative conditions were satisfied – whether, that is, he would have refrained from acting thus had they not been satisfied, or had he not been confident that they were satisfied; we might wonder, in some cases, whether he might have improperly encouraged or induced the patient to request death. Indeed, if we are concerned enough about these dangers we might formulate the law in a way that does require evidence of compassionate motivation, or that removes the defence from anyone who was motivated by profit. But that would not help the virtue theorist, since this would not be to say that the person who does act because the patient-relative conditions are satisfied, but who does so for the sake of profit rather than from compassion, deserves to be convicted in his own right; the point is rather that we need to refuse him a defence in order to prevent legally unmeritorious killers getting away with it. We can legitimately count as a murderer, in law, someone who kills in ignorance of the conditions that

[47] See above nn 13–14.

[48] A virtue theorist might point out that when the English Director of Public Prosecutions was required by the courts to publish guidelines covering the factors to be taken into account in deciding whether to prosecute those who assisted suicides, one of the factors specified as favouring prosecution was that the assister 'was not wholly motivated by compassion', but was, eg, motivated by the prospect of financial gain, whilst one factor 'tending against prosecution' was that the assister 'was wholly motivated by compassion' (www.cps.gov.uk/publications/prosecution/assisted_suicide_policy.html; February 2010, following *R (on the application of Purdy) v DPP* [2009] UKHL 45). But the guidelines can most plausibly be read (if we are to make legal sense of them) as concerning excusatory rather than justificatory factors.

would have justified him in killing, as 'reasons' theorists argue; but the law should not count as a murderer one who kills only when the law permits it, and only because the law permits it, even if his further and deeper motives are morally far from admirable.

If this is right, it undermines the virtue theorist's claim, and Huigens' claims about the relevance to criminal liability of the deeper dimensions of the agent's practical reasoning. It is still true, in a way, that 'retrospective assessments of criminal fault' involve 'evaluations of the quality of the defendant's practical reasoning':[49] in the context of justificatory defences, we need to judge whether he acted because the specified conditions were satisfied. But it is not true that we must judge the quality of his practical reasoning as a whole, in relation to this action, or attend to the final ends towards which his action was directed; our enquiry goes no deeper than the reasons specified in the law's definitions of the relevant offence and defence. To put the point in Aristotelian terms, a person whose practical reasoning exhibits nothing more than the 'cleverness' that even a weak-willed or vicious agent can display should still be able to plead a justificatory criminal defence, so long as the immediate reasons for which he acts are sanctioned by the law; he should not have to display any kind of *phronesis*.[50] The killing of a relative who has asked to be helped to die, or the freeing of the trapped child from the car, might involve a modest degree of calculation or cleverness: the agent needs to realise that this enterprise will serve his ends (will bring him a financial reward), and might need to work out the best means to achieve the death or the rescue. That certainly does not amount to an exercise of *phronesis*, since the reasoning is not grounded in his grasp of appropriate final ends; indeed, it is ethically corrupted by the way it connects this action to ends that are wholly inappropriate to the context. Nonetheless, the reasoning is adequate in the eyes of the criminal law: for it matches, in its logically final stages, the reasons that the law sanctions – and the law should look no deeper than that.

A virtue theorist who wants to argue that criminal liability is ultimately grounded in or focused on vice must confront the fact that the criminal law's offence definitions are not set in virtue-theoretic terms: they concern the shallower, more superficial aspects of the agent's conduct and motivations. One way to explain that fact away is to argue that in determining criminal defences we must make explicit reference to the virtues or vices that underpinned a defendant's action; and that what is made explicit in these contexts – that the defendant is to be convicted only if his action displayed a relevant vice – should be taken to be implicit in cases in which no defence is offered or available. I have argued, however, that whilst we can plausibly interpret some familiar excuses in this way, this does not show vice to be the object of criminal liability; and that justifications are not plausibly interpreted in virtue-theoretic terms – that a vicious deep motivation need not be a bar to a justificatory legal defence.

[49] Huigens (2012: 156).

[50] On the difference between cleverness and practical wisdom, see Aristotle, *Nicomachean Ethics*, Bk VI.12; see also Bk VI.9 on 'calculation' and 'deliberation'.

IV. CONCLUDING COMMENTS

This chapter was not intended to produce any determinate general conclusions about the role that virtue theory might play in criminal law; indeed, given the variety of different kinds of virtue theory, and the different roles that ideas of virtue and vice could play in criminal law (some of which have been discussed here), such general conclusions cannot be quickly or easily reached. I have argued, however, that on the one hand a virtue-theoretic approach to the aims of criminal law can be more deeply liberal than Yankah seems to allow. It need not, that is, involve the illiberal claim that we have reason in principle to criminalise every kind of virtue or vice, or conduct that hinders any virtue or fosters any vice; it can instead reflect a liberal distinction between the public and the private realms, and hold that the state, and thus the criminal law, have a legitimate interest only in that subset of virtues or vices that properly count as civic. On the other hand, when we ask whether and how vice should constitute at least part of the object of criminal liability, whether we should be convicted and punished *for* the vices that our criminal conduct displays, ambitious forms of virtue theory are on shakier ground. We can typically infer some defect of character, or some deficiency in the agent's practical reasoning, from the commission of a criminal offence; some familiar legal excuses can be most plausibly interpreted and rationalised in partly virtue-theoretic terms. However, that is not true of justificatory defences – which seriously undermines any claim that criminal liability is grounded in vice.

REFERENCES

Aristotle, R Crisp (tr) (2000) *Nicomachean Ethics* (Cambridge, Cambridge University Press).

Bayles, MD (1982) 'Character, Purpose, and Criminal Responsibility' 1 *Law & Philosophy* 5.

Brady, M (2010) 'Disappointment' 84 *Proceedings of the Aristotelian Society* (Supp vol) 179.

Brandt, RB (1985) 'A Motivational Theory of Excuses in the Criminal Law' in J Pennock and J Chapman (eds), *Criminal Justice* (New York, New York University Press).

Dagger, R (1997) *Civic Virtues: Rights, Citizenship and Republican Liberalism* (Oxford, Oxford University Press).

Duff, RA (2001) *Punishment, Communication and Community* (New York, Oxford University Press).

——(2002) 'Virtue, Vice and Criminal Liability' 6 *Buffalo Criminal Law Review* 147.

——(2007a) *Answering for Crime: Responsibility and Liability in Criminal Law* (Oxford, Hart Publishing).

——(2007b) 'The Virtues and Vices of Virtue Jurisprudence' in T Chappell (ed), *Values and Virtues* (Oxford, Oxford University Press).

Duff, RA, Farmer, L, Marshall, SE, Tadros, V (2007) *The Trial on Trial III: Towards a Normative Theory of the Criminal Trial* (Oxford, Hart Publishing).

Feinberg, J (1970) 'The Expressive Function of Punishment' in *Doing and Deserving* (Princeton, Princeton University Press).

——(1984) *Harm to Others* (New York, Oxford University Press).

——(1986) *Harm to Self* (New York, Oxford University Press).

Fletcher, G (1978) *Rethinking Criminal Law* (Boston, Little, Brown).
Fricker, M (2010) 'The Relativism of Blame' 84 *Proceedings of the Aristotelian Society* (Supp vol) 151.
Gardner, J (1998) 'The Gist of Excuses' 1 *Buffalo Criminal Law Review* 575.
—— (2007) 'Justifications and Reasons' in J Gardner, *Offences and Defences* (Oxford, Oxford University Press).
Gardner, J and Macklem, T (2001) 'Provocation and Pluralism' 64 *Modern Law Review* 815.
Hampton, J (1984) 'The Moral Education Theory of Punishment' 13 *Philosophy & Public Affairs* 208.
Holmes, OW (1897) 'The Path of the Law' 10 *Harvard Law Review* 457.
Horder, J (1992) *Provocation and Responsibility* (Oxford, Oxford University Press).
—— (1996) 'Crimes of Ulterior Intent' in AP Simester and AT Smith (eds), *Harm and Culpability* (Oxford, Oxford University Press).
—— (2004) *Excusing Crime* (Oxford, Oxford University Press).
Huigens, K (1995) 'Virtue and Inculpation' 108 *Harvard Law Review* 1423.
—— (2012) 'Motivating Intentions, Reciprocal Specification of Ends and the Assessment of Responsibility' chapter 8 of this volume.
Hume, D, (1978) *A Treatise of Human Nature* (ed. LA Selby-Bigge and PH Nidditch; Oxford, Oxford University Press).
Kahan, DM (1998) 'Ignorance of Law is an Excuse – But Only for the Virtuous' 96 *Michigan Law Review* 127.
Keating, H and Bridgeman, J (2012) 'Compassionate Killings: The Case for a Partial Defence' 75 Modern Law Review (forthcoming).
Lacey, N (1988) *State Punishment* (London, Routledge).
—— (2011) 'The Resurgence of Character: Responsibility in the Context of Criminalization' in RA Duff and SP Green (eds), *Philosophical Foundations of Criminal Law* (Oxford, Oxford University Press).
Moore, MS (1993) *Act and Crime: The Philosophy of Action and its Implications for the Criminal Law* (Oxford, Oxford University Press).
—— (1997) *Placing Blame: A General Theory of the Criminal Law* (Oxford, Oxford University Press).
—— (2009) 'A Tale of Two Theories' 28 *Criminal Justice Ethics* 27.
Morris, H (1981) 'A Paternalistic Theory of Punishment' 18 *American Philosophical Quarterly* 263.
Robinson, PH (1997) *Structure and Function in Criminal Law* (Oxford, Oxford University Press).
Shafer-Landau, R (1991) 'Can Punishment Morally Educate?' 10 *Law & Philosophy* 189.
Stephen, JF, White, RJ (eds) (1973) *Liberty, Equality, Fraternity* (Cambridge, Cambridge University Press).
Tadros, V (2005) *Criminal Responsibility* (Oxford, Oxford University Press).
von Hirsch, A (1993) *Censure and Sanctions* (Oxford, Oxford University Press).
Williams, B (1985) *Ethics and the Limits of Philosophy* (London, Fontana).
—— (1995) 'Internal Reasons and the Obscurity of Blame' in B Williams, *Making Sense of Humanity* (Cambridge, Cambridge University Press).
Wolfenden, J (1957) Report of the Committee on Homosexual Offences and Prostitution (London, Her Majesty's Stationery Office).
Yankah, E (2012) 'Liberal Virtue' chapter 9 of this volume.

IV.

Legal Fact-Finding: Aretaic Perspectives

11

Virtues of Truthfulness in Forbearing Wrongs: Client Confidentiality Qualified by Legal Symmetry of Past and Future Harm

HENDRIK KAPTEIN

I. INTRODUCTION

PHILOSOPHY OF LAW relating to adjudication and conflict resolution generally focuses on issues of law and legal interpretation. Conflicts between so many varieties of natural law and legal positivism on the status and meaning of legal rules have reigned supreme. The roles of fact-finding and facts in application of the law to the case at hand have received less attention. But the great majority of legal conflicts is about contested facts, not about contested law. Still, issues of evidence and proof are back on scholarly agendas, hopefully leading to an improvement in practice. One general drift of such developments seems to be a zeal to introduce scientific method and logical rigour in legal establishment of the facts of the case.

However, one fundamental difference between scientific (historical, archaeological, psychological, etc) establishment of the facts of a case on the one hand, and legal establishment of such facts on the other, is procedural in nature. Maintaining client confidentiality is regarded as an essential part of the lawyer's duties in adjudication and in legal procedure in general. But such client confidentiality may rather unscientifically 'hide' important facts in adjudication and other varieties of legal conflict resolution. Lawyers may tell clients that they need to be fully informed in order to legally stand by them. Clients, however, may fear the legal consequences of unwelcome facts. So, client confidentiality seems to offer the solution here: lawyers need to know everything that their clients know about the case, but lawyers will withhold from the courts and others any facts that do not serve their clients' causes.

But less facts may lead to less law. Parties may be monopolists in important pieces of evidence relating to facts that are decisive for the case at hand. Legal opponents may try to state evidence supporting their claims without being able to adduce conclusive proof. Thus an owner discovering asbestos in his apartment roofing not mentioned by the seller of the apartment may well have good reason to think that the seller already knew about it but remained silent in order to get more money. The same seller, refusing to pay back, may be asked by his lawyer to confidentially tell him the whole story. The lawyer may then hear and see things like: 'Yes, I knew about it and I even had a certified report made about this asbestos thing, here it is.' The court's decision in this case would of course be determined in great part by such a report, that is, if it would come to light.

Client confidentiality may even hide facts completely unknown to other parties who might greatly profit from knowledge of such facts. For example, the plaintiff may be claiming damages for harm caused by a road accident. The plaintiff's medical specialist discovers that he has a serious life-shortening condition. Such facts may be highly relevant to the amount of damages that is recoverable in more than a few jurisdictions. So the defendant and/or his insurance companies would rather like to know about this medical condition. But then apart from issues of medical confidentiality, the plaintiff's lawyer may remain silent on such life-shortening conditions.

Thus confidentiality, however important it may be in lawyer-client relationships, may in the end lead to less law and right. The apartment buyer may be wrongly forced to cope with the asbestos issue himself and the road accident victim may receive more compensation that he should, given his true life expectancy.

Thus hiding facts important to the outcomes of legal conflicts does not just have an air of the unscientific, but seems subversive against law and right as well. Indeed, opposition against client confidentiality is about as long-standing as the practice of it. Non-lawyers generally think such confidentiality stands in the way of justice, while lawyers zealously defend the same confidentiality, appealing to lofty ideas or even ideals of the need for clients' trust, lawyers' partisanship for legally unarmed lay people, etc. (To be sure, some such lay persons may be less principled in their opposition against client confidentiality as soon as they become involved in legal conflicts themselves, but this may not be really relevant to the issue at hand.)

Still, there is broad consensus on at least one important qualification of client confidentiality, both in legal and in non-legal circles, and not just limited to the sphere of the law. Clear and present danger is not to be covered by any confidentiality. Clients convincing their lawyers, medical doctors, clergypeople, or any other fellow human being for that matter, that they are going to kill or maim, are not to be protected by professional silence. In fact, several jurisdictions require this to be disclosed to the authorities.

But then the conflict on the past remains: confidentiality or the facts of the case? In order to solve this dilemma, an attempt will be made to compare avoidance of future dangers with compensating legally wrongful harm. These two spheres of action are rather different at first sight. Harm done is history, potential harm may still be avoided. History cannot be changed at will, as may be done with the future at times. If such differences are fundamental, there may indeed be differences in client confidentiality regarding the past or the future.

Here it will be argued that such asymmetries do not really hold. Thus, there will appear to be a – or one more – good reason to do away with client confidentiality concerning things past as well. Wrongful harm is the subject here. Still, the results reached may be relevant for legal conflict resolution in general, generally related as it is to wrongful harm in a wide sense, or there would be no conflict. Discussion of this will be structured as follows. First, a brief reminder of key roles of facts in legal conflict resolution may facilitate a better understanding of client confidentiality and its problems (section II). Such client confidentiality may be an important quality or even virtue of lawyers striving for realisation of their proper roles in legal practice, as is further explained in section III. Further issues of confidentiality will be discussed in terms of possible conflict with availability of facts relevant for justice in conflict resolution (section IV). Section V states convincing reasons for qualification of client confidentiality concerning future dangers. Next and central to the argument is the refutation of the supposedly categorical difference between past harm and future danger, in terms of what undoing harm comes down to in principle (section VI). Practical objections against ideals of compensating harm 'as if nothing happened', related to the impotence of criminal law and punishment against harm and otherwise, are discussed in section VII. Section VIII vainly tries to restore asymmetry by appealing to the fundamentally 'procedural' nature of the establishment of evidence and proof concerning the past in adjudication, accommodating client confidentiality, as contrasted with extra-legal or 'free' fact-finding concerning the future. But what about the need for clients' trust in their lawyers? These and other objections will be discussed in section IX. Finally, practical demands of qualified confidentiality will appear to appeal to a lawyer's sometimes difficult virtues in balancing interests and rights, on the basis of the facts of the case. So, and however academic it is, this scholarly contribution may be of some practical interest as well (section X).

Anyway, any reader not wishing to delve into issues of client confidentiality may be advised to skip the outer parts of this frame story and concentrate on the discussion of undoing the past. This may be of more general value and interest than just in the context of confidentiality.

II. NO ADJUDICATION WITHOUT THE FACTS OF THE CASE

There can be no law without facts, in several important senses.[1] Of course, law itself, or at least positive law, is a complex of facts, societal and otherwise, even if law may not be completely reduced to matters of fact. Undisputed anyway is the given fact that there can be no sensible adjudication or legal conflict resolution in general without recourse to something like the facts of the case.

Indeed, the great majority of court cases and other varieties of legal conflict resolution concern contested facts, not contested law.[2] Why are facts so important

[1] See Kaptein (1999) for a brief overview of this.

[2] See Golding (1984) for a principled discussion of this.

in adjudication, even if uncontested? A brief discussion of this may be in order, so as to pave the way for the clarification of client confidentiality as possibly at odds with ideals of adjudication. Adjudication will here be discussed as paradigmatic for legal conflict resolution, at least concerning the role of the facts of the case.

The core activity of courts is the application of law to the facts of the case, though some courts may create law as well of course. The facts of the case are not to be established as such by the court either. Ideal-typical as this may be, the primary logical form of any rule application in order to resolve legal conflicts is still *modus ponens* in principle, however formally and materially complex legal conflicts may be. The facts of the case are subsumed under a general legal rule or rules suitably interpreted, in order to derive a legally normative conclusion.

Modus tollens types of argumentation may also play important roles. Thus 'standard' rule application may lead to legally, morally or even humanly unacceptable consequences. If such consequences are regarded as undesirable, standard rule application has to go. This again is related to 'result oriented' adjudicative reasoning, for better or worse at times. Problems of logic in adjudicative argumentation and in legal argumentation in general will not be further discussed here.

Anyway, adjudication ought to be based on the facts of the case as they were, or are, or even will be. Facts may not only be more or less relevant; given legal rules, such facts may be coloured or even constituted by their legal roles and even definitions, like official documents, seals, oaths and much more.

Such and other facts may be and are often taken for granted for good reason. Legal presumptions and even fictions may constitute facts in adjudication as well. Parts of the problems of evidence and proof may be formalised this way, with practical results. Other facts of the case may be difficult or even well-nigh impossible to establish. Establishment of evidence and proof concerning such facts of the case may require some more logic and other kinds of expertise, not always put on display by courts having to decide hard cases concerning facts.

Disputed and/or uncertain evidence for the presumed facts of the case may be inquired into by the court and other official bodies, like the public prosecution office. Still, other facts may only be adduced by the parties concerned. Such division of labour may be different in different jurisdictions. Courts and other official bodies are monopolists in establishing evidence and proof concerning the facts of the case. Still such bodies depend on the parties' contributions to fact-finding in great measure, and not always for the better. Of course, important facts may be known by only the parties themselves, at least at the opening stage of court cases or other forms of legal conflict resolution. Whether courts will be able to establish sufficient evidence for such facts is another matter.

This inexorably leads to issues of client confidentiality. Parties involved may know about facts highly important for the case, but may be unwilling to divulge such facts to opponents and/or to the court. Such facts may be damaging not so much for their lawful rights, but for their interests, at least as such interests are perceived by such silent parties and their lawyers. As a result, legal proof of such facts or even the facts themselves may not be available to the courts and to other parties whose lawful rights may depend on them.

Why should availability of possibly decisive facts for the court depend on parties' discretion and their lawyers' legally condoned secrecy? Is this not at odds with the basic principle that any court case ought to be decided on the basis of all relevant facts, impartially and expertly decided upon, in the light of law and right, however difficult it may be to establish such facts? What interests served by client confidentiality may outweigh this?

III. CLIENT CONFIDENTIALITY: A VIRTUE AMONG OTHER LAWYERS' VIRTUES?

Traditionally, protectiveness of client confidentiality is taken to be one of the three qualities or even virtues of the lawyer. A good lawyer will not only be protective of client confidentiality but will be independent and confraternal as well.[3] But why? This leads to the real question: what are lawyers good for in the first place? Or: why is there something like a bar at all? Strangely enough this issue is seldom put forward in explicit fashion, let alone discussed adequately. But without meaningful ends there cannot be sensible virtues of any kind, not even of lawyers.

An answer may be reached along the following lines. The bar is a product, a cause and above all an indispensable part of the inevitable complexity of law. Lawyers derive their reason for being from a tragic paradox, if not even from an outright contradiction. Simple and generally comprehensible law cannot be just and effective, just and effective law must be complex and incomprehensible to lay people.[4]

This inability of lay persons to autonomously secure their rights is the lawyers' raison d'etre. Few people are versed and experienced in the law and legal procedure to a degree sufficient to serve their own legal interests in court and elsewhere. Thus there can be no just and effective legal order without lawyers.

Given this fundamental role of lawyers, important conclusions follow naturally. Lawyers are to see to it that their clients' rights are realised. It is to be kept in mind here of course that a primary purpose of law and legal procedure is to realise rights, however contested they may be. Lawyers are to play main roles in the realisation of this primary purpose. They are to state in terms as legally favourable as possible the claims of their clients, both to other parties and to the public prosecution and the court. It is not the duty or obligation of lawyers to further whatever clients' interests by whatever means. The bar has not been instituted in order to create a surplus of injustice. Courts are to determine who is to win or lose in the end, not lawyers using all kinds of tricks, confidentially and otherwise, in order to

[3] See on this more extensively Kaptein (1998).

[4] See for classical statements of this Montesquieu (1748) and Fuller (1969).

let their clients (and their own purses) win against the purpose of the law in the realisation of justice and fairness.

This leads back to the aforementioned three basic virtues of the lawyer: client confidentiality, confraternity, independence. Independence from the client follows naturally from the lawyer's role in the realisation of law and right: lawyers ought not to be hired hands, let alone guns. (The lawyer's independence of course also includes his relative autonomy in relationships with courts, public prosecution offices and other public and private bodies.)

Confraternity is another consequence. Lawyers are to stand not only by their clients, but also by the legal order and its justice and fairness, however imperfect. This implies that legal procedure is not to be hampered in ways unrelated to the material merits of clients' cases. Thus confraternity may imply that lawyers ought to cooperate, among other things in duly sharing information on potential hindrances on the way to outcomes acceptable from a material legal point of view.

Lastly, client confidentiality may indeed be important for the protection of clients and for conflict resolution on the basis of all relevant facts. Without client confidentiality, clients may be unduly hesitant to divulge important information which they do not know to be legally relevant. As clients are indeed generally unable to determine the legal importance of facts, it is in their best interest to 'tell everything', in order to enable their lawyers to present their cases as based upon all possibly relevant facts. Such facts may not be related to third parties, as the position of clients may then be undeservedly worse than in legal conflicts without lawyers at all. Trust between clients and lawyers implies openness, but then results of such openness may not be exploited by possibly mala fide opponents.

Thus understanding of proper roles in the realisation of law and right is of utmost importance for lawyers. In this sense, acting upon role understanding is not just realisation of professional responsibility, but also professional self-realisation, with attendant positive consequences for self-understanding or even well-being. In practice however even the most principled lawyer is inevitably and continuously confronted not just with less well-meaning colleagues and other officials, but also with so many imperfections in law and legal practice thwarting principled attempts to realise law and right.

Such role realisation presupposes at least two different but deeply related kinds of virtues. First there must be the virtue of fixed determination to live up to really professional standards of the bar as an important institution of legal procedure aimed at the realisation of material justice. Second, there must be complex virtue in application of human and technical knowledge and skills in professional environments containing so many obstacles on the way to realisation of lawyers' unique contributions to the realisation of law and right.

This complex professional virtue is the very essence of being a lawyer. So many legal and other rules may be so easily lived by – or violated for that matter. The real challenge is abiding by the principles, in a practically imperfect world, legally and otherwise, whatever seductions driven by self-interests and other vanities there may be.

Client confidentiality does look like an important part of this professional ideal of lawyers serving rightful clients' interests in order to let justice prevail in the end. Unanswered yet is the issue of potential conflict between such client confidentiality and the need for knowledge of all facts concerned as a presupposition for fair conflict resolution.

IV. CONFIDENTIALITY IN COMPETITION WITH THE FACTS OF THE CASE?

Even in the middle of the eighteenth century, Johnson did not judge the concept of confidentiality, let alone client confidentiality, fit for inclusion in his famous dictionary. Were these concepts secret in themselves? Certainly not so, given the already widespread assumption, at least in lawyers' circles, that client confidentiality is a good thing, furthering the business of legal advice and representation. Anyway, and to introduce discussion of client confidentiality, it may be of some interest to recount Johnson's classical definitions of importantly related concepts (as published in 1755):[5]

> CO'NFIDANT. *n.f.* [*confident*, French.] A person trusted with private affairs, commonly with affairs of love.
>
> TO CONFI'DE. *v. n* [*confido*, Latin] To trust in; to put trust in.
> He alone won't betray, in whom none will *confide. Congr.*
>
> CO'NFIDENT. *n.f.* [from *confide.*] one trusted with secrets.
> If ever it comes to this, that a man can say of his *confident*, he would have deceived me, he has said enough. *South.*
> You love me for no other end,
> But to become my *confident* and friend;
> As such, I keep no secret from your sight. *Dryden's Aureng.*

Still, client confidentiality is more or less in line with this. Indeed, it implies a lawyer's duty (or sometimes obligation) not to divulge to any third parties anything told or shown to them by clients. So lawyers are not expected to testify on such information either. Here it is important to distinguish between what clients may say or show, whether as parties in court or otherwise, and what lawyers may say or show concerning their clients. Thus in most civilised jurisdictions, criminal defendants have a right not to speak out against themselves. Civil litigation on the other hand is generally determined by the division of burdens of proof, determining the consequences of parties informing or not informing the court. Under disclosure rules in several jurisdictions, civil parties ought to inform the court of all facts pertaining to the case. Such disclosure rules may limit client confidentiality, prescribing that lawyers inform the court of anything relevant said or shown to them by clients (see section V for more on this). So, client confidentiality is not so

[5] Johnson (1755).

much an issue of what clients and their lawyers are to tell the court and/or other parties, but of what lawyers may divulge concerning what their clients have told them.

Some standard reasons for client confidentiality are as follows. First, it is contended that a potential client's trust in his lawyer is essential for his readiness to turn to lawyers, for a client's trust in his lawyer's zealous pursuit of his interests presupposes client confidentiality. This probably is the most common line of reasoning in favour of confidentiality. However, such reasoning leaves open the essential question of whether clients may trust their lawyers in anything, including fraudulent or even criminal schemes against third parties. In other words, the argument seems to rely on the deeply implausible idea that lawyers are to serve any interests of their clients just because they are their clients' interests.[6]

Second and in line with this, it is argued that clients are not to be worse off with a lawyer's professional assistance than without it. Talkative lawyers may harm their clients. Again, this leaves open the question of whether all clients with all possible plans are to be better off with lawyers than without them. Dryden's definition of confident as friend echoes here of course, but then a lawyer may not be a real friend in these respects.

Third, it is contended that lawyers are partial by definition. Thus, they are not expected to care for the opponents' interests and rights, a task best left to such opponents and to the courts. Against this it may be argued that parties and lawyers leaving out essential facts usurp adjudication by determining wrongful judicial decisions beforehand (but see also section VIII, on proceduralism accomodating client confidentiality).

Fourth, it is thought that confidentiality is an essential part of client-professional relationships in which clients are in dire need of help (Johnson's definition of 'confide' is related to this). Part of the first line of reasoning returns to the scene here. Analogously, people would not turn to clergymen for confession of their sins in order to be freed from them if they could not be unconditionally sure that these clergymen would remain silent. More or less the same may hold good for the medical profession. At least in legal contexts, this argument is not really plausible, if only because more than a few legal clients do not really seem to be that helpless at all. In more than a few cases, it is opponents who are helpless, as a consequence of a client's misconduct.

Fifth, considerations of privacy merit only brief mention here. However essential privacy may be in many respects, *petitio principii* looms large in privacy arguments in favour of client confidentiality. Such arguments do not seem to reach far outside of circular reasoning in terms of secrecy because of the good of secrecy. Still, clients may inform or even need to inform lawyers of intimate and other facts not to be revealed to the outside world, that is, as long as such facts may not be determinative of other parties' rights. Medical confidentiality is rather less questionable in this respect. Information protected by it may cover things inti-

[6] Kaptein (1998), among others.

mate and even shameful without touching upon third parties' rights (though dilemmas may arise here as well).

A sixth reason for client confidentiality may be found in the complexity of law and legal procedures and the concomitant legal ignorance of laypeople. As a consequence, most clients are unaware of the possible legal importance of different kinds of facts. Unless clients may be sure that nothing they confidentially reveal will reach the outside world, they will not be completely open toward their lawyers. If they do not tell their lawyers everything, legally important facts may not be duly considered, with possibly fatal consequences for such clients' cases. Thus regarded, confidentiality seems an important prerequisite or even essential part of fair trial.

Seventh, and not exhaustively so, lawyers may be unwilling to be surprised by clients' information divulged in court or otherwise, about which they knew nothing beforehand. Such ignorance may indeed hinder the effectiveness of their defence. Also, opponents may unexpectedly come forward with evidence expected to be produced by clients themselves, under disclosure rules or otherwise. Courts may draw conclusions from this, at the expense of such wrongly silent parties.[7]

Still there may be facts damaging for clients but essential for opponents or other third parties. Thus clients may tell their lawyers of fraudulent schemes so cunningly set up that the parties disadvantaged by them will be unable to offer convincing evidence for their cases. Client confidentiality does not really seem plausible anyway. Indeed, Bentham was quite clear on this:[8]

> English judges have taken care to exempt the professional members of the partnership from so unpleasant an obligation as that of rendering service to justice.

Again: without the facts of the case there can be no lawful adjudication leading to justice and right. So much seems self-evident. Thus regarded, client confidentiality is part of what may be the fundamental moral – or simply human – problem of the bar, expressed by Luban in terms of lawyers as accomplices in crime:[9]

> In his essay on Francis Bacon (1561–1626) Thomas Babington Macaulay (1800–1859) asked rhetorically 'whether it be right that a man should, with a wig on his head, and a band around his neck, do for a guinea what, without those appendages, he would think it wicked and infamous to do for an empire.' Perhaps the most fundamental moral problem implicated in the practice of law arises from the fact that lawyers, acting on behalf of their clients, may lie under a professional obligation to further unjust causes or employ means – such as impeaching the character and reliability of truthful adverse witnesses at trial – that appear immoral. The problem is heightened by the fact that the lawyer furthers client ends by argument and persuasion. Though the doctor enables unhealthy malefactors to continue their careers of injustice, the lawyer, unlike the doctor, seems to be their accomplice in injustice. . . . In contemporary terms, it might be said that the very point of legal practice – to stand by one's client without passing judgment on him or her – is its deepest defect.

[7] See Kaptein (2005) for more on arguments in favour of client confidentiality.
[8] Bentham (1827: ch V, para 2).
[9] Luban (1992).

Why then are lawyers and so many more legal professionals so adamant on the issue of client confidentiality? This leads to what may be called their 'real reason': the bar is a commercial enterprise in essence. If lawyers do not stand by their clients, there is no market for the bar left and no money to be made by lawyers, it is suggested. Why should lawyers be Good Samaritans for third parties? Such third parties may not be poor and powerless anyway. The law is not about supererogatory love for all fellow human beings, but about procedure to be exploited to the fullest. Lawyers are no judges, realising law and right. They present their cases before courts who are to realise law and right. Without proper division of labour there can be no fair procedure, etc.

How to tip the scales of such arguments pro and con, quite apart from the logical possibility that there are still more such arguments in different directions?

V. CLIENT CONFIDENTIALITY QUALIFIED: NOT TO COVER THREATS OF SERIOUS HARM

Client confidentiality is seldom, if ever, taken to be unconditional or even absolute. Disclosure rules may prescribe that parties and lawyers hand over all relevant information to the court, at least in civil and administrative cases. Several jurisdictions also prescribe notification to authorities of clients' data concerning money laundering, tax fraud, or even financial damage to private or public enterprise. Whether such rules are effective in commercial or even criminal lawyers' practice is another matter.[10]

Also, client confidentiality may not cover all information reaching lawyers from third parties. The lawyer's duty to remain silent on issues not related to court cases may be contested as well. Still, professional silence is the norm. This also implies the lawyer's exemption from any testimony in court related to subject matter covered by client confidentiality.

Even such relatively marginal restrictions on client confidentiality, imposed and sometimes enforced by legislatures and some bar associations, are enthusiastically criticised by lawyers and the legal community in general. One important exception however is generally accepted, at least in legal and medical practice, for good reason. Client confidentiality ought to be lifted in – relatively rare – cases of imminent danger to life and limb.

Thus clients may convince lawyers of their intention to illegally kill or maim third parties. In such cases, it may be reasonably certain that nobody else is aware of the threats involved. Lawyers and other professionals under duties of confidence are expected to speak out on such dangers, subject to conditions of proportionality and subsidiarity, in order to forestall serious mischief. Indeed, such information may not be related to any court case in which such clients are involved. This may furnish one more reason to lift client confidentiality in cases of

[10] See eg Robinson (1996) on confidential lawyers being money launderers' preferred brothers-in-arms.

imminent danger to life and limb. Some criminal codes and bar codes even prescribe this, with sanctions for non-complying professionals and others. Indeed, in relation to future dangers, lawyers and other professionals are generally regarded as being on equal ground with non-professionals.

It could not be otherwise, of course. Any client's interests or rights, and any general interests or even rights vested in client confidentiality, cannot outweigh any real threat of illegal killing or maiming. Even legal professionals are, or at least ought to be, fellow human beings if the need arises.

Difficult balancing issues may ensue. It may be quite hard to determine the seriousness of threats communicated to lawyers without the benefit of hindsight. Dangers to life and limb with possibly irreversible consequences may justify breaches of client confidentiality sooner than schemes to financially disadvantage unwitting third parties in any illegal fashion.

VI. LEGAL SYMMETRY OF PAST AND FUTURE IN FORBEARING AND UNDOING WRONGFUL HARM

All kinds of things past may still be covered by clients' and lawyers' silence, or so it seems. That is unless it can be demonstrated that the distinction between past and future, fundamental at first sight, is untenable at least in legal respects. Discussion of this will here concentrate on wrongful harm in a wide sense, as subject to litigation or other kinds of legal conflict resolution. This is not just limited to tort law, but may be interpreted as relating to contract law, property law, and other kinds of civil law. Adjudication in administrative law may relate to wrongful harm and compensation for it as well. Criminal law may deal with the most serious cases of harm, such as harm caused by killing and maiming. Legal conflicts not relating to any contested wrongful harm are relatively rare anyway. However, conclusions reached here may still be relevant for such issues.

First and foremost, how is legally relevant wrongful harm to be determined? Generally, this is done by comparing two futures: one actual and another potential. Or, harm is the difference between somebody's or some body's total future without any conduct (in a wide sense) having caused the harm, and the future including the consequences of the harmful conduct involved.

Such a counter-factually conditional concept of harm is not really necessary in simple cases of harm, as caused by breaking glasses and the like. However, consequences of bodily and associated mental and emotional harm may well need to be determined by comparison of different life expectancies. Also, and of course, only differences with monetary or otherwise legally relevant consequences count. Even this elementary concept of harm suffices to show that any categorical distinction between past and future is rather implausible, at least in legal respects. Related to this is the basic and uncontested function of compensation for wrongful harm: guaranteeing a future for the harmed person or body concerned as if no harm was ever inflicted at all.

This is one, or even the essential, function of compensation: undoing harm in principle. In adjudication, the basic issue is the restoration of the plaintiff's original position in the sense of bringing the wrongfully harmed person or body back to its state 'without the wrongful conduct'. Such 'undoing' of a harmful past is analogous to preventing harm in the future. Thus regarded, past and future are symmetrical from a legal point of view.

In many cases of wrongful harm, the payment of money may do, by way of restitution and/or compensation. In other cases, undoing mental and emotional harm may presuppose the identification of wrongdoers, to be made to pay for what they did wrong themselves.

Only when perpetrators are set to work to restore what they did wrong may victims come to forgive them, which may be an important prerequisite for mental and emotional well-being not just for victims, but for perpetrators as well. Slightly otherworldly philosophical as this may sound, the admittedly high costs of bringing perpetrators to task may be still worth it, at least in cases of serious and mala fide wrongdoing. Restoring victims to their rightful original positions and thus ensuring unencumbered prospects in the future for them may be the result. Victims may feel vindicated and move forward in the knowledge that justice has been done.

This is important not just in adjudication. In any case of wrongful harm without overriding excuses, tortfeasors (in a wide sense) better make good what they did wrong. In doing so they not just pay respect to their victims, but to themselves as well. Only if they rid themselves of their guilt by restoring victims to their original positions, can they be back to their own original position of respect as well. Thus regarded, the undoing of wrongful harm by the perpetrators who caused it in the first place is an important presupposition for respect and self-respect, being in turn parts of the 'cement' of society.

In practice, not much of this ideal of retributive justice may be realised; most perpetrators of harmful wrong being rather unwilling even to accept liability in public or their personal lives. Still, it is to be strived for by all means and to be enforced if the need arises.[11]

This way, retributive justice, whether enforced by courts or freely realised, changes the future and the past for the better. This is at odds with common sense which has it that the past is what it is and the future is what it may become. Interpretations of things past may be changed 'for the better', but still the past seems to be unchangeable in principle. This stance may be fundamental, in totally accepting everything that has happened:

> Happy the man, and happy he alone,
> He, who can call today his own:
> He, who secure within, can say
> Tomorrow do thy worst, for I have liv'd today.

[11] See Kaptein (2004) for more extensive discussion.

> Be fair, or foul, or rain, or shine,
> The joys I have possessed, in spite of fate are mine.
> Not Heav'n itself upon the past has power;
> But what has been, has been, and I have had my hour.

This is John Dryden's version of Horace's twenty-ninth ode (book 3), as cited by Thomas.[12] Even this kind of triumphant fatalism may be vanquished by changing the past for the better by undoing wrongful harm.

Wrongful differentiation between past and future may also be fostered by commonsensical tendencies to identify wrongful harm with wrongful conduct in the past, as contrasted with future conduct possibly causing harm and danger. For undoing harm, such differences in time are irrelevant. What matters is changing things for the better, as if nothing wrong ever happened or may happen. In line with this, it may even be contended that what matters in the end is the experience of wrongful harm, however caused. Such experiences may be largely irrelevant concerning matters of evidence and proof, necessarily related as these are to 'hard' facts like causes of harm and their tangible consequences. Still, if there is nothing like any negative experience related to facts with potential legal relevance like torts, there may be no relevant legal conflict either.

In line with this, and rather simplifying things, harm may be taken to be future harm only. All wrongful or even rightful harm done in the past may in a sense be reduced to present and future experiences of wrongful harm. If this holds good, all harm is present and future. Past harm is an empty notion then, or just identical to present and future harm. This way, there is not so much symmetry of harmful pasts and futures as elimination of all harm from the past.

Still more philosophical is the idea that if wrongful harm may be really undone, related to things past or future, there may be no negative attention to any worrying past or future either. Wittgenstein's remarks on this may stand for a long tradition on thinking about time and eternity in human life:[13]

> Wenn man unter Ewigkeit nicht unendliche Zeitdauer, sondern Unzeitlichkeit versteht, dann lebt der ewig, der in der Gegenwart lebt.
>
> Unser Leben ist ebenso endlos, wie unser Gesichtsfeld grenzenlos ist.

(If eternity is not taken to be an infinite period of time, but timelessness, then he who lives in the present, lives forever. Our life is just as infinite [without ends] as our point of view is boundless.) This echoes Dryden's 'for I have liv'd today.' High flying in philosophical skies maybe, but still an expression of an important aspect of human flourishing.

Anyway, the basic idea is clear enough. The past may be changed for the better after all. Not much sorcery, adjudicative or otherwise, is needed for this. So if there is to be no partnership in crime by client confidentiality concerning wrongful futures, then client confidentiality concerning things past is wrong in principle as well.

[12] Thomas (2009: 267).
[13] Wittgenstein (1921: 6.4311).

VII. CRITICISM: NOT EVEN CRIMINAL LAW AND PUNISHMENT CAN UNDO REALLY SERIOUS HARM

Changing the past for the better by the restoration of original positions probably does not really work in cases of serious killing and maiming. Given medical states of the art, not even the emotionally irreplaceable dead may be resurrected, just as having to drive or just ride around in a wheelchair cannot really be undone by any means. Criminal law and punishment may not positively add to civil law measures here. Even killing perpetrators cannot undo any earlier killing or maiming. So here it seems that the symmetry of future and past wrongful harm ends.

But then anything is better than nothing. Civil law measures in terms of sizeable sums of money paid by insurance companies in most cases may still ensure less humanly unacceptable futures for victims of serious crime in some senses. Criminal law cannot undo the consequences of crime, whatever other ends may be served by such punishment. Punishment is intended to let perpetrators suffer, for purposes of prevention and/or retribution. Such infliction of suffering may do their victims some good. Resentment or even desires for revenge may be more or less satisfied in such ways. Victims may gain by the criminal courts' authoritative establishment of perpetrators' liabilities. Otherwise, victims may think and feel that they are themselves guilty for their ordeal. Also, the purposes of special prevention and non-confrontation with victims may be well served by prison sentences.

Still, the essential element in undoing the past is lacking in criminal law, as there is nothing like compensation and restoration, or retribution in its original sense as quite distinct from retribution as infliction of pain. For this and other reasons, it is highly doubtful whether any system of punishment as infliction of pain may be really justified. Thus the high price to be paid in terms of the costs of imprisonment as the prime means of hurting convicts, both for these convicts and for society, may not be outweighed by any ends attainable by it at all. Again, Johnson aptly expressed a major part of this problem as follows:[14]

> The prosperity of a people is proportionate to the number of hands and minds usefully employed. To the community sedition is a fever, corruption is a gangrene, and idleness an atrophy. Whatever body, and whatever society, wastes more than it acquires, must gradually decay; and every being that continues to be fed, and ceases to labour, takes away something from the public stock.
>
> The confinement, therefore, of any man in the sloth and darkness of a prison, is a loss to the nation, and no gain to the Creditor.

Such concerns on imprisonment, concomitant idleness and suffering in the context of debts caused by loans hold good for any debt of course, as a consequence of wrongful harm or otherwise.

[14] Johnson (1758).

Indeed, reform of criminal law and punishment in restorative directions ought to be high on the agenda. Such restorative justice need not be 'soft' in any sense. Thus punishment as infliction of pain by incarceration may be better replaced by penal servitude, the proceeds of which may cover the costs of retribution, restitution and compensation for victims of crime. Nothing may ever undo all consequences of killing, maiming and other kinds of serious crime. Prevention of such wrongful harm remains infinitely superior to any attempt to undo it. Still, such restorative criminal law and punishment may do rather better than actual practice.[15]

Of course, many more criticisms may be put up against the principles and feasibility of undoing wrongful pasts. Probably the most radical version is denial of the very idea of undoing wrongful pasts as a humanly feasible and desirable end. The past is the past, however interpreted afterwards, only the present and the future may be changed for the better, it is contended. So, why not just care for such a better future, by trying to optimise positions for everybody and every body concerned? In such a radically 'futuristic' view of the role of things past, wrongful harm is no more than one of so many relevant factors determining the state of the present and the future.

Making perpetrators pay may still be motivated by considerations of special and general prevention. Knowing that one must pay for harmful wrongdoing may make potential wrongdoers think twice. Such prevention may not be totally effective and thus may not very forcefully back any legal measures against perpetrators, criminal or otherwise.

In such consequentialism, utilitarian or otherwise, no room is left for retributive justice in principle. Retribution is an essentially backward looking concept, at odds with any exclusive future orientation at first sight. Against this it may be put that victims' futures may be partly determined by memories of wrongful harm and concomitant resentment. Such negative factors may still be more or less undone by perpetrators' restoration of victims' original positions as far as possible. This may be more important in cases of intentional or otherwise mala fide wrongdoing with seriously harmful consequences than in cases of unintentional or otherwise bona fide wrongdoing without lasting consequences.

Still, even strict consequentialism may accommodate retributivism. Or better said, notwithstanding appearances to the contrary, retributivism may well be backed by utilitarian and other consequentialist considerations. All the better for retributivism of course, though it probably does not really need such unexpected support.

In civil law, consequentialism may be found in normative law and economics approaches rejecting retribution as restoration of original positions in favour of economic optimisation for everybody concerned, according to Kaldor-Hicks criteria or otherwise. Wrongful harm is not to be undone then, but is considered to be just one more factor determining cost-benefit optimisation strategies. Such and other alternative approaches to wrongful harm and its legal consequences, however implausible not just at first sight, are left out of account here.

[15] On this, see among others Kaptein (2004).

Also, retribution in whatever sense, by perpetrators' suffering or better by their undoing wrongful harm, may be thought to wrongly presuppose free will. Nobody and nothing can be held accountable for what had to happen anyway. On these and other grounds, abolition of criminal law and punishment has indeed been proposed. Such abolitionism does not seem to be a realistic option however.

Again, killing, maiming and consequences of other kinds of serious crime may never be really undone. But even the actual practice of criminal law and punishment may undo something of it, just as civil and administrative law, notwithstanding so many practical imperfections, may still undo parts of so many varieties of wrongful harm. Some symmetry may be left, against client confidentiality not to cover any kind of wrongful harm and its causes future or past.

VIII. NO SYMMETRY AT ALL FOR OTHER REASONS: PROCEDURALISM, OR RITUAL INSTEAD OF RIGHT?

However, one more fundamental objection against symmetry of client confidentiality issues past and future needs to pass muster. Even if symmetry is plausible from a material legal point of view, procedural law may imply that the establishment of facts in adjudication is fundamentally different from prediction of facts concerning threats in the future. Dealing with facts on possible killing, maiming and other specific harm in the future is best left to the police and to public administration bodies in general. Professionals and others may inform authorities of such threats, to be investigated and to be handled as the need arises, and within the rights and rightful interests of everybody concerned.

Establishment of facts in adjudication concerning past issues is quite another matter, or so it is contended. One basic rule of evidence law seems to put an end to debates on confidentiality ex post. Parties are expected to put forward evidence on their own behalf, if they want to obtain anything to which they feel entitled. Or, whoever wants to realise whatever rights against other parties in adjudication is to do the work needed for it, including collection of evidence, himself.[16] Also, defendants may put it that presumptions of good faith imply that they do not need to prove their innocence themselves (though this is rather problematic).[17]

Parties probably will not hide any information positively pertaining to their cases anyway. If they are unable to convince the court of their cases, they may expect answers like: 'You could have known about this before, next time you'd better care for documentation on your behalf.' In the asbestos case (see section I), the plaintiff may thus be told to be responsible for want of evidence and to be more careful in the future. In general, defendants may simply answer: 'Why are we to do plaintiffs' work at all?' So, client confidentiality may still cover information not serving parties' own causes after all. In a way this is an extension of the third ground for client confidentiality as mentioned in section IV.

[16] See Thayer (1890) for a classic discussion of issues of divisions of burdens of proof.
[17] On this, see eg Kaptein (2009).

However, such establishment of legal evidence and proof may be fallacious in its appeal to ignorance.[18] Why does the Monster of Loch Ness (or God for that matter) exist? Because there is no proof of their non-existence. This goes nicely the other way round as well: Why is there no Monster of Loch Ness? Because there is no proof of its existence (or again of the existence of God). Indeed, such appeal to lack of knowledge is fallacious inference of truth or plausibility of a statement from the absence of evidence for its denial. Such absence of course does not imply any impossibility of such evidence and proof in itself.

Indeed, plaintiffs unable to put forward convincing evidence may lose their cases. Courts may assume that the absence of sufficient evidence puts an end to their claims. But this cannot imply that such plaintiffs really had no case. They may simply have been unable to prove their cases, which is something quite different in principle. The asbestos case is a clear enough illustration here: the plaintiff was right, but he was unable to effectuate his rights as long as the defendant would not 'help' him out. This may seem at odds with the principle that adjudicative decisions ought to be based on the facts of the case as far as possible. So client confidentiality hiding unwelcome facts is under fire again.

Unless evidence law is further proceduralised. Then, issues of evidence and proof are no longer seen as relating to some or other objective reality, but to parties' contributions to convincing the court of the 'facts' of the case in principle, according to the rules of the game, which is evidence law. Under such 'proceduralism' different stories and their different rhetorical forces replace any appeal to historical or future realities as ascertainable independently of parties and courts concerned. It is even contended that at least in the context of adjudication there is nothing like 'the facts of the case'. What remains then are three different stories: the plaintiff's, the defendant's and the court's final version, deciding the case.

In such conceptions of legal evidence and proof in adjudication, issues of confidentiality are no longer problematic. If there are no facts of the case in principle, then there is nothing to be hidden by client confidentiality either. Likewise, fallaciousness of arguments *ad ignorantiam* presupposes the possibility that some or other evidence on the basis of facts of the case has not come to light yet. Again, if full proceduralism is right, there are no such facts in principle. Or, whatever story convinces the court best wins the case. Evidence and proof are not dependent on facts to be established some or other way but on courts' perceptions of parties' contributions complying with lawful procedure in adjudication. Or, legal realism extends to evidence and proof; the facts of the case are nothing more than what the courts establish as such. Johnson's sceptical remarks on client confidentiality and lawyers' doubtful roles in general may be taken to apply not just to law but to the facts of the case as well:[19]

> I asked him whether, as a moralist, he did not think that the practice of the law, in some degree, hurt the nice feeling of honesty. JOHNSON. 'Why no, Sir, if you act properly.

[18] On arguments *ad ignorantiam*, see, among others, Walton (1996) and Kaptein (2009).

[19] See Boswell (1793: 345–46).

> You are not to deceive your clients with false representations of your opinion: you are not to tell lies to a judge.' BOSWELL. 'But what do you think of supporting a cause which you know to be bad?' JOHNSON. 'Sir, you do not know it to be good or bad till the Judge determines it.'

In many ways such proceduralism is indeed a realistic depiction of what goes on in adjudication, fitting in nicely with general pictures of legal conflict as conflict per se. Which indeed is its fatally weak point in principle. If conflict resolution is nothing more than conflict itself, in which 'the facts of the case' totally depend on parties' rhetorical prowesses, then no reference points for any justice and fairness apart from the formalities of procedural law remain. Such meta-conflict will never really resolve conflict.

Please note that seemingly absurd consequences of 'pure proceduralism' in the establishment of evidence and proof cannot be criticised on the basis of common sense like: there was asbestos in the apartment roof or there was none and this may be established on the basis of historical evidence in principle. Against this it will be admitted that evidence law is no heuristically perfect procedural justice in the establishment of historical facts at all. 'But why take such facts for granted?', proceduralists may retort. Thus regarded, any appeal to any facts against proceduralism is a *petitio principii.*

That is, unless it may be shown that reliable evidence and proof on the basis of plain facts may be established in at least some cases. The asbestos case may be a hard one from an evidential point of view, not leading to any real historical certainty. However in other cases, courts may establish facts like fingerprints relating to one party and not to another beyond reasonable doubt. What is further done with such circumstantial evidence is another matter. Also, courts may indeed be dependent on parties' contributions in establishment of evidence to great extents. But then such contributions are not to be tested in terms of rhetorical force, but in terms of facts whenever possible. It just cannot be true that in all cases there is really nothing more than three stories and nothing like any facts of the case to be reliably established. Proceduralism cannot be the whole story.

Anyway, attempts to totally differentiate evidence and proof in court from any other evidence and proof, concerning future danger or otherwise, must fail, or adjudication would be nothing more than a stage act played according to the rules of the game, unrelated to any human reality apart from the all too human realities of just conflict – conflict as no more than conflict – continued in the court room. So the legal symmetry or even identity of past and future is back again. Problems of client confidentiality or whatever problem for that matter cannot be solved by procedural denial of anything like 'the facts of the case' in adjudication.

IX. CLIENTS' PERSPECTIVES IN AN IMPERFECT WORLD: CONFIDENTIALITY NOT TO BE DONE AWAY WITH AFTER ALL?

So, objections against client confidentiality based on symmetries of past and future wrongful harm still loom large, at least in principle. But, what would clients think of this, in their roles of plaintiffs or defendants in the actual practice of litigation and other kinds of legal conflict resolution? Even if they want to be completely honest in their causes and means to be deployed against opponents, their reaction may well be: 'All very nice this anti-confidentiality, but why hire lawyers if they cannot be trusted?'

If lawyers' services cannot be circumvented in the end, clients may well decide not to be open with their lawyers on everything they think relevant for their case, certainly not so if they think such information to be detrimental to their interests. Thus any abolition of client confidentiality, however plausible on paper, may be a paper tiger in practice.

This relates to the question of parties' openness on information pertaining to their case apart from any lawyer-client relationships (as already discussed in section IV). Criminal defendants have a right to remain silent while others are expected to speak out. But, how effective may burdens of proof or even disclosure rules be against parties expecting not to be caught out on any information they would rather keep to themselves? Even under oath, so many parties may lie without paying any price for it in this world. Clients may even conspire with lawyers, or lawyers with their clients, in hiding potentially decisive facts of the case at hand if this seems to serve their own best interests, however at odds with law and right. Opponents and courts may be unable to uncover such information.

Non-confidentiality, as far as it is effective at all, may have unwanted consequences as well. Most clients are unaware of the legal relevance of information concerned. So under non-confidentiality they may wrongly remain silent on facts that in fact further their causes. Thus an employer in The Netherlands who found out about a thieving employee by covertly operating a CCTV system did not even turn to a lawyer in order to get rid of this employee, due to the wrong supposition that improperly obtained evidence will be thrown out by the court. A lawyer might have told him otherwise, but the employer feared losing his case as a consequence of the court being informed of the CCTV system.[20]

So, non-confidentiality and attendant disclosure rules may be both ineffective and dangerous. This is not just a consequence of clients' silence. Unfair opponents may exploit the misplaced openness of weaker parties. Banks, insurance companies and other corporate players may misuse honestly divulged clients' information in litigation which is not perfect procedural justice for so many reasons. Adding to this is the problem of parties and lawyers willing to divulge information but confronted

[20] See also Luban (1988: 189 v) for a dramatic example in a murder case.

with opponents effectively hiding any unwelcome facts. What is justice and fairness in surrendering to such mala fide parties?

Public prosecution offices and courts unwilling or even unable to do justice on the basis of facts and law concerned cause part of this imperfection. Why speak out if there is no guarantee that openness on facts concerned will lead to the right results? May this not make lawyers want to be as silent as their clients if the need arises, even *contra legem* against disclosure rules or otherwise?

Adding to this are imperfections of material law, not always determinant for the right results, it seems. Thus the human price to be paid for criminal law and punishment as infliction of pain is high (see section VII). Criminal lawyers remaining silent on any client's incriminating information may well justify this by asking why they are expected to surrender clients to irrational or even inhuman consequences. Dangerous moralising in legal contexts maybe, but still in accordance with positive law upholding client confidentiality in criminal procedure.

X. LEGAL PRACTICE: VIRTUES OF TRUTHFULNESS COME FIRST

The uneasy upshot, not just from clients' perspectives in legal practice, may well be: however implausible client confidentiality may be in principle, it will not be abolished in the real world any time soon. Also, and however strong the symmetry argument against client confidentiality may be, its plausibility in principle may well depend on pro-confidentiality arguments which have not come to light yet (as noted before, see section IV). Such issues *ad ignorantiam* need not be worrying, however. Things may change as soon as better arguments pro client confidentiality are available, overriding arguments against client confidentiality not just based on the symmetry of past and future wrongful harm. Nothing much points in such a direction right now.

In the meantime, the practical consequence is: speak out, unless secrecy leads to better realisation of material law and right. This is backed not just by the legal symmetry of past and future. Again, without the facts of the case there can be no material law and right in legal conflict resolution. Remember that most conflicts are about contested facts, not about contested law. Virtues of truth and truthfulness come first, however difficult it may be to establish any truth in some cases. Which side is right may be contested, but not always contestable for that reason alone. But virtues of truth and truthfulness will not always do. Professional silence may still lead to more lawful results at times, against mala fide opponents, and/or before incompetent courts or even given wrongful law and legal procedure.

So, virtues in balancing such factors are important as well. Lawyers need to 'look forward' to possible results, both in terms of avoidance of danger and in terms of undoing wrongful harm as a consequence of things past. They ought to act from the knowledge that their professional conduct is at least partly determinant for courts' rulings as well. Drawing consequences from this may be extremely difficult, to be sure. What to divulge to other parties and to courts, and what not?

This may require lawyers' more or less solitary balancing of reasons, with attendant dangers of irreparable mistakes.

Important here is the intellectual and moral challenge not of living by the rules – if such rules are clear guidelines at all – but of positively exploiting opportunities offered by legal rules and procedures for realising material law and right. Whatever may be thought about relationships of law in the books and law in action, what counts in the end is the quality of law in terms of its realisation for human beings.

This may lead to professional disobedience or even instrumentalism in violating positive law for good reasons at times. Thus disclosure rules may indeed be disregarded in cases of undeservedly poor parties against mala fide opponents, just as criminal defendants may be confidentially protected against any punishment which may not be really justified. On the other hand, confidentiality however legally prescribed may be lifted if the main facts of the case leading to justice are to come to light in no other way.

Not just concerning confidentiality, but regarding procedural rules in general, it ought to be remembered that there is no such thing as perfect procedural justice. 'Lawful but awful' in any material sense may still be the result of sticking to procedure. Lawyers live by procedure. Other people, be they plaintiffs or defendants, may be interested in a fair trial, but will probably be more interested in material results in the first place. This of course was one of the driving forces between Bentham's anomism or abolitionism (as explained by him in 1812 and 1827), reaching much further than his objections against client confidentiality and not just in evidence law.

So professionally and humanly virtuous lawyers will always ask themselves what more or less rightful means may lead to rightful results, given the truth of the matter as far as it is available. Virtues not just of jurisprudence, but also of practical wisdom in a wider sense or 'moresprudence', are rather more important than observance of legal rules. Part of such moresprudence may still be determined by the need for clients' trust (in the line of Johnson's beautiful definitions, see section IV). Then again, there ought not to be trust in everything. There ought to be trust in the right outcome in the first place.

Against this it may be objected that lawyers are not to usurp the role of courts in determining what is law and right in casu or even in general. Sure, but let it be stressed again that lawyers withholding essential facts without further thinking are acting rather more like judges than their colleagues trying to realise law and right by balancing reasons for and against secrecy. Why? Again: because hiding facts determines the outcome of adjudication at least in part.

Of course, it is much simpler to stick to professional secrecy apart from extreme exceptions and not to think about consequences, for reasons like: 'this is no lawyer's responsibility, courts are there to correct wrongs', etc. Also, professional consciences are sometimes laid to uneasy rest by appeal to slippery slope arguments like: if clients can no longer trust lawyers, there will be no more lawyers' clients and so the sacred institution of the bar will come to an end.

This is not just fallacious, it is also a denial of the lawyer's roles in the realisation of material justice and right. Professional secrecy may be good for commerce, but the bar cannot be just about making money in the end. According to Kutz:[21]

> The ambition of law is to resolve conflict, exchanging the coin of private (and public) violence for its own currency. For idealists, law's currency is justice, and it resolves conflict by reference to morally grounded rights. For cynics, law's currency *is* currency.

If law's currency is justice (which it ought to be) then lawyers are to serve justice as well. They may, or even must be one-sided in this, serving their clients' rightful interests in the first place. Clients are not to be worse off with lawyers' assistance than without it, as long as they are not furthering any illegal or even criminal schemes. Sure, but the legal and moral qualities of the law and of society are not to be worse as a consequence of there being lawyers either (see section IV on this).

Of course, lawyers' virtues are not to be limited to zeal for the truth of the matter. Lawyers need to contribute to realisation of law, right and justice in many more ways. Thus they need to explain to some clients that their heartfelt causes are less just than such clients are deeply convinced of, and/or that such causes may not be worth the cost, time and hassle of court proceedings. Some cases may be better resolved by informal dispute resolution, etc. Mutual understanding and sometimes even sympathy may forbear lots of harm, procedural and otherwise. Communicative and even rhetorical virtues in winning everybody over to the right side are to serve such purposes.[22]

What matters in the end is cooperation of all concerned toward forbearing and solving legal conflict in a humanly acceptable fashion. Such cooperation presupposes common knowledge of the facts concerned, in as far as possible. Solidarity and social cohesion are not really compatible with secrecy and confidentiality, unless there are special reasons for hiding facts. The truth of the matter ought to be the common ground, not just in restoration of original positions for everybody and everybody concerned as presupposition of respect and self-respect (section V).

Lawyers are to play their own specific roles in this. Such a professional practice may be much more interesting and challenging in the end than just confidentially cooperating with any clients, however criminal, and going for their – or simply the – money. Also, lawyers' consciences do not need to be left in the driveway, as the saying goes, just as the same consciences will haunt lawyers less afterwards.

Finally, and for readers not liking this idealistic openness on confidential issues, remember everything to be found here against secrecy may be skipped, in order to concentrate on the timeless centre of this frame story. History may be reversed after all; harm may be undone even if it is better avoided in the first place.

[21] Kutz (2003).

[22] See also Kaptein (1998) and (2003) on lawyers' roles and lawyers' ethics.

REFERENCES

Bentham, J (1812) *An Introductory View of the Rationale of Evidence: For the Use of Non-Lawyers as well as Lawyers* in J Bowring and J Mill (eds) (1843) *The Works of Jeremy Bentham,* vol 6 (Edinburgh, William Tait).

——(1827) *Rationale of Judicial Evidence, Specially Applied to English Practice* (London, Hunt & Clarke).

Boswell, J (1793/1811) *The Life of Samuel Johnson* (London, Everyman's Library).

Fuller, LL (1969) *The Morality of Law* (New Haven & London, Yale University Press).

Golding, MP (1984) *Legal Reasoning* (New York, Alfred A Knopf).

Johnson, S (1755) *A Dictionary Of The English Language: In Which The Words Are Deduced From Their Originals And Illustrated In Their Different Significations By Examples From The Best Writers. To Which Are Prefixed, A History Of The Language, And An English Grammar.* In Two Volumes. (London, printed by W Strahan, for J and P Knapton; T and T Longman; C Hitch and L Hawes; A Millar; and R And J Dodsley).

——(1758) 'Debtors' Prisons (I)' 22 *The Idler*, also in S Johnson (2009) *Consolation in the Face of Death* (London, Penguin Books).

Kaptein, HJR (1998) 'Against Professional Ethics' in C Sampford, N Preston and CA Bois (eds), *Public Sector Ethics: Finding and Implementing Values* (Routledge Studies in Governance and Public Policy 1) (Sydney and London, The Federation Press/Routledge).

——(1999) 'Facts and Law' in CB Gray (ed), *The Philosophy of Law: An Encyclopedia* (New York & London, Garland Publishing).

——(2003) 'Just Criminal Lawyers? Professional Ethics and Problems of Punitive Justice: Restorative Perspectives' 88 *Archiv für Rechts- und Sozialphilosophie* 141.

——(2004) 'Against the Pain of Punishment: on Penal Servitude and Procedural Justice for All' in HJR Kaptein and M Malsch (eds), *Crime, Victims and Justice: Essays on Principles and Practice* (Aldershot, Ashgate).

——(2005) 'Secrets of Confidentiality: Adjudication *ad ignorantiam* against Material Rights and Justice?' in C Dahlmann and W Krawietz (eds), *Values, Rights and Duties in Legal and Philosophical Discourse* (*Rechtstheorie Beiheft* 21) (Berlin, Duncker & Humblot).

——(2009) 'Rigid Anarchic Principles of Proof: Anomist Panaceas Against Legal Pathologies of Proceduralism' in HJR Kaptein, H Prakken and B Verheij (eds), *Legal Evidence and Proof: Statistics, Stories, Logic* (Farnham & Burlington, Ashgate Publishing Limited).

Kutz, C (2003) 'Why We Obey the Law (Review of Jules Coleman, *The Practice of Principle*)' *The Times Literary Supplement* 3–6, 26.

Luban, D (1988) *Lawyers and Justice: An Ethical Study* (Princeton, NJ, Princeton University Press).

——(1992) 'Legal Ethics' in LC Becker and CB Becker (eds), *Encyclopedia of Ethics* (New York & London, Garland Publishing).

C-L de Montesquieu, *De l'esprit des lois* (1748) also in AM Cohler, BC Miller and HS Stone (eds) *The Spirit of the Laws* (Cambridge Texts in the History of Political Thought) (Cambridge University Press, Cambridge, 1989).

Robinson, J (1996) *The Laundrymen: Money Laundering the World's Third Largest Business* (London, Arcade Publishing).

Thayer, JB (1890) 'The Burden of Proof' 4 *Harvard Law Review* 2, 45, also in W Twining and A Stein (eds), (1992) *Evidence and Proof* (Aldershot, Dartmouth Publishing Company).

Thomas, K (2009) *The Ends of Life: Roads to Fulfilment in Early Modern England* (Oxford, Oxford University Press).

Walton, D (1996) *Arguments from Ignorance* (University Park, Pennsylvania, Penn State Press).

Wittgenstein, L (1921) 'Logisch-Philosophische Abhandlung' 44 *Annalen der Naturphilosophie* (and later editions and translations).

12

Virtuous Deliberation on the Criminal Verdict[1]

HO HOCK LAI

I. PROOF BEYOND REASONABLE DOUBT

TO CONVICT A person of a crime, the fact-finder[2] must be satisfied beyond reasonable doubt that she is guilty as charged. What does it mean to be satisfied beyond reasonable doubt? In England, the jury is told that it means 'being sure'. The model instruction states:[3]

> Model Jury Instruction: If after considering all the evidence you are sure that the defendant is guilty, you must return a verdict of 'Guilty'. If you are not sure, your verdict must be 'Not Guilty'.

The Model Jury Instruction is misleading in at least one respect: it is plainly insufficient that the fact-finder is sure of the defendant's guilt.[4] After all, an unshakeable belief may be completely irrational.[5] One might argue that the standard of proof is correctly applied if and only if on the evidence admitted in court, rational ground exists which would justify the fact-finder feeling sure about guilt. The Model Jury Instruction is better formulated as a Decisional Rule that speaks to the jury in these terms (emendations in italics):

> Decisional Rule: If after considering all the evidence, *you judge that there is sufficient rational ground for being sure that the defendant is guilty*, you must return a verdict of 'Guilty'; *otherwise*, your verdict must be 'Not Guilty'.

[1] This chapter expands on ideas sketched in Ho (2009).

[2] The fact-finder can be an individual (the judge at a bench trial) or a group of persons (the jury). Each juror, like the judge sitting alone, has to evaluate the evidence and make up her own mind. This chapter focuses on individual deliberation. For general discussion of group-deliberative virtues, see Aikin and Clanton (2010), and on the attribution of virtues to social collectives and institutions such the jury, see Fricker (2010) and Lahroodi (2007).

[3] Judicial Studies Board (2007: Specimen Direction 2).

[4] The Model Jury Instruction is also misleading in other respects. Verdict deliberation is sometimes constrained by legal rules which require or forbid the fact-finder to reason on the evidence along certain lines. Consideration of these legal rules falls outside the ambit of this chapter.

[5] In an English case, *Young* (1995) 2 Cr App R 379, some members of the jury used an ouija board to ascertain the facts of the case.

The Decisional Rule still leaves too much unsaid. How should the fact-finder go about 'considering . . . the evidence'? And when should she 'judge that there is sufficient rational ground for being sure that the defendant is guilty'? On matters such as these, the fact-finder should not be allowed to do as she pleases. For the sake of certainty and objectivity, so it has been argued, the law should provide a Deliberative Procedure, a set of instructions on how to evaluate the evidence and arrive at the verdict. Laudan gives as examples three possible forms of Deliberative Procedure (without, however, endorsing any of them). They are formulated respectively in terms of credibility, plausibility and reasonableness.

> <u>Deliberative Procedure</u>:
>
> *a)* If there is credible, inculpatory evidence or testimony that would be very hard to explain if the defendant were innocent, and no credible, exculpatory evidence or testimony that would be very difficult to explain if the defendant were guilty, then convict. Otherwise acquit.[6]
>
> *b)* If the prosecution's story about the crime is plausible and you can conceive of *no* plausible story that leaves the defendant innocent, then convict. Otherwise, acquit.[7]
>
> *c)* Figure out whether the facts established by the prosecution rule out every reasonable hypothesis you can think of that would leave the defendant innocent. If they do, convict; otherwise, acquit.[8]

If the choice of Deliberative Procedure is to be made according to the degree of accuracy (conceived say as the ratio of correct to wrong verdicts that following a particular procedure will achieve in the long run), how is one to know which is in fact the most accurate? Leaving this question aside, as two reviewers of Laudan's book have jointly noted, none of the three procedures set out above eliminates subjectivity from verdict deliberation; in their words:[9]

> [A]lthough the (intended) meanings of *credible*, *plausible*, and *reasonable* differ from *thought to be credible*, *thought to be plausible*, and *thought to be reasonable*, respectively, it is questionable whether the average juror has any way of determining whether the normative terms apply in a given case other than by seeing whether she herself finds various stories and hypotheses credible, plausible, or reasonable. In other words, jurors may have to see how they (subjectively) judge a given hypothesis or possibility in order to apply the normative terms in question. For this reason, it is doubtful whether presentation of these normative terms would enable jurors to get beyond reliance on their own subjective assessments, contrary to Laudan's intention. [Emphasis in original.]

Reasonable fact-finders faced with the same set of evidence may well arrive at different conclusions on whether a story or hypothesis is credible, plausible or reasonable. A major source of possible disagreement is the discretion that is imported by the non-binary nature of the operative criteria. For example, the Deliberative Procedure of form (b) above requires the fact-finder to consider whether 'the pros-

[6] Laudan (2006: 82).
[7] ibid.
[8] ibid 83.
[9] Goldman and Goldman (2009: 65–66).

ecution's story about the crime is plausible' and whether there is any 'plausible story that leaves the defendant innocent'. Since plausibility is surely a matter of degree, the fact-finder has to judge, amongst other things, whether a story that points to innocence is plausible *enough*, in the context of the case, to raise a reasonable doubt.

No acceptable Deliberative Procedure can do away with discretion. It is easy, of course, to think of a non-discretionary method of deciding on the verdict. We could simply toss a coin. But this method of decision is epistemically and ethically objectionable: it is arbitrary and hence both inaccurate and unjust. Notice also that this method of decision *excludes* deliberation, and it is only by doing so that it eliminates room for the exercise of discretion.

The most that any acceptable Deliberative Procedure can do is to give rational structure to deliberation and highlight the places where the exercise of judgement is called for. Judgement is an inescapable dimension of verdict deliberation. The quest for a Deliberative Procedure is not a quest for an algorithm of legal proof, understood as rules that are to be mechanically applied. What is sought is less ambitious: a rational framework on the directions of inquiry, the purpose of which is to identify the key questions that need to be addressed. Ultimately, the trier of the case must find answers to those questions, and the way to the verdict, by her own lights.[10]

Judgement in this context is exercised through the employment of various cognitive faculties, resources and skills. Deliberation requires imagination and creativity; these are needed, for instance, in the formation of factual hypotheses. Another cognitive resource is sensitivity; this can open up epistemic access to another person's emotions and consequently to an understanding of her behaviour. Insensitivity to the feelings of the rape victim may cause blindness to the possibility that the failure to make a prompt complaint (or, in old legal language, to raise a hue and cry) is other than a sign of fabrication. Perceptiveness is also an asset; a good judge of testimony is alert and responsive to cues to a witness's trustworthiness.[11] Depending on whether and how these and other cognitive faculties, resources and skills are deployed, a verdict deliberation may be appraised accordingly as well or poorly conducted.

While imaginativeness, creativity, sensitivity and perceptiveness are cognitive excellences, they would appear to be morally neutral; after all, I can be creative in manipulating a person by being sensitive to her feelings, striking at a time when I perceive the target to be at her most vulnerable. The thesis of this chapter is that

[10] I agree with Pardo (2008) that while models of legal proof 'may provide useful heuristics for understanding some aspects of the process, . . . they will not eliminate the need for the wise exercise of discretion and judgment by human decision-makers in evaluating evidence'. The *standard* of proof beyond reasonable doubt is exactly that, a standard rather than a rule. As Shiffrin has argued, although a standard is not as clear and does not provide as much guidance as a rule, it has the virtue of inducing 'moral deliberation and the deployment and exercise of moral skills' on the part of the person (in our case, the fact-finder) who has to apply the standard (2010: 1222), and this is to be welcome because, among other things, 'it directly promotes moral relations between agents' by demanding 'active engagement and understanding of the situations of others' (in our case, 'others' would include eg the accused) (ibid 1223–24).

[11] See the account of testimonial sensibility offered by Fricker (2007: 67–81).

verdict deliberation is open to ethical appraisal against standards of epistemic virtues that are – or partake of – a moral nature. On this approach, the appraisal does not turn on whether the verdict in fact hits upon the truth. A bit more will be said of the approach before an examination of the epistemic virtues is made.

II. AN ANALOGY: CLIFFORD AND THE 'ETHICS OF BELIEF'

William Kingdon Clifford began his famous 1877 essay 'The Ethics of Belief' with this scenario: a shipowner is about to send to sea a ship full of passengers. He knows that the vessel is old, not well-built, in a state of some disrepair and the long voyage ahead may be choppy. Doubts prey on his mind about the seaworthiness of the vessel. A delay will be both inconvenient and costly. Through self-deception, the owner brushes aside his doubts and convinces himself that it is safe to let the ship sail. The vessel sinks in mid-ocean and all aboard drown. According to Clifford, the sincerity of the owner's belief in the soundness of the ship does not absolve him of responsibility for the deaths:[12]

> It is admitted that he did sincerely believe in the soundness of his ship; but the sincerity of his conviction can in no wise help him, because *he had no right to believe on such evidence as was before him.* He had acquired his belief not by honestly earning it in patient investigation, but by stifling his doubts. [Emphasis in original.]

What if the ending was a happy one? Suppose instead that the journey went well and the ship reached her destination in one piece. Does this diminish the shipowner's culpability? According to Clifford: 'Not one jot.'

> The question of right or wrong has to do with the origin of his belief, not the matter of it; not what it was, but how he got it; not whether it turned out to be true or false, but whether he had a right to believe on such evidence as was before him.[13]

It seems that what matters in the assessment of the shipowner's culpability is not whether his belief happened to be correct; it is whether his holding of the belief was justified. Clifford stakes his reputation, for better or for worse, on this so-called principle of evidentialism: 'it is wrong always, everywhere, and for anyone, to believe anything upon insufficient evidence'.[14] His critics say that this principle overstretches.[15] It is not necessarily wrong to believe something without evidence, as in believing directly what you perceive. But I digress; it is not my intention to venture into the debate on evidentialism.

My purpose in citing Clifford's hypothetical example is to draw attention to the plausibility of a legal analogy. The shipowner's decision resembles in this respect

[12] Clifford (1879).

[13] ibid 178.

[14] ibid 186.

[15] For a rejoinder to Clifford, see James (1986: 60): 'Our passional nature not only lawfully may, but must, decide an option between propositions, whenever it is a genuine option that cannot by its nature be decided on intellectual grounds'. For a defence of evidentialism, see Feldman (2000) and Feldman and Conee (1985). For the opposing literature, see eg DeRose (2000).

the fact-finder's decision on the criminal verdict: each has a practical dimension, carrying a significant risk of harm to others. If the shipowner's prediction of a safe journey is incorrect, many lives will perish; if the fact-finder convicts a person whom she wrongly believes to be guilty, the person will be unjustly stigmatised and punished. Complications in the role of belief in trial deliberation need not detain us. For convenience, assume the following: the fact-finder must not find the accused guilty unless, on the evidence adduced, she judges and hence believes that the accused is in fact guilty.[16] By 'judgement', I mean the mental act that elicits belief. Unless a person is irrational, if she judges that p, she will come to believe that p. The 'ethics of belief' is better termed the 'ethics of judgement', or better yet, 'the ethics of deliberation'.

To be sure, we want the fact-finder's belief about the material facts to be correct. If she finds the accused guilty of murder because she judges and hence believes, amongst other things, that he killed the deceased, we want it to be true that, in fact, he killed the deceased. Even so, it must be remembered that when Clifford talked about the 'ethics of belief', he did not mean the correctness of the belief. That the shipowner was correct in his belief that the ship was sturdy enough for the voyage did not absolve him of moral culpability. Does the same apply to a guilty verdict? So far as the 'ethics of verdict deliberation' is concerned, are we to say that the truth of the fact-finder's belief that the accused killed the deceased is neither here nor there? The fact-finder can be culpable in *judging* and hence *believing* sincerely that the accused killed the deceased even when her *belief* is true and the accused did in fact kill the deceased. If it can be said that Clifford's shipowner acted unethically in quelling his doubt about the seaworthiness of his vessel, can it not also be said that the fact-finder acts unethically if, out of a malevolent desire to put the accused behind bars, a desire born of prejudice, she quells her doubt about whether he did kill the deceased? Although, as we are supposing, the truly guilty gets the outcome he deserves, the deliberation which led to the verdict was morally tainted.

III. VERDICT DELIBERATION AS THE OBJECT OF EVALUATION AND EPISTEMIC VIRTUES AS THE STANDARDS OF EVALUATION

The object of Clifford's moral appraisal was not, as such, the act of the shipowner in sending the vessel to sea; it was the shipowner's belief in the seaworthiness of the vessel, in the sense of his *believing* it or his *holding* of the belief. Clifford is widely taken to mean not just that it is epistemically wrong to believe something on no or inadequate evidence, it is also ethically wrong to do so: hence, the tantalising title of his essay, 'The Ethics of Belief'. But it is not obvious how the mere holding of a belief can in and of itself be ethically wrong.

I propose to take as the object of evaluation neither the holding of a belief (on one conception, a mental state) nor the acting on the belief (allowing the vessel to

[16] This is a simplification. See further Ho (2008: ch 3, part 1).

set sail), but the process of deliberation (a mental activity) which produced the belief. Further, and more on this in the next section, I propose to take epistemic virtues as the standards of excellence for verdict deliberation. In choosing this orientation, I take a leaf from the works of some virtue epistemologists of the 'responsibilist' variety. They include Hookway who has called for a move away from the 'doxastic paradigm' of epistemic evaluation (where the focus is on evaluating beliefs and their objects, concentrating on issues such as the justification for a belief) to a paradigm that treats epistemology as a 'theory of inquiry' (where the attention is on the agent and her conduct of evidential reasoning).[17] Guy Axtell, a proponent of 'zetetic responsibilism', offers a similar conception of epistemology and its central tasks by placing emphasis on the quality of the agent's motives and efforts in pursuing epistemic ends.[18]

There is some parallel between the evaluation of mental and physical performances. The excellence that is judged of a physical performance like dancing or acting is 'the excellence in the activity and not in some separable result'.[19] Can't something similar be said of verdict deliberation? There is at least one glaring difference. Unlike dancing and acting, deliberation has an end product, the verdict. A closer analogy would be the case of a fireman who risks his life to try to rescue a baby from a burning building. He fails despite doing all that was humanly possible to save the infant. Our sadness over the baby's death does not diminish the praise that the fireman deserves for his courage (even though the tragedy tempers, as it should, our celebration of his virtue or his virtuous act).

In much the same way, the court may, from the point of view of an all-knowing spectator, fail to reach the correct verdict: a person who is in fact innocent is convicted or someone who is in fact guilty is acquitted. Both results are wrong and bad, the first traditionally regarded as more deplorable than the second. The fact-finder may not be culpable for the mistake. Given that the court is rarely if ever presented with all of the relevant evidence (some may be missing and others may be deliberately withheld by the parties), given that honest witnesses may display idiosyncratic mannerisms that fit 'empirically reliable stereotype[s] of insincerity'[20] and, conversely, that mendacious witnesses may be highly artful in projecting an image of trustworthiness, and given how a skilful counsel can make even a truthful witness stumble under cross-examination,[21] the (as it happened) erroneous verdict may well be the one that a fair-minded, conscientious, careful, etc – in

[17] Hookway (2006a). See also Hookway (2003).

[18] See eg Axtell (2008).

[19] Annas (2003: 26).

[20] Fricker (2007: 41).

[21] Honest witnesses are perhaps especially prone to stumble. In the novel by Barnes (2006: 193), there is this dialogue between the accused and his solicitor:

> 'Mr Meek, I fear my parents were not good witnesses.'
>
> 'I would not say that, Mr Edalji. It is rather the case that the best people are not necessarily the best witnesses. The more scrupulous they are, the more honest, the more they dwell on each word of the question and doubt themselves out of modesty, then the more they can be played with by counsel like Mr Disturnal.'

short, the epistemically virtuous – fact-finder would reach. No person, however intellectually virtuous, is omniscient. And just as a wrong outcome may be arrived at virtuously, a correct outcome may be reached in a vicious way. Epistemic virtue is neither sufficient nor necessary for a right verdict. Truth or falsity in the outcome, viewed from the perspective of an all-knowing spectator, is not that by which the excellence of deliberation should be appraised.

An objection may be raised against my taking deliberation as the object of evaluation. Often we do not know how the deliberation was conducted or the real motivation for the verdict. What goes on in the jury room is secret. Even if members of the jury were biased or came to their judgement of guilt hastily, with callous unconcern for the accused, there is usually no way for us to know about it. At a bench trial, a judge who falls into the same vices may hide it from us by coming up with reasons, ex post facto, for the verdict that she thinks will meet public approval. But these raise issues of transparency and sincerity. While they are important, they do not undermine my claim about the normative standards of deliberative excellence. How well or badly I have deliberated is independent of whether others know how I have deliberated.

It might be said, as a further objection, that excellence of deliberation is not what really matters; it is the right outcome that matters most. A number of replies can be made to this. First, we want the fact-finder to deliberate virtuously because, on one view, the exercise of epistemic virtue is truth-conducive and reduces the likelihood of error. Secondly, while we value correctness in the outcome, it is not all that matters. That a guilty verdict was motivated by malicious ill-feeling is an independent source of grievance, one that is *additional* to the injustice that one suffers if convicted of a crime one did not commit.

Thirdly, another way of getting to the importance of excellence in deliberation is to move our attention away from the accused and to the fact-finder, the agent of deliberation. The fact-finder has a legal duty to deliberate well. This is true even though the duty may well be impossible to enforce (strict rules on jury secrecy in many jurisdictions is one obstacle) and the law is silent on much of the content of that duty. Quite apart from the fact that the law requires the fact-finder to deliberate well on the verdict, she should deliberate well in part because, to state it simply, exercising intellectual virtue is the right thing or a good thing for the epistemic agent to do. I will return later to say a bit more on this.

IV. VIRTUES IN DELIBERATION

Intellectual or epistemic virtues are required for excellence in verdict deliberation. On one conception of intellectual virtues, they are reliable cognitive faculties such as good memory and perception, or sound cognitive powers such as the capacity for a priori intuition and the ability to draw valid inferences. These reliable cognitive faculties or powers are *virtues* in the sense that they function properly or perfectly in congenial environments, and they are *epistemic* virtues because they are truth conducive. On this view, intellectual virtues are instrumentally valuable.

Take a juror whose memory is failing due to age and who is unable, at the time of deliberation, to recall accurately the testimony that was given at the trial. She is lacking in a cognitive faculty, and therefore in an intellectual virtue, that is needed to deliberate well, to be reliably successful in getting to the truth about the facts in dispute. That a person has poor memory, or for that matter, bad eyesight or hearing due to natural deterioration, is unfortunate; we do not regard any of these states as something for which she deserves blame and it sounds odd to call them intellectual 'vices'. It seems almost as odd, to modern ears at any rate, to praise innate cognitive faculties as 'virtues' when they function well.

The more interesting conception of intellectual virtues, the one on which I will concentrate, is modelled on moral or practical virtues. Moral virtues are commonly associated with character traits, aspects of personality that can be cultivated, and the exercise of which is under one's control. One is praiseworthy for the possession of a virtue, conceived as a deep and enduring disposition, and may be blamed for the lack of it.[22] The exercise or non-exercise of virtue on a particular occasion is also deemed a proper object of moral evaluation. Thus, one can be commended generally for being a brave person or specifically for acting courageously in saving a baby from a burning building; and, equally, one can be condemned generally for being a coward or specifically for acting dastardly in deserting one's comrade in the face of a danger that, with some fortitude, is surmountable. A person who lacks the stable disposition to exhibit courage (whose character cannot therefore be described as courageous) may yet act bravely on a particular occasion. The existence of character traits has been challenged.[23] But even if there is no such a thing as a courageous person, there is still such a thing as a courageous act. Since my argument is not that we should select virtuous persons to serve as fact-finders but that fact-finders should deliberate virtuously on the verdict, I will, following Hurka, 'treat virtue atomistically, finding it in occurrent desires, actions, and feelings regardless of their connection to more permanent traits of character'.[24]

The intersection of epistemic and moral appraisal is evident in the fact that many moral virtues and vices have direct epistemic analogues. Persons are sometimes criticised, *qua* cognitive agents, for their intellectual dishonesty and close-mindedness, and for unfairly jumping to conclusions and being biased or prejudiced in the analysis of evidence. At other times, they are praised for their fair-mindedness or for their intellectual courage, tenacity or humility.

One could take a deontological position and treat it as a matter of duty, a duty that is valued for its own sake, to exercise epistemic virtue (be intellectually honest, diligent, and so on) in one's theoretical deliberation. Or one could take a

[22] The problem of moral luck poses difficulties here if the development and persistence of virtues are affected by one's social situation: Adams (2006: 158–61).

[23] eg Harman (1999) and Doris (2002). Disputed by Sreenivasan (2002).

[24] Hurka (2000: 42). See also Hurka (2006).

consequentialist view and contend that the agent's exercise of epistemic virtue will generally promote (even though it will not guarantee) the acquisition of true beliefs, and cognitive accuracy, in turn, is good because it conduces in some way to the maximisation of utility. Or one could see epistemic virtue as intrinsically good in the sense that its possession and exercise is constitutive of a flourishing intellectual life, and this is good apart from whatever tendency it may have to promote the achievement of an epistemic end such as true belief. For present purposes, I need not choose amongst these ethical theories of epistemic virtues.

Many virtue epistemologists take as their project the analysis of core epistemic concepts such as knowledge and justified belief in terms of intellectual virtue, that is to say, in terms of the properties of the subject as a person rather than properties of the belief. Thus, and to put it roughly, they may define knowledge to include as a necessary element that the belief in question has its source in intellectual virtue. This chapter has nothing to do with that controversial project: it seeks only to study the role of some intellectual virtues in verdict deliberation and to explore how excellence of deliberation can be understood as the exercise of those virtues.[25]

It is impossible in this chapter to examine all of the relevant virtues and vices.[26] A few important examples will suffice. First, I will highlight two connected virtues, 'justice as humanity' and 'empathic care', which give the trial its humane quality and which bear on how one approaches the evidence and comes to a verdict. Secondly, I will discuss the various manifestations of a prominent vice in legal fact-finding, 'prejudice', and attend to its virtuous counterparts. Thirdly, I will consider the virtue of 'practical wisdom' and the roles it plays in virtuous verdict deliberation.

V. JUSTICE AS HUMANITY AND EMPATHIC CARE

A. The Virtue of Justice as Humanity

To give a guilty verdict is, first, to assert that the accused did commit the crime; this assertion is either true or false. Secondly, it is also to declare that she is guilty as charged. Such a declaration condemns the accused for what she did. Whether the person deserves to be condemned depends on whether she did in fact commit the crime: the justice of the declaration is contingent on the truth of the assertion.[27]

But justice may be conceived in a more complex way than simply as the state of affairs in which the truly guilty gets convicted and condemned or the innocent is

[25] This undertaking bears some affinity to the type of 'regulative epistemology' engaged by Roberts and Wood (2007).

[26] For a valuable discussion of epistemic duties and intellectual virtues in legal fact-finding, see Amaya (2008: esp 311–14).

[27] Ho (2006).

acquitted and released. On a richer view, justice involves recognising the humanity in another. Justice as humanity, as we may call this understanding of justice, both structures and enriches our relations with others, relations in which we respect each other's intrinsic worth and dignity. Contrary to its popular depiction, justice as so understood is decidedly not blind.[28] It is exhibited in empathic care,[29] an other-regarding affective attitude that supposes the capacity to take the position of a fellow human being and to experience the situation from her standpoint; where the situation is bad, this experience elicits in the virtuous a benevolent or caring response, one driven by concern for the person for her own sake.[30]

Gaita reminds us that the worst of criminals, the most recalcitrant, still deserves to be 'kept amongst us as our fellow human beings'.[31] This is notwithstanding the practical necessity of conviction and punishment.[32] The court has a duty to convict persons of the crimes that it is proved they have committed, mete out appropriate punishment and explicitly condemn criminal behaviour that warrants censure. But, even as the court does so, it should always respect the humanity of the accused. VK Rajah J set a good example in the Singapore High Court case of *PP v Chee Cheong Hin Constance*.[33] A woman was tried (without jury) for kidnapping and causing the death of a young girl who was the daughter of her lover and his wife. Rajah J returned a guilty verdict, not with spite and fury, but with admirable humanity. Sadness accompanied his verdict: 'This is a desperately tragic case'. The judge noted that the accused was herself a victim, describing her as 'a forlorn individual', 'an enigma wrapped and trapped in a serious ailment'; he observed that 'she [was] not well', was 'emotionally vulnerable', and that her lover had 'exploit[ed her] . . . and [taken] advantage of her vulnerability'.

Instead of treating *her* only as a problem, a dangerous element from whom the rest of us should be kept safe, the judge drew a picture of the accused as a person *with* serious problems, herself the victim of betrayal and exploitation. He took effort to understand her pain and anguish, to look at things from her viewpoint. We can feel her pain and anguish even though we cannot explain what pushed her ultimately to do what she did. Our ability to experience her pain and anguish connects us to her; in that shared experience, we recognise that she is as human as we are, notwithstanding the terrible thing she has done. Few things can be worse than the killing of a young and defenceless child. Empathic care did not blind the court to the horrible nature of her deed. Nor was it an obstacle to conviction and punishment: the court found her guilty after a meticulous examination of the evidence and stated unequivocally that 'the accused cannot be exonerated for her

[28] The blindfold that is featured in the popular icon of justice is open to many interpretations: Curtis and Resnik (1987: 1755–61).

[29] 'Empathic care' is different from 'empathy'; it is connected to 'sympathy' and, more closely, 'compassion', on which see Darwall (1998) and Blum (1980: 507–17) respectively.

[30] For conceptions of justice along this line, see Gaita (2000) and Dubber (2006). More generally, for a theory of the ethics of care, see Slote (2007).

[31] Gaita (2000: xvi).

[32] But *cf* Boonin (2008).

[33] [2006] SGHC 9; [2006] 2 *Singapore Law Reports* 24.

conduct'.[34] The judge rightly condemned her action and punished her for it; what is especially praiseworthy was how he kept firmly in his sight, and made us see, the humanity in Constance Chee.

I should forestall two related criticisms. First, lest it be misunderstood, I am not suggesting that the fact-finder should be motivated by empathic care only for the accused. That would be the mark of a biased judge, not a virtuous one. Other persons are affected by the verdict, such as the victim and her family, and they surely deserve empathic care as well.[35] (An example will be given later of a lack of empathy for rape victims.) Further, the virtuous fact-finder is not motivated only by empathic care. Many kinds of virtue bear on deliberation and, as we will see later, they require coordination through the exercise of practical wisdom. On a related note, we often praise the dispassionate dispensation of justice. It seems to me this is best read to mean not that justice should be dispensed without any empathic care for anyone at all but that empathic care should not be unfairly distributed when dispensing justice.

Secondly, some jury directions instruct jurors to divest themselves of 'any feelings of pity or sympathy for the accused or any other person who might be affected by [their] decision'.[36] This kind of direction is unobjectionable if it seeks only to prevent cases such as one where the jury acquits the accused out of pity for that person even though they believe her to be guilty, or, where the jury, appalled by the terrible injuries sustained by the victim and blindly desirous of getting someone to pay for the ghastly crime, gives the prosecution evidence more weight than it deserves. But if the direction means that deliberation on the verdict should be conducted without any trace of empathic care for anyone who might be affected by it, the direction strikes me as heartless.[37]

B. Deliberative Implications of Empathic Care

Empathic care for the accused shapes the conduct of verdict deliberation. (To bring this into focus, I will leave aside empathic care for others and the demands of other virtues in this discussion.) An important aspect of deliberation involves the selection of an epistemic threshold: 'What should it take, in terms of truth-related factors such as evidential support, to persuade me to accept the prosecution's case, to judge it true?' The epistemic threshold the fact-finder applies may

[34] ibid [113]. Constance Chee was sentenced to 10 years' imprisonment for the offence of culpable homicide and three years' imprisonment for the offence of kidnapping: *PP v Chee Cheong Hin Constance* [2006] SGHC 60; [2006] 2 Singapore Law Reports 707.

[35] Slote (2012: 288).

[36] Criminal Jury Instruction 2.2-3 (model direction on 'reasonable doubt') of the State of Connecticut (available at www.jud.ct.gov/JI/criminal/part2/2.2-3.htm, accessed on 29 August 2009). See also *Connecticut v Griffin* 253 Conn 195 at 204 (2000) (Supreme Court of Connecticut).

[37] A similar view is taken by Tanesini (2008: 79) ('A judge who is lacking in all emotion would not be impartial; in all likelihood he or she would be perceived as cold, perhaps even callous'). *cf* Bloomfield (2000: 34).

be influenced by, among other things, how much respect and concern she has for the accused, the degree to which she empathises with him – with the pain he would feel if he were wrongfully convicted – and on the importance she attaches to protecting him from that harm. All else being equal, the greater the empathic care the fact-finder has for the accused, the more it will pain her to convict him of a crime he did not do, and consequently, the more it will take to convince her to return a guilty verdict.[38]

Another aspect of deliberation involves answering two important questions: What relevant evidence do I have? Is it strong enough to satisfy the epistemic threshold?[39] In these respects, much will depend, to begin with, on how observant the fact-finder was during the trial. To be observant takes more than acute eyesight and good hearing; one must put in cognitive effort to exercise well one's perceptual faculties. The excellence of this cognitive performance requires the fact-finder to be attentive during the proceeding, to look out for relevant information, some of which (like subtle behavioural cues of a witness) can easily escape notice.[40] After both sides have made their closing submissions, the fact-finder will typically retire to deliberate on the verdict. She must now recall and go over all of the evidence admitted in court. Deliberation requires mental perseverance. The fact-finder must assess the credibility of the witnesses, check their testimony for internal and external consistency, draw evidential inferences, form factual hypotheses, appraise their explanatory power and coherence, and so forth. In the end, a conclusion must be drawn as to whether the epistemic threshold is satisfied. If done conscientiously, in all but the clearest cases, the fact-finder must expend considerable energy. Why would the fact-finder bother to exert herself? Empathic care for the accused provides her with a moral motivation to do so.

Emotions play necessary and proper roles in verdict deliberation. (They can also have very negative effects, on which more will be said later.) Doubt itself is an emotion, an epistemic feeling of anxiety about getting the facts wrong. This feeling arises because one is aware of and cares about the implications of error.[41] Where doubt is eliminated through reflective analysis of the evidence, the feeling of anxiety is quelled and replaced by the feeling of certainty or conviction or sureness about guilt. A fact-finder who has empathic care for the accused would be anxious not to do her wrong; this anxiety shapes the conduct of deliberation and engenders sensitivity to reasons for having doubt about her guilt. Emotions, according to Elgin, are 'sources of salience'; they direct attention, regulate delib-

[38] I do not claim that this is the only possible motivation for exercising caution in convicting the accused. Even someone concerned solely with deterring crimes would also want to exercise caution since convicting the wrong person or the appearance of having done so may undermine the deterrent effect of the criminal law.

[39] Studies suggest that what the fact-finder sees in the evidence depends on matters such as her culture, worldview and values. See generally Kahan and Braman (2008) and Kahan, Hoffman and Braman (2009).

[40] See generally Hookway (2006b).

[41] On doubt as epistemic anxiety, see Hookway (2008). On epistemic feelings, including doubt and certainty, see de Sousa (2008).

eration and have 'cognitive deliverances'.[42] The fact-finder who has empathic care for the accused is more likely for that reason to be patient in hearing her out, not to be dismissive of her story, and to be drawn to evidence that corroborates it; the same fact-finder is also less likely to carelessly overlook flaws in the prosecution case.

VI. THE VICE OF PREJUDICE AND ITS COUNTER VIRTUES (INTELLECTUAL INTEGRITY, OPEN-MINDEDNESS AND INTELLECTUAL HUMILITY)

I turn now to consider a cluster of virtues that counter the vice of prejudice in its various forms. Whether the accused is in fact guilty or not, the fact-finder is morally culpable if, like Clifford's shipowner, he acquires his belief not 'by honestly earning it in patient investigation, but by stifling his doubts'. There are different possible causes for this. Doubts may be stifled due to intellectual sloth, the irresponsible avoidance of the mental labour needed for the conduct of a thorough inquiry; or it may be due to impatience, an undue haste to shorten deliberation and be done with it, settling for quick and easy answers.

One of the more sinister causes of the stifling of doubt is prejudice. Imagine a trial where the fact-finder feels revulsion for the accused because of passing remarks the latter makes while in the witness box. Those remarks show the accused to be a bigot who is contemptuous of the racial group to which the fact-finder belongs. The accused is charged with a crime that is unrelated to his odious views. The intense dislike that the fact-finder has for the accused may cause her to be biased in her deliberation on the verdict, leading her to actively search for weaknesses in the defence, to magnify those that she supposes herself to have found, to overlook grounds for doubt which would otherwise have been apparent to her, and to dismiss alternative hypotheses which would ordinarily have undermined her confidence in the prosecution's case. She is less resistant to a guilty verdict than she should be and comes too quickly to believe that the accused is guilty as charged. The possibility of error does not give her much pause. Even if the accused is innocent of the crime, this will not cause the fact-finder much regret. In her eyes, the punishment the accused gets is only a fraction of what he deserves for being the person that he is.

This example shows how emotion can engender bad deliberation. Whether the accused is in fact guilty or not, we would think poorly of the fact-finder's deliberation. An ethical problem lies at the root; sometimes, as Gilson once said, 'men are most anxious to find truth, but very reluctant to accept it.'[43] The failure is not of sincerity but of rational self-mastery. Those who lack intellectual integrity 'want to believe that things are as they would like them to be: a goal best achieved by

[42] Elgin (1996: 149, 150 respectively; see also generally ch V).
[43] Gilson (1938: 61).

not looking into things too closely, and actively ignoring or . . . trying to explain away any inconvenient evidence [they] can't avoid'.[44]

One aspect of verdict deliberation is the making of credibility judgements. Prejudice may result in a deflation of the level of credibility that the fact-finder gives to a witness. A particularly pernicious form of prejudice is negative identity-prejudice. In Harper Lee's *To Kill a Mockingbird*, the racist white jury disbelieved Tom Robinson's testimony because he was black. In the film *The Talented Mr Ripley*, the sexist Herbert Greenleaf silenced his son's fiancé by dismissing her views as groundless 'female intuition'. Both are examples of what Miranda Fricker calls testimonial injustice.[45] Testimonial injustice results in epistemic harm to the *hearer*: prejudice prevents the hearer from receiving knowledge from the speaker. More than that, testimonial injustice is an intrinsic form of injustice to the *speaker*; it constitutes an insult to her. The speaker is wronged in her capacity as a giver of knowledge. As Fricker argues, the capacity to know is an aspect of the capacity for reason. Since 'our rationality is what lends humanity its distinctive value', 'to be wronged in one's capacity as a knower is to be wronged in a capacity essential to human value'.[46]

A notorious example of negative identity-prejudicial credibility deficit in law is the rule that used to exist which required the jury to be given a 'corroboration warning' about relying on the evidence of a sexual offence complainant. This rule was based on assumptions about the psychology of the female complainant. The judge had to warn the jury that it was dangerous to base a guilty verdict on her evidence unless it was corroborated by independent evidence which implicated the accused in a material particular.

This rule was endorsed by many judges and scholars. In the 1964 case of *Din v PP*,[47] Lord President Thomson, sitting in the Federal Court of Malaysia, found the rule entirely sound because, to his mind, '[t]he temptations of a woman to exaggerate an act of sexual connection are well known and manifold'. In 1972, the majority of the Criminal Law Revision Committee of England and Wales, which comprised entirely of men and mainly of senior judges and law professors, decided against abolition of the corroboration rule. They recommended that the jury be warned of the 'special need for caution' when relying on the word of a sexual complainant. The basis for this recommendation was 'the danger', which they must have thought a prevalent one, 'that the complainant may have made a false accusation owing to sexual neurosis, jealousy, fantasy, spite or a girl's refusal to admit that she consented to an act of which she is now ashamed.'[48]

Wigmore, widely extolled as one of the greatest scholars of evidence law, would have female sexual complainants treated as presumptive liars. Writing in 1940, he

[44] Haack (2005: 365). Further, ibid 362: the ideal of intellectual integrity rests on the difference 'between really trying to figure something out, and merely trying to make sense for a predetermined conclusion'.

[45] These examples are taken from Fricker (2007).

[46] ibid 44.

[47] [1964] *Malayan Law Journal* 300, 301.

[48] Criminal Law Revision Committee (1972: 113).

recommended: 'No judge should ever let a sex-offence charge to the jury unless the female complainant's social history and mental makeup have been examined and testified to by a qualified physician.'[49] Citing psychiatric studies, the science of his day, he said of young girls and women that:

> Their psychic complexes are multifarious, distorted partly by inherent defects, partly by diseased derangements or abnormal instincts, partly by bad social environment, partly by temporary physiological or emotional conditions. One form taken by these complexes is that of contriving false charges of sexual offences by men.

Such generalisations show an appalling lack of empathy with the victims. In 2000, they were rejected by Yong CJ in the Singapore High Court case of *Kwan Peng Hong v PP*.[50] According to the judge:

> [I]t is objectionable to argue that extreme caution is required because female witnesses are prone to fantasising, exaggeration and lies due to some sexual neurosis. . . . [T]he court will no longer entertain such an argument, whatever the attitude was twenty years ago. Such generalised categorisation of female witnesses in sexual offence cases . . . is not acceptable to a Singapore court today. . . . [I]t is both disingenuous and rather offensive in my view, and incongruous with the societal norm today.

Another example of testimonial injustice in the trial context is where the court disbelieves a woman who alleges rape because of her sexual history. When a woman claims that she did not consent to have sex with the accused on the occasion in question, should we disbelieve her because she has had consensual sex with other men on other occasions or even with the same man but on a different occasion? An assumption was once held in the law, which reflected the then socially entrenched view, that 'unchaste' women were, by the very fact of 'unchastity', dishonest. To make matters worse, double standards were employed. In a notorious passage, the Missouri Supreme Court declared:[51]

> It is a matter of common knowledge that the bad character of a man for chastity does not even in the remotest degree affect his character for truth, when based upon that alone, while it does that of a woman. . . . What destroys the standing of the one in all walks of life has no effect whatever on the standing for truth of the other.

The 'weakness . . . for sexual pleasure', the court went on to note, was 'an infirmity' shared by 'many great and noble men'.[52] For women, the virtue of truthfulness hinged on their reputation for chastity[53] whereas for men, the two were completely detached. The falsity and injustice of these sexist assumptions, especially in the context where a woman is alleging rape, are now well-recognised. In *R v Seaboyer*,[54] the Canadian Supreme Court 'debunked' the law of the 'twin myths', namely, that 'unchaste women were more likely to consent to intercourse

[49] Wigmore (1940: §924a).
[50] [2000] 4 *Singapore Law Reports* 96, [27].
[51] *State v Sibley* 131 Mo 519, 531; 33 SW 167, 171 (1895) (Supreme Court of Missouri, per Burgess J).
[52] ibid.
[53] On the history of the law on this, see Simon-Kerr (2008).
[54] [1991] 2 SCR 577; 83 DLR (4th) 193.

and in any event, were less worthy of belief'. In *R v A (No 2)*, a decision of the House of Lords, Lord Steyn declared: 'Such generalized, stereotyped and unfounded prejudices ought to have no place in our legal system.' He noted that such prejudices have 'inflicted unacceptable humiliation on complainants in rape cases.'[55] Prejudices of the sorts just discussed are objectionable not merely because they are likely to lead the court to the wrong verdict. These assumptions against the credibility of women are intrinsically objectionable because they are insulting and unfair to them.

The essence of identity prejudice is a pre-judgement about the members of a class of persons. Grounding the judgement is a generalisation about a defined class and an association of it with certain attributes. Thus, the prejudice may be directed at women generally (women are generally prone to sexual fantasy) or at the subcategory of 'unchaste' women (such women are dishonest). This judgement is a *pre*-judgement in the sense that it is made without proper regard to the evidence, or even in the face of counter-evidence. There is usually epistemic culpability in this resistance to evidence. But there may be ethical culpability as well. According to Fricker, the ethical flaw 'consists in the ethically bad motivation behind the irrationality'.[56] For example, some form of contempt for women may be at work.

The visceral impact of prejudice on a credibility judgement is typically unnoticed by the person making it. A prejudice may be so deeply ingrained and pervasive in the collective social imagination that persons living at that moment of history are excused for imbibing it. In these circumstances, no culpability attaches to the wrong of testimonial injustice. There is perhaps room for charity to Wigmore and company. As Fricker noted: 'A setting in which there is little critical awareness of the construction of gender . . . is a setting in which people are not generally in a position [to rise above] identity prejudice against women.'[57]

But the excuse should not be made too readily available. Frequently, we can rise above the social prejudices of our day when making judgements of credibility. We can do so by exercising the virtue that Fricker calls 'testimonial justice'. This virtue calls for 'reflexive critical awareness of the likely presence of prejudice'.[58] '[T]he disposition at the heart of [this] virtue is such that the subject is motivated to neutralize the impact of prejudice in her credibility judgements.'[59] The subject will revise her credibility judgement upwards to compensate for any negative prejudice that is detected. Testimonial justice is a facet of intellectual humility, where, in recognition of one's epistemic and ethical fallibility, one is disposed to self-monitor and check on the unreflective deliverances of one's testimonial sensibility.[60]

[55] [2002] 1 AC 45, [27].
[56] Fricker (2007: 34).
[57] ibid 99.
[58] ibid 91.
[59] ibid 121.
[60] However, as Fricker (ibid 7–8) acknowledges, 'there is a limit . . . to what virtues on the part of individuals can achieve when the root cause of epistemic injustice is structures of unequal power and the systemic prejudices that they generate. Eradicating these injustices would ultimately take not just more virtuous hearers, but collective social political change.'

There is a second form of epistemic injustice which Fricker calls 'hermeneutical injustice'. The source of this form of injustice is a gap in 'our shared tools of social interpretation'.[61] This gap obscures from collective understanding what the victim is experiencing. What can now be easily described as 'postnatal depression' was criticised as unreasonable or erratic behaviour before we had that critical concept. The victims of the present type of injustice lack the interpretive resources needed for proper comprehension of their own experiences and for intelligible communication of those experiences in contexts where it mattered that others understood what they were going through.[62] A hermeneutical gap is created when the class to which the victim belongs is denied equal participation 'in the practices through which social meanings are generated'.[63] Until women finally had their voices heard in socio-political discourse, sexual harassment was dismissed as innocent flirting.

The problem of hermeneutical gaps exists in legal fact-finding. A woman who kills her husband after years of being abused by him will typically find it difficult to explain why she stayed in the relationship. That she did not leave him might in turn prompt the fact-finder to doubt her claim of having been frequently beaten by her spouse. Expert evidence has helped to bridge the hermeneutic gap and to bolster the battered woman's 'credibility in the eyes of the jury by demonstrating that her experiences, which the jury would find difficult to comprehend, were in fact common to women in abusive situations.'[64] Such evidence can help to explain why the battered woman did not simply walk out on her husband and why her past experiences may render her particularly accurate in predicting the imminence of the attack to which she reacted.[65]

In situations where a witness is unjustly hindered in the attempt to make communicative sense of her experience, it is vital that the fact-finder exercises the virtue of 'hermeneutical justice'. The form that this virtue must take is an 'alertness or sensitivity' to the possibility that the difficulty a witness has in giving a coherent and persuasive account of her behaviour is not because she is crazy or lying but due to an inadequacy in our common resources of social interpretation: it may be that there is as yet no effective way of capturing and conveying in words the experiences that she has had, the emotions and thoughts with which she had to struggle. Fricker says it well: 'The point is to realize that the speaker is struggling with an objective difficulty and not a subjective failing.'[66] It is through the closing of the hermeneutical gap that the violent retaliation by a battered wife is now capable of being construed as the action of a reasonable person

[61] ibid 6.

[62] ibid.

[63] ibid.

[64] Schneider (1986: 209).

[65] 'There is ample literature to suggest that a battered woman may in fact be *accurate* in predicting an imminent threat of [serious bodily] harm . . . [O]ut of sheer instinctual self-preservation a battered woman must become highly sensitive to her abuser's behavior, and must learn to read the cues of an impending attack.' Krause (2007: 563) (emphasis in original).

[66] Fricker (2007: 169).

placed in a tragic situation rather than as an instance of irrational or deranged behaviour.

Testimonial justice and hermeneutical justice are related to or are aspects of open-mindedness. The latter involves, as Montmarquet explains, 'at least some resistance to one's own immediate reactions of unfamiliarity and even implausibility.'[67] When faced with a challenge to or with putative evidence that runs against an existing belief or assumption, a person who is open-minded is willing to question that belief or assumption, thus opening the way to the possibility of its correction. To facilitate such correction, one should actively search for and be receptive to alternative viewpoints.[68] Testimonial justice and hermeneutical justice are also related to or are aspects of the general virtue of intellectual humility. It is only when we are mindful of the possibility of epistemic blind-spots that we begin to question our beliefs and assumptions and do not hasten to attribute our difficulty in understanding what someone is trying to tell us to some subjective failure in the speaker. As the present Chief Justice of Singapore emphasised in an interview:[69]

> All of us have ingrained prejudices of one kind or another, some of which may be strong enough to influence the way we look at the evidence and find the facts or the justice of the case. The important thing is to recognise that we may have such frailties so that we can consciously put them aside in our fact-finding and decision-making.

VII. PRACTICAL WISDOM

Practical wisdom is a necessary aspect of virtue, the constitutive component that directs the relevant traits. Generosity is not simply the disposition to share wealth. While generosity calls for charity to the destitute, it is foolish rather than generous to give money to a gambler to feed her addiction. Generosity 'involves giving the right amount of the right sort of thing, for the right reasons, to the right people, on the right occasions'.[70] It is as bad to be prodigal is as it is to be stingy.[71] One who possesses the virtue of generosity has the practical wisdom to navigate between these two vices.

Practical wisdom is equally needed in the sphere of cognitive activity. Within that sphere, it plays a number of roles. First, we need practical wisdom, as Zagzebski puts it, to 'determine the mean between extremes in those cases in which the virtue is a mean'.[72] Thus, 'in the case of intellectual carefulness, it takes practical wisdom . . . to tell how much evidence is enough to support a belief'.[73] This general observation holds true in the context of a trial. Excellent deliberation on the verdict

[67] Montmarquet (1993: 25).

[68] Medina (2011: 29–30) suggests the active seeking of 'epistemic friction' as an antidote to the meta-blindness that causes hermeneutical injustice.

[69] Thian (2008: 7).

[70] Hursthouse (1999: 12).

[71] ibid 13: 'generosity contrasts not only with meanness or selfishness but also with being prodigal, too open-handed, a sucker'.

[72] Zagzebski (1996: 221).

[73] ibid.

requires practical wisdom in order to attain the mean between many opposed cognitive tendencies. Thus, intellectual scrupulousness does not require an impractical level of proof. To be scrupulous in the evaluation of evidence is about treading the right path between credulity and incredulity, feeble gullibility and stubborn scepticism. Intellectual humility contrasts with intellectual arrogance but is also different from intellectual timidity. The humble is mindful of her cognitive fallibility but is unlike the timid who, fearful of error and dirtying her hands, shrinks from making a judgment of guilt. A virtuous fact-finder does not allow an unreal risk of convicting the wrong person to defeat the courage of her conviction.[74] While the intellectually courageous has qualified confidence in her cognitive abilities, the intellectually reckless or arrogant has too much confidence, jumping to adverse conclusions and taking too lightly her responsibility for the fate of the accused. Practical wisdom thus plays an important role in mediating between virtues, as here, between intellectual courage and intellectual humility.

Further, practical wisdom is needed in order to accommodate the different directional pulls of a single virtue. As we saw, having empathic care for the accused does not prevent one from concluding that the person is guilty as charged and returning a guilty verdict: it is about exercising appropriate caution in deliberation and giving due recognition to the humanity of the accused, a recognition that encompasses an awareness of human imperfections, the potential in the accused, as indeed in all of us, to commit crimes.[75] Furthermore, the wise fact-finder who possesses the virtue of empathic care does not hold only the accused in her moral vision: that would be unfairly myopic. Included in the proper scope of concern are the welfare of those who will suffer from the inefficacious enforcement of criminal law (the public at large) as well as the dignity and well-being of particular persons other than the accused. Empathic care for the accused must be wisely balanced against empathic care for, amongst others, the victim and her loved ones.[76] The caring fact-finder maintains epistemic impartiality, keeps an open mind and exercises caution without making any pre-judgement. This attitude of balanced caring must be distinguished from the kind of one-sided affective attachment that, to borrow Goldie's phrase, 'skews the epistemic landscape' of the fact-finder.[77] Such cognitive distortion can arise as much when the affective attachment is to the accused[78] as when it is to the victim;[79] and it can be to either one of them personally or as a member of a particular class.

[74] There is some truth in Paley's tirade, callous as a whole, against the 'over-strained scrupulousness, or weak timidity of juries' who 'reject . . . proof' simply 'from a general dread lest the charge of innocent blood should lie at their doors'. Paley's views are discussed in historical context by Whitman (2008: 192) in his historical study of 'proof beyond reasonable doubt'.

[75] Feinberg (2002: 62–63).

[76] For an account of 'balanced caring', see Slote (2001: ch 3).

[77] Goldie (2008: 160). It has been argued that friendship involves epistemic partiality (Stroud (2006)) and even that it requires epistemic irresponsibility (Keller (2004)). These arguments rely on the loyalty that obtains between friends and such loyalty is one that we expect the fact-finder not to feel for any of the parties before the court.

[78] Thagard (2003).

[79] See example by Trianosky (1987: 131).

Lastly, practical wisdom serves to mediate between the intellectual and the practical. Deliberation on the verdict is a theoretical inquiry that is conducted in a practical context. The questions 'What am I to believe? Are the facts as the prosecution allege them to be?' are not posed in the abstract. They are raised for the purpose of answering 'What shall I do? Shall I return a guilty verdict?' It matters practically what the fact-finder judges and hence believes to be true about the facts of the case. The fact-finder fails to exercise practical wisdom as much when she is over-cautious as when she is incautious in judging what to believe on the question of guilt; the right amount of caution is relative to the practical context in which the question of truth arises for determination.[80] Since I care about doing justice to the accused more than I care about my plants, the epistemic threshold I apply to my belief about the accused's guilt is greater than that I apply to my belief about the health of my plants.[81] If this is uncontentious, it should be equally uncontentious that, within the same domain, the epistemic threshold may vary with the context. The threshold should be higher where the accused is charged with murder, attracting a potential sentence of life imprisonment or even death, than where she is charged with petty shoplifting. A virtuous fact-finder has the practical wisdom to align the epistemic threshold to what is at stake.[82]

VIII. CONCLUSION

I began this chapter by noting the desire for certainty and objectivity in legal fact-finding, in particular, for certainty and objectivity in the concept and application of the standard of proof beyond reasonable doubt. It would seem that the natural answer to satisfying that desire is to devise a suitable Deliberative Procedure. If, as I have suggested, excellent deliberation on the verdict – the process of evaluating evidence and coming to a factual conclusion – requires the exercise and coordination of numerous epistemic virtues in the particular circumstances of each case, and the careful avoidance of epistemic vices such as prejudice, there are greater inherent limits to what codification can properly achieve than we might think.

Instead of trying to tame the complexity of the deliberative process, we do better to embrace the complexity and strive to understand it better. And instead of despairing of the subjectivity that is involved, we should acknowledge and stress the personal responsibility that comes with it.[83] The fact-finder cannot evade

[80] Ho (2008: 196–213).

[81] Zagzebski (2004).

[82] That our practical interests bear on the appropriate threshold is consistent with the claim that the satisfaction of the threshold depends only on truth-related factors. See Grimm (2011).

[83] See Whitman (2008: 212): 'Open-hearted human beings condemn others in a spirit of humility, of duteousness, of fear and trembling about their own moral standing. That is what our ancestors, for all their bloodiness, believed; and it is why they spoke about "reasonable doubt".... Instructing jurors forcefully that their decision is "a *moral* one," about the fate of a fellow human being, is, in the last analysis, the only meaningful modern way to be faithful to the original spirit of reasonable doubt.' (Emphasis in original.)

ethical appraisal of her verdict deliberation by recourse to a context-independent set of formal and precise rules. Epistemic virtue is indispensable for excellent deliberation on the verdict, and appropriate emotions, wisely deployed, have an enriching and humanising role to play.

REFERENCES

Adams, RM (2006) *A Theory of Virtue – Excellence in Being for the Good* (Oxford, Clarendon Press).

Aikin, SF and Clanton, JC (2010), 'Developing Group-Deliberative Virtues' 27 *Journal of Applied Philosophy* 409.

Amaya, A (2008) 'Justification, Coherence, and Epistemic Responsibility in Legal Fact-Finding' 5 *Episteme – Journal of Social Epistemology* 306.

Annas, J (2003) 'The Structure of Deliberation' in Michael DePaul and Linda Zagzebski (eds), *Intellectual Virtue – Perspectives from Ethics and Epistemology* (Oxford, Clarendon Press).

Axtell, G (2008) 'Expanding Epistemology: A Responsibilist Approach' 37 *Philosophical Papers* 51.

Barnes, J (2006) *Arthur and George* (London, Vintage Books).

Bloomfield, P (2000) 'Virtue Epistemology and the Epistemology of Virtue' 60 *Philosophy and Phenomenological Research* 23.

Blum, L (1980) 'Compassion' in Amélie O Rorty (ed), *Explaining Emotions* (Berkeley, University of California Press).

Boonin, D (2008) *The Problem of Punishment* (Cambridge, Cambridge University Press).

Clifford, WK (1879) 'The Ethics of Belief' in Leslie Stephen and Frederick Pollock (eds), *William Kingdon Clifford, Lectures and Essays*, vol 2 (London, MacMillan and Co), first published in *Contemporary Review*, January 1877.

Criminal Law Revision Committee (1972) *Eleventh Report – Evidence (General)* (Chairman: Edmund Davies LJ, Cmnd 4991) (London, HMSO).

Curtis, DE and Resnik, J (1987) 'Images of Justice' 96 *Yale Law Journal* 1727.

Darwall, S (1998) 'Empathy, Sympathy, Care' 89 *Philosophical Studies* 261.

DeRose, K (2000) 'Ought We to Follow Our Evidence?' 60 *Philosophy and Phenomenological Research* 697.

de Sousa, R (2008) 'Epistemic Feelings' in Georg Brun, Ulvi Doğuoğlu and Dominique Kuenzle (eds), *Epistemology and Emotions* (Aldershot, Ashgate).

Doris, JM (2002) *Lack of Character: Personality and Moral Behavior* (Cambridge, Cambridge University Press).

Dubber, MD (2006) *The Sense of Justice – Empathy in Law and Punishment* (New York, New York University Press).

Elgin, CZ (1996) *Considered Judgment* (Princeton, Princeton University Press).

Feinberg, J (2002) 'Criminal Entrapment' in Joel Feinberg, *Problems at the Roots of Law: Essays in Legal and Political Theory* (Oxford, Oxford University Press).

Feldman, R and Conee, E (1985) 'Evidentialism' 48 *Philosophical Studies* 15.

Feldman, R (2000) 'The Ethics of Belief' 60 *Philosophy and Phenomenological Research* 667.

Fricker, M (2007) *Epistemic Injustice – Power and the Ethics of Knowing* (Oxford, Oxford University Press).

——(2010) 'Can There Be Institutional Virtues?' in Tamar Szabó Gendler and John Hawthorne (eds), *Oxford Studies in Epistemology*, vol 3 (Oxford, Oxford University Press).

Gaita, R (2000) *A Common Humanity: Thinking about Love and Truth and Justice* (London, Routledge).

Gilson, E (1938) *The Unity of Philosophical Experience* (London, Sheed and Ward).

Goldie, P (2008) 'Misleading Emotions' in Georg Brun, Ulvi Doğuoğlu and Dominique Kuenzle (eds), *Epistemology and Emotions* (Aldershot, Ashgate).

Goldman, RM and Goldman, AI (2009) 'Review of *Truth, Error, and Criminal Law – An Essay in Legal Epistemology*, by Larry Laudan' 15 *Legal Theory* 55.

Grimm, SR (2011) 'On Intellectualism in Epistemology' *Mind* (online advance access).

Haack, S (2005) 'The Ideal of Intellectual Integrity, in Life and Literature' 36 *New Literary History* 359.

Harman, G (1999) 'Moral Philosophy Meets Social Psychology: Virtue Ethics and the Fundamental Attribution Error' 99 *Proceedings of the Aristotelian Society* 315.

Ho, HL (2006) 'What Does a Verdict Do? A Speech Act Analysis of Giving a Verdict' 4 *International Commentary on Evidence* Article 1, available at www.bepress.com/ice/vol4/iss2/art1.

——(2008) *Philosophy of Evidence Law – Justice in the Search for Truth* (Oxford, Oxford University Press).

——(2009) 'Re-imagining the Criminal Standard of Proof: Lessons from the "Ethics of Belief"' 13 *International Journal of Evidence and Proof* 198.

Hookway, C (2003) 'How to be a Virtue Epistemologist' in Michael DePaul and Linda Zagzebski (eds), *Intellectual Virtue – Perspectives from Ethics and Epistemology* (Oxford, Oxford University Press).

——(2006a) 'Epistemology and Inquiry: the Primacy of Practice' in Stephen Hetherington (ed), *Epistemology Futures* (Oxford, Clarendon Press).

——(2006b) 'Reasons for Belief, Reasoning, Virtues' 130 *Philosophical Studies* 47.

——(2008) 'Epistemic Immediacy, Doubt and Anxiety: On a Role for Affective States in Epistemic Evaluation' in Georg Brun, Ulvi Doğuoğlu and Dominique Kuenzle (eds), *Epistemology and Emotions* (Aldershot, Ashgate).

Hurka, T (2000) *Virtue, Vice, and Value* (New York, Oxford University Press).

——(2006) 'Virtuous Act, Virtuous Dispositions' 66 *Analysis* 69.

Hursthouse, Rosalind (1999) *On Virtue Ethics* (Oxford, Oxford University Press).

James, William (1986) 'The Will to Believe' in Gerald D McCarthy (ed), *The Ethics of Belief Debate* (American Academy of Religion), first published in the New World, June 1896.

Judicial Studies Board (2007), *Crown Court Bench Book, Specimen Directions*, available at www.jsboard.co.uk/criminal_law/cbb/index.htm.

Kahan, DM and Braman, D (2008) 'The Self-Defensive Cognition of Self-Defense' 45 *American Criminal Law Review* 1.

Kahan, DM, Hoffman, DA and Braman, D (2009) 'Whose Eyes Are You Going to Believe? *Scott v Harris* and the Perils of Cognitive Illiberalism' 122 *Harvard Law Review* 837.

Keller, S (2004) 'Friendship and Belief' 33 *Philosophical Papers* 329.

Krause, JH (2007) 'Distorted Reflections of Battered Women Who Kill: A Response to Professor Dressler' 4 *Ohio State Journal of Criminal Law* 555.

Laudan, L (2006), *Truth, Error, and Criminal Law – An Essay in Legal Epistemology* (Cambridge, Cambridge University Press).

Lahroodi, R (2007) 'Collective Epistemic Virtues' 21 *Social Epistemology* 281.

Medina, J (2011) 'The Relevance of Credibility Excess in a Proportional View of Epistemic Injustice: Differential Epistemic Authority and the Social Imaginary' 25 *Social Epistemology* 15.

Montmarquet, JA (1993) *Epistemic Virtue and Doxastic Responsibility* (Lanham, Rowman & Littlefield).
Pardo, MS (2008) 'Witness Testimony Evidence: Argumentation, Artificial Intelligence, and Law' *Notre Dame Philosophical Review*, available at www.ndpr.nd.edu/review.cfm?id=14625.
Roberts, RC and Wood WJ (2007) *Intellectual Virtues* (Oxford, Clarendon Press).
Schneider, EM (1986) 'Describing and Changing: Women's Self-Defense Work and the Problem of Expert Testimony on Battering' 9 *Women's Rights Law Reporter* 195.
Shiffrin, S V (2010) 'Inducing Moral Deliberation: On the Occasional Virtues of Fog' 123 *Harvard Law Review* 1214
Simon-Kerr, J (2008) 'Unchaste and Incredible: The Use of Gendered Conceptions of Honor in Impeachment' 117 *Yale Law Journal* 1854.
Slote, M (2001) *Morals From Motives* (Oxford, Oxford University Press).
——(2007) *The Ethics of Care and Empathy* (London, Routledge).
——(2012) 'Empathy, Law and Justice' chapter 14 of this volume.
Sreenivasan, G (2002) 'Errors about Errors: Virtue Theory and Trait Attribution' 111 *Mind* 47.
Stroud, S (2006) 'Epistemic Partiality in Friendship' 116 *Ethics* 498.
Tanesini, A (2008) 'Virtues, Emotions and Fallibilism' in Georg Brun, Ulvi Doğuoğlu and Dominique Kuenzle (eds), *Epistemology and Emotions* (Aldershot, Ashgate).
Thagard, P (2003) 'Why wasn't O.J. convicted? Emotional Coherence in Legal Inference' 17 *Cognition and Emotion* 361.
Thian, YS (2008) 'In Conversation with the Honourable the Chief Justice Chan Sek Keong' *The Law Gazette* 6, first published in the *Subordinate Courts Annual Report 2007*.
Trianosky, GW (1987) 'Virtue, Action, and the Good Life: Toward a Theory of the Virtues' 68 *Pacific Philosophical Quarterly* 124.
Whitman, JQ (2008) *The Origins of Reasonable Doubt – Theological Roots of the Criminal Trial* (New Haven, Yale University Press).
Wigmore, JH (1940) *A Treatise on the Anglo-American System of Evidence in Trials at Common Law* (3rd edn, vol 3) (Boston, Little Brown).
Zagzebski, L(1996) *Virtues of the Mind – An Inquiry into the Nature of Virtue and the Ethical Foundations of Knowledge* (Cambridge, Cambridge University Press).
——(2004) 'Epistemic Value and the Primacy of What We Care About' 33 *Philosophical Papers* 353.

13

Must Virtue be Particular?

FREDERICK SCHAUER

RECENT YEARS HAVE seen a burgeoning interest in virtue ethics, and thus a focus on thinking of morality in terms of the appropriate moral attitude, or state of mind, or motivation, or character, or disposition, that an agent should possess.[1] Moreover, this focus on the agent's character is typically conjoined with the view that the virtuous agent recognises the irreducible complexity of life and life's moral implications, thus rejecting the notion that moral decisions can be made by following rules, whether those rules have a deontological or utilitarian foundation. Thus, the virtuous agent is a particularist, applying his virtuous moral character to each situation in itself and in its full detail, refusing to ignore in the name of some rule or principle or category any of the features of a situation that his moral virtue tells him are morally relevant.[2]

In 'Virtuous Deliberation on the Criminal Verdict',[3] Ho Hock Lai applies the lessons and methods of virtue ethics to decision-making in the criminal law,[4] and in particular to the decision-making character that a virtuous juror (or, I might add, a virtuous judge acting in her fact-finding capacity)[5] ought to have. And because

[1] Modern interest in virtue ethics begins with Anscombe (1958). Since Anscombe, however, the interest in virtue ethics has accelerated, and is still doing so. Noteworthy contributions include Adams (2006); Annas (1993); Crisp and Slote (2009); Darwall (2003); Foot (1978); Gottleib (2009); Hursthouse (1999); Slote (2001); and Swanton (2003).

[2] On particularism in ethics, see especially Dancy (2004) and (1993); Hooker and Little (2000); and McNaughton (1988). Although virtue ethicists are almost invariably particularists of some sort, see Swanton (2001) and Stangl (2008), particularists are not necessarily wedded to any version of virtue ethics. Indeed, Stangl, ibid, begins to explore the possibility of separating virtue from particularism, and there is some hint of this as well in Stangl (2010). And for a particularly effective challenge to many of the main themes and arguments in the particularist canon, see Sinnott-Armstrong (1999).

[3] Ch 12 of this volume.

[4] On the relationship between virtue ethics and the law more generally, see esp Solum (2003). See also Farrelly and Solum (2007); Huigens (1995); and Solum (1988). Some scepticism is expressed in Duff (2006). The conjunction between virtue and particularism is stressed in Solum (2006).

[5] Because he focuses on common law systems and on the criminal law, Ho appropriately writes in the context of jury decision-making about facts. But even in some common law systems, notably Singapore, South Africa and Israel, there are, with few exceptions, no juries. And even in legal systems in which there is a general right to jury trial in criminal cases, often the right is waived, and often the system requires juries only for major crimes. As a result, the judge as fact-finder and law-applier in common law criminal cases is a more substantial presence than is commonly assumed. See Schauer (2006b).

Dr Ho is especially concerned with cases in which courts have applied inappropriate gender- or race-based stereotypes in reaching their judgments, he offers virtue ethics not only as a way of thinking about the attitudes and dispositions that properly deliberating jurors ought to have, but also as a way of transcending the common tendency of people to adopt regrettable stereotypes in their decision-making. The particularism of virtue ethics is thus, for Ho, appealing as a way to focus jurors' attention on the particular aspects of particular cases, and especially on the particular characteristics of both defendants and the victims of crimes.

In enthusiastically adopting the particularism characteristic of modern virtue ethics, Ho avoids the question of whether it is possible to be virtuous without being particularistic. Indeed, that question, although admirably highlighted in Ho's analysis, is almost entirely absent in the entire virtue ethics literature. But it is precisely that question I wish to address here, and in this brief comment I want to suggest, *pace* Ho and many others, that the virtuous legal deliberator may not only not be required to be particularistic, but may also, at times, be required not to be particularistic.

I. THE RELEVANCE (OR NOT) OF ARISTOTLE

My goal in this chapter is not to engage in Aristotelian exegesis. It is plainly true that Aristotle, especially, is the canonical source of virtue ethics, and equally true that for Aristotle virtue was indeed particularistic. In his analysis of equity, Aristotle explains how rules, because of their generality, will inevitably produce non-optimal results in some instances, and that equity – for Aristotle much more a state of mind than an institution[6] – is the 'solution' to the inevitable coarseness of rules.[7] For Aristotle, a decision-maker is less virtuous just insofar as he avoids using equity to make the best decision for the particular case, regardless of the decision that might be indicated by an under- and over-inclusive rule.[8]

Aristotle's writings on equity, as well as various other parts of the Aristotelian corpus,[9] lend considerable historical and exegetical support for the conjunction of virtue ethics with particularism. And if we take the very phrase 'virtue ethics' to be an explicit reference to an Aristotelian perspective, then there would be no warrant for attempting to separate the two. Virtue ethics just *is* particularism, it could be insisted from an Aristotelian standpoint, because we have strong evidence from Aristotle's writings (and Plato's too)[10] that for him particularism was one of the

[6] The institutionalisation of equity came later, and Cicero's *De Oratore* 1.57 is a canonical source. See Frier (1985).

[7] Aristotle, *Nicomachean Ethics* 1131a-b, 1137a-b. A similar perspective can be found in Plato, *Statesman* 294a-b. An important analysis of Aristotle's equity and its relation to law is Shiner (1994). See also Solum (1994).

[8] On the under- and over-inclusiveness of rules, see Alexander and Sherwin (2001) and Schauer (1991).

[9] See Aristotle, *Rhetoric* 1374a-b.

[10] *Statesman*, above n 7.

primary virtues – maybe *the* primary virtue – that the ethical and virtuous decision-maker would internalise and exhibit.

But if virtue ethics is a topic about which Aristotle might be instructive but not authoritative – if virtue ethics exists as a concept independent of a label we might attach to certain of Aristotle's views – then the question remains open for analysis and argument whether virtue ethics must or even should incorporate ethical or moral particularism. And that is precisely the question I propose to address in this comment. Using Ho's valuable application of virtue ethics to legal factual deliberation[11] as a useful frame for the inquiry – or perhaps as a foil – I want to inquire into whether the virtuous decision-maker can be something other than a particularist.

II. HO ON VIRTUE

It is appropriate to commence with a description of Ho's own analysis. He begins by describing the process of deliberating as necessarily involving discretion.

> The most that any acceptable Deliberative Procedure can do is to give rational structure to deliberation and highlight the places where the exercise of judgement is called for. Judgement is an inescapable dimension of verdict deliberation. The quest for a Deliberative Procedure is not a quest for an algorithm of legal proof, understood as rules that are to be mechanically applied. What is sought is . . . a rational framework on the directions of inquiry, . . . Ultimately, the trier of the case must find answers to those questions, and the way to the verdict, by her own lights.[12]

The question is then how the virtuous deliberator is expected to exercise this discretion. Ho wisely recognises that the deliberative task involves taking on some combination of moral and epistemic virtues, but for him the epistemic virtues, at least in law, also have a moral component. Because in law a factual determination 'has a practical dimension, carrying a significant risk of harm to others',[13] the virtuous deliberator will be concerned with factors other than 'correctness in the outcome'.[14] Rather, excellence in deliberation, because of the 'intersection of epistemic and moral' factors, will, Ho argues, exhibit empathy, and thus recognise the 'humanity

[11] There is a bit of ambiguity about how we should best characterise the application of law to uncertain facts. We can understand an abstract legal question as a question of law, as when we ask whether the law should permit an injured consumer to recover against a manufacturer with whom she has had no direct relationship (*Donoghue v Stevenson* [1932] AC 562 (HL)). And we can understand a pure question of fact, as when we ask whether it really was a snail that tumbled into Mrs Donoghue's glass of ginger beer in *Donoghue v Stevenson*. But when we ask a judge or juror to apply the potentially uncertain law to facts that they must determine, as when we ask whether Mrs Donoghue, in particular, should recover damages against David Stevenson (the bottler) for the suffering she claims to have incurred at the Wellmeadow Café in Paisley, Scotland, on 26 August 1928, the task partakes some of legal interpretation and some of factual determination.

[12] This volume at 243.

[13] Ibid 245.

[14] Ibid 247.

in another'.[15] But although a substantial part of the empathic attitude will involve empathy for the accused, concern for others implicated by verdicts, 'such as the victim and her family, . . . surely deserve empathic care as well'.[16]

Ho's argument then moves from identifying the intersection of moral and epistemic factors, especially in the realm of the practical, to the identification of the admittedly emotional factor of empathy as one of the moral considerations that will guide virtuous deliberation. And then the subsequent step in the argument is the recognition that empathy requires taking seriously one's own doubts about the evidence. Stifling one's doubts is a bad thing, Ho says, and he identifies prejudice as an important cause of the inappropriate stifling of doubt. And he then argues, with a series of compelling examples of the racism and sexism embedded in numerous legal rules and judicial judgments past and present, that 'such generalisations show an appalling lack of empathy with the victims'.[17] His solution is thus to avoid 'pre-judgment about the members of a class of persons'.[18] And this in turn necessitates both making decisions 'in the particular circumstances of each case' and avoiding the prejudicial generalisations that are the concomitant of 'codification'.[19] 'The fact-finder cannot evade ethical appraisal of her verdict deliberation by recourse to a context-independent set of formal and precise rules.'[20] And thus an argument that commenced by postulating the importance of virtue in deliberation produces a conclusion about the importance of rule-free particularistic judgement. It is just this dimension of the argument I wish to discuss here.

III. THE NON-INEVITABILITY OF JUDICIAL DISCRETION

Initially, there is a question that needs to be asked about Ho's claim that the process of fact-finder deliberation is 'inescapably' discretionary, non-mechanical, non-rule-based, non-formalistic and non-algorithmic. So in order to pose the question, let us imagine a simple case, one in which the relevant rule of law specifies that anyone driving at a speed greater than 40 kilometres per hour above the posted speed limit is guilty of the crime of reckless driving. And then suppose that two police officers, working independently but at the same location, and with separate and recently tested and calibrated radar speed detection technology, both testify that the defendant was 'observed' (by the radar) traveling at 130 kilometres per hour on a stretch of highway plainly posted as having a speed limit of 80 kilometres per hour. The judge or jury is then required to determine whether the defendant is guilty of reckless driving.

[15] Ibid 250.
[16] Ibid 251.
[17] Ibid 255.
[18] Ibid 256.
[19] Ibid 260.
[20] Ibid 260–61.

On the above facts, it appears that the process of finding the defendant guilty is indeed quite mechanical. When the rule of law speaks in precise terms, and when there is no dispute about the facts, it seems odd to say that the process of reaching a verdict is in some way discretionary. And although this is an especially clear and hypothetical case, it is hardly unrealistic or unusual. Many criminal statutes are written in moderately to highly precise terms,[21] and it is often the case that the relevant facts are not in dispute. Yet even when the law and the facts are clear, there may still be reasons why defendants in such cases do not simply plead guilty and save the state the expense of a trial.[22] One is that some defendants might hope for mercy in sentencing, but if the factual deliberation is for the jury and sentencing for the judge, then the jury deliberation will still remain a largely mechanical process, even though it is a necessary prerequisite to arriving at the sentencing stage.[23] Or, as is commonly the case with many traffic or other minor (and some major) offences, the defendant may hope that the police officer or other complaining witness will simply not show up for the trial.[24] But if the defendant's hope that the prosecution's case will be deprived of its principal witness does not ensue, the trial will then proceed even though the deliberation to verdict will typically be straightforward.

Now it is of course possible to have a system in which jurors are permitted to exercise mercy in their own right, and to decide whether it is 'right' in the larger sense for this particular defendant to be convicted for this particular crime in light of a full array of moral and political factors not encompassed in the definition of the offence.[25] But granting such a power to the trier of fact is rarely the law in most countries,[26] and thus this aspect of discretion can hardly be called inevitable.

[21] 26 USC §5861(d) (2006) eg prohibits the possession of unregistered hand 'grenades' (see *United States v Freed* 401 US 601, 609 (1971)), and Florida Statutes §893.135(1)(b) (2008) makes it a felony to possess more than '28 grams' of cocaine.

[22] There is a vast literature on the selection effect, and the way in which, especially for civil cases, the incentives to appeal (or not to appeal) are such that only (or almost only) difficult or close or indeterminate cases make their way to appellate courts. See Lederman (1999); Priest and Klein (1984); and Schauer (1988). In criminal cases, however, the incentives are very different, partly because of the availability of appointed (and therefore free to the defendant) counsel, partly because of the felt need on the part of many defendants and their lawyers to put the prosecution to its proof in every case, and partly because non-finality – the notion that there is still hope, however small – may produce psychological benefits for the defendant during the period of non-finality.

[23] On the array of issues implicated by the question of when (and by whom), if at all, in a criminal proceeding it is appropriate to exercise discretion or mercy, see the important argument, offered in part from a virtue ethics perspective, in Bowers (2010).

[24] The situation is common for minor traffic offences, and defendants often appear in court in the not unreasonable hope that the prosecuting police officer will not be available to testify, or will simply not appear to testify. Moreover, and for an array of tragic psychological, social and economic reasons, complaining witnesses in rape and domestic violence cases often do not appear at trial (see *Davis v Washington & Hammon v Indiana* 547 US 813 (2006)), and thus a plainly guilty defendant would have an incentive to take the case to trial.

[25] Bowers (2010).

[26] Which is not to say that judges and juries may not at times exercise such a power, but whether they should is exactly the normative matter at issue, and does not follow from any necessary fact about legal language, legal rules, or the very idea of the criminal law.

Thus, although it is indeed often the case that the law is unclear, or that the facts are unclear, or both, such indeterminacy of law or indeterminacy of fact is a contingent fact about some prosecutions in some legal systems, and can hardly be called inevitable. Consequently, Ho's claim that particularised discretion is inevitable turns out to be best understood as a normative argument for the desirability of particularism in criminal law, an argument that is by no means implausible, but is also by no means a necessary component of law as we know it. It is in the nature of a legal rule that it will make some facts irrelevant, and it is in the nature of the under- and over-inclusiveness of rules that the facts that the rule renders irrelevant may be relevant to the best all-things-considered determination of some controversy. But whether in such cases the judge or jury should follow the rule to a suboptimal result or instead violate the rule in the service of the optimal or most equitable result is one of the enduring and deeply contested issues of legal theory.[27] It is indeed true that virtue in its particularistic sense – a conjunction I will challenge presently – will require the judge or juror to prefer the equitable result to the rule-generated one, but this follows from the normative stance of taking particularistic virtue to be an underlying goal of a legal system rather than from the simple fact that rule-application is inevitably discretionary or particularistic. If particularistic virtue is to be taken to render even the clearest application of the clearest rules defeasible in the service of equity, or justice, that is a conclusion in need of independent argument, and not a conclusion that follows from some supposed inevitable feature of legal rules or even of the law in general. Application of legal rules to individual conduct can indeed be mechanical or algorithmic, and if the system should avoid this possibility, it takes normative argument to explain why this should be so.

IV. GENERALISATIONS – GOOD AND BAD

With a series of compelling examples of racial and gender discrimination, Ho argues, correctly, that the law should not permit verdicts to be based on impermissible generalisations. But he then goes further and takes his conclusions about racial and gender discrimination as an argument for particularism, and in effect an argument that deliberation should not be based on generalisations at all. The first step in this argument is unexceptional, but the second is more problematic.

Racial and gender generalisations might be impermissible for one of two reasons, both of which I have explored at length elsewhere.[28] One is that many such generalisations may be false, in the sense of being statistically spurious. The view that people of certain races or ethnicities are more likely than people of other races and ethnicities or than people in general to be lazy, for example, has been

[27] Compare eg Schauer (2009: 13–35) and Manning (2003), who tend toward a 'yes' answer to the question in the text, with Dworkin (1986) and Fuller (1958), who tend toward 'no'. The issues are explored, albeit perhaps not from an unbiased perspective, in Schauer (2008).

[28] Schauer (2003).

a widely accepted view through the ages, but there is no evidence whatsoever supporting this conclusion. Similarly, and to take one of Ho's several examples drawn from actual decisions, the view that women are more likely 'to exaggerate an act of sexual connection'[29] than are men, or that women are more likely to engage in such exaggeration than any witness is to exaggerate in general, has no empirical support at all. We should reject the use of such generalisations for the same reason that we would reject inferences drawn from phrenology or astrology or numerology. That the defendant has a bump on one side of his head, or was born under the sign of Capricorn, or has a birthday on a date including the number '6' tells us absolutely nothing about his character or his behaviour. Such inferences are simply spurious, providing no information at all, and thus it is irrational to use them as any part of proof of a criminal act. To the extent that many racial and gender generalisations are of this variety, they are properly excluded from having any place in the legal process.

Moreover, at times we do, properly, exclude even statistically non-spurious generalisations based on race or gender, in part because their soundness as generalisations is itself based on previous discrimination, in part because norms of equality may demand that people be treated equally even when they are not empirically equal, and in part because a justifiable fear of overuse of certain race-based and gender-based generalisations will lead us to mandate underuse as preferable to that overuse. So although it may well be true that women at certain times and in certain places are or have been, on average, less adept at sophisticated finance than men,[30] such a differential is almost assuredly itself a function of discrimination in education and acculturation, and so we prohibit the use of such generalisations, even when they are sound.[31]

From these premises Ho draws the conclusion that there is something suspect about generalisations in general, but the move from the premises to the conclusion is, at the very least, open to question. We do not allow children to drive, drink, or vote because of generalisations about their abilities to engage in such tasks responsibly, and few would argue that the state acts impermissibly in refusing to allow a 13-year-old to claim that he should be permitted to drive because he is taller, smarter and more responsible than most 13-year-olds. Universities admit students based on generalisations about how people with certain test scores will perform in their studies, and few banks will employ convicted thieves as security guards, even though it is an imperfect generalisation that those convicted of theft will be tempted to steal again. Similarly, the law of evidence is replete with generalisations, and it is

[29] See p 254, this volume.

[30] Such was the basis for the Idaho law addressed by the US Supreme Court in *Reed v Reed* 404 US 71 (1971), and properly invalidated as a denial of the equal protection of laws.

[31] See *United States v Virginia* 518 US 515 (1996). For a generalisation to be sound is for it to have, unlike astrology, some predictive or indicative value. The generalisation that Swiss cheese has holes is a sound one even though some Swiss cheese does not, because knowing that a cheese is Swiss makes it more likely to have holes than knowing simply that it is cheese. Such generalisations – Volvos are reliable, Italians are demonstrative, cobras are dangerous – are so much a part of our linguistic, conceptual and perceptual apparatus that it is hard to imagine a life in which the only permissible generalisations were those that were universally accurate.

hard to imagine how it could be otherwise. Sometimes people do not do what they intend, but evidence of intentions is universally admitted as probative of the question on whether the person with that intention actually committed the act.[32] And we ordinarily admit evidence of flight because of a generalisation that people who run away from the scene of a crime, or from the authorities, are more likely to have been involved with the crime than are randomly selected members of the population, or than are those who do not run away.[33] Such generalisations are imperfect, but it is inconceivable that the criminal justice system, the law in general, or even human cognition could operate without them.

It is certainly true that a legal system or a criminal justice system can be more or less particularistic. But the fact that there are some generalisations that are spurious and others that are morally problematic hardly produces the conclusion that the generalisations that undergird the law itself are problematic just because they are generalisations. Driving in excess of the speed limit is a crime, after all, only because such driving probabilistically but not inexorably indicates a lack of care and safety. Many other crimes – at least the entire category of *mala prohibita*, and possibly much of *mala in se*, depending on one's moral theory[34] – are premised on a generalisation about the relationship between the particular type of act that is made criminal and the state's deeper concern. It is indeed wrong to base a legal judgment or an evidentiary rule on stereotypes about, for example, the veracity of rape victims, but the wrong lies in the content of the generalisation and not in the very idea of generalisation. The existence of empirically and morally unfortunate generalisations is a problem, but it does not come close to justifying the move from the problem with some generalisations to a problem about generalisation. It is true that Aristotle and modern particularists argue against generalisation per se, but these are not arguments that are based on the misuse of racial or gender generalisations, and the undeniable existence of such misuse cannot do the work that Ho wants it to in making the case against generalisation as such.

V. THE VIRTUES OF ANTI-PARTICULARISM

That the arguments from inevitable discretion and from the misuse of generalisations are unsuccessful does not mean, of course, that there is nothing to be said in favour of particularism, and indeed much of it has been said, from Aristotle's time to the present. But there is much to be said on the other side of the argument as well, and in the particular context of virtue in criminal law deliberation, one of those arguments is about the virtue in humility. Is there virtue in humility, and, if so, what does it mean, and what follows from this?

[32] See James (1941).

[33] See *United States v Rowan* 518 F2d 685 (6th Cir 1975); *United States v Ballard* 423 F2d 127 (5th Cir 1970).

[34] Thus, to the utilitarian all legal rules are probabilistic approximations of the acts whose prohibition will increase aggregate utility.

Ho admirably recognises that the virtuous deliberator will be sceptical, when appropriate, of the accounts of police officers and other officials, and even sceptical about the accounts of others, including defendants. And he recognises as well that the deliberator herself should be sceptical about her own first impressions. Indeed, he believes that such scepticism about one's own first impressions has great value, and is properly understood as the kind of attitude or state of mind that we should class as a virtue. Yet although Ho recognises the virtue in being sceptical about one's first impressions, he does not suggest that the virtuous deliberator should also be sceptical about her second impressions. That is, after the virtuous deliberator has reflected carefully and sceptically on her own first impressions, Ho appears to believe that she should have confidence in, and thus act on, her subsequent impressions and the decisions that follow from them. First thoughts may be systematically unreliable, but carefully considered second thoughts will and should form the basis for a decision.

Such a view of deliberation, however, seems potentially lacking in humility – or modesty – and in an arguably unvirtuous way. Against the view that the virtuous deliberator should have act-motivating confidence in her considered second impressions, we should ask whether perhaps the virtuous deliberator will recognise that others simply know more than she does, even more than she knows on careful and sober reflection – and if necessary, re-evaluation – on her first impressions. Or perhaps the virtuous deliberator will recognise that others have an expertise that she does not possess. Or perhaps the virtuous deliberator will acknowledge that many decisions have second-order and third-order and even more remote consequences that are real but which she cannot perceive. Or perhaps the virtuous deliberator will recognise that she is susceptible to various forms of bias, prejudice, irrationality and other forms of decision-making incapacities that her mere awareness cannot transcend. Recent research on implicit bias, for example, has suggested that some racial and gender prejudices may exist in even the agent who recognises them and seeks to avoid them.[35] And much of the research on heuristics and biases has shown that some of the supposed irrationalities of human decision-making – anchoring, for example – are substantially resistant to debiasing techniques, including debiasing by awareness.[36]

One consequence of all of this is that the virtuously humble and modest decision-maker, the one self-aware about her own inabilities even upon second thought and deeper reflection, may recognise that some decisions are better made by others. As Joseph Raz has powerfully argued over the years,[37] acceptance of authority may at times be a function of the recognition that others who share our goals might be better at making the decisions that serve those goals than we are ourselves.

[35] The literature is vast, see eg Banaji and Greenwald (1995); Greenwald and Banaji (1995); Greenwald, Nosek and Banaji (2003); and Nosek and others (2007), and has hardly been without challenge and controversy. See Mitchell and Tetlock (2006) and Tetlock and Mitchell (2008).

[36] See Wilson and others (1996). See also Hanson and Kysar (1999: 633).

[37] See esp Raz (1979) and (1975).

If humility in just this way – humility about one's own decision-making capacities even on second and reflective impression – is plausibly one of the virtues, then this allows us to see rule-based deliberation in a different and better light. The deliberator who follows the rule even though her own best all-things-considered judgement says otherwise might not be irrational. She might simply be modest. Or humble. Or self-aware. She might virtuously doubt that her own all-things-considered best judgement is better than that of the rule-maker who has considered a very large number of similar cases. She might virtuously doubt that her own view that this case warrants an exception to the rule is better than that of the rule-maker who, worried about the secondary consequences (the slippery slope, dangerous precedent, and so on)[38] of making exceptions, crafted a rule without them. And she might virtuously doubt that her own expertise is sufficient to decide when the empirical generalisations that undergird any rule are inapplicable. For all of these reasons she might prefer to apply a pre-existing rule literally, or formalistically, or mechanically. And she might prefer this not because of irrational and thus non-virtuous rule-worship or obsession with form, but because what looks to an outside observer (whose judgement may too be flawed) like irrational rule-worship may look to the rule-follower as a form of deference,[39] humility and modesty. To have such attitudes or the character that promotes them may not only not be irrational, but may indeed be an important virtue. And as a result, there may be more to be said for the virtue of rule-following, in the proper sense of virtue, than Ho and many others seem inclined to recognise.

Particularism, *pace* Aristotle and Ho, among many others, may therefore not always be virtuous. It may reflect a self-confidence in one's own decision-making and deliberative abilities that, in its more extreme form, partakes of arrogance. Generality in decision-making may accordingly reflect an appropriate and modest recognition that one's perceptions of *this* case may be flawed or distorted by this case's very this-ness.[40] And rule-following in deliberation may reflect a desirable and humble acknowledgment that others might be better at some tasks and decisions than are we. And insofar as this is so, there may be a virtue in generality and generalisation – and rule-following as well – that has all too often been ignored in the literature on particularism and virtue ethics.

VI. CONCLUSION

I have not in this brief comment dealt with all of the dimensions in Ho's rich and provocative chapter. Indeed, there is much in the chapter with which I agree. And I certainly have no quarrel with Ho's general moral posture towards racism and sexism or with his views about the examples he has so skilfully marshalled. But it is precisely the richness of his chapter that invites reflections about delibera-

[38] See Schauer (1985).
[39] On the complex and controversial virtues of deference, see Soper (2002).
[40] See Schauer (2006a) and Schauer and Zeckhauser (2011).

tion, particularism and virtue ethics even outside of the specific context of fact-finding in criminal cases. The conjunction between virtue ethics and particularism is ubiquitous in the virtue ethics literature, but if Ho's analysis has the unintended consequence of prompting challenges to this conjunction, then his chapter, ironically, will turn out to be even more important than he may have intended.

REFERENCES

Adams, RM (2006) *A Theory of Virtue* (New York, Oxford University Press).
Alexander, L and Sherwin, E (2001) *The Rule of Rules: Morality, Rules, and the Dilemmas of Law* (Durham, North Carolina, Duke University Press).
Annas, J (1993) *The Morality of Happiness* (New York, Oxford University Press).
Anscombe, GEM (1958) 'Modern Moral Philosophy' 33 *Philosophy* 1.
Aristotle, JAK Thomson (tr) *Nicomachean Ethics* (Harmondsworth, UK, Penguin, 1977).
——, JH Freese (tr) *The 'Art' of Rhetoric* (Cambridge, MA, Harvard University Press, 1947).
Banaji, MR and Greenwald, AG (1995) 'Implicit Gender Stereotyping in Judgments of Fame' 68 *Journal of Personality and Social Psychology* 181.
Bowers, J (2010) 'Legal Guilt, Normative Innocence, and the Equitable Decision Not to Prosecute' 110 *Columbia Law Review* 1655.
Crisp, R and Slote, M (eds) (2009) *Virtue Ethics* (Oxford, Oxford University Press).
Dancy, J (1993) *Moral Reasons* (Oxford, Blackwell).
—— (2004) *Ethics without Principles* (Oxford, Clarendon Press).
Darwall, S (ed) (2003) *Virtue Ethics* (Oxford, Blackwell).
Duff, RA (2006) 'The Virtues and Vices of Virtue Jurisprudence' in T Chappell (ed), *Values and Virtues: Aristotelianism in Contemporary Ethics* (Oxford, Oxford University Press).
Dworkin, R (1986) *Law's Empire* (Cambridge, MA, Harvard University Press).
Farrelly, CP and Solum, LB (eds) (2007) *Virtue Jurisprudence* (London, Palgrave Macmillan).
Foot, P (1978) Virtues and Vices (Oxford, Blackwell).
Frier, BW (1985) *The Rise of the Roman Jurists: Studies in Cicero's Pro Caecina* (Princeton, Princeton University Press).
Fuller, L (1958) 'Positivism and Fidelity to Law – A Reply to Professor Hart' 71 *Harvard Law Review* 630.
Gottleib, P (2009) *The Virtue of Aristotle's Ethics* (Cambridge, Cambridge University Press).
Greenwald, AG and Banaji, MR (1995) 'Implicit Social Cognition: Attitudes, Self-Esteem, and Stereotypes' 102 *Psychological Review* 4.
Greenwald, AG, Nosek, BA, Banaji, MR (2003) 'Understanding and Using the Implicit Association Test: I. An Improved Scoring Algorithm' 85 *Journal of Personality and Social Psychology* 197.
Hanson, JD and Kysar, DA (1999) 'Taking Behavioralism Seriously: The Problem of Market Manipulation' 74 *New York University Law Review* 630.
Hooker, B and Little, MO (eds) (2000) *Moral Particularism* (Oxford, Oxford University Press).
Huigens, K (1995) 'Virtue and Inculpation' 108 *Harvard Law Review* 1423.
Hursthouse, R (1999) *On Virtue Ethics* (Oxford, Oxford University Press).
James, GF (1941) 'Relevancy, Probability and the Law' 29 *California Law Review* 689.
Lederman, L (1999) 'Which Cases Go to Trial?: An Empirical Study of Predictions of Failure to Settle' 49 *Case Western Reserve Law Review* 315.

Manning, JF (2003) 'The Absurdity Doctrine' 116 *Harvard Law Review* 2388.
McNaughton, D (1988) *Moral Vision* (Oxford, Blackwell).
Mitchell, G and Tetlock, PE (2006) 'Antidiscrimination Law and the Perils of Mindreading' 67 *Ohio State Law Journal* 1023.
Nosek, BA and others (2007) 'Pervasiveness and Correlates of Implicit Attitudes and Stereotypes' 18 *European Review of Social Psychology* 36.
Plato, JB Skemp (tr) *Statesman* (Bristol, Bristol Classical Press, 1952).
Priest, GL and Klein, W (1984) 'The Selection of Disputes for Litigation' 13 *Journal of Legal Studies* 1.
Raz, J (1975) *Practical Reason and Norms* (London, Hutchinson).
——(1979) *The Authority of Law: Essays on Law and Morality* (Oxford, Clarendon Press).
Schauer, F (1985) 'Slippery Slopes' 99 Harvard Law Review 361.
——(1988) 'Judging in a Corner of the Law' 61 *Southern California Law Review* 1717.
——(1991) *Playing By the Rules: A Philosophical Analysis of Rule-Based Decision-Making in Law and in Life* (Oxford, Clarendon Press).
——(2003) *Profiles, Probabilities, and Stereotypes* (Cambridge, Massachusetts, Harvard University Press).
——(2006a) 'Do Cases Make Bad Law?' 73 *University of Chicago Law Review* 883.
——(2006b) 'On the Supposed Jury Dependence of Evidence Law' 155 *University of Pennsylvania Law Review* 165.
——(2008) 'A Critical Guide to Vehicles in the Park' 83 *New York University Law Review* 1109.
——(2009) *Thinking Like a Lawyer: A New Introduction to Legal Reasoning* (Cambridge, MA, Harvard University Press).
Schauer, F and Zeckhauser, R (2011) 'The Trouble with Cases' in D Kessler (ed) *Regulation vs Litigation: Perspectives from Economics and Law (National Bureau of Economic Research Conference Report)* (Chicago, University of Chicago Press).
Shiner, R (1994) 'Aristotle's Theory of Equity' 27 *Loyola of Los Angeles Law Review* 1245.
Sinnott-Armstrong, WP (1999) 'Some Varieties of Particularism' 30 *Metaphilosophy* 1.
Slote, M (2001) *Morals from Motives* (Oxford, Oxford University Press).
Solum, LB (1988) 'The Virtues and Vices of a Judge: An Aristotelian Guide to Judicial Selection' 61 *Southern California Law Review* 1735.
——(1994) 'Equity and the Rule of Law' in I Shapiro (ed), *The Rule of Law: NOMOS XXXVI* (New York, New York University Press).
——(2003) 'Virtue Jurisprudence: A Virtue-Centered Theory of Judging' 34 *Metaphilosophy* 178.
——(2006) 'Natural Justice' 51 *American Journal of Jurisprudence* 65.
Soper, P (2002) *The Ethics of Deference: Learning from Law's Morals* (Cambridge, Cambridge University Press).
Stangl, R (2008) 'A Dilemma for Particularist Virtue Ethics' 58 *Philosophical Quarterly* 665.
——(2010) 'Asymmetrical Virtue Particularism' 121 *Ethics* 37.
Swanton, C (2001) 'A Virtue Ethical Account of Right Action' 112 *Ethics* 32.
——(2003) *Virtue Ethics: A Pluralistic View* (Oxford, Oxford University Press).
Tetlock, PE and Mitchell, G (2008) 'Calibrating Prejudice in Milliseconds' 71 *Social Psychology Quarterly* 12.
Wilson, TD and others (1996) 'A New Look at Anchoring Effects: Basic Anchoring and Its Antecedents' 125 *Journal of Experimental Psychology: General* 387.

V.

Law, Empathy and Justice

14

Empathy, Law and Justice

MICHAEL SLOTE

IN RECENT YEARS, many people have pointed out the importance of empathy for jurisprudence and the law. We have been told, for example, that judges really need to be capable of empathy if they are to preside fairly in trials, etc and render just verdicts in the cases they have to deal with. All too often in the past, judges have been unwilling to look at or think about 'where people are coming from' in emotionally sensitive ways, and most of us nowadays recognise that this requires a capacity for or disposition toward empathy. Empathy has thus, to a certain extent, come into its own in law and jurisprudence, and that fact reflects, I believe, an increased awareness on the part of the public, and especially its more thoughtful members, of the general significance or importance of empathy. The term itself was not invented till the twentieth century (though in earlier times some philosophers, for example, Hume and Adam Smith, and presumably many non-philosophers too, were at least aware of empathy as a phenomenon). However, the earliest official usage of the term 'empathy' was in application to our understanding of and reactions to works of art; the widespread use of the term to refer to a desirable form of sensitivity to *other people* came much later. But when it came, latish in the twentieth century, it came in a torrent. Everyone talks about empathy nowadays – it is seen as part of emotional intelligence, as an important trait that is lacking in sociopaths, as necessary to the best sort of political leadership (Obama talks about it), etc.

In this chapter, I want to add a bit more about what empathy is and then to use what I have said for a much larger purpose than any (to my knowledge) to which the idea of empathy has been put, at least since Hume's time. Hume used the notion of empathy (for which he had to use the term 'sympathy') as the basis for his account of normative morality and of moral language, and I think his basic approach is in fact much more promising than it is typically given credit for. Even though Hume said a lot of things we all disagree with nowadays, I believe the notion of empathy has more potential life in it than most people think and more even than Hume himself might have recognised. But I will not be able to persuade you of all this in one chapter; in fact, what I am and shall be saying here summarises the general argument of a book, *The Ethics of Care and Empathy*,[1] though I

[1] Slote (2007).

shall focus or refocus that argument in the direction of legal and political issues and away from its main emphasis on questions of personal morality.

I am going to argue, or summarise an argument to the effect, that empathy and empathic concern for others can function as the basis, the entire basis, for a plausible understanding of legal and social justice (as I think they do for personal morality as well). And I have no doubt that your initial reaction to this idea is going to be sceptical or even more negative than that. We know that empathy can get us into trouble – a judge who is extremely empathic with the convicted felon she is about to sentence might well give a much lighter sentence than most of us would consider to be compatible with legal justice or with the judge's own sworn commitment to uphold the law. And much more generally, we are, most of us, suspicious of the idea that any set of emotions could be sufficient to justify or guarantee the general rights and liberties that we think a just society should ensure. Rather, we tend to speak and believe we need to speak of those widely-acknowledged basic rights and liberties as being discerned by reason and as having a rational and/or impartial moral basis. So what I am proposing here is really very much opposed to the rationalist/liberal/Kantian way of conceiving these matters that is so prevalent in Anglo-American jurisprudence and legal/political philosophy. Such a radical divergence from common ways of viewing things needs to be justified, and, of course and again, I cannot give the whole of such a justification here. But I am going to try to show that this new way of seeing things, with its strong emphasis on empathy, has some distinct advantages and is capable of accounting for basic legal and political phenomena more adequately than one might initially expect.

I have been led toward this kind of 'sentimentalist' approach to legal and political justice via certain recent trends within Anglo-American philosophical thought. In 1982, Carol Gilligan published a book called *In a Different Voice* that for the first time in living memory gave moral-sentimentalist notions a foothold in ongoing philosophical discussions of ethical issues.[2] Gilligan (and others who followed her lead) defended the idea of an ethics – called the ethics of care – that is not based on rational considerations or arguments, but rather depends, if you will, on the human heart. That human heart needs, of course, to be informed by facts; it does not work in a cognitive vacuum. But the fundamental idea was that the measure of one's morality lies in how caringly one treats others and that a failure to care does not indicate a failure of rationality, but rather shows ethically defective or deficient emotional sensitivities. And one thing that moved me in the direction of such an approach was my (previous) recognition of how odd and under-motivated it is to say that someone who does not care about (their moral obligations to) others automatically counts as irrational. That is not, in fact, how ordinary people typically regard such immoralists: they are thought of, perhaps, as heartless, but they are not commonly said to be irrational.

[2] Gilligan (1982).

My own purported contribution to care ethics has been to emphasise the necessary role of empathy in launching and sustaining our dispositions to care, altruistically, about others – a point that some psychologists had been making, but that philosophers and even care ethicists had not recognised in a full and general way. But then, you may ask, how can caring, and even caring based on or in empathy, help us understand political and legal issues? We may be morally required to be caring in regard to people we know, but surely this kind of thing cannot be generalised to the public/political sphere in any usefully systematic way.

Well, not so fast. Some care ethicists, the more recent Nel Noddings and my long-standing self among them, have argued that morally decent persons will not only care for their intimates and acquaintances, but also have some measure of concern for people, distant or otherwise, whom they do not know and are unlikely ever to know. And various forms of care ethics that take in the latter kind of caring have begun developing ideas about social justice on that basis. In my own writings, I have urged, as I shall be urging here, that such an extrapolation of care ethics to the public and political sphere is more easily and plausibly managed if one emphasises the empathic roots of concern for distant or unknown others. But I think I now need to say a bit about those roots.

In his book *Empathy and Moral Development*, the psychologist Martin Hoffman describes how empathy originates and develops in children.[3] To do this he has to distinguish empathy from sympathy, and for present purposes let me just say that empathy is what Bill Clinton (supposedly) exemplified when he said 'I feel your pain', whereas sympathy is a matter of feeling bad, say, about someone's pain and wanting to help them or see them helped. Thus empathy involves a kind of oneness or identification with others, and sympathy, however praiseworthy and desirable it may be, does not. Now Hoffman argues that our empathic tendencies are *partial* in certain ways that are in fact familiar to all of us. We tend to feel more empathy for those we know than for those we merely know about, and seeing someone in pain tends to cause a much stronger empathic reaction than merely learning that someone is in pain. But Hoffman argues that by their teenage years most children develop the capacity for feeling empathy with disadvantaged groups whose members they have never met – for example, the distant victims of famine or tyrannical rule (think of North Korea and the stunted growth of whole generations of children). But all this depends, of course, on increased cognitive sophistication; one has to know what a group is and how it can be disadvantaged by environmental events or human abuses.

So we are capable of empathy with people and groups we are not personally acquainted with, and it is possible, therefore, to argue that morality and justice require, either at the personal or at the governmental level, a concern, based in empathy, for possibly distant (groups of) people less fortunate than the individual whose morality or the society whose justice is at issue. This gives us the beginnings of what an ethics of care or any plausible sentimentalist approach can and should

[3] Hoffman (2000).

say about social and legal justice generally. But the devil (or is it God?) is in the details.

I want to show how a sentimentalist approach that emphasises empathy can help us understand and justify basic human rights and our most important ideals of social and legal justice. As a general criterion (and in parallel with what it wants to say about individual actions), such a view will hold that laws, institutions and social customs are just (and consistent with our basic rights) only if they do not manifest a lack of fully empathic concern for (groups of) other people on the part of those who promulgate, maintain, or participate in them. Let me, then, illustrate this (admittedly somewhat vague) general formula with respect to some important issues of social justice, and I would like to begin by saying something about the putative right to religious freedom.

It is usually thought that the right to worship as one chooses has to be based on rational or other considerations that are independent of human feeling and emotion – because, it is held, feelingful concern for fellow human beings, far from ensuring a respect for such religious rights or liberties, can actually move us toward denying them to people. It is frequently said that concern for the long-term welfare of others can make us deny them the right to worship freely on the grounds that such worship would be displeasing to God and lead to their eternal damnation, and this kind of thinking is sometimes applied, in particular, to the Spanish Inquisition. It is then frequently maintained that we need something other than sentiment, namely, rights grounded in rational considerations of autonomy, in order to defend religious rights and liberties in circumstances where well-meaning benevolent individuals would seek to deny them. (Both Thomas Nagel[4] and JL Mackie[5] have said this sort of thing.)

But such reasoning is, in fact, naïve or worse. As John Locke pointed out centuries ago, the 'dry eyes' of those who were supposedly torturing people for the sake of their souls gives the lie to the claim that they were motivated by benevolent concern for the welfare of those they tortured.[6] In fact, those who tortured and persecuted heretics and non-believers during the Inquisition typically had nothing but contempt and hatred for those they were persecuting; and this means, in fact, that they were very far from seeing things from the point of view of those they were persecuting. On the contrary, and more generally, one could say (following psychologist Albert Bandura)[7] that greater and humanly feasible empathy with 'out-groups' could have prevented every form and instance of religious persecution (and intolerance) that has occurred in human history. So the denial of religious rights or liberties is and has always been unjust by the criterion of empathic concern for others. (In certain imaginable science-fiction scenarios one can imagine it being morally acceptable, and not at all indicative of a lack of empathic

[4] Nagel (1991: 154–68).
[5] Mackie (1980: 28).
[6] Locke (1960).
[7] Bandura (2002).

concern for others, to deny people the right to worship as they choose. But this is not what happens in actual human cases.)

But even granting all this, the Kantian or liberal might still say that it is better to understand rights of religious freedom in rationalistic terms, rather than as grounded and justifiable via a sentimentalistic appeal to the notion of empathy. But if they do say this, they are in fact conceding quite a lot, and they are making a claim of superiority that stands in some need of justification. In fact, the typical liberal or Kantian appeals to the notion or ideal of (rational) autonomy as the grounding basis for their views, and I believe that such appeals are philosophically quite vulnerable. For example, certain care ethicists and feminists have argued that autonomy is best seen as dependent on the nurturing of others, especially parents, and although liberals and Kantians never explicitly deny this, they often speak of autonomy as if it were an automatic feature of human character and personality, as if it did not have to be *developed.* I believe that the more relational conception of autonomy that has been advocated by some feminist thinkers and care ethicists is in fact more insightful and tenable than what Kantians and liberals have to say on this subject.

This point is further illustrated by what liberals and Kantians frequently say about the value and validity of autonomy. The Enlightenment ideal of holding everything – every aspect of one's life and of one's surrounding culture and society – open to question treats one's critical capacities, one's autonomous ability to question anything and everything, as somehow prior to all the commitments, emotions, projects and relationships that the exercise of autonomy can lead one to doubt or question. According to this picture of individuals and their basic autonomy, one ought, ideally, to subject every feeling and relationship to critical scrutiny or questioning before one allows oneself to accept (or continue with) it, and any ethics of care and indeed any familiar form of moral sentimentalism will want to question this assumption.

We think, contrary to the Kantian liberal or Enlightenment rationalist, that certain feelings and relationships need not be and in fact should not be automatically questioned, for example, one's love of one's own children. In fact, and as I argued in *The Ethics of Care and Empathy*, to have the kind of vigilant attitude to each and every emotion, relationship and commitment that liberals and others recommend in the name of their ideal of (critical) autonomy is to have a somewhat stunted capacity for those emotions, etc.[8] Here the Enlightenment clearly clashes with an ethical sense of the importance of feeling that to some extent derives from the ideals of Romanticism, but that also, and unlike the latter, allows ample room for intelligently criticising emotions and relationships. If things are going wrong with a relationship in various ways, one should, to be sure, question or criticise that relationship. But to start questioning or engaging in a critique *before* anything goes or shows any sign of going wrong is to be closed off from certain valuable deep feelings and relationships, and so, once again, the sentimentalist thinks they have reason to question the ideal of

[8] Slote (2007).

autonomy that Kantian liberals, libertarians and others so often invoke as the basis for freedom of religion and other political rights.[9] The sentimentalist, or at least my kind of sentimentalist, invokes ideals of caring and/or empathy as the grounds for our belief in a moral right to free religious worship, and in doing so they can fully allow for the importance and value of emotions/feelings and the commitments and relationships they permeate, in a way that ethical rationalists seem incapable of doing. And there is an additional reason for understanding rights and justice in sentimentalist terms that stems from what the sentimentalist has to say or can say about the meaning of moral terms like 'right' and 'wrong'.

There is an interesting correlation between the arousal of empathy and what we commonly think about the strength of our moral obligations. We think it is morally worse not to save a child who is drowning in shallow water right in front of us than not to save some distant child from dying of hunger by making a contribution to (say) Oxfam. But empathy is typically more strongly aroused by the pain and danger we witness than by the pain and danger we merely know about, and the correlation between the strength of empathic reactions and the strength accorded to varying obligations in fact extends very broadly. To mention just one further example, we feel we have a stronger moral obligation to our children than to other people's children, and our empathy for our own children is usually much stronger than what we feel in regard to the children of others. I have elsewhere argued at considerable length that the best explanation of this wide correlation is that the notion of empathy and the realised capacity for empathy enter into the making of moral judgements (I use this term without any commitment to the objectivity of such judgements). In other words, if the very same empathy that makes us respond differently to different kinds of situations enters into our understanding of and claims about what is morally better or worse, that would explain why there is such a wide correlation between what is morally worse and better and what goes more or less against the grain of our ordinary developed empathic tendencies. (The hypothesis that moral language or concepts are grounded in empathy would also tell us, very plausibly I think, that a psychopath is not fully capable of making moral judgements and at best uses moral language in an 'inverted commas' way – in parallel with what we are inclined to say about blind people and their imperfect understanding of colour terms.)

In a recent book called *Moral Sentimentalism,* I extend or deepen this conclusion by offering a specific account of the meaning of 'right' and 'wrong' in terms that make reference to empathy.[10] However, there is no space to go into that here. Rationalists do not offer us any account of the meaning of moral terminology, and they would certainly want to deny that empathy is essential to our moral concepts and judgements. But to that extent, what they say flies in the face of the correlation between empathic tendencies and moral judgements that I have just

[9] A theory of legal justice that emphasises empathy will also disagree with the typically liberal 'autonomy defense' of hate speech in 'Skokie-type' cases and with some liberal views about the autonomy rights of abusive husbands/boyfriends, as well. But that further right cannot be discussed here.

[10] Slote (2010).

been illustrating, and at the very least I think that the correlation gives us some reason to take a sentimentalist approach to rights and justice seriously – even if its terms of explanation and justification are somewhat unfamiliar both to philosophers and to the general public. But it is time now to extend our sentimentalist analysis of justice to issues other than religious freedom. Questions of distributive justice lie at the heart of most conceptions of social or international justice, so it is important for any sentimentalist approach to be able to say something convincing or plausible about the justice or injustice of serious inequalities of wealth. However, it may help us in doing this if we first say something about the distribution not of wealth, but of political power.

In some societies a ruling elite denies most people a political voice, a vote. We consider this to be an injustice, and the injustice can, in fact, be unpacked in care-ethical sentimentalist terms, because the refusal to grant basic political privileges or rights always – I really think always – expresses and reflects a rather greedy and selfish desire, on the part of the elite, to retain their hegemony of power, privilege and (typically, though not always) wealth. This constitutes less empathic concern for the welfare of one's compatriots than would be reflected in a fully developed capacity for empathy with others, and so our approach can call such a situation or society unjust. But let me be just a bit more explicit now about what I am assuming here. I earlier mentioned Hoffman's discussion of how empathy with disadvantaged groups can develop in teenagers or young adults, but it is worth pointing out, as Hoffman and others have done, how moral education can play a role in sensitising us to disadvantaged groups either within or outside our own country. In schools, for example, children can be exposed to literature or videos that focus on groups of people who are disadvantaged in one or another way and thereby made more sensitive to the unfortunate situations the people of such groups are in. And a power elite that refuses to grant what we think of as basic political rights because of a greedy or selfish desire to hold onto its prerogatives at all costs shows, in fact, a lack of the kind of empathic concern for the disadvantaged that teenagers tend (to a certain extent) to develop and that a process of moral education of the sort just mentioned would tend to instil. Holding on to power at all costs is unjust, therefore, because it exhibits or reflects a lack of fully empathic concern for other people, in this case one's own compatriots.

Similar criticism can be made of a meritocratic society in which there is no (guaranteed) safety net for the poor, the challenged, or the unemployed. Even if such a society allows everyone to vote, a power elite may successfully oppose all proposals to provide economic help for the poor, etc, and it is plausible to suppose, once again, that such opposition reflects or exhibits a selfishness and greed on the part of the elite that is incompatible with a level of empathic concern for the worst-off members of society that seems well within our human capacities. To that extent, such opposition counts as unjust in strictly sentimentalist terms.

But of course it is possible to hold that injustice(s) of an economic kind can exist even when a social safety net is in place, so let us consider that possibility. A safety net is compatible with enormous differences of wealth and with a considerable amount of poverty, and a sentimentalist care ethics may well want to say that (distributive) justice requires *more* than a safety net, that it requires that the rich and those with high incomes be taxed *more steeply* than those at the lower end of the economic scale. Considerations of marginal utility offer us, in fact, a very good moral justification for preferring and instituting the kind of progressive taxation on the rich and those with high incomes that makes for greater economic equality within society as a whole.

Given decreasing marginal utility, when we tax a rich person's money, we typically do less harm than when we tax a poor person's money. But even more importantly, when we tax rich or high-income individuals for the benefit of those who are poorer, the latter tend to gain a great deal more than the former lose. This fact gives us some empathic grounds to favour redistributive progressive taxation, and I believe the justice of progressive taxation and the injustice of not instituting such taxation can both be accounted for in sentimentalist moral terms. (However, in taxing the rich we *deprive* them of something good and do not merely *allow* the loss of something good to occur, and empathy is sensitive, in fact, to this sort of distinction between doing and allowing. I shall say more about this at the end of this chapter, but let me here just mention that I think what I have just said about progressive taxation survives the moral point about doing versus allowing.)[11]

In any event, nothing we have just been saying indicates that justice requires, or even allows, the progressive tax rate to be as steep as possible, so that society comes progressively closer (excuse this pun!) to complete socio-economic equality. The highest or steepest rates of taxation and any general insistence on equality, or near-equality, of wealth or income might very well deprive people of incentives to work hard and quite possibly would cause society as a whole to lose greatly in economic terms. The latter fact is (also) one to which empathic caring is or would be sensitive, so our account of justice need not insist on the highest rates of progressive taxation and would instead claim that the issue of how steep progressive taxation should be has to depend on empirical considerations. But there is a further, very interesting complication that also needs to be mentioned at this point.

Utilitarians often make use of considerations of marginal utility to argue for progressive taxation, but in addition they hold that the rate of taxation should not be so steep as to diminish overall economic output or overall social utility. However, the utilitarian *also* holds that justice requires the passing of laws that do a great deal (only) for those who are already well off, when the only alternative is legislation that would do somewhat less good overall for those who are poorly, or less well, off, and this will seem morally unacceptable to many of us. Rawls's difference principle[12] is intended precisely to avoid what utilitarianism is counterintuitively committed to here, but I want to argue that our sentimentalist approach can also handle this issue more intuitively than utilitarianism does.

[11] All this is argued for in Slote (2007).

[12] Rawls (1971).

We tend to feel more empathy and empathic concern for people whose situation or condition is bad or unfortunate than for those whose situation or condition is merely not wonderful, and this difference can mean that we prefer to help the former even if we are in a position to do somewhat more good for the latter. Our sentimentalist ethics of empathic caring entails, then, that we should take both marginal utility and (what we can very roughly call) absolute positionality into account in determining what is moral or just; and since legislators (and framers of constitutions) who are fully empathic will have greater empathy and a special/greater concern for those in their society whose position is bad or terrible (or will be, if nothing is done to help them), our theory of justice mandates a much higher degree of economic equality than utilitarianism provides for or allows.

Put another way, our view requires laws and institutions that do not reflect a lack of compassion, for compassion is clearly sensitive to what I am calling absolute badness (for individuals or groups of individuals). (How hungry one feels and other aspects of what is bad for people may depend partly on comparisons one makes with how others are doing, but I think you should be able to understand, nonetheless, what I mean by talking of absolute badness here.) Other things being equal, we feel more empathy for, and have more tendency to act on behalf of, those who are in bad shape or circumstances, and the term 'compassion' takes in that aspect of empathy – we would not call someone compassionate if they wanted to do somewhat more good for those already well off rather than somewhat less good for those in horrible circumstances, and, in fact, a concern to better the situation of those already well off cannot be *described* as (a form or instance of) compassion. In any event, we can say that a kind of social compassion, or at least laws or institutions that do not manifest a lack of compassion, are a necessary condition of social justice, and all of this follows quite naturally from our sentimentalist moral emphasis on empathy.

I have so far been concentrating on the motives of legislators and others toward those who live in their own country. But many will hold that a just society, with just laws, institutions and customs, will not be indifferent or hostile to the interests or welfare of people in other countries, and that certainly seems to be correct. However, a theory of justice that stresses empathy should have no problem in addressing these issues. Just as morally decent individuals develop an empathic concern for people (whom they do not personally know) living outside their own country, fully empathic legislators will also focus to some extent on the welfare of people in other countries. Such legislators will presumably be less concerned with the citizens or inhabitants of other countries than with the citizens or inhabitants of their own – empathy is not impartial or impersonal in utilitarian fashion – but the laws or legislation they approve (for example, the level of humanitarian foreign aid they support) should at least reflect a substantial amount of concern for the well-being of people in other countries and for the welfare of the countries themselves considered in aggregate terms. (More accurately, it should not reflect or exhibit a lack of such concern.) And the theory I am outlining can explain why, on grounds of justice, this should be so.

We have so far focused primarily on issues of distributive justice, and a fully-developed sentimentalist approach to issues of law and justice would certainly also need to take on questions of tort and criminal justice. But there is no space to consider those issues here, and in any case what sentimentalism has to say about them is – in my own case at least – rather less well worked out than what it can say and has said on the topic of distributive justice and rights of liberty. What I do need, finally, to address at this point is a question about judges and legal adjudication that I raised earlier and then promptly dropped. I mentioned the possibility of a judge who would be so empathic with a given criminal that she ignored legal precedent and statute and (to the extent she could get away with this) gave that criminal a much lighter sentence than in all justice she should have received. We were worried that such examples could readily undercut any approach to law and justice that stressed feelings (or feeling mechanisms) like empathy, and at this point, it may be clear, or easily made clear, why such examples do not in and of themselves show there to be a problem with sentimentalism. The judge who gives such a light sentence may be highly empathic with the convicted criminal, but clearly such a judge demonstrates a *lack of empathy* for everyone else who has been affected or is likely in the future to be affected by that criminal's behaviour: in other words, those the criminal has already victimised and those likely to be victimised in the future. So if the standard of justice is fully empathic concern for others, then the more limited or blinkered empathy that the judge of our example demonstrates shows a lack of such concern and can be criticised as unjust in strictly sentimentalist terms.

But this sort of example raises other issues that we need to consider by way of bringing this chapter to a conclusion. Couldn't a completely unblinkered and powerful empathic concern for people generally lead a (different) judge to violate her oath of office in certain (other) cases, and wouldn't a sentimentalist approach to justice then lack the means to say what was wrong or unjust about her doing so? To answer this question, I need to refer us back to some issues of personal or individual morality that I have not emphasised much in this chapter so far. I earlier mentioned the fact that we are more empathically concerned with the pain or danger we perceive than with the pain or danger we merely know about, and I argued that perceivability is one of the modalities of our empathic engagement with situations and the people (or animals) in them.[13] Or, to put the matter somewhat differently, the pain or danger we perceive is more immediate for us than the pain or danger we do not perceive, and our sentimentalist approach, for reasons already mentioned, treats perceivability as relevant to the strength or degree of our moral obligation(s).

But empathy involves other modalities as well. Clear and present danger is more immediate for us than is danger that is just as certain but that lies in an indefinite future, and that is why we prefer to save miners who we know are in danger of dying in a collapsed mine rather than spend an equivalent amount of

[13] Slote (2007).

money to install safety equipment that will save, say, a somewhat greater number of future miners. So contemporaneity with one's agential concerns is another factor or modality that makes for greater or stronger empathic reactions. And this cannot be reduced to sheer considerations of perceivability because our moral preference for saving miners who are presently in danger need not depend on our being personally acquainted with those miners or somehow perceiving them while they are trapped underground.

However, there is another modality of empathy I have not yet explicitly mentioned as such. When we cause a death, kill someone, we are in causal terms more strongly connected to that death than if we merely allow someone to die. And the same holds more generally for the distinction between causing pain or harm and merely allowing them to occur. And we are in fact much more empathically sensitive to the pain or harm or a death we ourselves have caused or might cause than to the pain or harm or a death we would (merely) allow to occur. In other words, just as we are empathically more sensitive to *perceived* or *contemporaneous* (potential) pain, etc, so too do we seem to be empathically more sensitive to the pain or a death we might cause than to the pain or a death we might merely allow to happen. We emotionally *flinch* from causing or inflicting pain in a way, or to an extent, that we do not flinch from merely allowing pain, and in the light of what I have so far been saying about the connection or correlation between (the strength of) empathic reactions and (the strength of our) moral obligations, this gives us some reason to hold that we are under a stronger obligation to avoid causing pain, harm, or death than to avoid allowing these things to happen – which is exactly what deontology (on one central and familiar understanding of it) tells us.

Thus in addition to (the empathic modalities of) perceptual and temporal immediacy, there is also such a thing as causal immediacy, and if both the former can make a difference to the strength of our obligations, so too, I want to say, can the latter. But of course this difference is not absolute. We think it is wrong to kill one person in order to prevent four others from dying, but we are not so sure when 20 or 100 lives are at stake, and that is because even if empathy is more sensitive to killing people than to allowing them to die, it is also sensitive to sheer numbers of potential or actual human deaths (we speak of *tragic* events or disasters when many people are killed or die at the same time). Thus if we have a choice between killing two people and allowing 100 people to die, our empathic sensitivities come into strong conflict, and it is not at all clear that our empathic aversion to killing would not be overwhelmed or outweighed, in such a case, by our empathic aversion to seeing or allowing 100 people to die. But how is all this relevant to the obligations of judges, the subject that initiated our present discussion?

Well, I have just argued that the strength of our causal connection to something bad like death makes a difference to the strength of our empathic reactions and of our moral obligations, but when a judge violates her oath of office her causal connection to that bad event is a much closer one than if she merely *allows* someone else to violate *their* oath of office. And, more generally, it can be argued on the basis of empathic considerations that it is morally worse to make and break a promise than to allow someone else to do so. Now following MacCormick and Scanlon, I have elsewhere also argued that what is bad about the violation of oaths and the breaking of promises can be unpacked in terms of disappointed/dashed expectations and resultant harms or ills.[14] But it is not important for our purposes today to spell out this whole scheme of justification. What is important is to notice that a deontology based on distinctions of causal immediacy that empathy is sensitive to can defend the special force of oaths of office and promises more generally. This means that where a judge, because of her empathic sensitivity to the welfare of all of those who are involved in a given case, is reluctant to pronounce sentence in accordance with settled law or explicit statute and is thus tempted to violate her oath of office, there is (or is likely to be) a psychological counterweight to such violation in the judge's own empathic reluctance to disappoint all the expectations she herself gave rise to by taking her oath of office in the first place. We are reluctant to kill, even when doing so is the only way to let certain other people live, because we are more sensitive to killing than to letting die; and by the same token, I think, a judge may be highly reluctant to violate her oath of office even if, in a given case, her empathic understanding of and concern for those involved tempts her in that direction.

Once again, however, I have to insist that this reluctance cannot and should not be thought of as absolute. Just as there are circumstances where the sheer weight of numbers makes it permissible to kill, there can, I assume, be cases where a judge morally should violate her oath of office because of the anticipated enormity of the consequences of her not doing so. If that is a weakness of the present approach, so be it. But this kind of moral flexibility might rather, on the contrary, be seen in positive terms, that is, be seen as indicating that an empathy-based approach to the law and justice allows for a desirable sensitivity to particular circumstances that can sometimes for exigent reasons override legal rules, established precedents, or a highly literal reading of a country's constitution.

But let me also mention one objection that might be lodged against the present sentimentalist account of deontology and the moral importance of oaths of office. I have said that we are more empathically sensitive to killing, for example, than to letting die, and have used that presumed fact to argue for the deontological force of the distinction between killing and letting die. But couldn't one argue that the just-mentioned differential sensitivity *presupposes* deontology: that we flinch more from killing than from allowing someone to die precisely because we already think it is wrong to kill and think it worse to do so than (merely) to allow someone to die? Well, one could indeed argue this way and conclude, as a result, that our proposed sentimentalist justification of deontology is viciously circular; but I think certain considerations having to do with moral education may persuade us that it would be a mistake to do so.

In *Empathy and Moral Development*, Hoffman describes a process of moral education (he calls it inductive discipline) in which a parent whose child has hurt another

[14] Slote (2007).

child firmly and calmly makes the child aware of the pain he has caused.[15] According to Hoffman, this will elicit or evoke an empathic reaction on the part of any normal child, and in particular make the child feel bad about the harm or pain he has caused. But this whole process does not require any use or mention of moral concepts or terms: empathy is aroused and the child feels bad because of the harm or pain he has caused, but the idea that the sort of thing he did is *wrong* need not enter the picture. But a child will feel worse if he can see the person whose pain he has caused, see him writhing in pain or crying; and that fact reflects our greater empathic sensitivity to the harm we perceive than to the harm we merely know about, a sensitivity that in no way depends on our making use of moral concepts or thinking in terms of explicitly moral precepts or injunctions. And by the same token, I want to say, our empathic bad feelings, what Hoffman calls empathic guilt, can be more readily and strongly aroused in reaction to (what our parents show us to be) the pain we have caused than in reaction to (what they show us to be) the pain we have merely (though unnecessarily) allowed to happen. And none of this depends on any moral precepts or concepts; it is a matter, rather, of our basic empathic repertoire, of modalities of our empathic interaction with people and situations that are psychologically prior to or independent of explicit moral thought. So what I have been saying about the empathic bases of deontology is not really threatened with circularity, and our sentimentalist account, therefore, of certain judicial obligations, however impressionistic and incomplete, does not, I believe, suffer from that particular philosophical infirmity.

Finally, I should say something about how what I have been saying relates to virtue ethics. I have not used that expression up till now, because I wanted to focus on the potential that moral sentimentalism has for dealing with issues of social and legal justice. But the sentimentalism I have been preaching and practising in or under the name of care ethics is in fact also a form of virtue ethics. The criterion of justice offered earlier ties the justice of laws and institutions to the motives and, in particular, the empathic sensitivity or insensitivity, of those who promulgate the laws or participate in the institutions, and this is clearly virtue-ethical. So the present theory actually has a double, even a triple, burden. Given its anti-democratic tendencies in ancient times and before its recent revival, philosophers and political theorists have been sceptical about whether *virtue ethics* can address important political issues in relevant contemporary terms. They have also questioned whether *care ethics* can be extended beyond its focus on individual lives and relationships to deal with larger and less intimate issues of public policy and social justice. And, finally, given the problems of 'Hume's circle' and of Hume's extreme political conservatism and given the seeming disconnect between law and human feeling, people have been inclined to dismiss the possibility or prospects of any contemporaneously relevant *sentimentalist* understanding and justification of political/legal norms. I hope, however, that this chapter will have made you less sceptical about all these possibilities. It seems to me that a suitable

[15] Hoffman (2000).

deployment of the notion of empathy can help us toward a rather promising way of seeing justice and human rights, and though I have only offered a sketch of how this would work, I hope that it will at least whet your appetite for hearing or seeing more.

REFERENCES

Bandura, A (2002) 'Reflexive Empathy: On Predicting More Than One Has Ever Observed' 25 *Behavioral and Brain Sciences* 24.
Gilligan, C (1982) *In a Different Voice* (Cambridge, MA, Harvard University Press).
Hoffman, M (2000) *Empathy and Moral Development: Implications for Caring and Justice* (Cambridge, Cambridge University Press).
Locke, J (1960) *Second Essay on Government* in P Laslett (ed), *Two Essays on Government* (Cambridge, Cambridge University Press).
Mackie, J L (1980) *Hume's Moral Theory* (London, Routledge & Kegan Paul).
Nagel, T (1991) *Equality and Partiality* (New York, Oxford University Press).
Rawls, J (1971) *A Theory of Justice* (Cambridge, Mass, Belknap Press).
Slote, M (2007) *The Ethics of Care and Empathy* (London, Routledge).
——(2010) *Moral Sentimentalism* (Oxford, Oxford University Press).

15

Empathy in Law (A Response to Slote)

JOHN DEIGH

'EMPATHY' ENTERED THE English language a century ago as a translation of a German word, 'einfühling', that originated as a term of artistic criticism. Its meaning has shifted considerably since then and is still somewhat unsettled. Indeed, it is currently something of a vogue term, so loose use of it is likely to continue for some time. Social and developmental psychologists, however, have come to recognise in their work two distinct meanings. They either define 'empathy' as a cognitive state or as an affective state. Martin Hoffman, in his important book on empathy, remarks that psychologists define the term either as 'the cognitive awareness of another person's . . . thoughts, feelings, perceptions, and intentions' or as 'the vicarious affective response to another person'.[1] These two meanings are recognised by philosophers as well.[2]

Michael Slote, in his contribution to this volume, takes 'empathy' to have this second meaning. But in adding that it 'refer[s] to a desirable form of sensitivity to other people', he converts it into a term of ethics.[3] Apparently, Slote's view is that empathy is a vicarious affective response to another that implies benevolence toward that person, though perhaps Slote does not strictly mean that, as a response to another, it is in itself a praiseworthy state. Perhaps, he means only to capture the positive attitude we typically have toward empathy because it usually shows that one is benevolently disposed toward the person to whom one is responding. In that case, it is not a term of ethics. This, I think, is the better approach, for it is commonly observed that sadistic torturers get additional pleasure through empathy with the pain of their victims, and such empathy is plainly not praiseworthy. In any event, I will not be using 'empathy' as a term of ethics in the discussion that follows. For me, it is a term of positive psychology.

In an article[4] I wrote some years ago, 'Empathy and Universalizability', I took the term to have the first of the two meanings Hoffman identifies. Empathy so understood, I argued, has a crucial but unacknowledged role in the ethics of

[1] Hoffman (2000: 29–30). See also Wispe (1987: 17–37).
[2] See eg Nussbaum (2000: 301–02) and Darwall (2002: 54–66).
[3] Slote (2012: 279).
[4] Deigh (1996: 160–80).

certain rationalist philosophers. My argument proceeded through an inquiry into the deficiency in moral feeling and moral motivation that characterises the psychopathic personality. Psychopaths are commonly described as amoral agents who nonetheless know right from wrong. My idea was to use an inquiry into their deficiency to distinguish a kind of moral judgement, the capacity for which they lack – thus accounting for their amorality – from the kind they are commonly recognised as being capable of making – thus accounting for their commonly being said to know right from wrong. The kind they lack is the kind moral philosophers since Kant have identified as categorical imperatives. These are categorical judgements about what one ought to do that a person cannot make without being moved to act accordingly. Such judgements, I argued, cannot, *pace* Kant, be understood as products of purely rational processes. That is, they cannot be judgements that consist entirely of the mind's applying a formal operation to a plan of action or what Kant called a maxim of action. If they were, then psychopathy would have to consist at least partly in the inability to apply such operations to maxims of action, yet on the assumption that a completely egocentric outlook characterises psychopathy,[5] one can show that nothing about psychopaths, specifically, nothing in their failure to make moral judgements of the kind Kant identified as categorical imperatives, precludes their applying such operations to maxims of action. In other words, on this assumption, one can show that such operations as the Golden Rule and Kant's first formulation of the Categorical Imperative imply, yield judgements of this kind only if the agent's application of them to some maxim of action is informed by his regarding those people with whom he is contemplating interaction from their perspectives. Such operations require, in other words, empathy with others, if they are to yield categorical imperatives.

In making this argument, I had in mind Piaget's distinction between the early and later stages of moral development in children.[6] At the early stage, on Piaget's account, when a child's parents exercise absolute authority over him or her, the child sees the rules they lay down as fixed limits on his or her behaviour, limits that require obedience by virtue of their authority. At the later stage, when children have left the shelter of their parents' domain and entered into social relations with peers that are free of close adult supervision, they come to see rules as variable regulations by which cooperative activities, chiefly with peers, are organised. This development in moral thought that Piaget records consists in the child's abandoning an egocentric view of the world of which the rules his or her parents have imposed are structural parts and acquiring a view informed by the perspectives of others as well as his or her own in which the rules are instruments of the common good. Older children, then, Piaget held, being aware of these different perspectives and of the need sometimes to balance the different claims that arise from them if the common good is to be promoted, acquire a sense of justice about

[5] Egocentricity is one of the chief indicia of psychopathy. See Hare (2003).

[6] Piaget (1965).

how the rules apply. Their sense of justice thus entails a capacity to see situations that come under the rules from the perspectives of the different people involved. It entails, that is, a capacity for empathy with them in the sense given in the first meaning that Hoffman identified. Consequently, the exercise of a capacity for empathy, on Piaget's account, is essential to making moral judgements of the kind that characterise the child's thinking at this later stage of moral development. It is essential to the child's acquiring a sense of justice.

Such judgements are essential to sound legal thought. This is plainly true if one's idea of law matches that found in the natural law tradition, for in this tradition laws necessarily have as their ultimate end the advancement of the common good. But it is true as well if one's idea of the law matches that found in the tradition of legal positivism, provided that standards of justice are then understood as paramount in the evaluation of law and so in the determination of how to apply law to situations that do not neatly fall within it. In either case, because judgement about a law's application in such situations entails balancing conflicting claims that arise from the perspectives of the different people who are affected or are liable to be so, it requires, to be sound, taking those perspectives so as better to determine the strengths of these conflicting claims. Hence, one way in which empathy has an important role in law is through the perspective-taking required in making these judgements. And when it is not exercised and the judgement is made instead by relying on a 'strict' reading of the law, then the outcome is as likely as not to be grossly unjust.

A good example is *Ledbetter v Goodyear Tire & Rubber Co*[7], a case of sex-based discrimination that the US Supreme Court decided in 2007. Lilly Ledbetter held a managerial position at a Goodyear plant, a position of a type that men normally filled. She began at the same pay as the men who held similar positions, but due to poor performance reviews her annual raises were less than theirs. After nearly 20 years at Goodyear, she was the only woman in that type of position; her salary was significantly less than the next lowest paid man in that type; and it was about three-fifths that of the highest paid man. The performance reviews that resulted in her receiving smaller annual raises were conducted by supervisors who were biased against women and consequently gave them poorer evaluations than men. In light of this fact and the cumulative effect of these smaller raises, she sued. Goodyear, she alleged, had violated her rights under Title VII of the 1964 Civil Rights Act. She won at trial, and the jury awarded her backpay and damages.

The decision, however, was then reversed on appeal on the grounds that the complaint she had filed was untimely. Title VII requires that a complaint like hers be filed with the appropriate government agency, the Equal Employment Opportunity Commission (EEOC), within 180 days 'after the alleged unlawful employment practice occurred',[8] and because more than 180 days had passed since the last discriminatory decision by Goodyear about an annual raise, the

[7] 550 US 618, 127 S Ct 2162 (2007). I give a more detailed analysis of the opinions in this case in Deigh (2011).

[8] 42 USC §2000e – 5(e)(1).

appellate court ruled that she had failed to meet the deadline. The Supreme Court agreed and upheld the reversal. The issue, which Ledbetter raised in her appeal to the Supreme Court, was whether the monthly payment of her salary could also count as a discriminatory act, for if it did, then she had met the law's deadline. The Court held that it did not. Justice Alito, writing for the majority, reached this conclusion by relying on precedents in several cases in which the law was interpreted as defining the period in which a complaint may be filed as 180 days after a discrete intentional act of discrimination had occurred. None of these cases, however, involved discrimination in pay. Alito, nonetheless, thought this difference was irrelevant. So the rule he located in these precedents applied and controlled the Court's decision.

Alito's opinion, though it opens by acknowledging that the case is one of first impression, is nonetheless strikingly devoid of any attempt to understand from Ledbetter's perspective what would be a reasonable trigger of the EEOC's 180-day filing period. Nowhere, that is, in the opinion does Alito take Ledbetter's perspective and attempt to understand at what point someone in her situation would realise that she had been the victim of sex-based discrimination in pay and that the harm was great enough to warrant taking action.[9] Rather, his opinion is almost entirely devoted to locating in prior cases a fixed authoritative rule by which to determine, for the purpose of applying the EEOC's deadline, what counts as an unlawful employment practice. It is the authority of these cases that matters to Alito and not whether extending their holdings to pay discrimination serves the central aims of Title VII or of justice. Indeed, these aims never figure in his reasoning about the case. It is no wonder then that Justice Ginsburg, in her dissent, criticises the opinion for being 'a cramped interpretation of Title VII'.[10]

Ginsburg's dissent is a model of the role of empathy in sound legal thought. Trying to understand Ledbetter's situation, Ginsburg observes:

> Comparative pay information . . . is often hidden from the employee's view . . . Small initial discrepancies may not be seen as meet for a federal case, particularly, when the employee, trying to succeed in a nontraditional environment, is averse to making waves . . . It is only when the disparity becomes apparent and sizable, eg, through future raises calculated as a percentage of current salaries, that an employee in Ledbetter's situation is likely to comprehend her plight and, therefore, to complain. Her initial readiness to give her employer the benefit of the doubt should not preclude her from later challenging the then current and continuing payment of a wage depressed on account of her sex.[11]

[9] Alito never takes Goodyear's perspective either. He is, in this respect, even-handed in his abstaining from trying to understand empathetically either party's situation. He does at one point observe that filing deadlines, like the EEOC's 180-day time period, 'protect employers from the burden of defending claims arising from employment decisions that are long past' (quoting the decision in *Delaware State College v Ricks*, 449 US 250 (1980)). But here too (550 US 618 (2007) 630) he makes the observation by citing precedents regarding the policy considerations that support statutes of limitations.

[10] 550 US 618 (2007) 661 (dissent).

[11] ibid 645 (dissent).

These and similar observations make it evident, Ginsburg argues, that Ledbetter's case is not on a par with cases in which the unlawful employment practice that triggered the filing period was a discrete act whose adverse consequences for the victim are immediately apparent, like the denial of tenure or the setting of seniority upon rehiring. The cases from which Alito drew the rule on which he based his opinion all have this feature. In each of them the allegedly unlawful act that triggered the filing period was a discrete act that employees who it adversely affected could easily identify. Further, its discriminatory character was not hidden from them, and its chief adverse consequence, the loss of a job (*Delaware State College v Ricks*),[12] the assignment of lesser seniority (*United Air Lines, Inc v Evans*),[13] or the imposition of disadvantages due to a change in a seniority system (*Lorance v AT & T Technologies, Inc*),[14] was a direct result of the act. So the rule ill fits Ledbetter's case. The injustice of applying it is palpable once one takes up her perspective, as Ginsburg did, and asks whether under this rule someone in her position would have a fair opportunity to file a complaint.[15]

Ginsburg's observations and the way they lead to her judgment about the unfairness of applying the rule that controlled the Court's decision to Ledbetter's situation exemplify sound moral thought as well as sound legal thought. They exemplify, as I indicated, the proper use of standards of justice in deciding novel cases and the role of empathy in applying those standards. In particular, such thinking, as my argument in 'Empathy and Universalizability' was meant to show, is essential to moral thought on those accounts of it, like Kant's, on which moral judgement primarily consists in the mind's applying a formal operation to a plan of action. These accounts represent one major strand of rationalist ethics, and their reliance on empathy is worth noting because one could easily infer from the way sentimentalist ethics is commonly opposed to rationalist ethics that empathy has no place in a rationalist account of moral judgement. The opposition Slote stresses between his sentimentalist ethics and rationalist ethics is a good example. Of course, what may have no place in a rationalist account of moral judgement is empathy on the second of the two meanings Hoffman identifies, the meaning that corresponds to Slote's understanding of empathy. So the point is that rationalist ethics at least in the Kantian tradition excludes empathy, if at all, only when empathy is understood as an affective rather than a cognitive state. If understood as a cognitive state, it is, to the contrary, an essential component of moral thought on this tradition's account of it. And similarly, when Slote declares that his sentimentalist account of legal justice is 'very much opposed to the rationalist/liberal/

[12] 449 US 250 (1980).

[13] 431 US 553 (1977).

[14] 490 US 900 (1989).

[15] Ginsburg also, in regards to Alito's observation of the protection that filing deadlines provide employers, takes up Goodyear's perspective and notes that the discrimination that triggered the complaint in this case did not occur in the distant past and that employers have various defences available to them when the complaint alleges cumulative harm due to discriminatory acts that occurred over a long period of time: 550 US 618 (2007) 657 (dissent).

Kantian' account,[16] one could easily take this to imply that empathy has no place in the latter. But this would be true at most when empathy was understood as an affective state. As a cognitive state, it has, as we have seen, an important place in traditional liberal jurisprudence.

Slote, in opposing his sentimentalist ethics to rationalism, harks back to an eighteenth century dispute over the nature of our capacity to distinguish good from evil and virtue from vice. Moral sense theorists, like Hutcheson and Hume, held that this capacity was at bottom a matter of feeling; rationalists, like Clarke and Kant, attributed it to reason. Slote believes that the ethics of care that educational psychologist Carol Gilligan formulated as the result of her observations of the differences between the moral thought of boys and that of girls has rejuvenated the moral sense theorist side of this dispute. An ethics based on caring, if caring is understood to be supported by empathy for strangers as well as family and friends, empathy, that is, in the sense of shared affect, is adequate, Slote believes, for much if not all of ethics, both personal and social. Therefore, he concludes, an ethics of care vindicates Hume's thesis that, as Hume put it, 'Morality . . . is more properly felt than judg'd of'.[17]

Slote's idea of reinforcing the ethics of care with the capacity for empathy in the sense of a capacity to experience vicariously the feelings, thoughts, sensations, etc of others, especially strangers who belong to groups socially if not also geographically distant from oneself, is admirably innovative. Using it, Slote is able to meet one of the main objections to care ethics, that it is limited to personal relations and cannot yield an adequate account of social justice. At the same time, Slote's thesis that the ethics of care, on his reconstruction of it, reintroduces into ethics a powerful version of Hume's moral sense theory is questionable. Indeed, it appears to me to derive from Slote's running together different theses on which Hume built his moral sense theory.

The main problem is that Hume's sentimentalism is inseparable from his subjectivist account of virtue and vice, and it is doubtful that on the most cogent version of the ethics of care it is a subjectivist ethics. By Hume's subjectivism about virtue and vice, I mean his thesis that a personal trait is a virtue or a vice because one who regards its exercise from a general view takes a certain pleasure or displeasure in it and not the other way round. The other way round would be the thesis that the trait's being a virtue explains the pleasure that a person who regards its exercise from a general view takes in it. On this latter position, which Hume opposes, virtue is conceived of as existing independently of any emotional response to it, and the pleasure it gives to one who regards its exercise from a general view – like the pleasure that a spectator at a ballgame takes in a brilliant play by a player on the opposing team – is merely an effect of beholding it. Such pleasure, one might say, is the appropriate emotional response to the virtue, just as fear is the appropriate emotional response to danger. On Hume's subjectivism, by con-

[16] Slote (2012: 280).
[17] Hume (1739–1740: bk III, pt 1, s ii).

trast, one cannot conceive of virtue as something independent of the pleasure it gives to those who regard its exercise from a general view. The pleasure it gives is not an effect of its being a virtue, but rather constitutes it as such.[18] And as a consequence, one cannot say that pleasure is an appropriate emotional response to the trait: something that is such as to give pleasure to a person who regards it from a general point of view cannot also make appropriate the pleasure that the person takes in it – a point that Hume himself makes. There is no need, however, to make this Humean position part of an ethics of care. And nothing in the ethics of care particularly invites it.

On an ethics of care, caring for other people in a way that is responsive to them as individuals and sensitive to the responsibilities toward them that one's relationship with them entails is the fundamental standard of moral goodness and moral decency. To say this, however, is not to say that such caring for other people has moral value because a sober judge of moral matters feels a certain way about those acts or about the kindheartedness and responsiveness they manifest. Specifically, such caring for other people does not have value because the emotional response of such a judge is the response of a caring and empathic person. It should be obvious that on such an explanation of the theory's fundamental standard, the theory would collapse under its own weight. An explanation of such caring as the fundamental standard of moral goodness and moral decency must include an explanation of its being an authoritative standard, a standard of conduct that *ought to be* realised. In the argot of contemporary moral philosophy, it must include an explanation of its normativity. Presumably, a successful explanation appeals to the special value or intrinsic worth that each and every human being possesses, a value or worth each has that makes caring for them, should one have entered into a relationship with them, appropriate. But in any case, the sort of explanation that Humean subjectivism yields is now widely recognised as having serious problems meeting this condition. Incorporating such subjectivism into the ethics of care would seem then to saddle the theory unnecessarily with these problems.

I suspect that Slote's conception of the ethics of care as a kind of sentimentalism is due to his having misidentified Hume's moral sense theory with one of the two major theses on which it rests. The first is Hume's thesis that reason is motivationally inert.[19] Call this Hume's anti-rationalism about moral agency. The second is his thesis that morality is essentially practical.[20] Call this his internalism about moral judgement. It is Hume's anti-rationalism about moral agency that Slote expressly

[18] On a weaker version of Humean subjectivism, the pleasure does not constitute the virtue, but direct awareness of the virtue requires it. I do not think Slote's view of the ethics of care as a form of moral sense theory would be any more credible if it incorporated this weaker version of Humean subjectivism. The problem of the authority or normativity of the ethics' fundamental standard, which I point out below, would remain. On the weaker version of Humean subjectivism, see McDowell (1985: 110–29) and Wiggins (1991). For criticism of Humean subjectivism including McDowell's and Wiggins's versions, see Deigh (2008: 72–102).

[19] Hume (1739–1740: bk II, pt 3, s iii).

[20] ibid bk III, pt 1, s i.

endorses and attributes to the ethics of care when he observes that much immorality is due to heartlessness and not to deficiencies in reason,[21] and it is this thesis I suspect that he takes as qualifying the ethics of care as a kind of sentimentalism. But one can endorse this thesis without also holding that moral standards have no rational basis. Questions about the truth or validity of moral standards are independent of questions about the kinds of motive on which agents who guide their conduct by these standards act. Hence, as long as one accepts the possibility of someone's grasping the truth or validity of moral standards without being moved to act as they require, one is not compelled to agree with Hume that the moral properties we attribute to people and actions in making moral judgements result from projections of our feelings onto them. One's theory, then, may agree with Hume's anti-rationalism about moral agency, but that alone would not make it kin to his moral sense theory.[22]

Slote, in much of his chapter, presents the basics of his sentimentalist programme for the ethics of care and shows how in a few cases it works to give explanations of commonsense judgements of personal morality as well as commonsense principles of social justice. These explanations exemplify the problems I referred to above. Thus, consider his explanation of the commonsense judgement that the obligation to save a child drowning in a shallow pool right before one's eyes is more stringent than the obligation to save a child dying of malnutrition in some foreign land thousands of miles away. According to Slote, what explains this judgement is that 'empathy is typically more strongly aroused by pain and danger we witness than by pain and danger we merely know about'.[23] As an explanation of why people feel more compelled to save a child drowning in front of their eyes than to save one living thousands of miles away whose imminent death they know about only from reports of famine in the child's homeland, this is unexceptionable. It is, as far as it goes, an accurate description of human psychology. But it no more provides grounds for the judgement that our obligation to save the child in the first case is more stringent than our obligation to save the child in the second[24] than the repulsion people commonly feel when witnessing two men passionately kissing is grounds for the judgement that such kissing between men is wrong, not at any rate without some explanation of why one kind of feeling people have in

[21] Slote (2012: 280).

[22] Slote, in effect, accepts Hume's internalism about moral judgement when he remarks that the amorality of psychopaths is like the unfamiliarity with colour of people blind from birth (Slote (2012: 284), since to explain psychopathic wrongdoing as due to a kind of ignorance is to say that the psychopath's lack of moral motivation is due to his or her failure to make the relevant moral judgement. But nothing in the ethics of care leads to this analogy. Slote's acceptance of internalism about moral judgement is thus independent of his embrace of the ethics of care.

[23] Slote (2012: 284).

[24] Indeed, the case was originally presented to confound the commonsense judgement about the relative stringencies of these two obligations. See Singer (1972: 229–43). After all, if neither child has more intrinsic worth as a human being than the other and if the sacrifice one must make in saving either is no greater than the sacrifice one must make in saving the other, then each, it would seem, has the same claim to being saved by those in a position to do so as the other. So what could justify the greater stringency of the obligation to save the drowning child? To say that we feel more intensely the drowning child's distress than we feel the malnourished child's does not seem to be any more satisfactory an answer than that one child is spatially closer to us than the other.

reaction to some event or situation is evidence of how they ought to act with respect to that event or situation. Two centuries ago the spurs and reproaches of conscience were generally taken as authoritative determinants of duty, but thanks to Mark Twain, among others, they no longer are. I see no reason to think that empathy in the sense of a vicarious affective state has any stronger claim to being such an authoritative guide.

REFERENCES

Darwall, S (2002) *Welfare and Rational Care* (Princeton, Princeton University Press).

Deigh, J (1995) 'Empathy and Universalizability', *Ethics* 105; reprinted in John Deigh (1996) *The Sources of Moral Agency* (Cambridge, Cambridge University Press).

——(2008) 'Emotions and Values' in John Deigh, *Emotions, Values and the Law* (Oxford, Oxford University Press).

——(2011) 'Empathy, Justice, and Jurisprudence' 49 *Southern Journal of Philosophy* 73.

Hare, RD (2003) *Manual for the Revised Psychopathy Checklist*, 2nd edn (Toronto, Ontario, Multi-Health Systems, Inc).

Hoffman, M (2000) *Empathy and Moral Development* (Cambridge, Cambridge University Press).

Hume, D, Selby-Bigge, LA and Nidditch, PH (eds) (1978) *A Treatise of Human Nature*, 2nd edn (Oxford, Clarendon Press, 1978).

McDowell, J (1985) 'Values and Secondary Qualities' in Ted Honderich (ed), *Morality and Objectivity* (London, Routledge & Kegan Paul).

Nussbaum, M (2000) *Upheavals of Thought: The Intelligence of Emotions* (Cambridge, Cambridge University Press).

Piaget, J, Gabian, M (tr) (1965) *The Moral Judgment of the Child* (New York, The Free Press).

Singer, P (1972) 'Famine, Affluence, and Morality' *Philosophy & Public Affairs* 1.

Slote, M (2012) 'Empathy, Law, and Justice' chapter 14 of this volume.

Wiggins, D (1991) 'A Sensible Subjectivism' in David Wiggins, *Needs, Values, Truth*, 2nd edn (Oxford, Blackwell).

Wispe, L (1987) 'History of the Concept of Empathy' in Nancy Eisenberg and Janet Strayer (eds), *Empathy and Its Development* (Cambridge, Cambridge University Press).

16

On Empathy as a Necessary, but Not Sufficient, Foundation for Justice (A Response to Slote)

SUSAN J BRISON

IN 'EMPATHY, LAW and Justice', Michael Slote makes a compelling case for the importance of empathy in law, just as he argued convincingly in his recent book, *The Ethics of Care and Empathy*, that empathy is necessary for personal morality. He claims, however, to have established that 'empathy and empathic concern for others can function as the basis, *the entire basis* [my emphasis], for a plausible understanding of legal and social justice', and, of this, I am not (yet) convinced.[1]

Before presenting my reasons for scepticism about the claim that empathy alone can provide a sufficient basis for an adequate understanding of justice, I want to say how refreshing this chapter is after the firestorm sparked by US President Obama's invoking of empathy in a press conference held on 1 May 2009. In announcing Justice David Souter's intention to resign from the US Supreme Court and sketching the qualifications he would look for in Souter's replacement, Obama said, among other things:

> I will seek someone who understands that justice isn't about some abstract legal theory or footnote in a casebook. It is also about how our laws affect the daily realities of people's lives – whether they can make a living and care for their families; whether they feel safe in their homes and welcome in their own nation. I view that quality of empathy, of understanding and identifying with people's hopes and struggles, as an essential ingredient for arriving at just decisions and outcomes.[2]

Obama's subsequent nomination of Judge Sonia Sotomayor to replace Souter fanned the flames of what some in the press had already labelled the 'empathy

[1] In a book published after the conference at which this paper was presented, Slote (2010) further defends the view that justice can be understood in sentimentalist terms, concluding that '[o]ur ideals of justice . . . can be anchored in the normative idea that actions, laws, customs, and institutions are morally objectionable if and only if they exhibit a lack of full-blown empathic concern for others (on the part of individuals or groups)': Slote (2010: 159). I do not discuss these further developments in this commentary, but recommend to readers interested in empathy and the law *Moral Sentimentalism*, especially ch 9 on 'Justice'.

[2] Available at www.nytimes.com/2009/05/01/us/politics/01souter.text.html.

wars'. Sotomayor's Republican critics accused her of being too empathetic and used the word 'empathy' interchangeably with the words 'bias', 'prejudice', 'partiality' and 'identity politics', claiming empathy to be at odds with justice which, as they reminded us, is, or at least should be, blind.

During her confirmation hearings, Sotomayor was quick and adamant in her rejection of Obama's 'empathy standard'. When asked by Republican Senator Jon Kyl whether she agreed with Obama when he said (in 2005) that in a certain percentage of judicial decisions, the key ingredient is 'what is in the judge's heart', Sotomayor said, 'No, sir, I wouldn't approach the issue of judging the way the president does . . . I can only explain what I think judges should do, which is judges can't rely on what's in their heart . . . It's not the heart that compels conclusions in cases. It's the law.'[3]

Sotomayor emerged victorious from the confirmation, but the idea that empathy is compatible with, let alone necessary and/or sufficient for, justice took a serious and very public beating. Republican Senator Jeff Sessions even claimed a kind of victory for his party in declaring that '[b]y the end of the hearing not only Republicans, not only Democrats, but the nominee herself ended up rejecting the very empathy standard the president used when selecting her. This process reflected a broad public consensus that judges should be impartial, restrained and faithfully tethered to the law and the Constitution.'[4] That (now-)Justice Sotomayor actually (in her heart) repudiated the role of empathy in judging, however, is as inconceivable as Justice Clarence Thomas's claim (made during his confirmation hearings) that he had never discussed – or even formed an opinion about – *Roe v Wade.*

It is unfortunate that the public debate around Sotomayor's nomination did not elucidate how empathy is compatible with and, indeed, required for, justice, but that is a job for philosophers and we can be grateful that Michael Slote has performed it admirably. I agree with him that 'laws, institutions, and social customs are just (and consistent with our basic rights) only if they do not manifest a lack of fully empathic concern for (groups of) other people on the part of those who promulgate, maintain, or participate in them'.[5] That is to say, empathy is necessary for justice. The problem, for Slote's position, is that empathy alone is not sufficient for justice.

First we need to determine what Slote means by 'empathy'. Although he does not give a definition of 'empathy' in his chapter, he does say that the chapter summarises the general argument in his book, *The Ethics of Care and Empathy*, in which he writes that 'empathy involves having the feelings of another (involuntarily) aroused in ourselves, as when we see another person in pain. It is as if their pain invades us'.[6] That this empathic connection does not imply sympathy for the

[3] Available at www.npr.org/templates/story/story.php?storyId=106569335.

[4] Available at www.latimes.com/news/nationworld/nation/la-na-sotomayor7-2009aug07,0,4571672.story.

[5] Slote (2012: 282).

[6] Slote (2007: 13).

other in pain, on Slote's view, is clear from the next sentence: 'However, we can *also* [my emphasis] feel sorry for, bad for, the person who is in pain' and this 'amounts . . . to sympathy for them, and it can happen even if we aren't feeling their pain'.[7] I take his definition of empathy to be similar to that employed by Martha Nussbaum, who holds that empathy is an 'imaginative reconstruction of another person's experience, without any particular evaluation of that experience'.[8]

On Slote's view, empathy, unlike sympathy, 'involves a kind of oneness or identification with others'.[9] It should be noted, though, that empathy also requires a certain degree of detachment. As John Deigh points out, 'it is distinctive of empathy that it entails imaginative participation in the other's life without forgetting oneself'.[10] I assume Slote agrees with this, though I doubt that he would go as far as Nussbaum, who asserts that, typically, 'empathy is like the mental preparation of a skilled (Method) actor: it involves a participatory enactment of the situation of the sufferer, but is always combined with the awareness that one is not oneself the sufferer'.[11] Empathy requires, on Nussbaum's view, 'a kind of "twofold attention", in which one both imagines what it is like to be in the sufferer's place and, at the same time, retains securely the awareness that one is not in that place'.[12] I do not know if good Method actors actually feel their characters' pain, but Nussbaum's view of empathy sounds here more like the view that it is merely cognitive awareness, since it is difficult to know how a secure awareness of the fact that one is *not in the position of* [my emphasis] the sufferer is compatible with actually feeling the sufferer's pain.

In any case, it seems that, on Slote's account of empathy, X's empathising with Y's pain involves three stages:[13]

(1) X feels pain as a result of X's awareness that Y is feeling pain.
That more than mere awareness that Y is feeling pain is required for empathy is clear, since X could be aware that Y is in pain even if X has never experienced pain (provided X knows how to read Y's pain-related behaviour and how to use the word 'pain' appropriately), just as X could be aware that Y is seeing green (as opposed to red) even if X is colour-blind. But in this case, it would be odd to say that X empathises with (rather than, say, merely comprehends) Y's pain.

[7] ibid.

[8] (2001: 302). Nussbaum elaborates that 'empathy is simply an imaginative reconstruction of another person's experience, whether that experience is happy or sad, pleasant or painful or neutral, and whether the imaginer thinks the other person's situation good, bad, or indifferent (separate issues, since a malevolent person will think the other's distress good and her happiness bad)' (2001: 302).

[9] Slote (2012: 281).

[10] Deigh (1995: 759).

[11] (2001: 327).

[12] ibid 328.

[13] These stages need not be temporally distinct, and could perhaps more accurately be labelled 'components'.

(2) X judges that Y views feeling pain as desirable or undesirable.[14]
(3) X's feeling Y's pain prompts a moral sentiment that (typically) is (or leads to) a correct moral judgement (provided X has a sufficiently developed and appropriately exercised capacity for empathy).

It is important to note the potential for error at each of these three stages. At stage (1), error could come in if X misreads Y's signs (or Y is a very good actor). At stage (2), error could arise if, unbeknownst to X, Y is a masochist and actually desires the pain. And error could arise at stage (3) if, say, X is aware that Y desires the pain and so judges that Y's feeling pain is morally good, but Y's desiring the pain results from and exacerbates Y's low self-esteem which, in turn, negatively affects her overall well-being.[15]

One might reply that these ways in which empathy might lead one astray are all correctable or that, even if they are not, empathy could still *be* the basis for morality/justice even if we cannot be sure *when* it is. But, once we acknowledge that empathy is sometimes an unreliable guide, we point to the need for something beyond empathy as a basis for morality/justice.[16]

A further problem is that neither X's feeling Y's pain, nor X's judgement about Y's attitude (affective or cognitive) toward it – nor both taken together – can suffice, absent other considerations, to determine the 'absolute goodness' or 'absolute badness' of the pain, to use Slote's phrase.[17] Take the case of someone whose attitudes, including self-assessments of well-being, are distorted by adaptive preference formation. If Jane is, in terms of what Slote calls 'absolute positionality,' worse off than Joe, but is more content with her lot in life than Joe is with his, what does empathy (with how Jane and Joe *feel*) tell us about the strength of our moral obligations to Jane and Joe? Suppose women in a certain region are, again, with respect to 'absolute positionality', worse off than men in that region, but express higher levels of satisfaction with their lives.[18] Empathy with what they are feeling is not an adequate guide to what justice requires in our treatment of them.

Furthermore, giving any account of 'absolute positionality' that would enable us to characterise degrees of 'absolute badness' and 'absolute goodness' would require us to go beyond empirically-based empathy to an account of human flourishing, in which case, empathy would not be providing the (sole) basis for the theory of justice.[19]

[14] I am not sure this stage is essential, on Slote's view.

[15] I am not suggesting that all masochists suffer from low self-esteem, but only that the particular masochist in this thought experiment does.

[16] Someone (not me) might argue, as Descartes did with respect to sense perception, that, since empathy can be misleading, it should never be relied upon (as a basis for justice), but I doubt this is what Obama's Republican critics had in mind in asserting the incompatibility of empathy and justice.

[17] Slote (2012: 281).

[18] See Elster (1983) and Sen (1992), esp at 55 where Sen discusses the effects of entrenched inequalities and deprivations on preferences.

[19] Sen's capability theory is an attempt to provide such a theory. Supposing one can empathise with another's hunger (but could one 'feel their hunger' in the way that one might 'feel their pain'?), the sense of one's moral obligation arising from this will depend on one's knowledge of whether the person is hungry from starving or fasting, since it makes a moral difference whether the person had the capability to be well-fed but chose not to achieve that functioning.

Additional difficulties for an account of justice based solely on empathy arise upon examination of what Slote observes to be the 'interesting correlation between the arousal of empathy and what we commonly think about the strength of our moral obligations'.[20] Others suffering in close proximity to us arouse greater empathy than those suffering at a (geographic or temporal) distance. This correlates with our intuition that it is morally worse not to save a child drowning right in front of us than it is not to save a child starving in some distant place. Even if we agree with Slote that, in this case, empathy correlates positively with moral obligation,[21] in other cases, the arousal of empathy is not a reliable guide to moral obligation – or to what justice requires. We have a tendency to empathise more readily and more strongly with those who are similar to us – even when, as in the case of ethnicity, for example, the similarity is not morally or legally relevant. A judge who experienced – and then made decisions based on – greater empathy for members of her own ethnic group than for other similarly-situated persons of different ethnicities would not be acting justly. Sometimes, greater empathy for certain others leads us morally astray. I do not consider this to be a reason to reject empathy as something that should inform our views about justice. But it does indicate that empathy, by itself, is not enough.

The development of empathy can be thwarted, for example, by pernicious social constraints such as prejudice and hatred. Undeveloped or untutored empathy can lead to bad moral judgement, and even mature empathy – that of someone who has completed, for example, Martin Hoffman's process of moral education – can be dangerously selective. We need an independent standard to determine when empathy is sufficiently developed (for purposes of morality or law) and this cannot be the simple, overall maturity of the individual(s) in question.

Slote concedes that we need moral education in order to achieve 'a fully developed capacity for empathy with others'.[22] But this suggests that empathy must be modified, tempered, or disciplined with reason or some other moral measure. This is clear not only in cases where empathy for a particular group is insufficiently developed,[23] but also in cases where (fully developed) empathy for different people (or groups) pulls us in different directions.

Slote is unquestionably correct in his observation that 'we are more empathically concerned with pain or danger we perceive than with pain or danger we merely know about',[24] but it does not follow that this greater empathic concern for actually perceived danger implies a greater degree of moral (or legal) obligation to

[20] Slote (2012: 284).

[21] I am accepting Slote's claim for the sake of argument, but it is not obvious that we do have a greater moral obligation to the drowning child. And, even if we do, the fact that we feel greater empathy for the drowning child does not explain *why* we have a greater moral obligation to save her, as John Deigh points out in his comments (2012: 300–01).

[22] Slote (2012: 285).

[23] One wonders whether empathy for a particular group can be *over*developed (as Sotomayor's critics assumed her empathy for Latinas was).

[24] Slote (2012: 288).

prevent (or ameliorate or redress or otherwise address) it.[25] If present degree of empathic concern is what warrants degree of moral obligation, there would seem to be no moral imperative to expand our imaginations (and our purview) to be better able to perceive and thus feel empathic concern for potential victims of previously unseen dangers.

And yet, as Critical Race Theorists and others have argued, justice requires us to expand our imaginations and to try to put ourselves in the position of those unlike ourselves. As I have argued,[26] first-person narratives of victimisation and oppression can facilitate greater empathic concern than a perusal of arguments and statistics alone can and, thus, play a critical role in furthering our understanding of what justice requires. Seeking out and reading such narratives is especially important for those of us in dominant groups, since our lives do not, typically, require us to educate ourselves about the experiences of those in marginalised groups. Members of marginalised groups, in contrast, more readily acquire awareness of the dominant group's experiences since those are taken to be the norm for the culture (and are conveyed through education and reflected and reinforced by the mainstream media).[27]

Reason alone does not give us enough imaginative access to others' experiences to enable us to determine, on the basis of it alone, what justice requires. If rationalism is the view that reason is all that is required for justice, and if sentimentalism is simply the view that rationalism is false, then I am in agreement with Slote that sentimentalism is correct. However, if sentimentalism is the view that empathy provides a necessary and sufficient basis for justice, then, although Slote has not persuaded me that sentimentalism is correct, he has certainly 'whet[ted] [my] appetite for hearing or seeing more'.[28]

[25] The 'flinch' test Slote suggests (2012: 289) is notoriously unreliable. I flinched when watching my infant son get necessary immunisations, while I was and am capable of reading about countless distant children dying of famine or disease without flinching (which is not to say that I am not concerned about them).

[26] Brison (2002).

[27] I suspect this more fully developed imaginative repertoire on the part of marginalised minorities is what Justice Sotomayor had in mind when making the comment, for which she was skewered by her critics, that she would 'hope that a wise Latina woman with the richness of her experiences would more often than not reach a better conclusion than a white male [judge] who hasn't lived that life'. Sotomayor's comment was taken from a speech she gave in 2001 to a group of Latino lawyers and law students. 'I was trying to inspire them to believe that their life experience would enrich the legal system', Sotomayor said during her confirmation hearings. 'The words I spoke created a misunderstanding. I want to state upfront, unequivocally, I do not believe that any racial or ethnic group has an advantage in sound judging'. She pointed out that she made the comment in contrast to former Supreme Court Justice Sandra Day O'Connor who was known for saying that she did not view herself as a female jurist and said that a wise old man and a wise old woman would reach the same result as judges. Later, Sotomayor said, 'I was trying to play on [O'Connor's] words – my play fell flat. That was bad. It left an impression that life experiences commanded a result in cases, but that is not what I do as a judge'. (Available at www.features.csmonitor.com/politics/2009/07/14/sotomayor-wise-latina-a-bad-choice-of-words/).

[28] Slote (2012: 292).

REFERENCES

Brison, SJ (2002) *Aftermath: Violence and the Remaking of a Self* (Princeton, NJ, Princeton University Press).

Deigh, J (1995) 'Ethics and Universalizability' 105 *Ethics* 743.

—— (2012) 'Empathy in Law' chapter 15 of this volume.

Elster, J (1983) *Sour Grapes* (New York, Cambridge University Press).

Hoffman, ML (2001) *Empathy and Moral Development: Implications for Caring and Justice* (New York, Cambridge University Press).

Nussbaum, MC (2001) *Upheavals of Thought: The Intelligence of Emotions* (New York, Cambridge University Press).

Sen, A (1992) *Inequality Reexamined* (Cambridge, MA, Harvard University Press).

Slote, M (2007) *The Ethics of Care and Empathy* (New York, Routledge).

—— (2010) *Moral Sentimentalism* (Oxford, Oxford University Press).

—— (2012) 'Empathy, Law and Justice' chapter 14 of this volume.

17

Reply to Deigh and Brison

MICHAEL SLOTE

IN HIS COMMENTS on my chapter, John Deigh says that the term 'empathy' is nowadays used to refer either to a cognitive or to an affective state; and he also says that he disagrees with sentimentalists like myself in preferring to work entirely with the first kind (or concept?) of empathy. But this is a bit too simple. As Martin Hoffman points out, our affective, empathic responsiveness is mediated by the concepts and conceptual skills we possess: to take the simplest case, in order to 'feel your pain' in any kind of normal manner, I have to be cognitively aware of you in various ways. So Hoffman speaks of 'mediated' associative (affective) empathy, and I want to follow him in that.[1] The kind of empathy I am mainly speaking of is not, *pace* Deigh, entirely or simply an affective state – but he is certainly correct to assume that it involves affect or feeling.

Here is another misunderstanding. Deigh says that as a sentimentalist I follow Hume in holding that 'Morality . . . is more properly felt than judg'd of.' But this particular claim of Hume's is standardly taken to imply that moral claims are either subjective or emotive, and as a sentimentalist I want to argue, rather, that sentiment, feeling, fixes the reference of moral claims but is not their subject matter. A sentimentalist can hold that moral claims are every bit as objective as rationalists think they are, and I spent a great deal of time in my recent book *Moral Sentimentalism*[2] explaining how this can be true (Kripke's views on how the reference of natural kind terms is fixed come in in an important way). So it is a mistake to see the sentimentalism I defend as saddled with the subjectivity or non-cognitivity that Hume is often presumed to have embraced. And in fact the moral semantics I want to defend treats moral claims as more objective than even an ideal-observer or response-dependent interpretation of Hume's view can allow. I agree with (most) rationalists that we have reason to want to account for and justify our sense of the objective validity of morality, but if I am on the right track, then rationalism is not the only way one can attempt to do this.

Given these points, it is a mistake to think that I am forcing care ethics into a more subjective interpretation of moral claims than it might or should feel

[1] Hoffman (2000).
[2] Slote (2010).

comfortable with (though Nel Noddings in her book *Caring*[3] is rather quick to accept such a subjective view of the morality of caring). And then there is the issue of normativity. Deigh asks how the fact that we tend to be more empathically concerned with dangers we are immediately aware of than with dangers we merely know about can translate into the moral conclusion/claim that it is (*ceteris paribus*) morally worse not to save a child who is drowning right in front of one than not to save a distant child (say, from hunger) whom one merely knows about. But we do commonly believe this kind of moral claim, and the assumption that empathy is relevant to normative morality helps us to begin explaining why that conclusion is correct. Also, and as I pointed out in the final chapter of *The Ethics of Care and Empathy*,[4] the meta-ethical hypothesis that empathy *enters into our moral concepts* would help us explain why the fact that ignoring the child drowning right in front of one goes more against the grain of empathy than not helping the distant child is relevant to our typical conclusion/belief that the former is morally worse than the latter. I say much more about this in *Moral Sentimentalism*, but the principal idea there is that empathy is essential to normative morality through being essential to meta-ethics.

Both the books I have just mentioned also speak to the question of the normativity of morality and to related questions about the motivating force (or lack of it) of moral judgements. To be sure, and unlike many forms of rationalism, sentimentalism cannot say that it is *irrational* to act immorally. But this may actually be an advantage. Ordinary people do not think that the immoral are necessarily irrational and are much more likely simply to characterise them as heartless or cold-hearted. That fits with what the sentimentalist wants to argue, but (although there is no space to say more here) this does not mean that sentimentally-understood moral judgements lack objectivity or appropriate normativity.

Let me conclude my reply to John Deigh with a question. Deigh says that the strictly cognitive kind of empathy is relevant to categorical moral judgements and is notably absent in psychopaths. However, he also states that sadists are capable of empathy with the pain of their victims, and it is well known that sadistic psychopaths are often very capable of getting inside the heads of their intended victims. But why, then, does that not show that psychopaths are capable of strictly cognitive empathy? And if it does, then the psychopath's lack of such empathy cannot, *pace* Deigh, be the explanation of why they cannot make appropriate moral judgements. On the other hand, psychopaths *are* ordinarily thought to be incapable of affective empathic reactions/receptivity, and that may well mean that sentimentalism is in a better position to explain their moral incapacities than Deigh's 'empathic rationalism' is capable of doing.

Susan Brison thinks empathy may well be necessary to acting morally or justly, but she offers some arguments for holding that it is not sufficient for being moral or just. She begins by telling us that empathy can sometimes be misleading, as

[3] Noddings (1984).
[4] Slote (2007).

when another person very convincingly feigns being in pain. But in such cases I think it makes more sense to say that our empathy is *misled*, and the non-culpable ignorance that is involved here does not affect our moral judgement. If a person is innocently misled by someone feigning intolerable pain and on that basis barely misses, say, an appointment they have with some third party, we are not inclined to criticise what they have done in moral terms – so to that extent the empathy criterion seems adequate to our considered moral judgements. Similar points apply where a masochist is not known to be a masochist, but Brison also wants us to consider whether the empathic concern criterion is morally adequate for cases where someone is adaptively contented with what most of us would consider a terrible situation: say, a wife who dutifully accepts her husband's authority and her lack of any right to a career of her own. How, Brison wants to know, can empathy give us a morally adequate response to what is wrong with this situation?

But why does Brison take the idea of adaptive preference formation and contentment so uncritically, so much at face value? Surely, many, most, perhaps even all women who become deferential and selfless in the above manner have become so through being treated disrespectfully under patriarchal conditions. As Carol Gilligan puts it, such women have not been really listened to, really heard – as when, having expressed the desire to become a doctor, they are told by their parents that they would really rather be something more feminine like a nurse or housewife.[5] Such treatment shows a lack of empathy for the ideas and aspirations, for the points of view, of girls or women, and if we understand normative morality in terms of empathy, then we shall have reason to say that the 'preferentially adaptive' woman has been treated unjustly and is morally owed something by way of compensation. More important still, perhaps, is the question of whether such deferential women really are contented. As Kristin Borgwald has pointed out to me, if they have not been listened to, such women may be angry with the way they have been treated, yet lack the means or self-confidence to say that or why they are angry (and unhappy). This last capability is what consciousness-raising groups were supposed to make possible for women, so the whole idea of adaptive preferences seems in need of deeper interpretation; and if it receives such interpretation, I think empathy's status as a moral criterion will be enhanced rather than called into question. And in the light of these points, I remain unconvinced that a theory of objective welfare needs to be invoked to supplement empathy as a criterion, a sufficient condition, for acting morally/justly. (This is supposed to apply to institutions as much as to individual actions.)

Brison goes on to note that empathy for certain others can lead us astray, and with that I absolutely agree. That is why the criterion I offer for morally acceptable action is not ordinary people's empathic concern for others, but, rather, a 'fully-empathic' concern for other people. People who have developed in a normal way in our society may have a good deal of empathy, but (as Brison herself indicates) given the amount of hatred and prejudice (and ignorance) that exists in

[5] Gilligan (1982).

our society and the world more generally, I do not think we can assume – and I myself have not assumed – that most 'normal' 'mature' adults are fully empathic. For example, a person is not fully empathic, is somewhat lacking in empathy, if she does not empathise with (groups of) people who are very different from herself and who may live far away from where she lives. I spend a lot of time in *The Ethics of Care and Empathy* talking about ways in which children can be made more fully – more widely and deeply – empathic through moral education in schools (and there are obviously issues about how or whether parents can be brought into this process). And it is only this fuller, wider, deeper empathy that I am claiming to be a sufficient condition of acting morally.

Of course, and as Brison mentions, there are cases where empathy tugs in two or more directions. But this is only a problem for my criterion if there is a definite moral obligation in one specific direction or another in such situations, and I do not think there is any reason to hold that this has to be the case. In such situations, more than one course of action (*either* helping the poor *or* providing one's own child with a tutor in algebra) may be morally acceptable. So on the whole I think the moral criterion I offered is in considerably better shape than Susan Brison has suggested.

REFERENCES

Gilligan, C (1982) *In a Different Voice* (Cambridge, MA, Harvard University Press).

Hoffman, M (2000) *Empathy and Moral Development: Implications for Caring and Justice* (Cambridge, Cambridge University Press).

Noddings, N (1984) *Caring: a Feminine Approach to Ethics and Moral Education* (California, University of California Press).

Slote, M (2007) *The Ethics of Care and Empathy* (Abingdon, Routledge).

—— (2010) *Moral Sentimentalism* (Oxford, Oxford University Press).

Index

www.ingramcontent.com/pod-product-compliance
Ingram Content Group UK Ltd.
Pitfield, Milton Keynes, MK11 3LW, UK
UKHW020238290926
15470UKWH00002B/604

9 781849 461757